ARCHAEOLOGISTS & AESTHETES

in the Sculpture Galleries of the British Museum 1800–1939

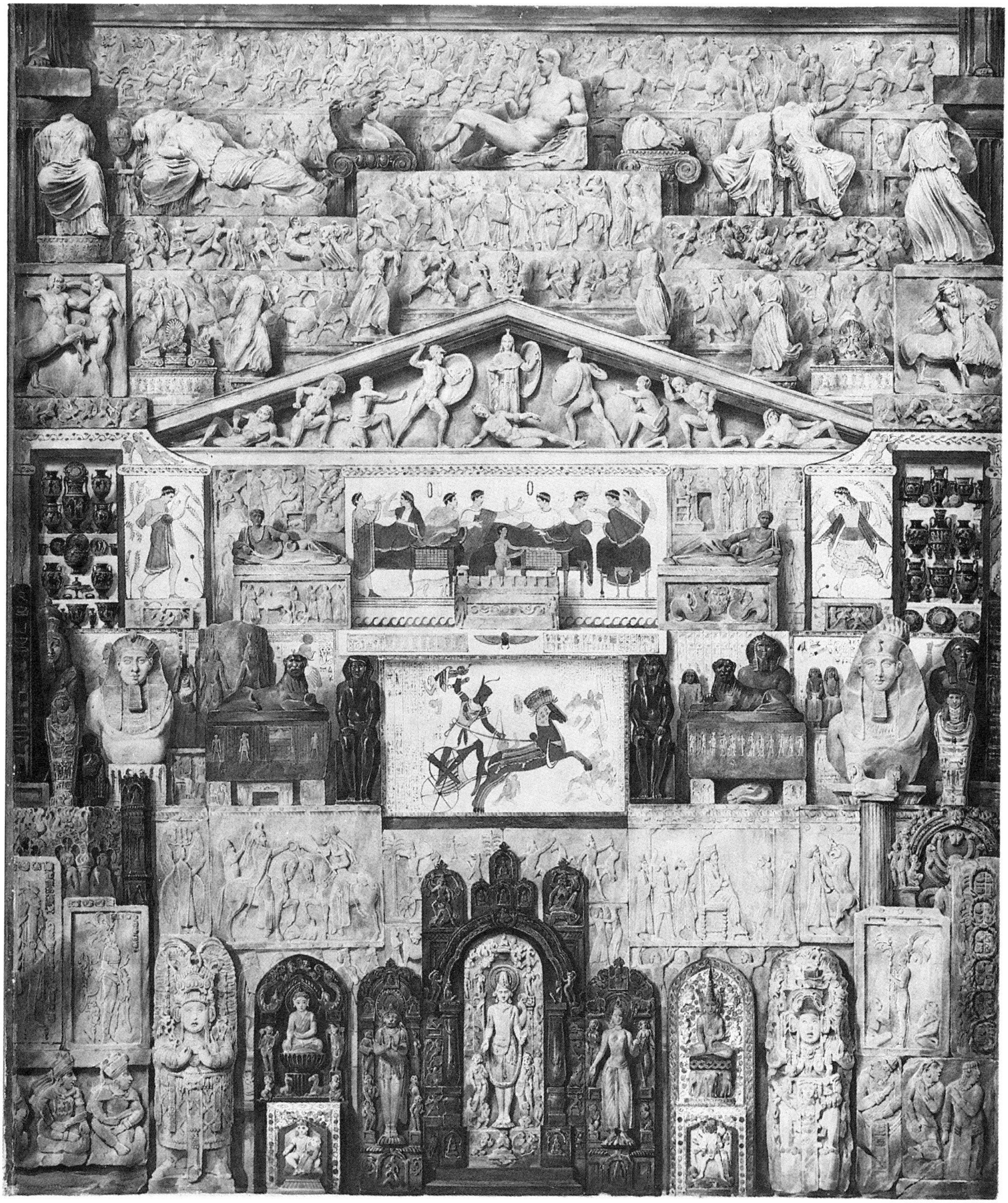

'An Assemblage of Works of Art in Sculpture and Painting', by James Stephanoff. Watercolour, exhibited 1845. Private collection (see Colour Plate VI).

ARCHAEOLOGISTS & AESTHETES

in the Sculpture Galleries of the British Museum 1800–1939

Ian Jenkins

Published for the Trustees of the British Museum
by British Museum Press

The Trustees of the British Museum are grateful to the Caryatids and to the author for their generous contributions towards the production of this book.

Published by British Museum Press
A division of British Museum Publications Ltd
46 Bloomsbury Street, London WC1B 3QQ

British Library Cataloguing in Publication Data
A catalogue reference for this book is
available from the British Library
ISBN 0–7141–1299–2

Designed by James Shurmer

Printed in Great Britain by
The Bath Press Ltd, Avon, Bath

Contents

IN MEMORY OF

ANTONY AND MOLLIE DUNKELS

Acknowledgements

This book has been made possible by the help of many friends and colleagues. It began as an idea for a doctoral thesis that grew out of an interest in Museum history shared with Brian Cook, Keeper of Greek and Roman Antiquities. My first debt is to him for support and encouragement, without which the project would certainly have foundered.

I must also thank my thesis supervisor, Joseph Mordaunt Crook, and examiners, Francis Haskell and Geoffrey Waywell, all of whom gave help and guidance.

In the preparation of both thesis and book I have drawn liberally on the knowledge, skills and patience of numerous colleagues. I am grateful to Janet Wallace and the staff of the Museum's Central Archive, and to Christopher Date, in particular, for the benefit of his specialist knowledge of the Museum's archival photographs. I would also like to thank Marjorie Caygill, fellow enthusiast for the history of the Museum, whose knowledge has been indispensable on a great many points.

Other friends and colleagues who have given help and advice include Donald Bailey, Morris Bierbrier, Sue Bird, Lucilla Burn, Frances Carey, William Cole, Paul Dove, Wolfgang Ernst, Antony Griffiths, Professor and Mrs Michael Jaffé, Sheila O'Connell, Julian Reade, Jeffrey Spencer, Lindsay Stainton, Hafed Walda, Susan Walker, Hilary Williams, Susan Woodford and Wladimir Zwalf.

For the production of the photographs I am grateful for the endless patience of Tom Cochrane, Paul Gardner, Christi Graham and Philip Nicholls.

The tireless efforts of Teresa Francis, who edited the text, have made it a better book than it might have been. All remaining faults and errors are my own.

I must also thank Carole Cosgrove and the staff of the British Museum typing pool, and Beverley Fryer, Peter Lassey and Marian Vian, all of whom helped in the production of the manuscript.

Finally, I wish to acknowledge my debt to Frances Dunkels for her support and companionship through the eight years this book has been in the making.

IAN JENKINS

Introduction

This book tells the story of the British Museum's sculpture collections as they were amassed in the nineteenth century. It presents a detailed account of the acquisition and arrangement of the collections, and describes the architectural development of the Museum as it strove to contain them.

The growth of the sculpture collections was an important part of the process by which the Museum was transformed from something resembling a cabinet of curiosity into an institution dedicated to the scientific pursuit of art history and archaeology. In the course of this transformation a central theme emerges: the desire to chart through the sculpture galleries of the British Museum the 'Progress of Civilisation' in antiquity. This was the name given by the sculptor Richard Westmacott to the pedimental composition set above the entrance to the Museum.

The idea of Progress was conceived in terms of a 'Chain of Art' in which the rise and fall of ancient art and civilisation could be traced link by link. The Chain was a metaphor adapted from the old eighteenth-century 'Chain of Being', an image used to describe the taxonomy of the natural world. Disagreement over how the Chain of Art should be arranged as a physical sequence in the sculpture galleries of the British Museum gave rise to a revealing conflict between two interested parties. These were, on the one hand, conservative *aesthetes* committed to a traditional neo-classical system of fixed values and, on the other, a new breed of professional *archaeologists* influenced by Darwinian evolutionism and radical science.

At the centre of every proposed new arrangement of the collection were the Elgin Marbles, revered in the nineteenth century with near religious awe. Lord Elgin was one in a long line of ambassadors to the Sublime Porte at Constantinople who, through the resources of the diplomatic service and the Royal Navy, was responsible for the enhancement of the collections of the British Museum. In the seventeenth century Sir Thomas Roe assisted, among others, Thomas Howard Earl of Arundel in his quest, as Henry Peacham put it in *The Compleat Gentleman*, 'to transplant old Greece into England'. After Elgin, Stratford Canning, later Lord Stratford de Redcliffe, was responsible for the transmission of both Greek and Assyrian sculptures to the British Museum. 'To transplant old Greece into England' was a peculiarly British idea. In the seventeenth and eighteenth centuries it was expressed in the ruined landscapes of English formal parks and in poetry; in the nineteenth century Arcadia became enshrined at Bloomsbury in the great 'Temple of the Muses' designed in Greek Revival style by Robert Smirke.

British fascination for ancient Greece, and Winckelmann's Platonic concept of ideal beauty in particular, dominated the Museum's thinking. Even radicals who could appreciate the importance of so-called primitive or barbarian cultures, such as the Assyrian, Meso-American or Oriental Indian, tended to see them in terms of a hierarchy culminating in the rise of Greek art. As early as 1777 J. G. Herder had challenged Winckelmann's premise that Egyptian art should be judged according to the standard of the Greeks.[1] He put forward a relativist view based upon a plea for recognising the function of Egyptian art as an expression of native religious belief. Interest in the symbolic function of so-called primitive art had preoccupied the antiquaries of the late eighteenth century, when, among others, D'Hancarville and Richard Payne Knight took what might today be called an anthropological approach to the Greeks and Romans in search of meaning in classical erotic imagery. This interest led to a greater understanding of, and sympathy for, non-Greek art. The eighteenth-century treatment of sexually explicit Hindu sculpture represents a phase in the history of the reception of Indian art which contrasts favourably with what Partha Mitter describes as 'the subsequent reassertion of Christian prejudice' in the Victorian period.[2] Sensitivity to the artistic intent of other cultures must depend upon acceptance of the determining role of other values. This was something Hellenists, who dictated what little theorising there was in the Museum, were disinclined to do.

Herder's criticism of Winckelmann, although relativist, did not deny the concept of art as a fixed and universal term: his position was that the art of one culture could not provide the standard of another. To reconcile the premise of art as a constant, with the idea of cultural relativism became, as Michael Podro has shown, a central problem in German critical art theory of the nineteenth century. It was not, however, a problem that exercised the minds of dogmatic Hellenists for whom Art was not a concept that could be shared or applied outside the classical tradition. Winckelmann's Platonic vision was the guiding force and, later, that of such classicists as Karl Otfried Müller and Heinrich Brunn. Their work – with necessary modification – continued in the conventional mode of *Meisterforschung*, the ongoing search for the lost masterpieces of classical antiquity.[3]

Greek art was the norm and appealed because its supposed purity provided a model of western, even British, moral values. The standard *History of Greece* of the day was that of George Grote, who was a trustee of the Museum from 1859 until 1871. Published in twelve volumes between 1846 and 1856, its treatment of the Athenians provided what many Englishmen saw, in Frank Turner's words, as 'a reflection of their own best selves'.[4] At the end of the century another generation of classicists including Jane Ellen Harrison, Francis Cornford, A. B. Cook and James

Frazer would once more turn to explore the dark side of the Greeks and rediscover links that narrowed the gulf between them and the so-called primitive cultures. This new wave of classical anthropologists, in showing the Greeks as also being 'other' and in possessing values that were alien to contemporary western philosophies, did something to assist in the disintegration of the British Museum's old hierarchy of cultures.

In this century the merits of non-Greek art have come to be judged according to their own terms of reference. This tendency towards a relativist understanding of ancient cultures coincided with the disruption of the Museum galleries occasioned by two world wars. In the climate of revisionism brought about by world events, the process of arranging the sculptures in a chronological progressive sequence, which had been continuing since the early nineteenth century, lost momentum. The idea of serialising ancient civilisation as one continuous narrative ceased to compel archaeologists as it had done. The image of the Chain of Art, once charged with meaning for those who thought they could see the connection between ancient cultures, has now fallen entirely into disuse. It is, however, a powerful force in the history of ideas, and these pages endeavour to record the part it has played in shaping the sculpture collections of the British Museum.

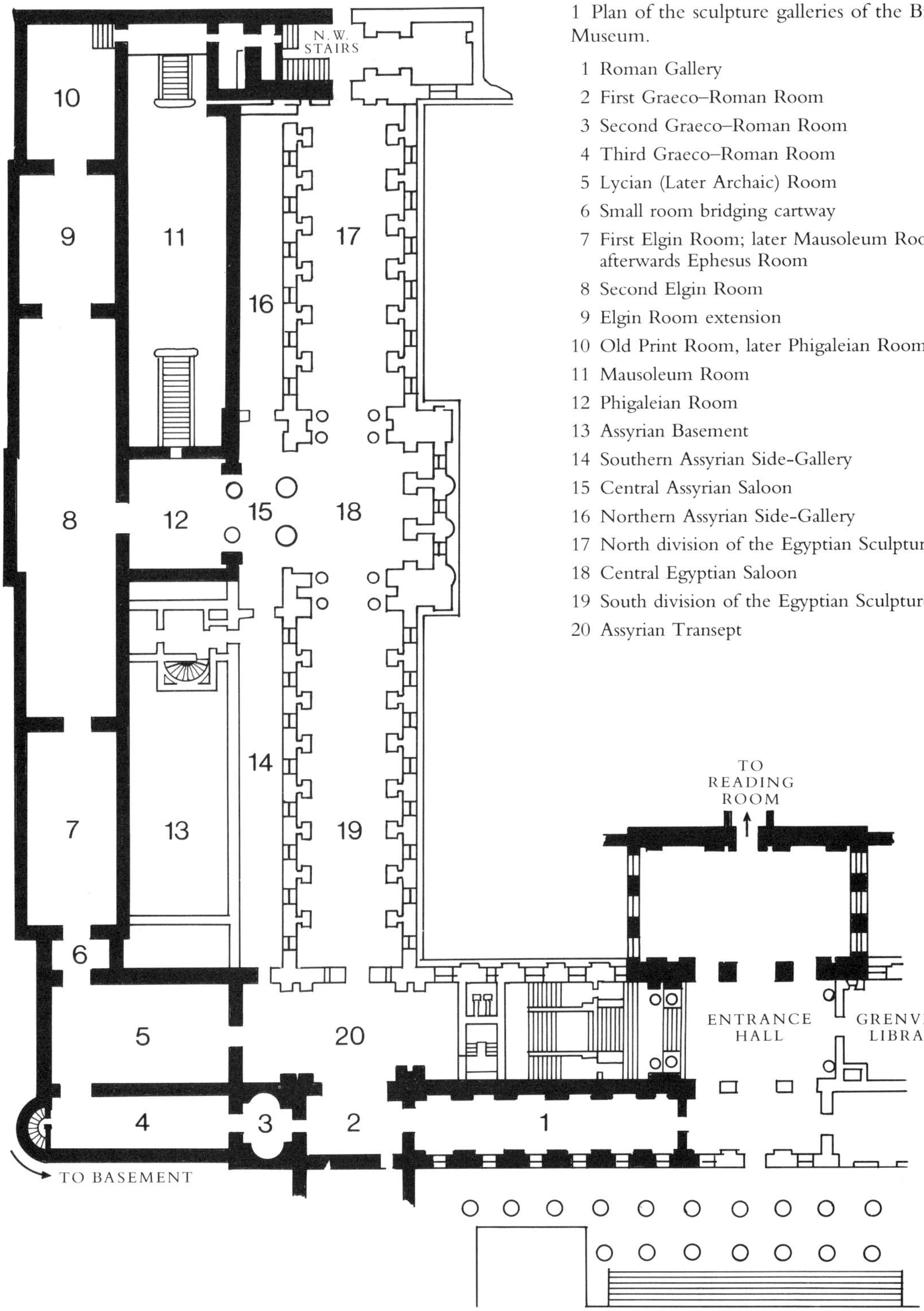

1 Plan of the sculpture galleries of the British Museum.

1 Roman Gallery
2 First Graeco–Roman Room
3 Second Graeco–Roman Room
4 Third Graeco–Roman Room
5 Lycian (Later Archaic) Room
6 Small room bridging cartway
7 First Elgin Room; later Mausoleum Room; afterwards Ephesus Room
8 Second Elgin Room
9 Elgin Room extension
10 Old Print Room, later Phigaleian Room
11 Mausoleum Room
12 Phigaleian Room
13 Assyrian Basement
14 Southern Assyrian Side-Gallery
15 Central Assyrian Saloon
16 Northern Assyrian Side-Gallery
17 North division of the Egyptian Sculpture Gallery
18 Central Egyptian Saloon
19 South division of the Egyptian Sculpture Gallery
20 Assyrian Transept

PART I

1 'The Triumph of Excellence'

'Pheidias belongs to Peace'[1]

During the first half of the nineteenth century the British Government assembled in its national Museum the most comprehensive and important collection of ancient sculpture to be found anywhere in the world. The success of British foreign diplomacy and the strength of the Mediterranean fleet were the means by which this great body of material was brought together, and yet it was done without any obvious political intent. The British Museum was never a Roman-style 'Trophy of Conquest' as the Louvre during its Napoleonic period unequivocally became. French imperial ambition justified the plunder of Italy in historicist terms as the prevailing of military virtue over spiritual decadence. Modern events were seen as comparable with the supposed defeat of the Egyptians by the ancient Greeks, and of the Greeks in their turn by the Romans.[2] Certainly, a great deal of national pride was invested in the British Museum also, and competition with the French provided a constant incentive for archaeological activity. Yet, the material culture of the great civilisations of antiquity was not gathered out of any sustained motive for national self-aggrandisement, but rather through a series of remarkable accidents. The composition of the Museum's collections reflects not so much the acquisition policy of a nation, as the enterprise of a few extraordinary individuals who, all too often, were obliged to enter into protracted negotiations in order to persuade a reluctant British Parliament. Some chances were missed altogether, and it was to be a constant source of regret that the Aegina marbles went to Munich when, if it were not for the bungling of the British attempt to purchase them, they might have become the natural 'archaic prelude' to the Elgin Marbles.[3] Again, the Greek vase collections of Berlin and Munich are the richer because of England's failure to acquire, when she could, the best of the vases Napoleon Bonaparte's brother Lucien had discovered in the ancient Etruscan tombs unearthed on his Italian estate in 1828–9.[4]

Here the primary concern is with successes and not with failures, and these are nearly always linked with the name of a particular personality. Thus we remember Elgin for his eponymous sculptures; the architect and antiquary Charles Cockerell for the Phigaleian Marbles; the Paduan engineer and explorer Giovanni Belzoni for the Egyptian sculptures; Charles Fellows for the Lycian; Stratford Canning (later Lord Stratford de Redcliffe) for the Mausoleum frieze; Austen Layard for the

Assyrian sculptures; Charles Newton for further sculptures from the Mausoleum at Halicarnassus and from nearby Didyma and Cnidus; Robert Murdoch Smith and E. A. Porcher for those from Cyrene; Richard Pullan for the sculptures from the Temple of Athena Polias at Priene and John Turtle Wood for those from the two temples of Artemis at Ephesus.

To members of this illustrious company and others may be attributed the greatness of the sculpture collections of the British Museum, but that is not to underestimate the importance of the contribution made by the British Foreign Office and the Navy. Not a few of those listed above achieved what they did as a direct consequence of a diplomatic appointment. Moreover, nothing could have been achieved without the enlistment of the services of the ships and men that conveyed the often difficult and dangerous cargoes to safety in London. The role of the Royal Navy in the progress of classical archaeology would make a book in itself. Featuring large in such a study would be the role of Captain (later Admiral) Beaufort, commander of the hydrographic survey that produced the first detailed charts of the coastlines on or near whose shores the remnants of the great ages of classical civilisation lay scattered. Beaufort first surveyed the coast of Asia Minor in 1811–12, while the French and the English were still at war.[5] The defeat of the French fleet by Admiral Howe off Ushant on the 'Glorious first of June' 1794 established the supremacy of the Royal Navy that was to prove vital in determining not only the eventual outcome of the Napoleonic Wars, but also the future of the British Museum. On 1 August 1798, Nelson destroyed the French fleet at the Battle of the Nile, effectively denying Napoleon the success of his ill-fated Egyptian expedition. Following their defeat on land, in the summer of 1801 the French were forced to evacuate Egypt and thus surrender to the victors the antiquities intended for the Louvre. Napoleon's Egyptian campaign was a visionary scheme of conquest and scientific exploration. His appointed artist and antiquary, Dominique Vivant Denon, had recorded the expedition in numerous brilliant drawings which were later to form the basis of his handsome *Description de l'Égypte*.[6] He also collected a number of sarcophagi, sculptures and inscriptions, including the celebrated Rosetta Stone discovered during the building of fortifications at Alexandria. The antiquities reached England in 1802 and thus became the first major acquisition of ancient sculpture, effectively founding the Museum's collection. In this defeat, however, France lost a greater prize still, for she had ceded to England a political advantage of inestimable value.

At this time, the Ottoman empire, although a power in decline, occupied the greater part of the eastern world of classical antiquity, including mainland Greece itself. Egypt was counted among its territories, and it was therefore against the Sultan in Constantinople that Napoleon had directed his Egyptian offensive. The failure of that campaign would afford the British a unique opportunity, and Lord Elgin's embassy to Constantinople, with its French-style entourage of artists and antiquaries, was well timed to coincide with Britain's military role as the saviour of Egypt. The firman authorising the removal of sculpture from the Athenian Acropolis reached Elgin only weeks after the capitulation of the French forces in Egypt.[7] Thus the acquisition of the Elgin Marbles by the British Museum in 1816 was a direct consequence of preceding political events. Subsequently, there was something of a cooling off in Anglo-Turkish relations, but during the 1840s and 1850s, under Sir Stratford Canning's skilful tenure of the embassy at Constantinople, British diplomacy would again prevail in facilitating the favourable disposition of the Ottoman Porte towards the removal of antiquities from Asia Minor and elsewhere.[8]

In 1815 the war with France was brought to an end by the defeat of Napoleon's
2 army at Waterloo. No time was lost by the allies in ensuring the dismantling of the Musée Napoléon and the restitution of its artworks. W. R. Hamilton, who as secretary to Lord Elgin had played a leading role in the acquisition of the Elgin Marbles, now attended Castlereagh's mission to Paris in the capacity of Under-Secretary of State for Foreign Affairs. He was very active in assisting the Pope's agents to claim back what had been taken from the Italian museums nearly twenty years before. Denon, who was now Director of the Louvre, recognised Hamilton as his natural enemy and complained of the unusual enthusiasm with which he pursued the act of dismantlement.[9]

The Italian marbles reached Rome in January 1816, the year in which it was decided to purchase the Elgin Marbles for the British Museum. France's loss was matched by England's gain, and the dawning of *Pax Britannica* was heralded as a new age of cultural prosperity. Thus an anonymous contributor to the popular *Gentleman's Magazine*[10] submitted the following plea for the 'Building of a Temple or Palace of the Arts':

> At this proud era, when the steady valour and preserving energies of Great Britain have sustained the tottering foundations of States and Empires, and in restoring peace, order, and confidence of the civilised world, has stamped her fame in arms, wisdom, and diplomatic skill; no longer let it be said the Muses have no abode with us; no longer let us hear we have no establishment suitable for their reception – but let the public munificence now completely establish our triumph of excellence, both in the possession and execution of the Fine Arts; and prove to the surrounding nations that our native talent need not blush when placed in competition with the finest performances of the Old School, and make the magnanimous display of the celebrated works which we now possess.

In this manner were sown the seeds from which would grow the great Temple of the Muses built to a neo-classical design by the architect Robert Smirke. The response was by no means immediate; fourteen years passed before the Elgin Marbles, which the author clearly had prominently in mind, were displayed in a new Grecian hall. It

Numbers in the margin refer to illustrations

was literature, moreover, rather than art that prompted the British Government finally to provide the funds for the gradual replacement of Montagu House, the unsuitable building that had served as the British Museum since it first opened its doors to the public on 15 January 1759. In 1823 the presentation of the King's Library to the nation provided the excuse for drafting a general scheme for the Museum's renewal. Robert Smirke was asked to present designs, which he did in the pure Greek style then in vogue. The first section of the new building, the receptacle for the King's Library and the Museum's considerable manuscript collection, was completed in 1827.[11]

The priority given to manuscripts and books was traditional. At its inception the Museum had been established not as a show-place for works of art but rather as a public reference collection of books and manuscripts, as well as natural history specimens and other 'rarities'. Its foundation in 1753 was not announced with any grand declaration of museological doctrine but as a matter of expediency to provide a repository for the collection of Sir Hans Sloane, bequeathed to the nation on his death on 11 January 1753, and also for the valuable manuscript library of the Cotton family which had become public property through an Act passed as early as 1700. To these two collections was added the important manuscript collection built up by the Earls of Oxford, Robert and Edward Harley. Having been inherited by the Duchess of Portland, the Harleian manuscripts were purchased from her for £10,000 by the same Act that founded the British Museum, passed on 7 June 1753.[12]

The Sloane collection was the largest and most important of the three founding collections, containing in addition to drawings, manuscripts and books, a full range of natural history specimens. When it was visited by John Evelyn in 1691 it included 'plants, fruits, corails, minerals, stones, earth, shells, animals and insects'.[13] To these was added an important collection of antiquities including a few sculptures and stone inscriptions, which together made up a cabinet of curiosities in the old seventeenth- and eighteenth-century tradition. Sloane was a physician, and like others of that profession had built up a reference collection of 'Natural and Artificial Rarities' – the essential apparatus of a learned gentleman.

The emphasis of the early Museum upon books and the natural sciences is indicated in the appointment and titles of its officers. Thus, apart from the governing body of Trustees, the daily affairs of the Museum would be conducted by a Principal Librarian, assisted by three Under-Librarians, two of whom were also physicians. There was then no separation of the natural history and archaeology collections, these 'specimens' being all lumped together as 'Natural and Artificial Productions'.[14] For the first fifty years of its history the Museum remained without a person specifically appointed to deal with the collection of antiquities and, in particular, the growing cabinet of coins. On the recommendation of Charles Townley, the important collector of classical sculpture, Taylor Combe was appointed in 1803 but still as

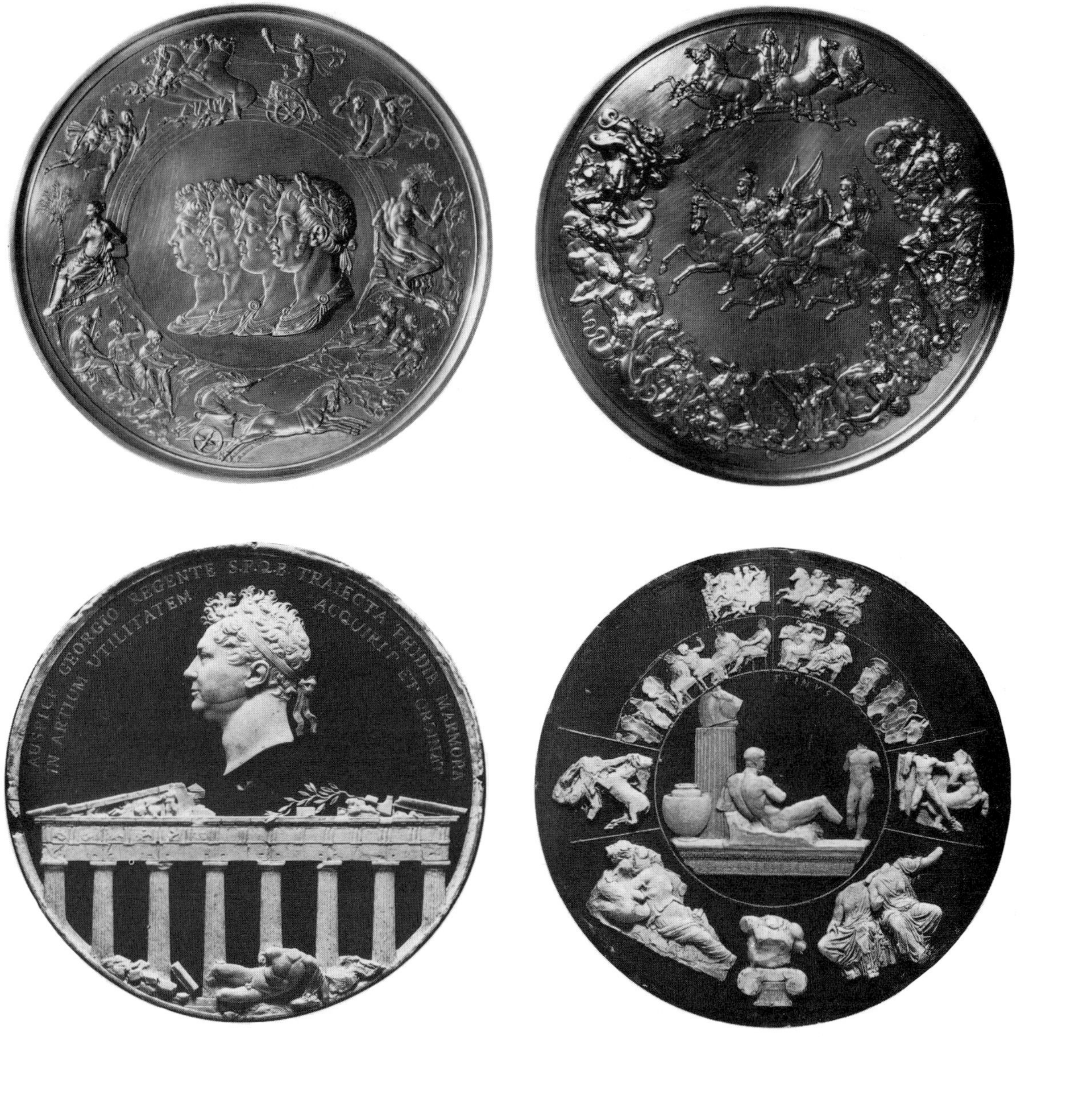

2 Waterloo became England's Battle of Marathon and the Elgin Marbles her 'Triumph of Excellence'. Commemorative medal by B. Pistrucci (*top*) celebrating the Battle of Waterloo (British Museum, Department of Coins and Medals), and wax models for a medal (never struck) celebrating the acquisition of the Elgin Marbles (Rome, Museo della Zecca).

an Under-Librarian in the Department of Natural History. Only in 1807 was the Department of Antiquities formed, with Combe as its first Keeper.[15]

Although tastefully arranged in the picturesque rooms of old Montagu House, the collections of the British Museum tended to be regarded primarily as a *Wunder-* rather than a *Kunstkammer*, representing a spectacle of curiosities for the casual visitor or a scientific reference collection for the serious student. Only by degrees did the establishment take on the identity of a collection of art and archaeology. Eventually, this would become the dominant feature, and the scientists grew to resent the cuckoo that would finally force them altogether from the nest.

The rise of the Department of Antiquities must be related directly to developments across the Channel. On 18 Brumaire, Year IX (9 November 1800), the Galérie des Antiquités, gorged on the booty seized from the capitulation of the Italian states, was opened to the public.[16] Here in close proximity were to be found the three most famous sculptures of the day: the Laocoon group and Apollo Belvedere from the Belvedere courtyard of the Vatican Museum and the Venus de' Medici from the Uffizi Gallery in Florence. In spite of the great wealth of antique sculpture that had been salted away in the private collections of the English country houses, there was no comparable public collection here. The nearest approximation was Charles Townley's house-museum in Westminster, to which visitors were admitted upon application. Following the Treaty of Amiens in 1802, marking a brief respite in Anglo-French hostilities, English visitors are said to have flocked to Paris, among them the young Robert Smirke.[17] In 1803 the first appointment was made at the Museum for the curatorship of the antiquities. At the same time plans
were drawn up for a new gallery to house the Egyptian sculptures recently arrived 33
from Alexandria. In 1805 the design of the new gallery was altered to accommodate,
in addition, Charles Townley's collection, which was purchased for the nation upon 36–7
his death.

The Townley Gallery, as it became known, was opened in 1808, a year after Taylor Combe had been appointed as the first Keeper of Antiquities. In 1816–17 a temporary apartment was tacked onto the west side of the Townley Gallery for the exhibition of the Phigaleian and Elgin Marbles. Thus were laid the foundations of the sculpture collections of the British Museum. The French boasted of transferring Rome to Paris, but with the Elgin Marbles in Bloomsbury some would deny the need for Rome at all. England sought another paradigm for her 'Triumph of Excellence', the ancient School of Hellas, Periclean Athens. If France had identified herself with the conquering ambitions of Rome, England took as her model the freedom-loving Athens of Pericles's day. The association is made explicit in a remarkable passage in the Report of the Select Committee which sat in 1816 to determine the future of the Elgin Marbles. In 1851, lest anyone should forget why it was that the most famous body of sculpture in the world had been chosen for the

British Museum, the following extract was republished in volume I of the new journal *Museum of Classical Antiquities*.[18]

Your Committee cannot dismiss this interesting subject, without submitting to the attentive reflection of the House, how highly the cultivation of the Fine Arts has contributed to the respect, character, and dignity of every government by which they have been encouraged, and how intimately they are connected with the advancement of everything valuable in science, literature, and philosophy. In contemplating the importance and splendour to which so small a republic as Athens rose, by the genius and energy of her citizens, exerted in the path of such studies, it is impossible to overlook how transient the memory and fame of extended empires and of mighty conquerors are, in comparison of those who have rendered inconsiderable States eminent, and who have immortalized their own names by these pursuits. But if it be true, as we learn from history and experience, that free governments afford a soil most suitable to the production of native talent, to the maturing of the powers of the human mind, and to the growth of every species of excellence, by opening to merit the prospect of reward and distinction, no country can be better adapted than our own to afford an honourable asylum to these monuments of the school of Phidias, and of the administration of Pericles; where, secure from further injury and degradation, they may receive that admiration and homage to which they are entitled, and serve in return as models and examples to those who, by knowing how to revere and appreciate them, may learn first to imitate, and ultimately to rival them.

The possession of the Elgin Marbles by the British Museum was contrasted with the recently returned French spoils of imperial conquest. Early in 1817, the comparison was made explicit by an anonymous contributor to the *Gentleman's Magazine*. Announcing the imminent opening of new temporary accommodation in the British Museum, the article goes on: 'they are a proud trophy, because their display in the British Metropolis is the result of public taste, and also a pleasing one, because they are not the price of blood shed in wanton or ambitious wars'.[19] J.J. Winckelmann, writing around 1750, had attributed the greatness of Greek art to the freedom of the Greeks themselves, by whom he had principally in mind Athens after the
2 Persian Wars. Waterloo became England's Battle of Marathon, and acquisition of the Elgin Marbles by the British Museum was hailed as confirmation of the ancient claim that liberty and the arts rise and fall together.

Winckelmann and the pursuit of ideal beauty

The acquisition of the Elgin Marbles is arguably the single most important event in the history of the British Museum and certainly in the course of nineteenth-century European *Antikenrezeption*. At the time of their arrival in this country, the manner in which sculpture was seen and discussed was founded upon the literary tradition of antiquity itself. The pursuit of ideal beauty, the major concern of neo-classical theorists, depended ultimately upon a *quasi* Platonic hierarchy of forms, through which art was elevated above nature. Reynolds, Fuseli and Flaxman all expressed in their respective theoretical systems the notion of ideal perfection as a fixed standard and goal, against which all art, ancient and modern, might be measured. Plato and later critics such as Cicero, Quintilian and Plotinus provided the ancient philosophical authority for this *credo*.[20]

Reynolds's philosophy of art made especial use of the Platonist belief that ideal beauty existed only in the mind. It was an unattainable truth: 'the sight never beheld it, nor has the hand expressed it; it is an idea residing in the breast of the artist, which he is always labouring to impart, and which he dies at last without imparting.'[21]

The paradox that perfection can be both the source and the goal of beauty was a common belief among ancient theorists, many of whom were more optimistic than Plato had been about an artist's power to reproduce ideal beauty. Plato had a poor opinion of art which, as an imitation of nature, was at two removes from that abstract beauty of which nature itself was a copy. Here by contrast is Cicero praising Pheidias's extraordinary abilities: 'When he created his Zeus or Athena, he did not contemplate any persons from whom he drew a likeness, but rather a sort of extraordinary apparition of beauty resided in his mind, and concentrating on it and intuiting its nature, he directed his art and his hand towards reproducing it.'[22]

The idea that classical Greek sculptors had been gifted with a divine intuition or *phantasia* was developed first by Hellenistic Greek theorists who in turn passed it on to their Roman successors.[23] Post-Renaissance neo-classicism adopted the notion as the fundamental premise of beau-idealism, the system of critical theory that came to represent the ground rules of art. The goal of art was not, however, to be achieved by rules alone and that peculiar beauty or Grace possessed by such ancient statues as the Apollo Belvedere was encapsulated in academic art-circles by frequent recourse to the beau-idealist catch-phrase: *je ne sais quoi*.[24] Even the ancients themselves, as Alexander Pope had observed in his *Essay on Criticism*, 'their rules invade'. And in so doing, 'Great wits sometimes may gloriously offend ... And snatch a grace beyond the reach of Art.'

The most important figure to emerge from the eighteenth-century Greek revival and the theorist who would exert the greatest influence on the nineteenth century was Johann Joachim Winckelmann. Without rejecting the concept of the absolute, 3
he emphasised the importance of observation in detecting in actual examples the presence and progress of beauty upward to its 'source'. Winckelmann, like Aristotle, was interested in the mechanics of beauty, in particulars as well as universals. An understanding of the individual parts of a statue was therefore essential for comprehending the whole. The ideal unity of Greek sculpture, as he saw it, depended upon the Greek genius for selecting the most perfect forms in nature and combining these into an ideal whole. A consequent interest in close observation and the comparison of the actual remains of antiquity is what makes Winckelmann's *History*

of Ancient Art important as the foundation stone of modern empirical archaeology.

In stressing Winckelmann's particular claim to celebrity it would be wrong to lose sight of his beau-idealist orthodoxy. For both Plato and Aristotle beauty, as represented by the harmonious whole, was ultimately a metaphysical concept predetermining the proper ordering of parts. In Plato's theory of *mimesis* ideal beauty pre-exists the efforts of artistic imitators,[25] and Winckelmann similarly treats ideal beauty as both the goal and the inspiration of art. 'Beauty seemed to beckon me', he wrote in explanation of his desire to chart the rise of Greek art in antiquity, 'probably that same Beauty which exhibited itself to the great artists, and allowed itself to be grasped and figured, for I have sought and longed to recognise her in their works.'[26] Winckelmann's philosophy of art was, however, less defeatist than that of Plato. He

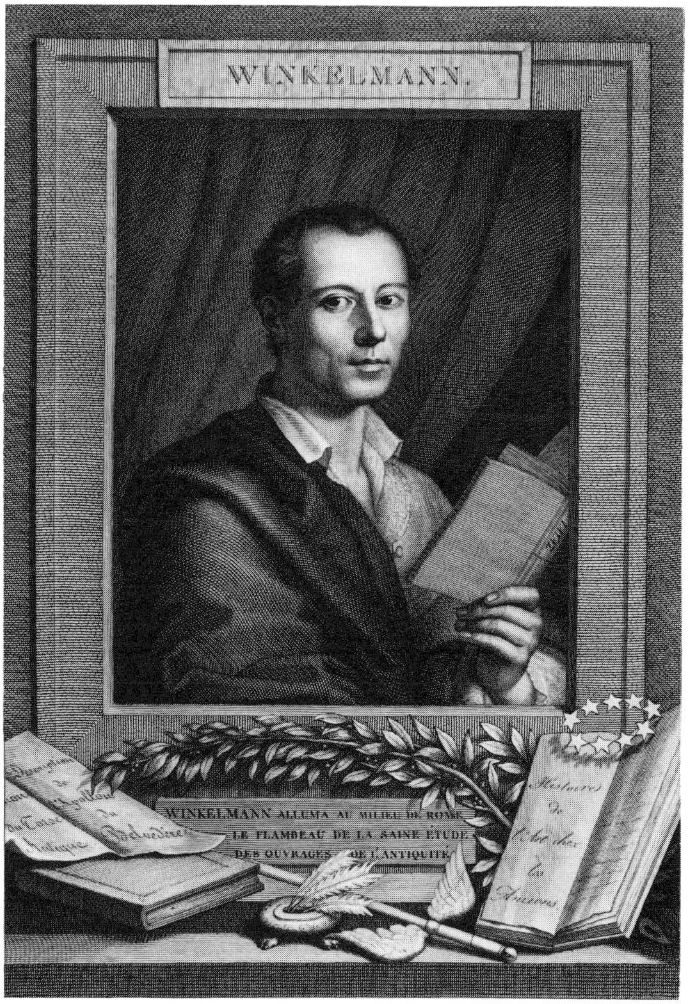

3 Johann Joachim Winckelmann (1717–68), the most important influence upon nineteenth-century British thinking about classical sculpture. Engraving by M. Blot after A. R. Mengs, 1815.

certainly knew and admired the works of the first of the Greek philosophers to turn his mind in earnest towards a definition of ideal beauty, but in detail Winckelmann's own philosophy derives more from the works of such later figures as the third-century Roman neo-Platonist Plotinus.[27] He differed from Plato in affording artists and their creations a more exalted role. According to Plotinus, material things could possess 'Intellectual Beauty'. A single quotation will suffice: 'Now it must be seen that the stone . . . brought under the artist's hand to the beauty of form is beautiful not as stone – for so the crude block would be as pleasant – but in virtue of the Form or Idea introduced by the art.'[28]

The especial importance of Winckelmann for the rise of classical scholarship, therefore, lies in the fact that he was the first to work up the ancient commentaries, in particular that of Pliny, into a 'modern' system of criticism, marrying the literary tradition of art theory to the monuments themselves. In so doing he established an empirical scheme for discussing the development of ancient sculpture within the traditional literary and philosophical framework. His connoisseurship coupled with Plato's inspirational vision of transcendental beauty was to remain the overriding influence upon the critique of classical sculpture. His system for tracing the rise and fall of Greek art was to be challenged and modified, while by some it was rejected altogether. And yet, even today – and notably in Germany – Winckelmann remains the presiding genius of classical archaeology. In particular, it is his insistence on the supremacy of Greek over Roman art that persists as the lasting legacy of his influence. Only in the art of the Greeks, and in the best period, could be found that approximation to ideal beauty that represented the goal of art.

At its simplest, Winckelmann's scheme for the stylistic development of Greek art may be divided into four periods: first, the 'straight and hard', which characterises the severe lines of the archaic period; second, the 'grand and square' style of the Pheidian era; third, 'the flowing beauty' exemplified by the idealised naturalism of the softer Praxitelean period; finally, the merely imitative and decadent copying of nature that characterised the decline of the arts in the Roman period.[29] E. Gombrich has shown how Winckelmann's system of progress in the arts is consistent with the history of human civilisation, as conceived by Gian Battista Vico, 'the founder of Cultural History', who in his *Scienza Nuova* of 1744 had proposed as one of his axioms that, 'The character of nations is first rude, then severe, then benign, then delicate and finally dissolute'. Whether or not Winckelmann had read Vico is not important since, as Isaiah Berlin has pointed out, 'ideas travel without labels'. What is certain, however, is the fact that Winckelmann's four styles of Greek sculpture draw upon the ancient testimonies of Cicero and Quintilian, where the development of oratory is compared with that of sculpture and is seen to evolve from 'hardness' to 'softness'.[30]

Whatever the inspiration, Winckelmann's *History* was worked out in practice on the basis of Roman copies of Greek sculpture, which he mistook for the originals. These copies were to be found in the Albani and other Italian collections; he never visited Greece. Among the first to point out the likely truth about the works Winckelmann had hailed as originals was his friend the painter Raphael Mengs. He argued that among those statues listed by Winckelmann as the exemplars of Greek sculpture there were, in fact, a number of later copies belonging to the inferior Roman period.[31] These revelations did not, however, weaken the prevailing conviction in the supremacy of Greek art; rather the reverse. A growing awareness of the remoteness of the Greeks served to intensify reverence for them. Winckelmann acknowledges in the closing passage of his *History of Ancient Art* that 'the authority of antiquity predetermines our judgement', and what follows seems to prepare his reader for the possibility that our longing for what the ancients knew may lead us astray:

> Just as a maiden standing on the shore of the ocean, follows with tearful eyes her departing lover with no hope of ever seeing him again, and fancies that in the distant sail she sees the image of her beloved. Like that loving maiden we too have, as it were, nothing but a shadowy outline left of the object of our wishes, but that very indistinctness awakens only a more earnest longing for what we have lost, and we study the copies of the originals more attentively than we should have done the originals themselves if we had been in full possession of them. In this particular we are very much like those who wish to have an interview with spirits, and who believe that they see them when there is nothing to be seen.

Ultimately, therefore, Winckelmann's understanding of ancient sculpture depended not upon the presumed surviving models of Greek beauty but upon a nostalgia for the metaphysical perfection of Greek art that transcended mere material paradigms.[32] His approach to antiquity was charged with a melancholy of longing for a lost golden age. The beauty of this world serves only to remind us of that which we have lost.

Winckelmann's authority was paramount but did not go unchallenged. A powerful dissenter was Ennio Quirino Visconti who, while accepting the greatness of Greek art in the classical period, yet declined to accept that the sculpture of the Hellenistic and Roman periods must be judged inferior. He considered that the standard of art established by Pheidias had continued through the so-called Macedonian period and on into the time of the Roman emperor Hadrian. He acknowledged the lateness of the sculptures that since the Renaissance had been held up as the paradigms of antique art, but insisted that they were not imitations so much as ideal adaptations. This last is a view recently revived by some modern champions of Roman art, who invoke a similar principle of *imitations perfectionnées* in defence of Hellenised Roman sculpture.[33] It provides an archaeological alternative to the science of *Kopienkritik* with its often seemingly obsessive pursuit of lost Greek originals.

Time alone will tell whether the current bid to promote the reputation of Roman copies will have a lasting influence. As for Visconti, his attempt met with barely more success than did Richard Payne Knight's declaration that the Elgin Marbles were Roman works of the Hadrianic period.[34] As Napoleon's court archaeologist, Visconti was committed to the collection of the Louvre which, even after the restitution of the pieces removed from the Papal collections in Rome, remained rich in Roman copies. In summing up 150 years of archaeological scholarship, Adolph Michaelis explained Visconti's particular interest in seeking to promote Roman copies:

The Musée Napoléon was the last magnificent example of a Museum exhibiting a Roman character. It marked the end of the old system of conducting Museums. The Napoleonic empire had represented itself as the heir of the Roman Caesars. Philology and Ancient History had also for centuries cultivated in a one-sided manner Rome and Roman literature .... On the horizon, however, the splendour of another dawn was visible. Simultaneously with the Roman Musée Napoléon, the British Museum in London was developing as the most illustrious centre of Greek art.[35]

It was partly in response to the debate engendered by the proposed acquisition of the Elgin Marbles by the British Museum that Visconti refined his aesthetic doctrine into its final form. In the report commissioned from him by Lord Elgin, he could afford to be generous and fulsome in his praise since, in the words of Jacob Rothenberg, his aim was 'to make the Elgin Marbles a historical source and prelude for the professed excellence of later Greek and Roman art'.[36] In fact, the view that was to prevail acclaimed the Elgin Marbles not as a 'prelude' but as the summit of artistic achievement, against which all else would be measured.

The shock of the new

The arrival of the Elgin Marbles in England and the publicity surrounding them presented a new challenge to Winckelmann's authority. From 1807 the collection went on show in a makeshift museum at Park Lane. Here for all to see, viewed as it were 'in the flesh', was the living link with the lost art of the Greeks. Ancient authority assigned the major public works of Perikles's building programme to the supervision of Pheidias, and these were sculptures if not from his own hand, then from his workshop. What immediately struck all those who saw the Parthenon sculptures for the first time was their likeness to nature. Far from being 'grand and square' according to Winckelmann's classification, the art of Pheidias appeared to take inspiration directly from nature.[37] This was something the painter Benjamin Robert Haydon took as cause to abandon the 'false beau-ideal' of traditional art theory based upon the repertoire of Graeco-Roman models. He hailed the arrival of the Elgin Marbles as marking the commencement of real art, based upon the twin exemplars of the Parthenon sculptures and Nature. In so doing he flew full in the face of the academic tradition of Joshua Reynolds and the Academy, which had placed ideal above actual form.[38] Another critic who saw an opportunity for promoting the professed beauty of particular as against generalised nature was William Hazlitt, essayist and biographer of Bonaparte, who described the Elgin Marbles as 'the best answer to Sir Joshua Reynolds's discourses'.[39] The central thesis of an important study by Jacob Rothenberg of the reception of the Elgin Marbles regards the opinion of such radicals as Haydon and Hazlitt as being all part of a rising Romantic spirit that saw in the Elgin Marbles the means with which to douse the already dying flame of neo-classicism. The storm of debate over the Marbles represents the gathering of opposite forces. 'The Elgin Marbles', writes Rothenberg, 'arrived in England at the height of the transition from neo-classicism to Romanticism. In this milieu they served as a focal point around which the most significant aesthetic and critical issues of the day were fought out ....'[40]

It is arguable whether such a 'transition' did, in fact, take place, when eighteenth-century classicism can be seen living on well into the nineteenth century, playing a part in the remarkable aesthetic eclecticism of that age. Suffice it to say that on the particular matter of the Elgin Marbles, it is dangerous to put too much emphasis on the energetic but exceptional voice of Haydon. Largely as a result of his outpourings in various tracts, diaries and biographies, it has become a commonplace to say that their arrival and public display caused a revolution in taste, overturning at a stroke the former canon. This needs qualification. Certainly, the Marbles created a dilemma for beau-ideal traditionalists, but in reality there was little to fear.

In assessing the worth of the Elgin Marbles as a potential purchase for the nation, the pressing question for the Parliamentary tribunal of 1816 was whether, in addition to their acknowledged natural beauty, they possessed anything of the ideal. Most of those who were called upon to give witness before the committee hedged around the problem. Few who openly admired them and were in favour of their purchase were willing to use the actual word *ideal*. The sum total of their testimony, however, hinted at what was to come, for far from representing a threat to the established view, the Elgin Marbles could serve to endorse traditional academic theory. In Antonio Canova's words, 'I admire in them the truth of nature combined with the choice of the finest forms'; in Joseph Nollekens's, 'I look upon them as ideal beauty *and* closeness of study from nature'; in Richard Westmacott's, 'That which approaches nearest to nature, with grand form, artists give preference to'. For Thomas Lawrence they were superior to the Apollo Belvedere because 'there is in them a union of fine composition, and very grand form, with a more true and natural expression of the effect of action upon the human frame.'[41]

On the face of it these carefully phrased evaluations of the Elgin Marbles may seem to suggest Haydon's own view. In 1840 he wrote of their possessing 'that combination of nature and idea which I had felt so much wanting for high art . . . . I saw in fact the most heroic style of art combined with all the essential detail of actual life . . . .'[42] In reality, however, Haydon and traditionalists like Westmacott were looking at their subjects from different ends of the telescope. Haydon's aim, as F. Cummings observes, was to train his students to understand 'the vitality, energy and inner life of the figure', rather than to admire it for its 'correctness'.[43] It was the 'system' of beau-idealist theory that Haydon's romantic and visionary temperament found objectionable. His inspirational search for the inner truth of a figure is the very opposite of that expressed by Winckelmann, whose search for classic poise contrasts with Haydon's Romantic frenzy. The much-quoted passage in which Winckelmann attributes to Greek art 'a noble simplicity and a quiet grandeur' was written with the Laocoon group in mind, a work he took to be the original admired by the ancients. It goes on: 'as the bottom of the sea lies peaceful beneath a foaming surface, a great soul lies sedate beneath the strife of passions in Greek figures.'[44]

The archaeological revelation that many of the sculptures he had admired as originals were in fact copies had shown up a potential weakness in Winckelmann's thesis and thereby posed a threat to the beau-idealist cause. The arrival of the Elgin Marbles in England came as a *deus ex machina* to fill the stage that was already being prepared for them.[45] A last-ditch attempt to preserve the reputation of the Apollo Belvedere at the expense of the Elgin Marbles was made in the summing up of the Report of the Parliamentary Committee seeking to draw the distinction between 'grandeur of style combined with close observation of Nature' – as perceived in the Elgin Marbles – and the qualities possessed by the Apollo, which make it 'the highest and most sublime representation of ideal form and beauty which sculpture has ever embodied'.[46] The old tune had begun to sound rather tired, however, and soon this accolade would be preserved for the Elgin Marbles alone, whose intrinsic merit had the ultimate imprimatur of the name of Pheidias.

Quatremère de Quincy

Far from being overthrown by the Elgin Marbles, as Haydon had hoped, the beau-idealist tradition took new life from their arrival and, with some necessary adjustment, ensured survival by attaching itself to new gods. One theorist who found virtue in this necessity was the French politician and beau-ideal archaeologist Antoine-Chrysostôme Quatremère de Quincy. For him the pursuit of ideal beauty had been made more piquant by the arrival of the Elgin Marbles, at a time when taste was tiring of the old repertoire of statues with the same style copied over and over again.[47] His evaluation is of particular interest, being communicated in a series of letters to his friend the sculptor Antonio Canova, in June 1818, when the Elgin Marbles were already installed in the British Museum. Quatremère had come to

England for the sole purpose of seeing the Marbles, and the letters penned after each visit are full of fresh and original insights. He was, for example, one of the first to point out the correct placement of the Iris figure in the west pediment, which, by an error of Visconti, had been given to the east.[48]

In 1814 Quatremère had published his *Jupiter Olympien*, a pioneering work of the rising interest in Greek as opposed to Graeco-Roman antiquities. It relied heavily, however, upon the evidence of ancient literary sources and, for all its great learning, lacked the revelationary impact of confrontation with the art of Pheidias as displayed in the British Museum. He had previously pronounced the Elgin Marbles to be of relatively little importance by virtue of their status as sculpture intended for a building. He later admitted to Canova that this opinion, formed upon the basis of James Stuart's engravings, the Comte de Choiseul-Gouffier's casts in Paris and the slab from the east frieze brought to Paris by the latter, was inadequate and premature.[49] He was struck by the great difference it made to the eye seeing architectural sculpture at close quarters. He compared the Elgin Room of the British Museum to the sculptor's workshop, where it was possible to lay hands on the sculptures.[50] This privileged view was one that had not been enjoyed since Pheidias's own day. We are reminded of a passage in Plutarch's *Life of Pericles* where Athens's premier statesman is said to have entertained his friends by taking them into the sculptors' workshops to preview the sculpture before it was put up on the building.

Charles Cockerell, architect and one of the discoverers of the Aegina marbles, had no misgivings about the importance of architectural sculpture and had argued the case for the celebrated Niobid group in Florence being a pedimental composition. Quatremère de Quincy had at first found improbable the suggestion that this important body of sculpture, traditionally attributed to Scopas, had belonged to a building. Seeing the Parthenon sculptures, however, had removed all his doubts.[51]

Quatremère was very interested in the effect of viewpoint on perception and on the question of whether the marbles should be seen at close quarters or at a distance. The acknowledged authenticity of the marbles as fifth-century originals depended upon the fact of their having been removed from a classical Greek temple. No one who had seen them from a distance or who was familiar with them from drawings or engravings alone could guess at the remarkable subtleties of modelling. All the same, the authentic viewpoint had to be that of the onlooker on the ground peering up. Quatremère therefore favoured the creation in the Elgin Room of plaster mock-ups of the entablature completed with casts of the sculptures in order to illustrate their original context. The choice between, on the one hand, displaying the Elgin Marbles as art and, on the other, presenting them as architectural elements was one which would continue to exercise the minds of those responsible for their arrangement throughout the rest of the century, and well into the next.[52] The desire to find a satisfactory solution to the problem of accommodating in a museum gallery the foremost relics of original Greek sculpture, which also happened to be the surviving fragments of the sculpted ornament of the most important Greek building, was to give rise to constant experiment.

Ultimately, however, what mattered about the Elgin Marbles was that they provided a touchstone of authenticity for the true Greek style. Those who saw them displayed at eye-level in the Elgin Room of the British Museum felt themselves to be in immediate contact with the art of Pheidias. This sense of intimacy is to be found in the testimony of Quatremère, and twenty years later we find it repeated by Charles Newton. In a remarkable lecture to the Oxford Art Society in 1849, Newton urged his listeners to 'make the sculptures of Pheidias your personal friends, live with them, commune with them, become acquainted with every fold in the drapery, every change in the curves of the muscles, know the colossal outlines of the torsos as the mountaineer knows the outlines of his hills, learn to distinguish each horse in the tumultuous throng of the friezes as a shepherd knows his flock.'[53]

An island of calm

Immediately following the installation of the Elgin Marbles in their temporary gallery at the British Museum, the initial wave of Parthenomania subsided into a more sedate reverence. Keats's 'indescribable feud' and 'dizzy pain', expressed in his *On Seeing the Elgin Marbles*, was transformed into the quieter, more comtemplative mood of the *Ode on a Grecian Urn*, where we find 'silent form . . . in the midst of other woe'.

It has become usual in the study of the British reception of the Elgin Marbles to point out that they did not succeed in becoming a new 'School of Art', as some hoped they might. There was no great renaissance of British history painting, as Haydon had proclaimed there would be.[54] At the same time, however, the Parthenon sculptures maintained and, indeed, increased their reputation as the highest form of classical art. Thus we witness the separation of art theory from art practice which would cause commentators later in the century to acknowledge that the study of art history has little to do with the process of painting and sculpture itself. The importance of the Elgin Marbles was not, therefore, so much that they caused a revolution in art, as that they constituted a major contributory factor in the separation of art from academic theory. In Rothenberg's words: 'The Elgin marbles were venerated by all but emulated by few.'[55] Haydon's drawing school where an artist's ability was measured in relation to how well he drew from the Parthenon sculptures, was the exception. Those who attended were a renegade group who disregarded the conventions of the Academy Schools.[56] Once their attendance had dwindled, the Elgin Gallery became an island of calm, where, 'in calmness of mind, all passion spent', art could be seen to have reached an inimitable perfection.

It was this inimitability that had ensured that the Marbles remained unrestored, and the decision not to restore them was crucial in determining their future status.[57] It set them apart from the Graeco-Roman sculptures of Rome and Paris, and from the Townley Marbles in the British Museum. Even the Aegina marbles, which – next to the Phigaleian – were the only comparable body of original Greek sculpture, had been made whole again according to Thorvaldsen's neo-classic taste. The Elgin Marbles, however, were to retain an archaeological purity of form that appealed not so much to the senses as to the intellect. They came to represent a fixed standard of beauty for the nineteenth-century Hellenist, both in the physical and abstract sense. Their physical condition as fragments made them difficult of access to the mass of the people, but this served only to increase their appeal to an élite class of cognoscenti, who could see beyond the ruin to a purer truth. As the most beautiful man-made creations in existence, they were the nearest thing to an earthly manifestation of that unseen beauty pursued in Plato's Theory of Forms. If in the repertoire of ancient sculptural paradigms the nineteenth century could invoke a greater model still, it would be the lost and invisible art of Pheidias, the chryselephantine Athena from the Parthenon and the Zeus from the temple at Olympia. Reverential awe for these lost originals surpassed even that felt for the Elgin Marbles. Having part of a statue, one might say, turns out to be second best only to having no statue at all.

Idolatry of the Elgin Marbles must, however, be taken in its context. Too few people, in the words of Edmund Oldfield, were sufficiently cultivated to appreciate 'the admitted merit of the marbles of the Parthenon in their actual fragmentary state'. Most people preferred 'an inferior though complete statue to a fragment of higher art'.[58] The Elgin Marbles had usurped the supremacy previously enjoyed by models such as the Laocoon, the Apollo Belvedere, the Torso Belvedere and the Venus de' Medici. Few would now deny their superiority, and yet old habits died hard. Far from being shunned, the Graeco-Roman sculptures continued to be preferred as the basis for an artist's training. As Francis Haskell and Nicholas Penny have pointed out, Haydon was exceptional in feeling that the defence of the 'new' necessitated the abuse of the 'old'.[59] We see this clearly reflected in the practice of art students drawing in the British Museum during the first half of the nineteenth century.

2 The Museum as a Drawing School

The British Museum and the Royal Academy

Throughout the nineteenth century the British Museum enjoyed a close relationship with the Royal Academy. The President was *ex officio* a trustee of the Museum and he could exert a powerful influence. For its part, the British Museum provided a training ground where students of the Academy Schools, or those seeking admission, could practise their skills upon the sculptures, mainly the Col. Pl. I
Graeco-Roman or Townley Marbles.

In 1808 the opening of the Townley Gallery resulted in a flood of applications from pupils of the Royal Academy wishing to draw the sculptures, and this raised the 36–7
question of regulations governing their admittance.[1] To begin with, these were rather constricting, but the rules were later relaxed and in the Parliamentary Return for 1833 we read that artists were admitted to the sculpture galleries every day between the hours of nine and four except Saturday.[2] One of the advantages of utilising the British Museum galleries was that it reduced pressure for space around the casts in the Royal Academy. The sculptures also extended the range of the Academy cast collection, which seems never to have been much developed. In 1813 Prince Hoare, honorary Foreign Secretary to the Academy, remarked upon the inadequacy of the institution in this respect: 'Scanty is its supplies of models and plaster casts; the latter crowded into so narrow a space, that it is difficult for the students even to obtain a proper view of them . . . .' In 1816 casts from sculpture in the Vatican were acquired through Pope Pius VIII and the Prince Regent, but even then the editor of the *Annals of Fine Arts* was to lament that the new arrivals must be consigned to 'smoky dingy rooms . . . liable to the carelessness of house-keepers, porters and idle boys'.[3]

Special Academy stools were provided for the use of the artists.[4] Easels were permitted for the first twenty years or so, but shortly before Christmas 1831, 'on a dark day', two fingers were snapped off the Townley Venus in the first rotunda of the Townley Gallery. The digits so rudely displaced were found the next morning hidden behind the statue base.[5] A falling easel was suspected and use of the device suspended; after two or three similar incidents, it was banned altogether, boxes being allowed instead.[6] Only in 1856, following a request from George Annesley on behalf of lady students, was use of the easel reinstated. A design was submitted to the 51 scrutiny of the Keeper of Antiquities, who set a limit on the permissible height as no more than 4 feet, 6 inches; twenty-four were ordered. Even then, artists were required to carry them 'underhand'.[7]

From the Annual Parliamentary Returns we can trace year by year the numbers of
4 students admitted to draw in the sculpture galleries. At first the record was presented in terms of the number of tickets issued; later the number of actual visits was counted. From these figures we can identify broad trends in the popularity of the sculpture galleries. From 1818 to the end of 1829, for example, 920 students were issued with tickets, 223 in the first year immediately following the opening of the temporary Elgin Room in 1817. In subsequent years far fewer applications were made, averaging around 60 per year.[8] From 1831 onwards these figures are replaced by the number of actual visits per annum. Thus from 4,398 in 1831, the figure rises to 7,052 in 1836; but then decreases to 5,655 in 1841 and slumps to 3,508 in 1847. The decline in numbers was remarked upon in *The Builder*, but no explanation was offered.[9] The reason is, however, not hard to find. The last vestige of the old Townley Gallery, which had probably provided the best setting the Museum ever had for the Graeco-Roman sculptures, was pulled down at the end of 1846. There
6 had been disarray in this quarter for some years, as the slow march of Smirke's new classical building displaced Saunders's outmoded Palladian design. The Townley

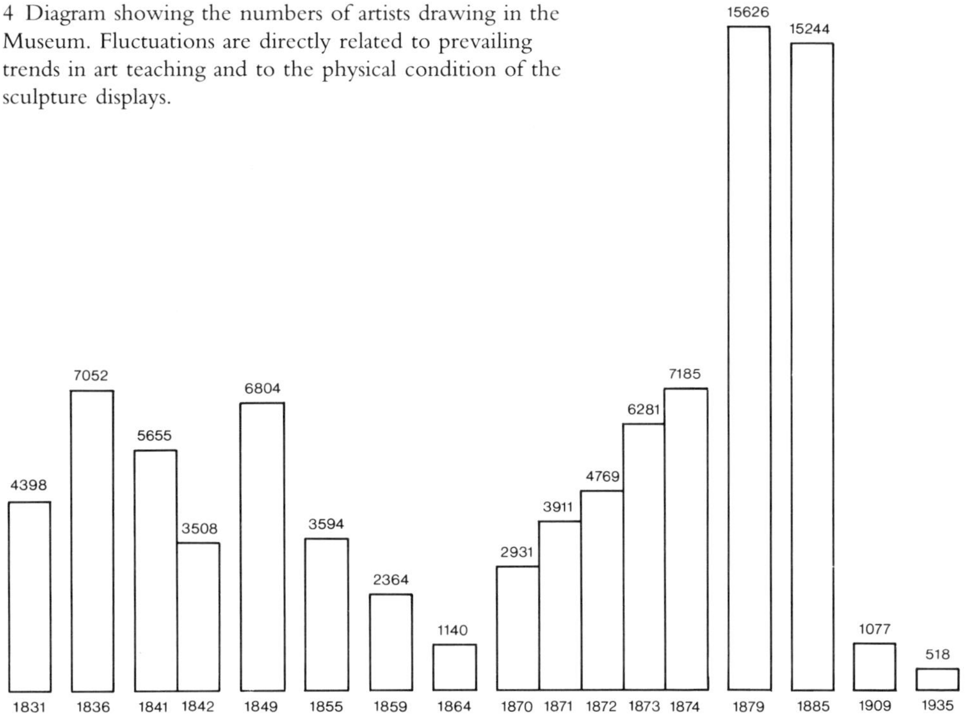

4 Diagram showing the numbers of artists drawing in the Museum. Fluctuations are directly related to prevailing trends in art teaching and to the physical condition of the sculpture displays.

sculptures were given temporary refuge either in the recesses around the Grand Central Saloon or in the newly completed Long Gallery (1 on Fig. 1) running between the Front Hall and what is now the Assyrian Transept. These new galleries, being over-tall and ill-lit, were unsympathetic to the Townley Marbles, and the sculptures must have lost much of the glamour afforded them by the more appropriate dimensions and top-lighting of the old Townley Gallery.

By 1849 some semblance of order had been restored to the arrangement of the sculptures and the attendance rose accordingly to 6,804 in 1849, remaining around that figure until it slumped again in 1855 to 3,594; in 1859 it had fallen as low as 2,364. The decline continued until 1864, when as few as 1,140 visits were made. The figures for the remainder of the 1860s show some improvement, but never reached the 3,000 mark. The decline in the mid-1850s is in part due to the fact that the Townley Marbles were on the move again, this time into a permanent home comprising a suite of galleries immediately to the south of the Lycian Room (2–4 on 48–56
Fig. 1). The sustained drop in attendance figures during this period, lasting until the

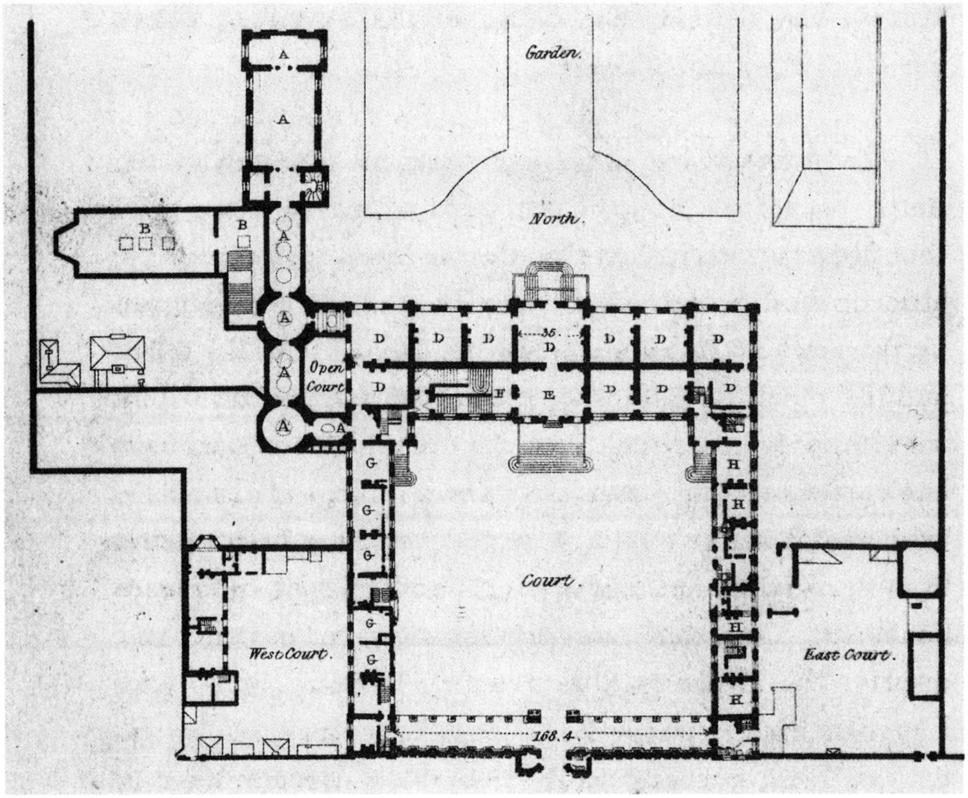

5 Plan of old Montagu House showing the Temporary Elgin Room, marked B, tacked onto the west side of the Townley Gallery, marked A. From Britton, pl. I.

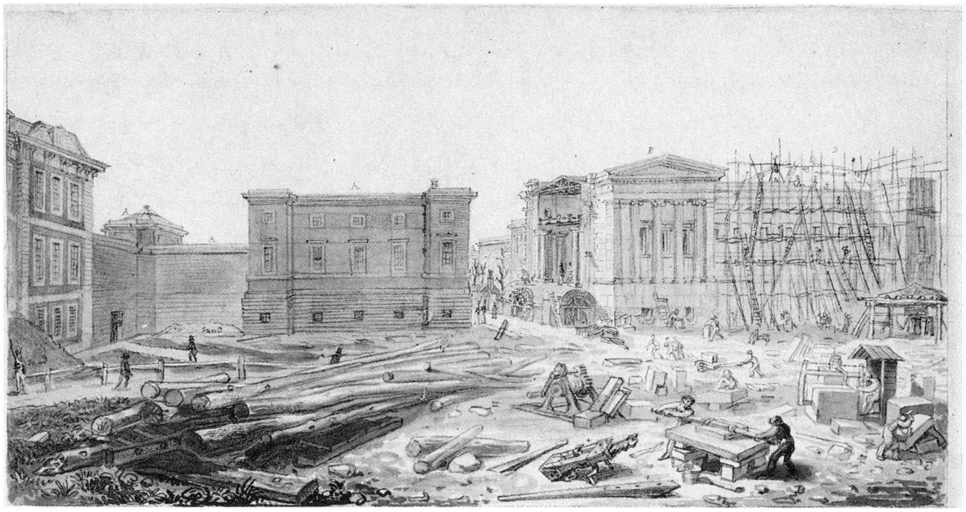

6 George Saunders's Townley Gallery (left) and the north division of Robert Smirke's Egyptian Sculpture Gallery (right). The 'permanent' Elgin Room, as first built by Robert Smirke, may be seen extending into the distance, westwards from the Central Saloon of the new building. It is clearly visible just to the right of the northern extremity of the Townley Gallery. Its long walls were afterwards torn down and the design adapted to accommodate the Parthenon frieze (compare Fig. 23). Watercolour signed G. Scharf, July 1828. British Museum, PD 1862–6–14–626.

1870s, is, however, curious. It may be due in part to the opening of the cast courts in the Crystal Palace at Sydenham,[10] or, more probably, to the reorganisation by Henry Cole of the casts belonging to the Government School of Design at Marlborough House.[11] For the first half of the nineteenth century London's artists had been without a representative collection of classical casts. The School of Design, which can be roughly equated now with the Royal College of Art, had acquired under the directorship of Charles Heath Wilson a collection of casts. But these were never well displayed and, following his dismissal in 1847, they fell into neglect. In 1852, when Henry Cole was brought in as General Superintendent to revive the flagging fortunes and spirits of the Government School, the casts were scattered throughout the cellars of Somerset House 'in a neglected and ruinous condition.'[12]

Before the creation of the cast courts at the Crystal Palace the best collection of casts in the British Isles was in Edinburgh, formed under the aegis of the Board of Trustees for the Encouragement of Manufacturers.[13] The lack of a similar collection in England is surprising when we reflect upon how formal art training was then based upon the copying of casts of classical sculpture. In his evidence to the National Gallery Parliamentary Commission of 1853, W. R. Hamilton considered the best training an artist might receive was to be given 'half a dozen of the very best works of art, either in casts or originals for study at home with their master.' This was

considered far preferable to 'turning them loose into a Museum where their minds are distracted by the great variety of style and quality.'[14] To the question 'Are the originals not preferable for study?' he was unequivocal in his reply: 'I believe not, with regard to broken fragments and others, likewise, I should presume that casts are preferable to the originals, because they cast a purer and a more direct shadow, whereas in a fragment of ancient sculpture you can hardly distinguish the dirt, as it were, from the shadow.' Richard Westmacott, Professor of Sculpture, was of the 13
same opinion: 'Students, whether of painting or sculpture should be taught from casts.' He conceded that drawing from sculpture had its place, but this should not be allowed too early in an artist's career. Currently, he felt, the students went too soon to the British Museum, and he agreed with Hamilton that a selection of casts of what were regarded as the finest works would be better than the statues themselves. A student, J. Davies, was called in and examined. He was one of those who went to the British Museum to draw, but would have preferred to draw casts.[15] J. Loft was also consulted. He had been a student at the Academy when it was combined with the National Gallery at Somerset House. Subsequently, having taken over Angelo Sarti's business in Dean Street, he had supplied casts to students and the general public. He remarked upon the great increase in the demand for casts, agreeing with the view that original sculptures were valuable as examples of the best art of the ancients but considering their use 'very limited for the purpose of study'.[16]

By 'the best art' Loft obviously had the Elgin Marbles in mind, and it is clear that they were not popular for art training. Even Benjamin Robert Haydon would not turn his students loose on them until their competence had been tested on other works. So far as the Academy was concerned, not only were novices advised against copying the Elgin Marbles, but the regulations actually prevented them from doing so. A second Parliamentary Commission sat in 1857 to investigate further the future of the National Gallery, and during his interrogation Edward Hawkins was asked: 7
'Do you find that the students study the Elgin Marbles as they would study perfect works?' He replied, 'I think they do now more than they used; because formerly the Royal Academy had a rule which prevented their students ever working in the Elgin Room at all. They insisted upon the students bringing a copy of a perfect statue.[17] Now, the Elgin Marbles do not afford a perfect statue and, therefore, though I think the Elgin Marbles are more valuable than all the sculptures in the world put together as a school of art, yet they were never much used by the students.' He goes on, 'It was quite dreadful to see a thing that they called a drunken faun (though it was not really a drunken faun) which was regularly wheeled into the room. Whenever, I saw it, I knew that the admission to the Academy was approaching.'[18] Asked why he thought the drunken faun was studied, Edmund Oldfield replied simply, 'Because it appears perfect.'[19]

The perfect statue could be afforded by a whole marble or by a cast. The British

Museum did not at this time display casts for the sake of artists. The policy of the Antiquities Department was quite simply that no cast of any sculpture that could be seen in a European museum should be exhibited in the galleries.[20] Exceptions were
14, 16 made only for the Aegina pediment sculptures and the Selinus metopes, considered essential for the sequence illustrating the rise of Greek art. Some thought that the Museum had not gone far enough in completing its chronological series of sculptures by the addition of casts.[21] Others, like Charles Eastlake, advocated the attachment of a cast gallery to the British Museum for the purposes of art training.[22] In investigating the future of the British Museum and the National Gallery collections the Parliamentary Committee was left in no doubt that given the choice between a gallery of casts of sculptures brought from all over the world and a collection of the best sculptures in the British Museum, the former would be considered more useful.[23]

The British Museum had a role to play not only in exhibiting models for the artist

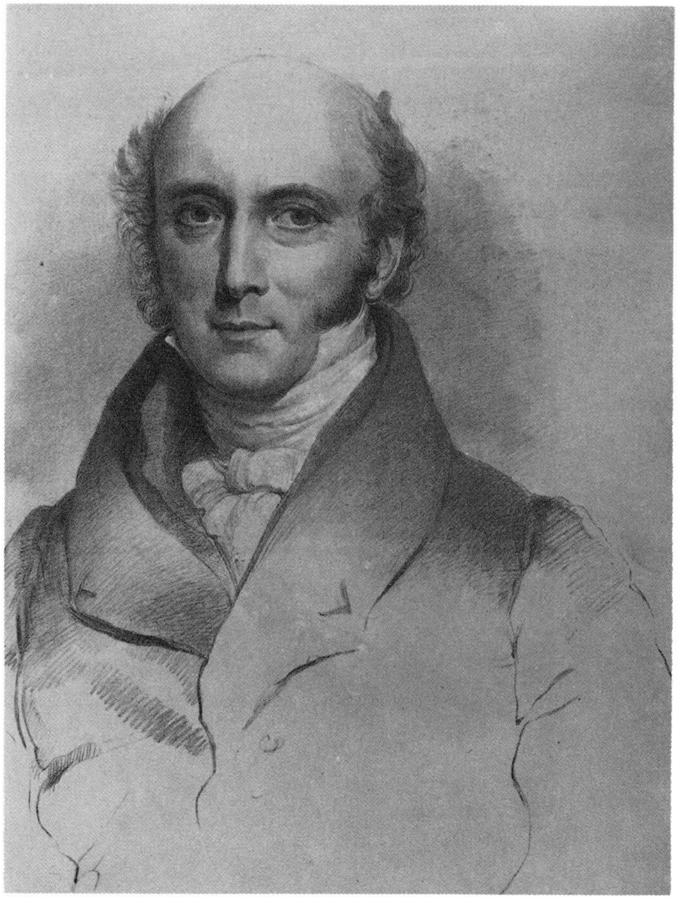

7 Edward Hawkins (1780–1867), Keeper of Antiquities 1826–60. Lithograph published by Colnaghi, 1833. *Illustrations of the British Museum*, vol. I. British Museum, Central Archive.

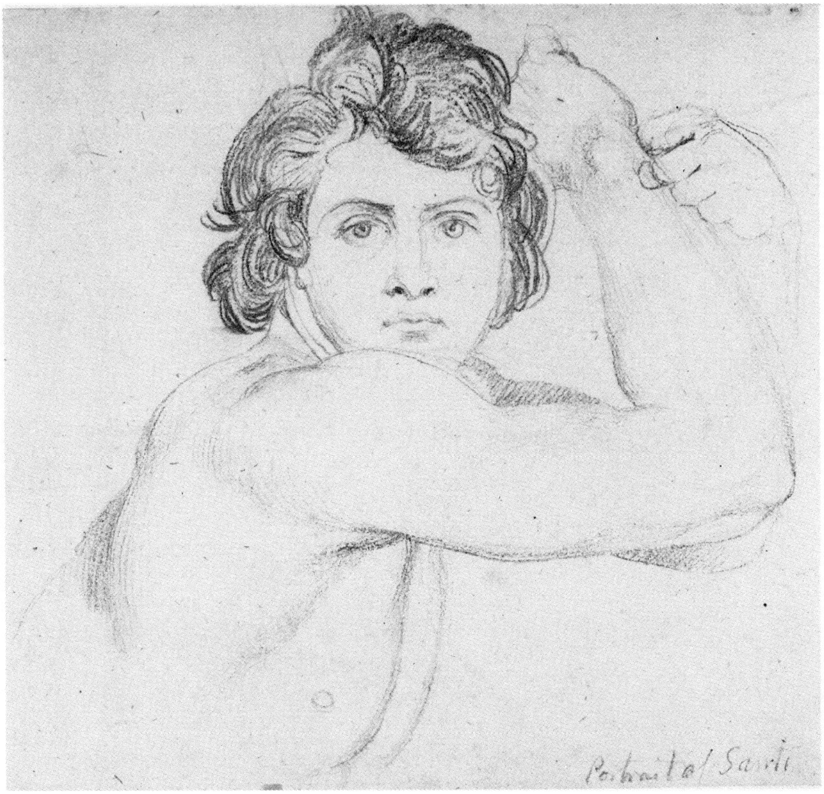

8 Angelo Sarti, the Museum's first official plaster-cast maker. Drawing by J. Flaxman. Boston, Museum of Fine Arts.

to copy, but also in the supply of casts to other institutions.[24] Demands by foreign institutions for casts of the Elgin Marbles prompted the establishment of a *formatore*'s workshop. At first the contract for moulding the Museum sculptures was given on an *ad hoc* basis to Richard Westmacott. Subsequently, however, the business was put on a more regular footing. At a Parliamentary Select Committee on the management of the Museum's affairs in 1835, Edward Hawkins, the Keeper of Antiquities, was quizzed as to why the Museum had no cast service such as that attached to the Louvre. The Committee considered the provision of casts a means for promoting national good taste, and there seems to have been added concern that Westmacott was running an extortionate monopoly. In June 1836 Hawkins attended the sale of the Durand vases in Paris and there had the opportunity of consulting the Comte de Clarac on how things were managed at the Louvre. Later that same year a contract was drawn up and Angelo Sarti, who had formerly been in the employ of West- 8
macott, became the Museum's first official *formatore*. His immediate task was to mould a new set of casts from the Elgin Marbles.

While the proliferation of casts from the Parthenon sculptures served to increase their reputation, yet casts of the Townley Marbles continued to be preferred as ornaments for domestic interiors and in the training of young artists. The immediate aftermath of the installation of the Elgin Marbles in the British Museum did not see any significant change in the practice of drawing from the antique. Although generally regarded as the greatest man-made creations on earth, when it came to the academic training of young artists they were shunned in favour of more traditional models. While Haydon had claimed them as his inspiration, others seem to have been almost intimidated by their peculiar blend of natural and idealised beauty. Haydon had hopes of their encouraging a new school of history painters, but by the

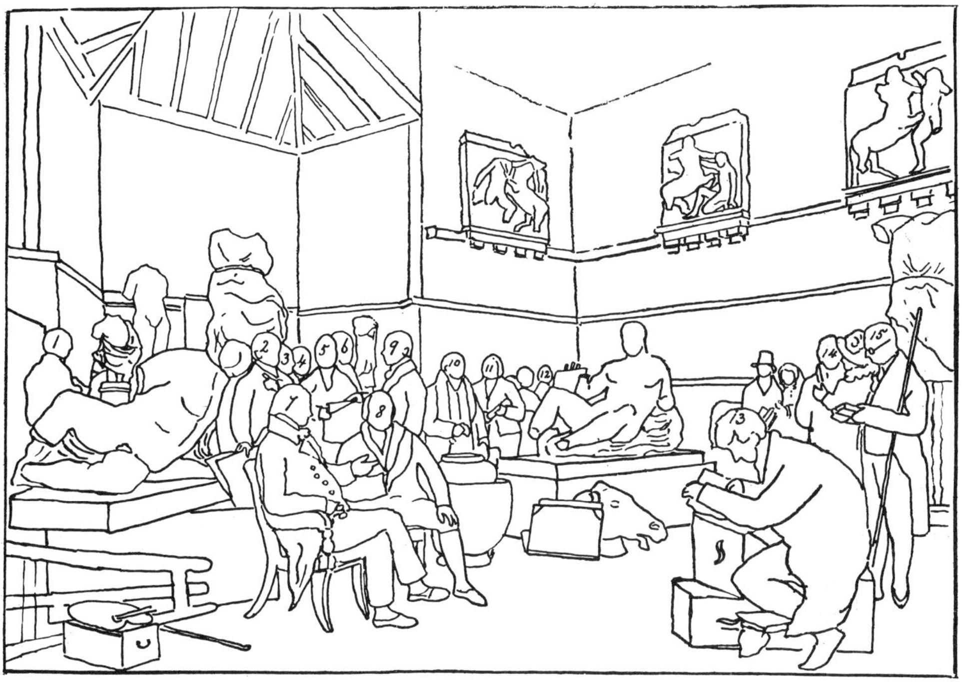

9 Key to Archibald Archer's painting of the Temporary Elgin Room (see Colour Plate II). From Smith (1916), pp. 353–4. **1**. Benjamin Robert Haydon (1786–1846). **2**. Sir Charles Long (?), afterwards Lord Farnborough (1761–1838), Paymaster-General. **3**. The Rev. James Bean, Assistant Librarian 1812–26. **4**. The Rev. Thomas Maurice (1754–1824), Assistant Librarian, Department of Manuscripts, 1799–1824. **5**. Sir Henry Ellis (1777–1869), Assistant Librarian 1805; Secretary 1814; Principal Librarian 1827–56. **6**. John George Children (1777–1852), FRS, Assistant Librarian 1816. **7**. Benjamin West (1738–1820), first elected President of the Royal Academy 1792. **8**. Joseph Planta (1744–1827), Under Librarian (Keeper of Manuscripts) 1776; Principal Librarian 1799–1827. **9**. Taylor Combe (1774–1826), Assistant Librarian 1803; Under Librarian (First Keeper of the Department of Antiquities) 1805–26. **10**. The Rev. Henry Harvey Baber (1775–1869), Assistant 1810; Under Librarian (Keeper of Manuscripts) 1812–37. **11**. John Thomas Smith (1766–1833), Extra Assistant Librarian (Prints) 1816–33. **12**. John Edward Gray (1800–75), Assistant, Department of Natural History, 1824; Keeper 1840–74. **13**. Archibald Archer, the artist. **14**. Charles Dietrich Eberhard Konig (1774–1851), Assistant Librarian, Department of Natural History, 1807–13; Under Librarian, Natural History (Minerals), 1813–51. **15**. John Conrath, Attendant from 1816.

time the Elgin Marbles were acquired for the British Museum the great vogue for neo-classic painting in Britain was already over. Archibald Archer's 'Elgin Room at Col. Pl. II
the British Museum' of 1819 celebrates the union of the Academy and the Museum, with the elderly figures of the British Museum's Principal Librarian and the President 9
of the Academy in the foreground, but it seems to mark the end of an era rather than the dawning of a new age.[25] Landscape and portraiture were to become the dominant schools, and the 1840s and 1850s saw the waxing and waning of the anti-classical Pre-Raphaelite Movement. There would, however, come a time when the Elgin Marbles became the centrepiece and inspiration for a new classical movement.

The later Victorian Greek Revival

During the 1860s a new generation of painters turned to the Parthenon sculptures with fresh admiration for Pheidias and the art of Periklean Athens. G. F. Watts, 10
having become disaffected from the Academy school early in his career, had kept the flame of Haydon's vision burning since the latter's tragic suicide in 1846, and was joined now by younger talents like those of Albert Moore and Frederic Lord Leighton.[26] Their story has been told many times and need not be repeated; all that matters here is that, broken or not, whether in the original or in cast, the Elgin Marbles exerted a new influence over the classical painters that would last until the great upheaval of the First World War.

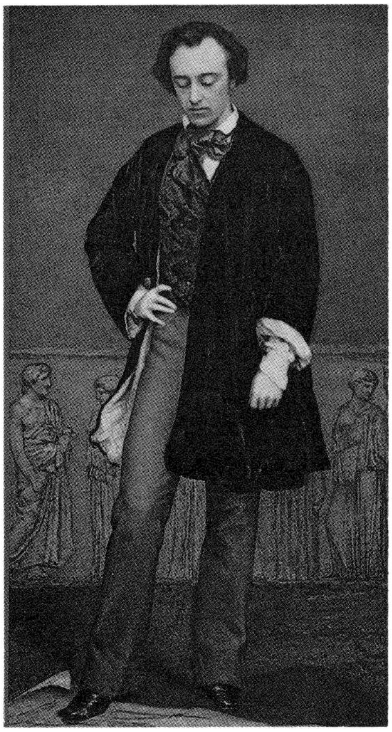

10 G. F. Watts as a young man, by Charles Couzens. Watercolour, *c.* 1849. Compton (Surrey), Watts Gallery. Watts is standing in front of a cast of a slab of the Parthenon frieze, now in the Louvre.

This new interest in classical art was accompanied by a dramatic rise in the number of students drawing in the sculpture galleries of the Museum. In 1870 the
4 annual number of visits stood at 2,981. As the new decade dawned, so the numbers began to rise: 3,911 in 1871; 4,769 in 1872; 6,281 in 1873; 7,185 in 1874; until in 1879 the increase peaked at an almost incredible 15,626. During the 1880s similar high numbers attended. The increase was remarked upon by Charles Newton in his reports to the Trustees, and he affords us supplementary figures of the actual numbers of students involved. At the beginning of 1876 he reported that during the previous year 267 students had been granted admission, of whom 166 were entirely new applicants. In the course of 1876 the number had risen to 516, of which 183 were new admissions.[27] In 1878 Newton was to remark, 'the galleries are now so crowded with easels, that on public days it is exceedingly difficult to keep a clear gangway . . . .'

At this time the galleries were closed to the public on Tuesdays and Thursdays and on Saturday mornings, and it was on these days that the students enjoyed exclusive access. Newton was very eager that this privilege should continue and, indeed, he had personally persuaded the Trustees to extend the time allowed to the students on Saturday morning. By opening the galleries to the general public at 12 noon instead of 11 a.m., Newton expressed the hope that the Museum might become a 'School of Drawing'. Newton, it must be remembered, had himself been married to an able draughtswoman, Mary, daughter of the painter Joseph Severn. He was also a close friend of George Frederic Watts and Frederic Lord Leighton. There was, nevertheless, opposition to the system of Museum closed days, and against an attempt to raise the matter in Parliament, Newton had protested that, as a consequence of the privilege enjoyed by artists in the Museum, there had been a marked improvement in the quality of drawing, 'so much so that in open competition for admission to the Royal Academy last month twelve out of fifteen successful candidates were students of the British Museum.'[28] This was certainly rhetorical, for the privilege had been enjoyed by artists since 1808. At no time, moreover, could the artists who frequented the British Museum be considered its students, but the idea is charming all the same.

There does, however, seem to have been a positive policy of encouraging students to draw in the galleries. By 1886 the Museum was at last allowing the introduction of casts expressly for the purpose of providing set pieces for drawing. In March 1886, the year in which Newton retired as Keeper, his successor Alexander Murray applied to the Trustees for permission to introduce a cast of the Venus de' Medici, 'the figure being one of those which the Academy accepts as a test of the drawing of the candidate for admission'.[29] A cast of the Venus de Milo and the Hermes of Praxiteles had already been installed for the same purpose and the intention was to relieve some of the overcrowding round these two figures.[30]

The Hermes of Praxiteles had been found at Olympia in 1877 and had become an instant success. The drawing of this naked male figure by ladies in the presence of gentlemen caused offence in some circles. A vicar by the name of J. Henry Skewes – Trollope could not have named him better – engaged the support of his local Member of Parliament to lobby the Trustees of the British Museum with a view to having a fig-leaf affixed to the Hermes. Mr Skewes's objections were deemed unreasonable and Murray dismissed them with a laconic 'Hitherto the Museum has done without the fig-leaf'.[31]

The great rise in the number of artists drawing in the sculpture gallery must be accounted for by the renewed interest in classical sculpture which accompanied the high Victorian revival of classical painting. Newton implies that the impetus was coming from the Academy Schools but no doubt students (or those seeking admission) also attended from other institutions, such as the Slade School opened in 1871, where students were subjected to a rigid drill of drawing from casts. Stuart MacDonald remarks how forty years after Edward Poynter's appointment as Director of the South Kensington School, 'galleries of casts of the classical nude became the central feature in major art schools'.[32] The great rise was followed, however, by a corresponding fall; from 15,244 in 1885, the number had slumped to 1,077 in 1909. There was, not surprisingly, a further substantial fall to 249 in 1916, and during 1917 and 1918 wartime measures to protect the sculptures from air-raids prevented any drawing at all. In 1919, 368 artists attended and during the 1920s there was a relative revival of interest, although numbers never reached the 2,000 mark. The figures show another fall during the 1930s, with as few as 518 attendances in 1935.

It is not difficult to find the causes of this decline in the rise of modernism. Antiquity no longer held its fascination for art teachers and their students. The modern art movement denied classical sculpture the supreme status formerly attributed to it and, although drawing from the antique was not altogether abandoned, it ceased to be the only standard by which an artist's ability could be measured.

Following the Second World War the Townley Marbles, which had supplied the principal focus of artistic practice in the Museum, failed to re-emerge from wartime basement storage. Only recently have they gone back on public exhibition in the new suite of Wolfson Galleries of Classical Sculpture. This, combined with a new post-modern, neo-classical movement, has created something of a revival of the old habit of drawing in the Museum sculpture galleries. Whereas before, however, the classical repertoire was almost exclusively deemed suitable, nowadays Egyptian, Assyrian, Indian and Ethnographic subjects are all included, and what has happened cannot be mistaken for a return to old values. Nor can a time be foreseen when casts will be readmitted to the galleries of the British Museum for the purpose of art training.

3 Light, Colour and Dirt

Lighting

Related to the role of the sculpture galleries as a training ground for artists are questions of lighting and of the colouring of walls. In general, ideal studio effects were not permissible in the galleries and were thought to conflict with the interests of the more general visitor. Occasionally this gave rise to rancour, as it had done in the planning of other European museums, namely the Louvre, the Munich Glyptothek and Schinkel's Altes Museum in Berlin.[1] The most fully documented discussion is that between J.M. von Wagner and Leo von Klenze over the lighting of Ludwig of Bavaria's Glyptothek.[2] Klenze opposed Wagner's desire to see a form of 'art-school' lighting with the observation that, 'A Museum is no drawing office, academic menagerie and studio.' Rather, he insisted, it exists, '... for all kinds of visitors ... more an institution for the nation, than for the student of art, suited to divert art into life and mix it with life.'[3]

Wagner had favoured a high diagonal light throughout the galleries, falling from an aperture set in one wall only, suitable for creating strong shadows. Klenze did, in
12 fact, introduce such a system into the Aegina Room and the other rooms containing the finer pieces of supposed Greek sculpture. Elsewhere in Ludwig's suite of rooms, however, he employed side-lights or top-lighting.

Klenze's principle of general, as opposed to studio lighting, was also that preferred in the British Museum, but here more use was made, from the beginning, of top-lighting, both in Saunders's Townley Gallery and in the new Smirke rooms. In the former the Townley Marbles were lit either by lanterns in the rotundas or by
38 roof lights in the intervening long galleries.[4] The space reserved for Egyptian sculpture, however, was side-lit from the long walls of the gallery, which were able, accordingly, to carry an upper storey.

The decision to deny the Egyptian sculptures the advantage of top-lighting was consistent with the view that Egyptian antiquities, being essentially non-artistic, did
34 not require the best setting. Indeed, some thought funereal gloom positively becoming. A reviewer of the Townley Gallery in *The Gentleman's Magazine* felt the Egyptian sculptures should not have been exhibited on the ground floor but should more appropriately have been consigned to the darkness of a basement.[5] In the
41, 45 Smirke gallery the Egyptian sculptures were again lit by a confused cross-lighting

from windows on both sides. In submitting his report to the Parliamentary Commission of 1853, Klenze excused this fact on account of the nature of the objects, and went on to express his general approval of the British Museum's top-lit galleries.[6] Even James Fergusson, who was generally scathing of the Museum as a whole, found nothing to quarrel with here: 'the light is sufficient and sufficiently diffused, and for Egyptian sculpture it is of very little consequence how or in what direction the light falls. The artists on the banks of the Nile never aimed at Aesthetic beauty of form, so that the sculptural products of their art scarcely depend more on their shadows than architectural members do.'[7] Modern visitors to the British Museum who have enjoyed the sight of some of the colossal Egyptian and, indeed, Assyrian sculptures lit artificially by night will wonder at the apparent short-sightedness of this statement.

Fergusson, although indifferent to the lighting of the Egyptian sculptures, was
violently critical of the classical sculpture galleries, making much play of the ac-
knowledged deficiencies in the Elgin Room.[8] His simple prescription was a north-
ern light falling at an angle of 45 degrees. Hawkins, the Keeper of Antiquities, had
his own reservations about the success of overhead lighting, as is shown in his
attempts to remedy the situation in the Elgin Room,[9] and in his objections to
Charles Barry's proposal for glazing over the central courtyard of the Museum and 72
turning it into a sculpture gallery: 'To give artistic effect to sculpture, distinction of
light and shade is essential; the light should fall only in one direction; there should
not be any cross-light; and the objects should be isolated, each having its own proper
background.'[10] The argument that none of these conditions was attainable in Barry's
proposed Hall of Antiquities is rather specious, since nowhere in the Museum had
such ideal conditions ever been achieved.

By 1858 Hawkins seemed more positive towards top-lighting, perhaps because he was no longer in the position of fending off Barry's interference but also, no doubt, because of the influence of his young and energetic assistant Edmund Oldfield, who had firmly stated his preference for it and who at this time was providing much of the power behind the throne of the Department of Antiquities. According to Hawkins, galleries with windows on both sides, such as the Egyptian sculpture galleries of the British Museum, necessarily forced freestanding objects to be illuminated by a series of awkward cross-lights. If windows were kept to one side only, then objects placed against the blank wall were in light, while those placed under the windows were necessarily cast into shadow. There was also the question of restriction on the Museum's natural growth: 'Galleries lighted from the sides require far greater building space than galleries lighted from the roof: for whilst any number of galleries with skylights may be built side-by-side, galleries with side-windows only must be separated by wide intervening spaces.'[11]

Here, Hawkins had in mind the Egyptian Sculpture Gallery which, since the

Reading Room had occupied the inner court of the Museum, was darkened beyond the gloom normally tolerated where these sculptures were concerned. The system advocated by Hawkins was entirely compatible with Oldfield's proposal to the 1853 Parliamentary Commission for a new Museum of Sculpture in galleries arranged in parallel lines. Thus Oldfield himself had told the Commission, '. . . the sculpture should have skylights, which after many experiments, and much observation I should say are indispensable to a well arranged gallery of sculpture.'[12] Newton came to the same conclusion when in 1859, on the way out to Rome to take up his commission as British Consul, he visited Berlin. There he reported on the effect of seeing casts of the Elgin Marbles displayed in the Greek Room of the Neues Museum, just completed with tall windows on one side of the gallery only. Here there seemed to Newton to be no *chiaroscuro* and the casts did not have the advantages of the top-lit setting in the British Museum.[13]

Top-lighting would remain the preferred method for the remainder of the century and all new sculpture galleries were to be thus illuminated. Towards the end of the century, however, an event occurred that would ultimately transform the Museum's approach to the problem of lighting its sculptures. On 28 January 1890 a

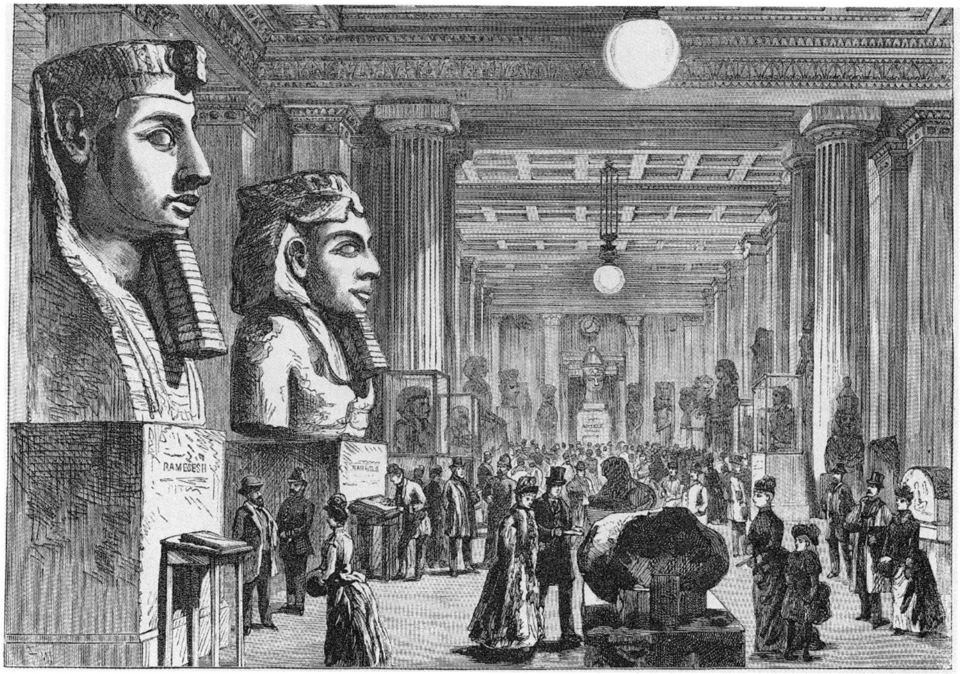

11 An evening opening of the Egyptian Sculpture Gallery, illuminated by newly installed electric lighting. Gas lighting had been considered too dangerous, and was never admitted into the galleries. *The Illustrated London News*, 8 February 1890.

private view was held, with 3,000 invitees, to witness the Museum lit by electricity. 11
Experiments had been going on for some years and the Reading Room had been lit artificially since February 1879. This was, however, the first occasion when the entire Museum was lit by electricity.[14] On dark afternoons in winter, especially when the London air was thick with smog, the new lighting proved indispensable. It did not, however, greatly affect the look of the galleries, which continued to rely upon their roof-lights as the principal source of illumination. The eventual change brought about by electricity is a relatively recent one, namely the introduction of the spotlight. It is this device which, in concentrating controlled, direct light onto the sculptures at all times of the day and night, has not only changed the manner in which the sculptures are lit, but also the look of the galleries themselves. Since the 1960s false ceilings, hanging panels and tracking disfigure or conceal altogether the ceiling mouldings and roof-lights of many exhibition rooms. In some cases, natural light is blocked out completely, thus solving by drastic remedy the old struggle against the unpredictable, shifting and transient rays of an English sun. Today, the tide of taste is happily changing once more as, increasingly, ceilings are being uncovered and natural daylight readmitted.

Colour

There is no detailed account of the colouring of the walls and ceilings of the Museum in the early years of the nineteenth century but from scattered sources we can piece together the evidence for the sculpture galleries. It has been said that the Townley Gallery, when opened, was a pastel green.[15] There were, certainly, experiments with paper imitating green granite before the Townley Gallery was finished,[16] but in the end the walls were distempered in a light grey granite colour. A water-
colour by George Scharf shows a greenish tint, but the reason for this is given in a Col. Pl. I
retrospective account by Richard Westmacott junior explaining how the original grey was later 'badly varnished to a dark yellowish or greenish tint'. Even so, he adds that the effect was generally 'cheerful'.[17]

A similar grey was probably employed in the northern Egyptian Gallery of 41
Smirke's new Museum (17 on Fig. 1) which we are told was a 'stone colour'. The Elgin Room was a somewhat darker, mottled purplish grey.[18] The tendency towards grey walls in the early Museum is consistent with some Continental museums, for example, the Museo Pio Clementino in the Vatican, whose walls are said originally to have been a pale greyish colour, and the Louvre, which employed 'granit gris mêlé de taches roses'.[19] Elsewhere in Europe, however, colour was more in evidence, particularly in the form of decorative marble wall-panelling or stucco, painted to imitate coloured marble. Notable were the greens, greys and yellows
introduced into the walls, ceilings and architectural members of Klenze's Glypto- 12

thek and Schinkel's Altes Museum. The British Museum was never so sumptuous in its polychromy, but after the middle of the century the walls of the sculpture galleries were almost uniformly red and green, and the ceilings variously ornamented.

For Museum men like Edward Hawkins the reason for this was partly practical. The sculptures darkened by London soot and grime, although washed frequently, had after about 1850 a permanently dingy appearance, which could only be offset by a strong contrasting background. This requirement, however, also fell in with the taste of the times, and in his evidence to the 1857 Parliamentary Commission John Ruskin remarked that, 'Beautiful sculpture should be set off beautifully – i.e. with dark walls round it to throw out its profile, and you should have all the arrangements made there so as to harmonize with it and to set forth every line of it.'[20]

There was, however, another consideration, namely the desire for archaeological correctness in the Museum interior. By 1850 the advance in knowledge of ancient architectural polychromy made it possible for Sydney Smirke to attempt an authentic reconstruction of Greek temple colouring in the Museum's interior decoration.[21] In so doing he employed the same principle of adherence to the code of ancient practice as his brother Robert had in choosing the Museum's plastic ornament. The naked purity of Greek architecture, however, seemed by the mid-1840s less acceptable to contemporary Victorian taste than it had done in the heyday of the Greek Revival. Increasing awareness of the extent to which the ancient Greeks painted their architecture and also the manner of their doing so, now made the Museum seem unfinished to the informed eye. While work was in progress a contributor to *The Builder* observed: 'The general effect ... when the walls are completed will be satisfactory as to colour; at all events far superior to the blank white walls and ceilings formerly in vogue.'[22]

On 19 December 1846, having just taken over from his brother Robert the commission of completing the building of the British Museum, Sydney Smirke noted that since the scaffolding had been taken down in the new hall and staircase, the plain surfaces of the walls and ceiling appeared to beg some relief.[23] He recommended that this be achieved by painted decoration which 'if done sparingly and cautiously, in strict conformity with the ancient examples, and confined chiefly to the mouldings' would be certain to bring a satisfactory result. Smirke acknowledged that there might be doubts as to the 'propriety of this kind of embellishment in the exhibition rooms', but he felt that the essentially *architectural* interior of the Front Hall demanded it.[24] The Trustees ruled that, so long as no figures were to be introduced, it was a matter that could be left to the discretion of the architect. Accordingly, Sydney Smirke commissioned a scheme from L. Collman and his partner Davis.[25] Their proposal was put into practice and, in spite of Smirke's original reservations, the result was to have far-reaching consequences.

The scheme of decoration in the Front Hall is shown in a watercolour drawing in the Department of Prints and Drawings and is described as follows in an article in *The Builder* published in 1849:[26] Col. Pl. III

The order is Grecian Doric. The ceiling is trabeated and deeply coffered, and is enriched with Greek frets and other ornaments in various colours painted in encaustic . . . The centre flight is seventeen feet wide, flanked by two pedestals of grey Aberdeen granite, highly polished. On the first landing are pedestals and carved vases of huddlestone stone. The balustrades are the same. The ceilings and walls are painted partly in oil and partly in encaustic colours, the former being trabeated and coffered to correspond with the Entrance Hall, and similarly decorated.

The polychromatic enrichments have been applied with very considerable success. The sunk panels are blue, with a yellow star in each; the enrichments are variously coloured – red and white predominantly, and the stiles, beams etc. are covered with frets, guilloche and scrolls in flat colours, for all of which precedents were sought in the Museum collection. These decorations were executed by Messrs. Collman and Davis.

Encouraged by the obvious success of the ceiling decoration in the Front Hall and Grand Staircase, in the summer of 1850 Sydney Smirke ventured to suggest an extension of the scheme.[27] The great gallery to the south of the Egyptian Sculpture Room (19 on Fig. 1) was nearing completion. Once the temporary partitions had been removed, the eventual space thus opened up would amount to some 380 feet in length and 41 feet in width. The unprecedented size of this gallery would, however, be likely to require relief from the total absence of colour. The sculpture itself, remarked Smirke, was as colourless as the building. The southern gallery of the west wing, it must be remembered, was intended for the Graeco-Roman sculptures at this time.

By way of reassuring the Trustees of his good intentions, the architect invoked antiquity as his source, namely, 'the type of Greek temple which has been favoured in the architecture of this Gallery'; and he further promised to use only such colour as the Greeks themselves would have used. If the Trustees were agreeable, then it would go without saying that the colouring would need to be extended throughout the whole gallery. The Egyptian Sculpture Gallery, he commented, had not been painted since it was first opened, and the southern and northern parts would have to be treated as one. The cost he estimated at £500, plus the cost of the ordinary redecoration. Smirke repeated his request in the following August[28] and it was then approved.

By November 1850 the ceiling painting of the new gallery was begun and still in progress, when Smirke wrote to say that he had been conferring with Sir Charles Eastlake as to the most suitable colour for the walls.[29] Both were agreed that 'the fittest colour for the background of the sculpture will be a strong red'. Smirke went on: 'Had the sculpture been clean and more nearly of the natural colour of marble, a lighter background would have sufficiently relieved them, but their dingy hue renders a deep-toned background unavoidable. The upper part, however, of the walls against which no sculpture can be placed should be painted in lighter tints, more in unison with the ceiling . . . .'

London dirt had become a major factor in the discussions about the colouring of the galleries. Thus Hawkins was to observe that since the London atmosphere would always render the sculptures dirty in appearance, the walls should be 'a very dark rich colour', so as to reduce as far as possible the contrast between the gloomy appearance of the sculpture and the tone of the background. The pilasters of the new southern division of the Egyptian Sculpture Gallery, he remarked, were currently light in tone, and the sculptures placed in front of them appeared very dirty. It was also to be observed that the deep recess of the pilasters created a dark perpendicular shadow that tended to present the statues in a 'very disagreeable manner'. This effect could be avoided if the pilasters were treated in a dark colour.[30]

A general conference was held with opinions taken from Eastlake, Westmacott and Sydney Smirke as to what colour the present Egyptian Sculpture Gallery and its new extension should be. Portions of the new room were accordingly painted in different colours, and statues tried against them.[31] The result of these deliberations is not recorded in contemporary papers, but we learn retrospectively from a future round of discussions that it was a 'strong red colour',[32] at least so far as the immediate background of the sculptures was concerned, for here – as elsewhere – the upper walls were probably broken up into panels of colour outlined in red or black. The following account taken from *The Builder* must apply to all the major galleries of the south and west wings, or at least those equipped with pilasters:

> The decoration of the new western galleries (by Mr Collman under Mr Smirke) is now nearly completed . . . The ceiling of the new galleries is formed like those of the other galleries into a series of small deeply-sunk panels: the ground of these is coloured blue, and upon this, in the centre of each star, is a gilt star, or a composition of four honeysuckles placed alternately (these patterns are from Greek fragments). The plaster bed-moulds around each panel have red in them, and on the soffit of the main beams forming the larger divisions of the ceiling, panels are formed by green lines. The frieze on the walls has a white honeysuckle pattern on a quiet ground, but where it runs out over the projecting piers, frets are substituted for the honeysuckle. The upper part of the walls is coloured sage-green, with panels formed by red lines, and the lower part (the podium) is to be coloured dark red, as a background for the sculptures. The decoration of the Elgin Room will be richer, – the walls wholly red.[33]

As early as 1839 red had been chosen for the walls of the Elgin Room. It was natural, therefore, that since a harmony of red walls and polychromatic ceiling had been achieved in the Egyptian Sculpture Gallery, a similar treatment should be given to the Elgin and Phigaleian Rooms. Before this work could proceed, however, a doorway had to be cut in the partition wall between the Elgin Room and a new gallery nearing completion to the south.[34] The opening must have been made by the following May, when the architect reported that he had 'received a distinct promise from Messrs. Collman and Davis, who are engaged in the painting and gilding of the Elgin and Phigaleian Rooms, that the Elgin Gallery will be completed by the 31st, and the Phigaleian Room a few days afterwards, and that the painting throughout the west wing will be completed by the 12th of June.' It is uncertain whether the walls, as well as the ceilings, of the Elgin Gallery were painted at this time. If they were, then it is unlikely that the colour differed much from that of the 1839 repainting. There must, however, have been some dissent voiced over the colour as a suitable background for the Parthenon sculptures, for Hawkins seems to have experimented with the idea of erecting a screen of a different (unspecified) tone behind the pedimental figures. This screen was to be a portable device which could be moved whenever the need arose to inspect the backs of the figures. The screen stood from June until November 1851, when it was removed by order of the Trustees.[35] In his annual report for the year ending December 1851, Hawkins declared that the painting of the entire west wing was complete.[36]

This initial phase of ornamental painting in the sculpture galleries was to be carried on for all new western galleries, as and when they were completed.[37] Nor was the practice to be restricted to the downstairs galleries, for towards the end of the decade the upper galleries of the western wing, at least in the northern division, had been similarly treated with polychromatic ceilings and red walls.[38]

Polychromania

Sydney Smirke's polychrome decoration had been carried out at the height of the mid-century debate over polychromy. The archaeological discovery of ancient colour in both classical and medieval architecture and sculpture had given rise to the question as to whether contemporary architects and sculptors should introduce colour into their works also.[39] In England curiosity had first been aroused in the late 1820s and early 1830s following a wave of interest on the Continent among travelling architects who had visited the temples of southern Italy, Sicily and Athens and witnessed and recorded vestiges of their applied colour. In 1836 a committee had been formed to discuss the question of whether the Elgin Marbles retained any traces of colour. The results of these deliberations, published in *Transactions of the Institute of British Architects*, were largely negative.[40] Nevertheless, in 1839 the walls of the Elgin Room were painted a strong red seemingly, in part at least, in answer to revelations of colour on the Parthenon and other Athenian monuments.

During the next decade interest in Greek polychromy tended to subside as the emphasis shifted towards Gothic architecture and its colouring.[41] Around 1850, however, the old enthusiasm was revived with renewed vigour. No fewer than three meetings at the Institute of British Architects in 1852 were devoted to the

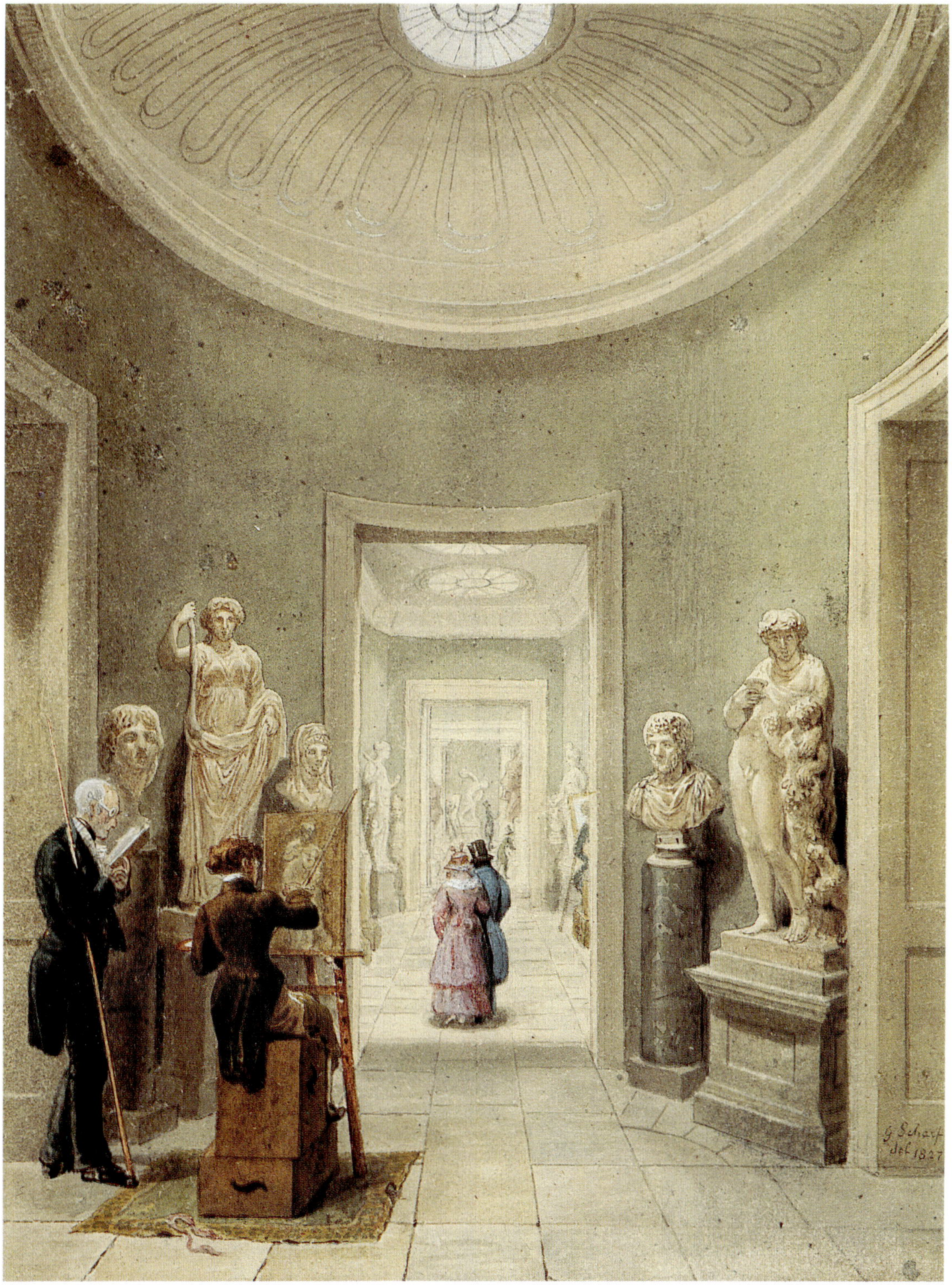

Plate I Room IV of the Townley Gallery, looking north. According to Richard Westmacott junior, the colour of the walls was an accident of varnishing. Watercolour signed G. Scharf, 1827. British Museum, PD 1862-6-14-632.

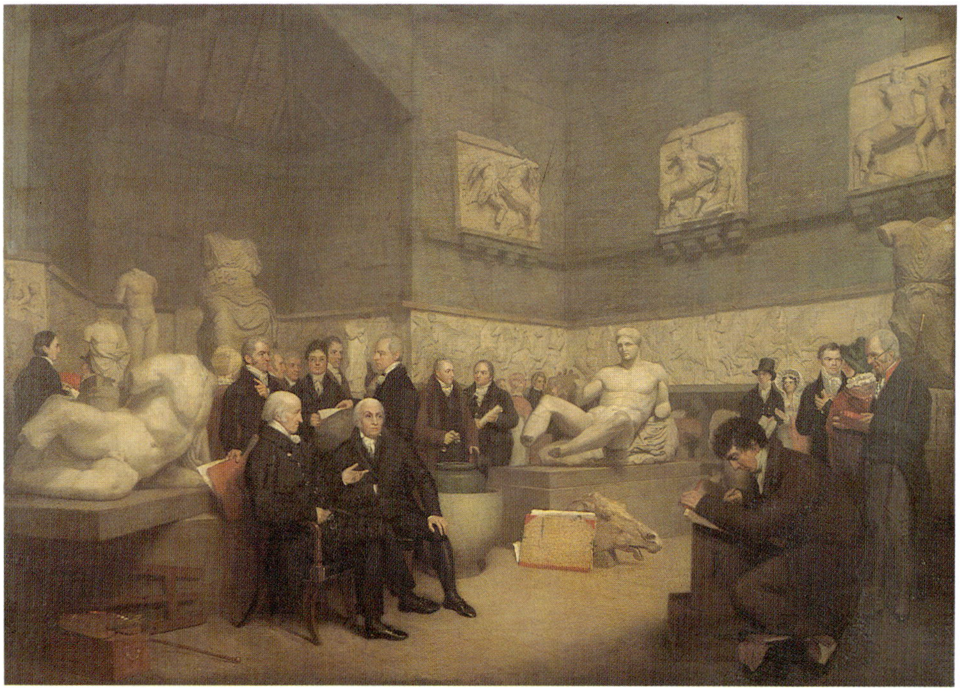

Plate II The Temporary Elgin Room. Oil on canvas, signed Archibald Archer, 1819. British Museum. See also Fig. 9.

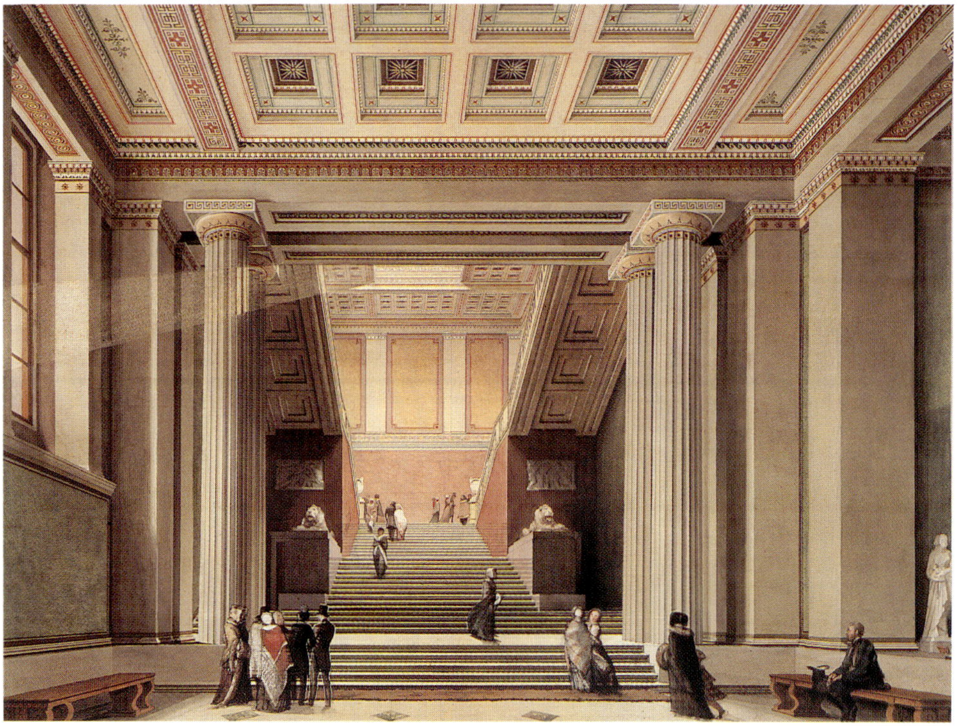

Plate III Scheme for the polychrome decoration of the Front Entrance Hall, by L. Collman. According to Sydney Smirke, the walls and ceiling of the newly completed Front Hall 'appeared to beg some relief'. Watercolour, 1847. British Museum, PD 1902–1–29–1.

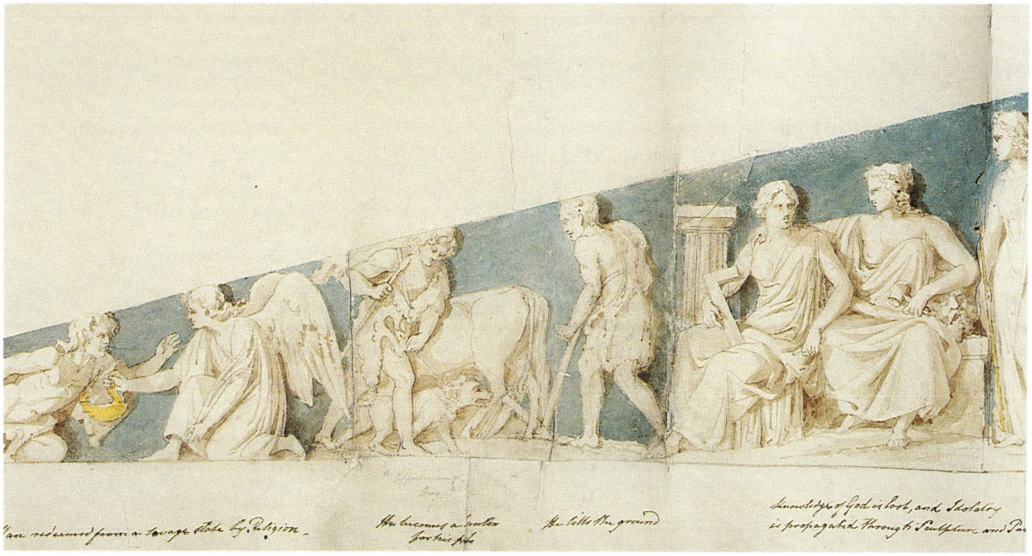

Plate IV Detail from 'The Progress of Civilisation', Richard Westmacott's design for the pediment sculpture of the British Museum. The blue colour was never added to the tympanum. Watercolour, *c.* 1846. British Museum, PD 1887–5–2–1.

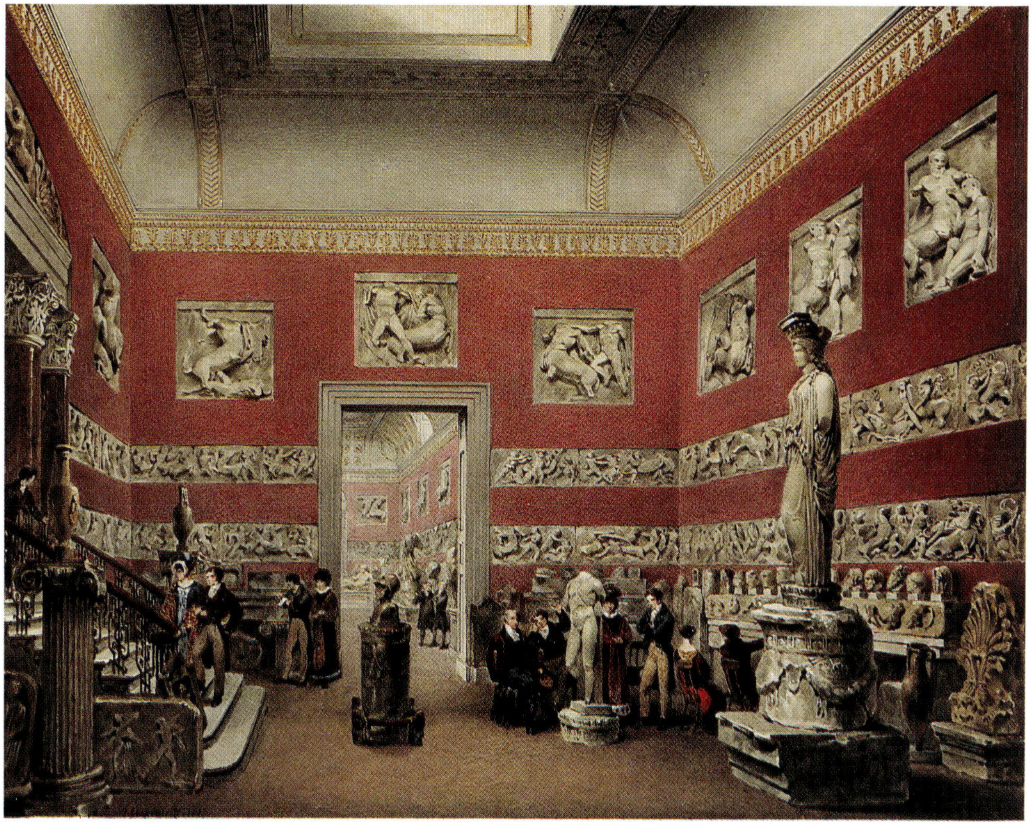

Plate V The Temporary Phigaleian Room, idealised by James Stephanoff, who transformed the makeshift apartment of real life into a splendid interior. Watercolour, exhibited 1818. British Museum, PD 1935–3–9–3.

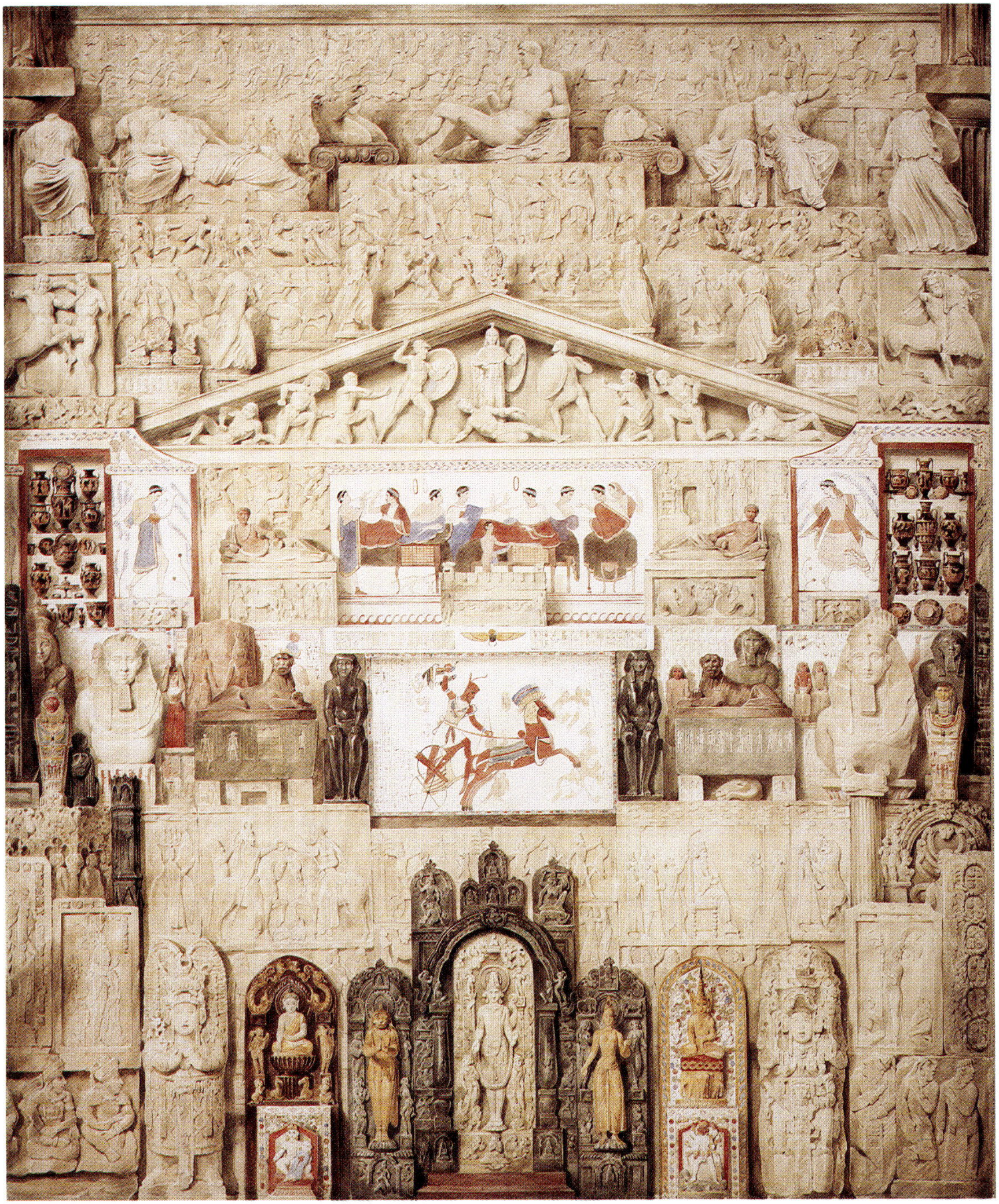

Plate VI 'An Assemblage of Works of Art in Sculpture and Painting', by James Stephanoff, showing the sculptured art of antiquity rising from a primitive beginning in oriental Indian and Central American civilisation to the supremacy of the Parthenon sculptures. Watercolour, exhibited 1845. Private collection.

polychromy issue, following publication in the previous year of Hittorff's *L'Architecture Polychrome chez les Grecs* and Penrose's *Principles of Athenian Architecture*. At the second meeting T. L. Donaldson, President of the RIBA and a veteran of the polychromy debate, paid tribute to 'the highly satisfactory instance of the British Museum, in which sculptures had received new life and animation by the coloured backgrounds introduced under the direction of Mr Sydney Smirke. The ceilings of the sculpture galleries in the Museum had been so skilfully decorated, in unison with the walls, and it was at length possible, in some degree, to estimate the effect of such embellishment in Greek buildings . . . .'[42]

To the voice of approval was added that of no less a figure than Leo von Klenze, who during a sojourn in England was invited by the Parliamentary Commission to comment upon the merits of the British Museum. He found the colouring to his taste and in accord with the principles of ancient practice. Klenze was himself a pioneer of the rediscovery of ancient polychromy and the interiors of his own museum buildings had reflected his archaeological interests.[43]

Sydney Smirke, for his part, had made his position absolutely clear in a letter to the President of the RIBA.[44] In general he was averse to the transfer of Mediterranean tastes to 'our cloudy zone'. He was therefore opposed to external polychromy on enviromentally determined grounds: 'The tastes, feelings and habits of men conform to the circumstances of external nature; even in the plumage of birds, and in the fur of animals, how wary of colour is Dame Nature herself in our cold, grey climate, and yet how lavish in the sunny south!'

As to the value of *internal* polychromy Smirke had no doubts, and the 1850s were to see a remarkable transformation of the colouring of the western galleries of the British Museum. The most ambitious scheme for ornamental painting in the Museum at this time, however, went unrealised. This was the Keeper of Printed Books, Antonio Panizzi's proposal for the dome of the new Reading Room which, if effected, would have transformed that vast canopy into a grandiose display of allegorical painting and marble statuary.[45] In the event the emptiness of the great space was to be relieved by gilding alone, applied under Smirke's guidance on the same general principles as those according to which polychromy had been introduced into the ceilings of the sculpture galleries:

> My belief and firm conviction is that by moderately gilding the mouldings, a general warmth and richness of effect would be produced which would abundantly compensate for the absence of strong coloured decorations . . . bringing into harmony the Dome and the walls which support it; those walls consisting wholly of books, whose bindings collectively produce a rich warm and somewhat deep tone, very strongly opposed to the cool light tint of the Dome.[46]

Richard Westmacott junior – chromophobe

Although red now predominated as a colour for the walls in the galleries of the Antiquities Department, it seems some felt there was still need for further experimentation, while others were positively opposed to the colour. Early in 1858, following the changes that were made in the arrangement of the sculptures, the question arose as to whether the Elgin Rooms should be repainted.[47] The Trustees decided not to proceed, but they accepted Sir Charles Eastlake's suggestion that it was desirable to obtain 'accurately coloured drawings showing the colouring and decoration of walls in foreign museums of such rooms as are appropriate to the reception of antique sculpture.'[48] A letter was drafted to the Secretary of State for Foreign Affairs requesting him to obtain information respecting the colouring of walls in foreign museums. When laid before the Trustees, however, it was deferred to the Sub-Committee on Antiquities to see whether the information might not be otherwise procured without troubling the Foreign Secretary.[49] Thus Eastlake's proposal foundered and we are denied his survey which, if carried out, would undoubtedly have made interesting reading.

The matter of colour for the walls of the British Museum, however, was far from laid to rest and in the ensuing debate some reference, at least, was to be made by the principal protagonists to their experience of colour in foreign museums. The controversy began with an invitation from the Trustees to Richard Westmacott junior to say what colour he thought suitable for one of the sculpture galleries about to be painted. The younger Westmacott had inherited from his recently deceased father the professorship of sculpture at the Royal Academy, which carried with it the privilege of advising the Museum upon the repair and display of its sculpture. The gallery in question is not specified in his report, but it seems to have been 'the small Graeco-Roman Saloon'.[50] Westmacott's reply to this seemingly modest request was nothing short of a personal manifesto for the principles he thought fundamental to the question of decorating public galleries.[51] In a report dated 30 December 1858, he argued that the question of colour for the walls could not be discussed without also taking into consideration the manner and the amount of light in the room; nor without consideration of the colouring of the ceilings, plinths and frames for the statues. On the matter of lighting, Westmacott was all in favour of direct top-lighting from a ceiling giving, as much as possible, the effect of being open to the sky. The sculptures must be 'viewed in an *atmosphere* of light', by which he meant that there should be as few interior shadows and dark corners as possible. The available light should be diffused over the largest possible area, and this meant harnessing reflected as well as direct light. Dark walls and pedestals tended to absorb or neutralise light, whereas lighter tones reflected it back evenly into the room. Thus, 'dark reds, chocolates, browns, ochres and their compounds' were to be avoided.

Hawkins had complained, when the question was debated some years previously, of the dirty appearance of the British Museum sculptures when seen against light walls. Westmacott contended that rather than attempt to offset the natural darkening of sculpture in the London atmosphere by darkening the walls, a virtue should be made of the contrast by rendering the walls as light as possible. If the sculptures could have been kept clean he would have been prepared to consider a reverse contrast, i.e. between the relative lightness of the marble and the darker tint of the background, for such, he thought, had been the custom in setting the architectural sculpture of ancient Greece. This last observation, however, begged the question as to whether the architectural sculpture of antiquity was not itself painted. Westmacott was violently opposed to the suggestion. In the discussions that were to take place in the following year as to the appropriate manner for displaying the pedimental sculptures of the Parthenon, Westmacott made it clear that he conceived the pediment of the Parthenon as something resembling a Wedgwood plaque with cream-coloured sculpture against a blue background. The sculptures themselves had not, he believed, been enlivened by painted detail but by the coloristic effects of the light and shade of natural daylight. Westmacott was to oppose any suggestion of a pedimental reconstruction in the Elgin Room, since he felt it would be impossible to recreate the effect of seeing the sculptures *en plein air*.[52]

Westmacott had an abhorrence of polychromatic sculpture, both ancient and modern.[53] This comes out clearly in a lecture read at a meeting of the Archaeological Institute of Great Britain and Ireland held at Cambridge, and in a chapter devoted to the problem in his book *The Schools of Sculpture Ancient and Modern* published in 1864. His assertion in this last that the archaeologist Charles Newton had been mistaken in confusing 'mere stains' for colour on the sculptures of the Mausoleum of Halicarnassus was to be publicly rebuffed. Newton was then Keeper of the newly formed Department of Greek and Roman Antiquities and this slight ensured that Richard Westmacott junior would not enjoy the intimacy with the Museum that his father had.

Although he had to admit the use of colour in some ancient sculpture, Westmacott generally played down its extent and importance, and was contemptuous of attempts by contemporary sculptors to revive it. He refused to accept that the orange patina still visible on the Parthenon sculptures was anything more than natural.[54] He called it a *warm* tone and argued, accordingly, that the appropriate background contrast for dark, warm sculptures was 'light in colour and cool in tone'. He went on to specify 'French and other whites, slightly veined or grained, blues or greens very light, and even lakes . . . .' Ceilings should be similarly light so as not to appear disproportionately dark in relation to the walls. He approved of picking out mouldings in light 'contra-strong' colours, and even gilding was admissible. He was, however, strongly opposed to heavy panelling in what he called positive colours.

In general, Westmacott objected to the sombre tomb-like effect then prevailing in the sculpture galleries of the British Museum, which he attributed to the dark, heavy ceilings and dark, light-absorbing walls and 'the lines of dark pedestals'. He particularly disliked the dark, heavy bases on which the Parthenon pediment sculptures were set and was to argue in favour of the suggestion that they be replaced by a cornice, which he thought should correspond in form and colour to the original horizontal cornice of the Parthenon.[55]

Finally, Westmacott made an appeal to the standards set by foreign museums, where he claimed light colours prevailed. He also considered a proper example to have been set in the Palace of Industry, which had formed part of the Great Exhibition of 1851, and in certain rooms of the Crystal Palace at Sydenham. He harked back to the days of the old Townley Gallery, where the rooms had been painted a light grey granite colour.

Westmacott's report offered a direct challenge to the two persons most responsible for the current appearance of the sculpture galleries, namely Edward Hawkins and Sydney Smirke. For some twenty years Hawkins had striven to obviate what he saw as the ill-effects of top-lighting coupled with light-coloured, reflective walls and flooring. Only of late, and with Sydney Smirke's co-operation, had a degree of success been achieved. Smirke was the first to reply, in a report dated 5 March 1859.[56] He succinctly reiterated all the now familiar arguments against light walls and the consequent evils of reflected light. He mentioned specifically the fact that when the walls of the Egyptian Sculpture Gallery had been very light, they had the appearance of being cold, unfinished and dirty. Sculpture was best seen with light coming from one source or direction; what Westmacott was advocating amounted to the effect of placing the sculptures outside on a dull day. On the question of what was done in foreign museums, Smirke contested that red was far from an exceptional colour. He cited as examples the galleries at Berlin and the recent colouring of the Assyrian sculpture galleries in the Louvre.

The Sub-Committee on Antiquities met in order to reconcile this difference of opinion, but succeeded only in ruling that the controversy should be settled between Smirke and Westmacott by experimenting in the 'alcove Room' (Second Graeco-Roman Saloon, 3 on Fig. 1).[57] The resulting experiment, we may infer from a note of Smirke's, tended to favour Westmacott's scheme.[58] Even so, Smirke warned, its apparent success in this room, where the effect of lightness was tempered by the shadows of the alcoves, would need to be reconsidered if applied to the large flat expanse of the Elgin Rooms.

Eventually Hawkins entered the fray with a written report dated 5 May 1859 in which he set out to ridicule Westmacott's attempt to offer what he dubbed the 'drawing-room' approach to sculpture galleries.[59] Such a system might be appropriate to the varied colour of modern furniture, mirrors, ornaments and female dresses, but it was quite inappropriate as a background for a series of ancient marbles: 'whilst the general impression sought to be conveyed in a drawing-room, that of gaiety and festive brilliance, is the reverse of what good taste would prescribe in the halls of a museum, and in the presence of monuments which bade every intelligent mind to reflection rather than to festivity.'

Having thus belittled his opponent, this veteran of many previous similar skirmishes then proceeded to patronise him:

> Fortunately Mr Hawkins can appeal to experience in support of the principles here-stated. The experiment proposed by Mr Westmacott has long been tried both in England and abroad. When the Elgin Room was first opened the walls were painted in a very delicate and in itself, agreeable colour, the sculptures were not merely thoroughly washed, but cleaned with soaplees. Yet hardly had they been exhibited to the public when complaints were raised of the dirtiness of the marbles. The consequence was that when the room came to be repainted, the Trustees reconsidered the style of decoration adopted; various specimens of colours were painted on portions of the walls; Sir Richard Westmacott, Sir Francis Chantrey and other authorities were consulted, and the result was that Mr Robert Smirke was directed to select the darkest hue of the whole.

Like Sydney Smirke, Hawkins contested that, far from being out of step with Continental practice, the Museum was setting an example that was being followed elsewhere. Thus at Rome, about two years before, the backgrounds to the most important sculptures in the Belvedere of the Vatican had been painted red. At Paris, red hangings had been draped behind the Venus de Milo. Finally, Hawkins appealed to the example of the Royal Academy itself where, in spite of the marbles being new and bright, for exhibition purposes the sculptures were fitted up with red baize and set against dark walls. This last sarcasm was aimed directly at Westmacott who, as Professor of Sculpture in the Royal Academy Schools, appeared to be arguing against his own practice.

Westmacott was stung into a reply.[60] He discounted the relevance of the Royal Academy's Sculpture Room, whose function as an exhibition gallery was only occasional. Its real purpose was to accommodate the Life School and its dark colour, which was in any case the accidental product of an accumulation of soot from the gas-burners (presumably to keep the models warm), was only tolerated because it served as a convenient background against which to set the undressed model. Then with a nice wit, Westmacott concluded that he could not conceive that Hawkins, who had been so contemptuous of the *drawing-room* approach, would wish to see the Museum set up as if it were a *Drawing School.* The joke was a good one but, as we have seen, there was a very real case for attempting to provide conditions suitable for art students in the sculpture galleries. Hawkins had striven to achieve those very studio effects that were now under attack. Ironically, the challenge came from a representative of the institution whose interests Hawkins had at heart.

At last the Trustees determined to settle the argument by putting the matter to a vote at a meeting of the Standing Committee. A motion was therefore put, 'That the general colour of the walls of the Sculpture Galleries in the Museum be red.' Six voted for the motion, and four against. It was ordered, accordingly, that the lower part of the Roman Gallery be painted red, and the upper part some lighter colour.[61] Col. Pl. VII

Dispelling Victorian gloom

Thus ended a decade of controversy. The sculpture galleries were to be red and so they remained for the rest of the century and well into the next, until the great changes that took place in the years between the two world wars. In general, it seems, the effect of polychromy in the British Museum's galleries was darker and heavier than it was in the Munich Glyptothek. When, therefore, in the 1920s and 1930s there was a reaction in taste against Victorian and Edwardian gloom, it was to Munich that advocates of a lighter, brighter Museum looked for inspiration. Comparing the effect of polychromy in the two institutions, one commentator summarised the effect of the British Museum as follows:

> In England, the colouring of Classic buildings was interpreted into a more sober range than in Germany. At the British Museum the predominant colour on the walls is dark terracotta red paint, with the upper walls and ceilings of buff or tan yellow ochre. While the intention was no doubt praiseworthy, the effect was to reproduce in the British Museum, with singular faithfulness, not the clear vibrant spectrum of the Mediterranean but a rich atmosphere of London fog.[62]

Now, this is not strictly fair, as Smirke's evaluation of internal as opposed to external polychromy quoted above, makes clear. It is true, however, that the British Museum lacked the richness of the decoration of the Glyptothek, whose walls of 12
coloured marble, or scagliola painted in imitation of marble, produced a mottled effect, less heavy on the eye. The floors, too, were not the monochrome York stone flags that were almost ubiquitous in the sculpture galleries at Bloomsbury, but a rich display of coloured marble mosaic. The ceilings were predominantly white with mottled decoration picked out in colours or gilded, and this greater use of white further distinguished the Glyptothek from the more sombre British Museum.[63]

One factor that may have made the colouring of the British Museum seem darker than intended was the deterioration of the colours through exposure to light and London dirt. The Elgin Room in 1929 was said to exhibit 'no colour at all'.[64]

When the Elgin Marbles were brought back from sanctuary in the Aldwych Underground railway tunnel and reinstated after the Second World War, the colour of the walls was sky-blue in obvious response to the taste for lighter shades which had been already introduced into some galleries before the war.[65] The pre-war programme of repainting galleries was initiated in 1928, when the first

Graeco-Roman Room, the Assyrian Transept and Nimrud Central Saloon were redecorated during the latter part of that year and the next. In 1930 experiments were conducted in the Archaic Room (5 on Fig. 1) with grey stippled over a red ground, 'with details in buff and terracotta'. At the same time the small room (6 on Fig. 1) linking it with what was then the Ephesus Room was painted a sky-blue mottled with white. This was subsequently considered a failure and was replaced by a mauve-grey. The Roman Gallery, where relief was needed from the darkness caused by the columns outside the windows, was tinted apple-green, while the second and third Graeco-Roman Rooms, being well-lit, were painted a deep slate-grey.[66] The result was, it seems, pleasing to the press and in one notice, in particular, we find a remarkable echo of the past:

> Walls of the sculpture rooms at the British Museum are being painted in 'art' shades to provide the best background for the exhibits and bring a new lightness and brightness to the sombre building. Gradually the dull red with which generations of Londoners have been familiar is to give way to delicate blends of greys, blues, mauves and greens. For it has been found that the art works of ten centuries or so B.C. are best shown in an ultra-modern colour setting such as might be found in a fashionable West End drawing-room.[67]

Pastel shades are exactly what Westmacott junior had suggested some eighty years previously and now, at last, the dark, 'archaeological' red was removed. Only in recent years has the pendulum of taste begun to swing in the opposite direction, and some have urged the Museum to restore, at least to some rooms, the splendour of nineteenth-century polychromy.

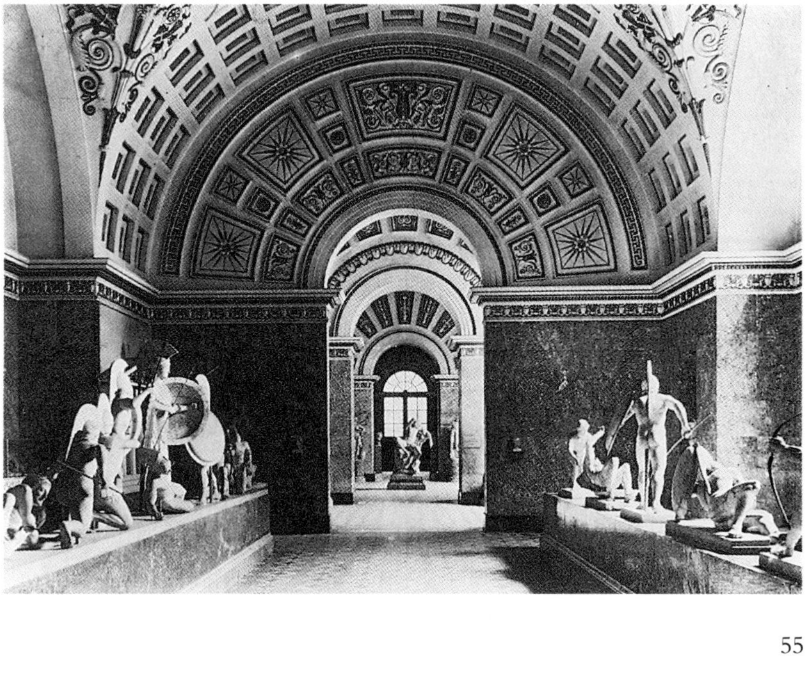

12 The Aegina Room of the Munich Glyptothek, completed in 1829. Munich, Glyptothek.

4 The Chain of Art

From the setting up of the Townley Gallery (completed 1808) until his death in 1856, Richard Westmacott the elder was responsible for the arrangement of the 13
sculptures in the galleries of the British Museum. At first he acted virtually independently of the Keeper of Antiquities, consulting instead with the Museum architect Robert Smirke or the President of the Royal Academy about the lighting and colouring of the galleries. This was to be a source of deep resentment within the Antiquities Department and in the course of his long Keepership Edward Hawkins gradually weakened Westmacott's authority and asserted the archaeological over the picturesque approach to displaying the collections.

Westmacott was a beau-idealist trained in the Academy tradition and, although he came to respect the historical sequence of civilisations represented by the sculptures, his primary interest in their arrangement was aesthetic. The distinction between his approach and that of the more historically minded Hawkins is shown up most clearly in the arrangement of the Lycian sculpture. Westmacott was to treat Fellows's Xanthian discoveries as a by-way of Greek art, while Fellows himself, and his friend Hawkins, wished to see the Lycian-style monuments shown as historical documents of a new culture, complete with its own language and individual architectural style. The Greek-style monuments from Xanthos – the Nereid and Harpy Tombs – they wished to see displayed separately. Westmacott, however, arranged everything together in picturesque fashion, giving pride of place to the Nereid monument while cramming together the Lycian sculptures and inscribed stelae.[1]

Cultural differentiation was one consideration in what became known as the 'scientific' approach to the sculpture galleries; another was chronology. By the middle of the nineteenth century it had become the overriding concern of the Department of Antiquities to see its sculptures arranged in chronological order. This was the arrangement first adopted by Leo von Klenze for the sculptures in Ludwig of Bavaria's Glyptothek, where the Aegina marbles formed the key or pivotal element in a developmental series leading from Egypt to Rome.[2] The system was to win lasting approval and came to be revered as a model. Towards the end of the nineteenth century Adolph Michaelis remarked that 'the Munich collection emphasises even in a greater degree than the British Museum the motive which should govern the future of all museums: a visible representation of the development of ancient art'.[3] Even allowing for Teutonic partisanship, this was probably fair. The British

Museum would strive for a century – from around 1840 to the great dismantlement at the time of the Second World War – to achieve a chronological arrangement of its sculpture, but with only limited success. Ludwig's collection was assembled by J. M. von Wagner within a relatively short period, but the difficulty confronting the British Museum was the great quantity and diversity of sculpture collected over more than half a century from four continents. Although it was conceived of as a piece, Smirke's original idea of a Museum arranged around four sides of a quadrangular court took thirty years to complete. Unlike the Munich Glyptothek or Schinkel's Altes Museum in Berlin, it was not designed around the collection but rather grew by accretion in a vain attempt to keep pace with the growth of the collections. The officers of the Antiquities Department would feel increasingly at odds with the building until the crisis of the 1850s, when there was strong support for the wholesale transfer of the collections to another site.[4] The British Museum was not, however, the only institution to be criticised for its lack of system, as F. Pulsky observed:

> In the Glyptothek at Munich, and in the Museum at Berlin, the collections are formed on a more general, but not on a complete plan; for the predilection for architectural effect and for the display of royal grandeur, forbade gaps in the monumental history of art being filled up with plaster casts, though these would have transformed the Museum into a school of arts and into an authentic archive of its history. They are noble proofs, therefore, of princely display, but they lack that civilising influence on the people, which, if duly arranged they might easily impart.[5]

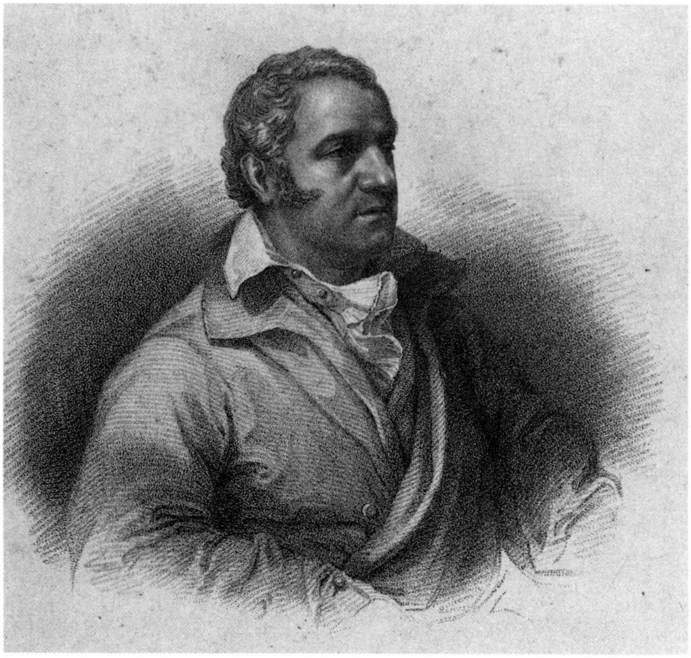

13 Richard Westmacott (1775–1856), sculptor. For fifty years Westmacott was responsible for all the displays of sculpture in the British Museum. *Illustrations of the British Museum*, vol. I. British Museum, Central Archive.

Charles Newton was another who saw the value of casts as a means of physically 68 portraying the history of art. In 1848 he observed of museums in general that, 'little has, as yet, been done to carry out in collections of sculpture the great principle of chronological arrangement', and in this respect he properly pointed out that even in the Munich Glyptothek a compromise had been necessary in order to accommodate those works that, being copies of lost Greek originals, could not be assigned with certainty to any particular date, 'but must be grouped around some one central object of kindred subject and of more detailed style'. Of the Vatican he was even more critical, dismissing it simply as a 'wilderness'.[6]

The grouping of sculpture according to subject had been the traditional method, as exemplified in the Villa Albani and the Museo Pio Clementino in Rome, and in the Louvre.[7] It provided a ready and obviously picturesque method for displaying sculpture that could only be classified imprecisely as Graeco-Roman and, besides, the chronology of classical art had not always been the burning question. Eighteenth-century theorists had frequently discussed ancient sculpture according to a hierarchy based upon iconographical divisions of divine, hero and mortal. Thus a distinction might be drawn between naturalistic style, on the one hand, suitable for the rendering of mortals and heroes, and, on the other, ideal style suitable for gods.[8] Since the prevailing neo-classical doctrine required that art should be elevated above nature in order to approximate as closely as possible to ideal beauty, it follows that the highest forms of ancient art were sought among representations of gods and goddesses, notably the Apollo Belvedere as the noblest form of male divine beauty and the Venus de' Medici as the most beautiful female.

As late as 1850 the Graeco-Roman sculptures of the Townley collection in the 49–56 British Museum were newly arranged by subject. The system was chosen, however, for want of a better, since by that date the Museum had assembled the most important chronological series of sculptures in the world, and chronological arrangement had long been the preferred method.[9] The desire for a chronological arrangement of the sculpture galleries of the British Museum was, no doubt, inspired in part by the Glyptothek, but there were other influences. One whose importance it would be easy to overlook is numismatics. Of the coins of the Hellenistic or 'Macedonian' period, Newton wrote: 'Where a number of the finest specimens are arranged in chronological order, this series, in reference to the history of art, forms a continuous chain of evidence, each regal coin may be regarded as a bas-relief in miniature, which tells us by its inscription when and where it was executed.'[10] The discipline of numismatics was vital to the training of the officers of the Antiquities Department. Taylor Combe was appointed in 1803 with special charge of the cabinet of coins before becoming the first Keeper in 1807 of the new Department of Antiquities. His successor, Edward Hawkins, had charge of all the collections, which in his day 7 included everything from drawings to ethnography, but he was first and foremost an expert in coins and medals. Charles Newton, who succeeded Hawkins as Keeper in 1861, joined the Department in 1840 and was consigned to years of routine, registering and arranging coins. It was a natural extension of the habits of a numismatist – sorting and arranging coins into chronological series according to like types – that the idea should occur of doing something similar with the growing sculpture collection.

Winckelmann and the idea of progress

Numismatics certainly played a part in shaping the Museum's chronological approach towards its sculpture collection, but it would be wrong to imply that no more was intended than a simple sequence in order of time. Just as Winckelmann's *History of Ancient Art* published in 1764 eschewed 'mere chronicle', so too the Museum's sculpture galleries aimed to present, in Winckelmann's words, 'a system ... to show the origin, progress, change, and downfall of art, together with the different styles of nations, periods and artists, and to prove the whole, as far as it is possible, from the ancient monuments now in existence'.[11] So far as coins were concerned, Winckelmann admitted to being bored by Roman ones because, it seems, they lent themselves too readily to being classified by date. Greek coins were less inclined to present a continuous series, and for this reason Winckelmann found scope for his particular mode of enquiry:

> Moreover, in the study of these antiquities, the learner will not waste his thoughts on trifles if he considers them as the productions of men whose thoughts were of a loftier and more manly strain than ours; and thus viewed, the investigation of them is able to elevate us above ourselves and above our age. A thinking person, on the shore of the wide sea, cannot occupy himself with low ideas; the illimitable view expands also the bounds of the soul, which, though at first seeming to be lost, returns again enlarged.[12]

That is not to say that Winckelmann had no regard for detail. On the contrary, large tracts of his *History*, particularly where it deals with Greek art, are virtually unreadable on account of the minute scrutiny of statues and their individual parts. He was deeply critical of scholars who failed to rest their assumptions about Greek art on precise observation of details of anatomy or drapery. He complained of the mistakes that had been made from 'inattention to restoration', and goes on to list a number of salient errors, adding that 'a large volume might be written about mistakes of this kind'.[13]

Winckelmann's particular genius lay in his ability to see the whole of a subject through its parts, and there is an obvious parallel to be drawn between, on the one hand, the artistic model of a harmonious whole and its parts and, on the other, Winckelmann's own *History of Ancient Art* seen as a great construct forged out of the various phases of man's artistic endeavour. The sweep of his historical perspective looks back to the sixteenth-century French scholar J. J. Scaliger, whose *De Emendatione Temporum* (1583) and *Thesaurus Temporum* (1606) employed contemporary advances in astronomy to provide a historical chronology of the ancient world.[14] Scaliger's chronology aimed at providing a scientific universal history combining the history of Greece and Rome with that of the biblical world. As Winckelmann himself acknowledges, the idea of history as a vast organic whole goes back to the earlier scholar, but in the wake of Scaliger, Winckelmann could also look back on a century and more of speculation upon the origins of the World and the history of Man's part in shaping it. Paolo Rossi's evocatively entitled book *The Dark Abyss of Time: The History of the Earth and the History of Nations from Hooke to Vico* shows how in the seventeenth century, and indeed earlier, 'the history of man was conceived as coextensive with the history of the earth'.[15] Natural and cultural history were seen as all part of the same process.

The rise of Greek art in Winckelmann's *History* is set within the framework of Egyptian, Phoenician, Persian, Etruscan and Roman civilisation, and metaphors of living plants and flowing streams abound, reinforcing his characteristic image of *art* as *life*. The influence of Plotinus is felt here: in *Enneads* we read of how the world is to be defined as a 'sort of life stretched out to an immense span, in which each of the parts has its own place in the series, all of them different and yet the whole continuous ....'[16] For Winckelmann, history is organic and the history of art traces the growth and development of humanity. At the outset of his great work we read:

> In the infancy of art, its productions are, like the handsomest of human beings at birth, mis-shapen, and similar one to another, like the seeds of plants of entirely different kinds; but in its bloom and decay, they resemble those mighty streams, which, at the point where they should be the broadest, either dwindle into small rivulets or totally disappear.[17]

Like Vico, Winckelmann conceived of human history as a progression from crude beginnings to refinement. Thus, he implies, the whole span of ancient civilisation stretching from Egypt to Rome may be mapped like the course of a stream, or traced like the life-cycle of a plant. And yet, when it came to discussing the precise relationship of the art of Greece to that of Egypt, Winckelmann was reluctant to subscribe to the view – put forward by another eighteenth-century protoarchaeologist, the Comte de Caylus – that a continuous thread linked the two and that the origins of Greek art were to be located in that of Egypt. Caylus in his *Recueil d'Antiquités* had described a chain of art, whose links led from Egypt through the Etruscans to the Greeks, whom the Romans in their turn both plundered and imitated. Winckelmann, by contrast, argued that, although early Greek art is similar to that of Egypt, the connection is largely one of appearances. The peculiar, autochthonous genius of the Greeks, which set them apart from the Egyptians, was the capacity exhibited in their art for *progress*.[18]

The Progress of Civilisation

The idea of progress as the natural condition of civilisation is today taken for granted. It is difficult for us to think outside the fundamental belief in the principle of material and social improvement inherited from our Victorian forbears, but it has not always been so. E. R. Dodds in an important essay demonstrated that the ancients lived largely without it, and J. B. Bury devoted a stimulating volume to the causes of the modern concept of progress, which he located in the social and political upheavals of the later eighteenth century.[19]

In selecting the subject for his pedimental composition over the entrance to the British Museum, Richard Westmacott could have chosen none more appropriate to
Col. Pl. IV his age than 'The Progress of Civilisation'. With its corner figure of primitive man emerging towards the light, and the central group of figures – some based on the Elgin Marbles – representing the intellectual and manufacturing arts, it is both a celebration of nineteenth-century pride in human achievement and an eloquent statement of belief in the idea of progress.[20]

Another eloquent image of a nineteenth-century idea of progress is a drawing by
Col. Pl. VI the watercolourist James Stephanoff showing the sculptured art of antiquity rising from a primitive beginning in oriental Indian and Central American civilisation to the supremacy of the Parthenon sculptures.[21] Each division, minutely observed, overlaps with the next and thus we pass through the Achaemenid, Egyptian, Etruscan, early and later Greek, until we come to the crowning glory of the Elgin Marbles and the age of Pheidias. The title of this extraordinary compilation earned a lengthy explanation in the exhibition catalogue when the drawing was shown at the Old Watercolour Society in 1845:

> An assemblage of Works of Art in Sculpture and Painting, from the earliest period to the time of Phydias, 1845.
>
> At the base of the picture are specimens of Hindu and Javanese sculpture, and on either side are the colossal figures and bas-reliefs from Copan and Palenque; those above them are from Persepolis and Babylon, followed by the Egyptian, Etruscan, and early Greek remains, and surmounted by the pediment from Aegina; bas-reliefs and fragments from Xanthus and Phygalia; the Theseus, Ceres and Latona, the Fates, and other figures from the Parthenon; and terminating in a portion of the equestrian bas-relief of the Panathenaic procession to the Temple of Minerva.

Stephanoff's own explanation implies a chronological progression, but the reality is a system based upon analogous styles. Thus the Hindu gods of Java and India are assimilated with the Mayan culture of Central America. The latter had recently been discovered by John L. Stephens, and Stephanoff took his examples of their art direct from the illustrations that were published with the account of Stephens's travels.[22] Further up the register in the drawing we find Achaemenid palace reliefs arranged as being somehow 'aesthetically prior' to the sculptures of Pharaonic Egypt, although they were known to post-date them. Higher still, we find Etruscan sculpture and tomb-painting and, above that, the severe Greek style of the group from a pediment of the temple of Aphaia at Aegina. Then, curiously, we are given the high-classical sculptures of the Nereid monument of ancient Lycia, newly arrived in the Museum;[23] next the frieze of the Temple of Apollo at Bassae and, finally, out of chronological sequence with the Phigaleian sculptures, the Parthenon sculptures.

In spite of his claim to the contrary, Stephanoff's picture does not heed even the sketchy chronology then available, but rather relies upon an intuitive perception of the ascent of the arts through the various civilisations represented. We only have to consider the position of the Elgin Marbles in relation to those placed immediately under them to see that the guiding principle of Stephanoff's system is the relative status he afforded each category of sculpture according to a hierarchy of artistic accomplishment. This hierarchy, as mapped in Stephanoff's drawing, appears to derive from two principal sources. First, from the real-life assemblage of the British Museum itself, in which many of the examples were to be found, either in the original or in cast form; second, from contemporary aesthetic theory.

Stephanoff took an intimate and sustained interest in the growth of the sculpture collection at the British Museum and will have witnessed the gradual piecing together of the assemblage of the arts brought into the Museum from the far-flung corners of the world in the first half of the nineteenth century. It is not only the content of his drawing, however, that is derived from the galleries of the British Museum but also something of the manner in which each category is presented in relation to the next. For although the Museum was firmly committed to the principle of chronological display, this had barely been realised in practice. There was therefore a similar clustering of analogous styles in, for example, the sometime placement of Mexican antiquities in the Egyptian Sculpture Gallery. By the same reasoning the arts of oriental civilisations were displayed side by side with 'curiosities' from Africa and Oceania.[24] Also to be found in the actual Museum was the use of a later style of Greek art as an introduction to the Parthenon sculptures. Thus in both the temporary and permanent display of the Phigaleian and Elgin Marbles, the former – although known to be chronologically later – were placed in an ante-room forming an entrance court to the principal room where even greater 14
treasures might be found. When chronology became the governing principle of arranging the sculptures, the officers would strive to correct this solecism, but the Phigaleian Marbles in their *atrium*-like hall would long remain a picturesque prelude to the greater glory within.

The British Museum's own galleries, therefore, are likely to have been the immediate inspiration for Stephanoff's drawing. There are, however, other possible influences. The Museum's officers and advisers were subject, as we have seen, to

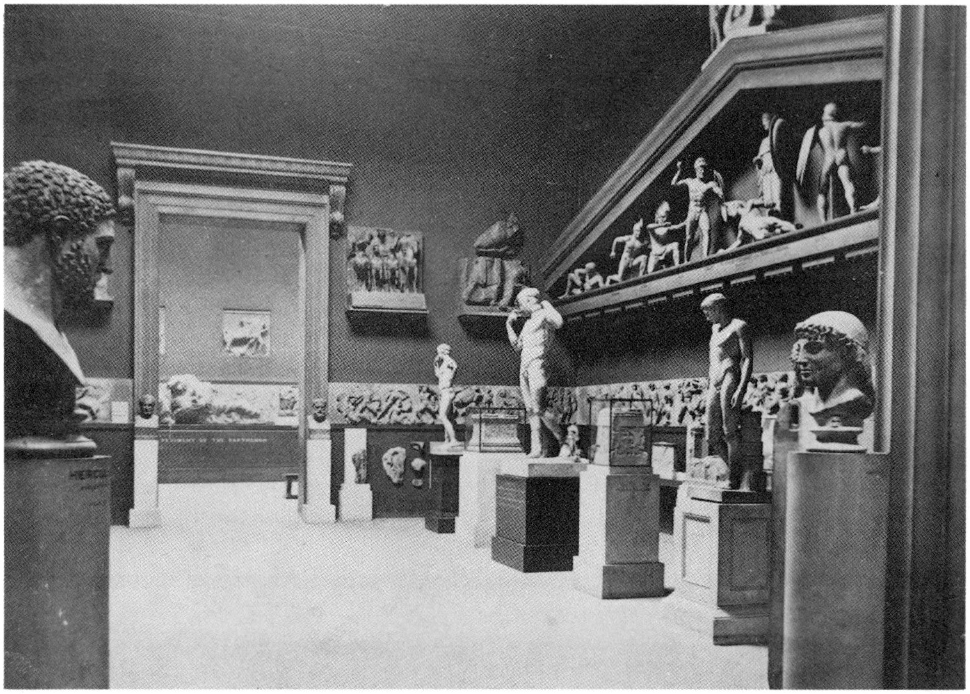

14 The Phigaleian Room (12 on Fig. 1), looking west into the Elgin Room, *c.*1875. The Phigaleian Marbles in their *atrium*-like hall provided a picturesque prelude to the greater glory within. To the right of the doorway are casts of the Selinus metopes; on the extreme right casts of the Aegina sculptures. Photo by F. York. British Museum, Department of Greek and Roman Antiquities.

certain 'external' trends in approaching the art of antiquity and Stephanoff was no doubt also open to these. He describes his compilation of the arts of antiquity as an 'assemblage' and nowhere uses the word 'progress'. The ordering of the individual groups, however, and the manner in which they are overlapped one with another implies the idea of a linear progression from primitive origins to the flowering of the arts at the time of Pheidias. This teleological view of art history was typical of both the eighteenth century and Stephanoff's own time. An influential thinker in Stephanoff's day was Hegel, who regarded the civilisations of the Orient, i.e. of India, China, Egypt and Persia, as the primitive forerunners of the Greeks. Unlike Winckelmann, however, Hegel conceived of civilisation as a continuous process; its course could be mapped by the passage of an itinerant 'spirit' moving from one nation to another, through the various civilisations that experienced the progressive awakening of man. This idea of continuing progress differed from that of Winckelmann, who had conceived the progress of art – and, therefore, of civilisation – in terms of a rise and fall, with classical Greece representing the paramount, pivotal point. Hegel, according to one strand of his complex philosophy, conceived of

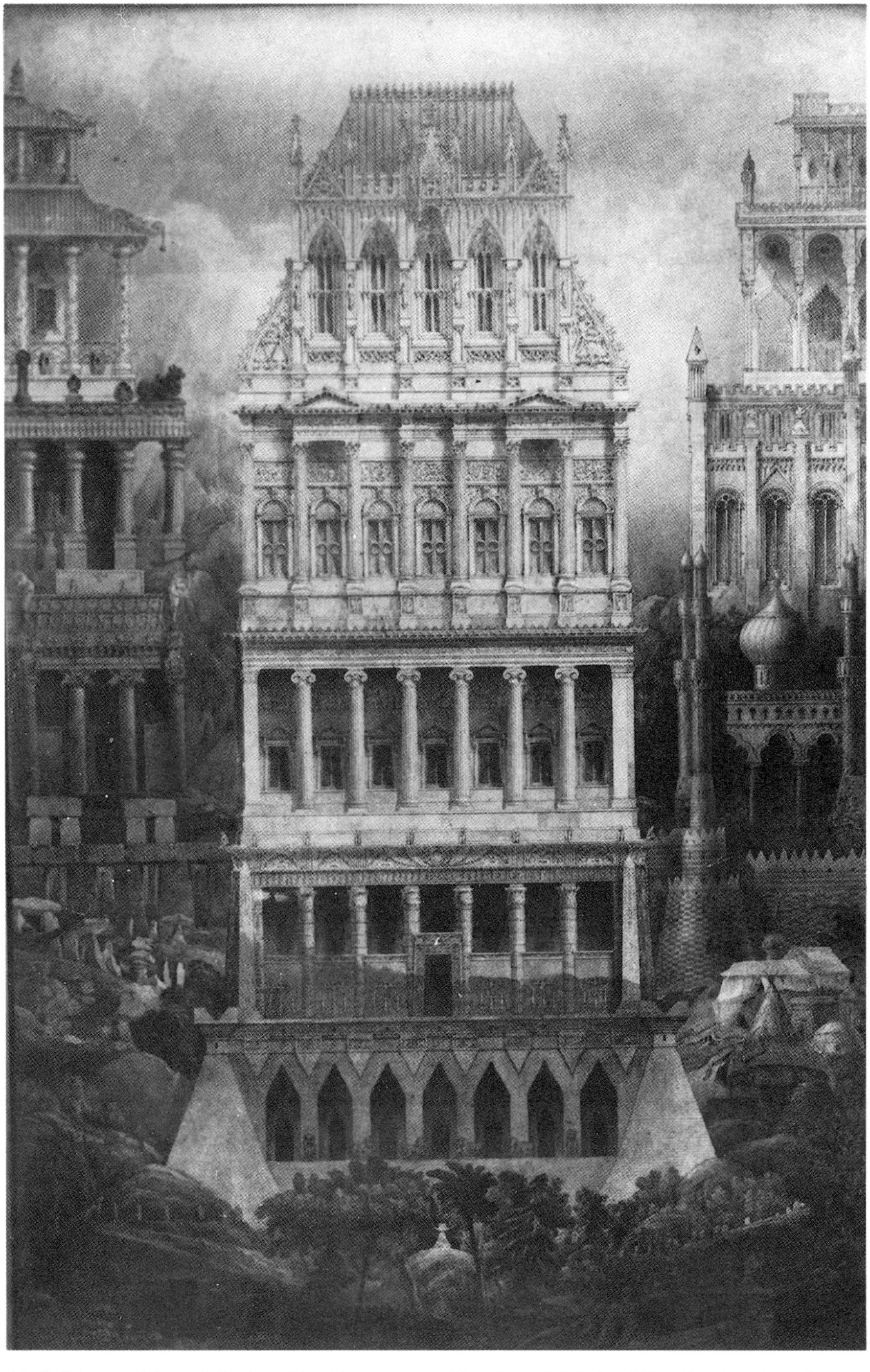

15 'Thirteen Selected Styles of Architecture etc.' by Joseph Michael Gandy, showing the rise of architecture from its primitive beginnings to a summit represented by medieval Gothic. Watercolour, exhibited 1836. London, Sir John Soane's Museum.

progress extending beyond the primitive and classical phases of civilisation into the medieval and modern age. His purpose was overtly nationalist, to show the Prussian monarchic state as the fulfilment of the destiny of the spirit of civilisation.[25] Stephanoff, like Hegel, subscribed to the illusion of finality, but terminates his rise of civilisation with the Elgin Marbles. The art of the Romans, who would necessarily have represented cultural decline, is conspicuously absent.

A more Hegelian scheme, and one which perhaps inspired Stephanoff's own, was
15 J. M. Gandy's 'Thirteen Selected Styles of Architecture', exhibited in 1836, a year after Hegel's *Philosophy of Fine Art* appeared.[26] It shows the rise of architecture from its beginnings in primitive forms to a summit represented by medieval Gothic. About this time Gothic architecture was enjoying a vogue which, some would claim, set it above the classical style. Medieval sculpture and painting enjoyed a similar revival but there was to be no serious challenge to the supremacy of Greek art. James Stephanoff's drawing is a remarkably articulate expression of the nineteenth-century approach to Greek and, in particular, Pheidian art as the goal of civilisation.

The Chain of Art

Throughout the nineteenth century the arts of antiquity were perceived in terms of
Col. Pl. XI the origin of Greek art. Thus, when in the 1840s Austen Henry Layard began to make his startling revelations of the forgotten art of the ancient Assyrians, his discoveries were immediately hailed as a potential missing link in the chain of art tracing the rise of Greek art from its primitive beginnings. In 1850, as the fruits of Layard's labours were piling up in the overcrowded galleries of the Museum, Sydney Smirke published an article in *The Builder* in which he argued that the traditional role of Egypt as the mother of Greek art should be relinquished to the Assyrians.[27] In his simple comparisons between Assyrian and Greek 'ornament', he was responding to what classical archaeologists would today call the orientalising phase in the development of early Greek art. In essence, however, Smirke's claims for Assyrian art were less positivist than those of the modern archaeologist, for they were made in the spirit of a theoretical system that had been current since the eighteenth century. Assyrian art fitted neatly into this system as the immediate successor of Egyptian and the precursor of archaic Greek art. The latter was represented in the Museum by the Harpy Tomb brought to the Museum by Fellows, by casts of the archaic metopes
14, 16, 79 from Selinus,[28] and by casts of the archaic pedimental figures from the temple of Aphaia on Aegina.[29] These casts were among the few that were tolerated by Hawkins in the exhibition galleries of the Museum during his tenure of the Keepership. The principle employed by him governing the display of casts was to exclude any piece the original of which was exhibited in a public gallery elsewhere in Europe. This was clearly stated in 1840 when the Museum was offered a cast of

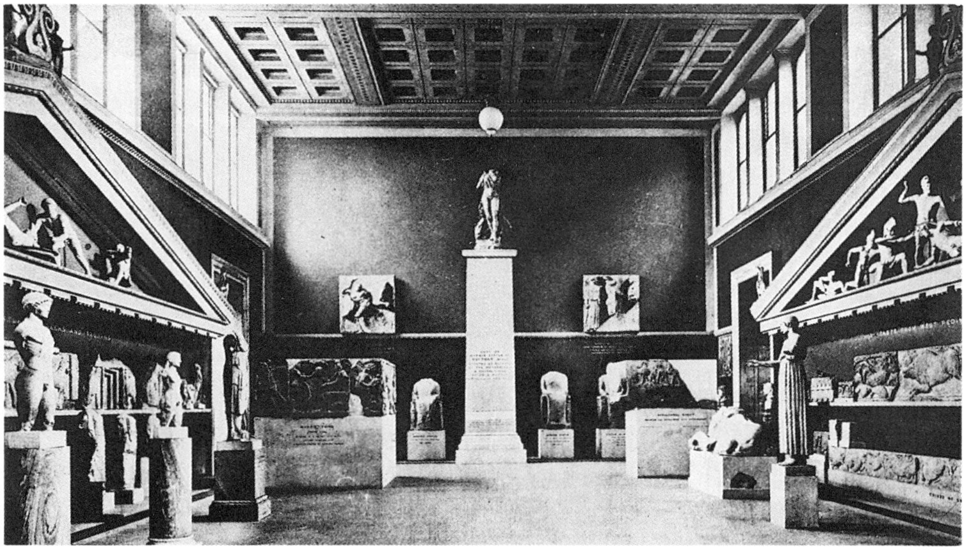

16 The 'Archaic' Room (5 on Fig. 1), looking west, *c.*1900–1908. The cast of the Nike from Olympia was removed about 1908 and replaced by a reconstruction of the doorway from the Treasury of Atreus. The ceiling and windows of this room (3 in the current scheme) are today hidden by a mezzanine floor. Photo British Museum, Department of Prints and Drawings.

the Apollo Belvedere formerly owned by George Saunders, architect of the old Townley Gallery.[30] The Aegina and Selinus casts were the exception by virtue of their unique importance for the rise of Greek art and the overriding principle of chronology.

Through Charles Fellows's activities in Asia Minor the Museum had already acquired the Harpy Tomb, which contributed a rare example of Greek art before its full flowering in the Elgin Marbles; to mark the immediate aftermath of the Pheidian era he had provided the sculptures of the Nereid monument. Charles Newton in his turn was to add to the repertoire of archaic forerunners the seated figures from the Sacred Way leading to the temple of Apollo at Didyma, while the sculptures of the Mausoleum and from Cnidus would provide superb examples of the post-Pheidian style. Thus every new acquisition was judged in relation to the standard of the Elgin Marbles and allocated its place within the shadow of their magnitude. The sculptures of the Parthenon were the embodiment of the peak of ancient civilisation. The arts of all other civilisations and all inferior forms of Greek art led up to or away from this one supreme moment.

A metaphor frequently used to describe the interconnection of cultures represented in the sculptures of the Museum was that of a chain. It was invoked especially when, periodically, suggestions were made for breaking up the Museum collections and dividing them according to their status as documents either of archaeology or of art. In 1826, defending the Museum against one such proposal, the Principal Librarian Henry Ellis wrote to Sir Charles Long as follows:

The Antiquary and the scholar ... would feel little contented with this separation; they would deem that an unnecessary and an untrue preference was given to the artist; that the chain of comparison for the purposes of illustration was broken; and that though fine art was valued, the gradations by which it was acquired were neglected and despised.[31]

This is a remarkably early affirmation of the principle of an archaeological over an aesthetic approach to the Museum's collections, a principle which was to become increasingly important in defending their integrity. The same argument would be expressed more fully by Charles Newton a quarter of a century later, when he joined in the defence against a similar attempt to break up and divide the Museum's collections according to their merits as art or archaeology. For Newton the peculiar excellence of the Museum's collections was the opportunity they afforded: 'for the illustration of that primeval period in the history of art which precedes, as it is believed, the earliest productions of Greek civilization, and reveals thus two distinct sources from which that civilization may have been derived ...' – namely, Egyptian and Assyrian art.[32]

Newton's perception of antiquity, like that of his immediate predecessors, was overtly Hellenocentric. His primary interest in Egyptian, Assyrian and Etruscan art was the light it shed upon the art of the Greeks. Such a view now seems extraordinarily narrow, but it did at least afford Assyrian sculpture a positive role in the unfolding of the history of art. Thus F. Pulsky put it very well in his startlingly incisive essay 'On the Progress and Decay of Art; and on the Arrangement of a National Museum':[33]

In the present state of knowledge when we feel that there is a common link which connects the civilized nations of all ages, a Museum cannot satisfy public expectation, which contains only some more or less important specimens of Greek, Etruscan, or Roman art. We see that Egyptian antiquities, excluded in the last century from the history of art and considered only as curiosities, are now everywhere added to the public collections. Nay, the works of eastern nations, as the Persians, the Assyrians, and the Hindoos, even the productions of the yellow race of China and Japan, excite attention, though despised by some artists for their unconformity with the Greek ideal.

Pulsky's prescription for a universal museum, exhibiting the arts of all civilised nations in chronological order, is rooted in Hegel's theory of limited artistic progress among all the civilised nations. In attributing the capacity for progress to all non-Greek art, Pulsky had deviated from the system of Winckelmann, that allowed no progress among the Egyptians and only a little among the Persians.[34] There are, moreover, some hints of quasi-modern cultural relativism of the kind which, in the twentieth century, would lead to the emancipation of so-called 'primitive' art from previous unfavourable comparison with the art of the Greeks:

Such a collection would be the most convincing proof of the affinity of all civilised peoples, of the unity of mankind. We should see that the first beginning of art is the same with all nations; and though, from the peculiar circumstances of each, its development was carried out in different ways and under different forms towards perfection, yet we should be able to detect a close affinity and connexion between the masterpieces of every national art, clearly showing that the feeling of the beautiful is the same in all ages and in all countries, and that the imitative arts of all nations, so soon as they break the thraldom of conventionality, which protected them in their infancy, but hindered their further development, are the most noble offspring of human genius, whether in Japan or Athens, whether on the Nile or the Arno, on the Euphrates or the Tiber.[35]

Pulsky conceived the Progress of Art as a series of peaks and troughs marking the rise and decline of each successive phase of civilisation. The prevailing image of the nineteenth century, however, was of one great rise and a corresponding fall. We may seek a parallel in Charles Eastlake's inclusion, during the 1840s, of the earlier schools of Italian painting into the National Gallery, admitting their role as the forerunners of Raphael.[36] So, Assyrian bas-reliefs and the Aegina marbles were deemed the precursors of the Elgin Marbles in a system that assessed all earlier and later art in relation to one ideal model.

The alternative approach taken by many theorists towards, for example, the art of the Assyrians, was to deny its value as art at all, and to reduce its importance to a mere 'curiosity' affording a pictorial record of the Bible. Richard Westmacott the elder, who favoured the separation of the Museum's collections, stressed what he saw as the artistic ineptitude of Assyrian art. In the contrast between his view of the Museum's collections, as presented in his testimony to the Parliamentary Commission of 1852–3, and that of Newton, we encounter at startling first hand the great rift that had developed by the middle of the century between the understanding of art, on the one hand, from a historical and documentary viewpoint and, on the other, from the outlook of the artist and aesthetician.[37] In the principle established in the 1840s and 1850s that a museum might be a reference collection for the study of history of art and archaeology rather than a collection arranged in picturesque fashion for the practice of art and the promotion of public taste generally, we may locate the origins of the British Museum's current cherished role as an academic institution.

For Newton the Museum was 'a vast comparative scheme of the Material productions of man'.[38] As to the place of the Elgin Marbles in this scheme he was in no doubt; remove them and the continuity of the series is destroyed. He likened them to the keystone of an arch which itself symbolised the rise and fall of the progress of ancient art.[39] The waxing and waning of the ancient arts was also expressed in terms of the metaphor of a life-cycle, 'the art of schools and races being, like the life of individuals, subject to a certain law of growth, maturity and decay'. Newton went on to urge a search for the origins of perfection in art through the entire repertoire of 'extant specimens', beginning with the earliest: 'We should thus see how perfection in art is the result of a long series of previous trials and failures; how the climax of success has never been reached *per saltum*, but is rather the legacy of many generations of artists; with what rapidity, after this culminating point has been attained, the first symptoms of decline begin to show themselves.'[40]

In these remarkable sentences Newton seems to reveal an awareness of contemporary thinking in the Natural Sciences. Indeed, he has been credited with a developmental view of art along evolutionary lines, foreshadowing Darwin's *Origin of Species* with its vision of the ascent of man through the process of natural selection.[41] We should be unwise, however, to take the analogy too far, for although he might borrow from the language of radical science, Newton was ultimately a traditionalist whose thinking was rooted in the ancient literary and philosophical view of art as interpreted by Winckelmann. The art-as-life metaphor fits easily with Winckelmann's idea of art history in which he regarded the Greeks as representing the youthful flowering of man's creative urge, while the Romans could be compared with his wearied old age.

Newton's view of the progress of art, therefore, was the traditional one, albeit embellished with observations based upon his own experience. This is shown up clearly in the report of his tour of European museums, conducted in the autumn of 1848, when he had set off in pursuit of the origin of Greek art armed with a mental image of the Elgin Marbles as the touchstone of excellence. The account of his researches is a fascinating document of British Victorian *Antikenrezeption*, amounting to a *musée imaginaire* arranged 'in one great chronological series'.[42] Newton's was a voyage of exploration but it was also one of demonstration, for he had set out confident in the belief that he would nowhere find anything to compare either with the perfection of the Elgin Marbles in the British Museum nor with that Museum's ability to illustrate the material process through which such perfection was achieved. Nevertheless, there were lessons to be learned, and in general his text represents a reworking of the received Winckelmann system tracing the rise and fall of Greek art from the earliest to the Roman period. He concluded his essay with an appeal for his imaginary museum to become reality through the assemblage of a scientifically arranged series of casts. Acknowledging the fallibility of the human memory in adequately recalling all that it had seen, he observed: 'Nothing would so much supply this deficiency in the natural powers of the mind as a well-selected *Museum of casts of sculpture, not disposed, as is too often the case, merely to please the eye, but so as to develop, by a series of transition specimens, the chief features of successive styles.*'[43]

At a lecture delivered to the Oxford Art Society shortly after returning from his tour of European museums, Newton urged the establishment of a museum of casts, not of whole pieces but of *membra disiecta*. His model was the collection of casts presented to the Oxford Architectural Society by Thomas Rickman, the pioneering historian of architectural style, who had shown the importance of 'smaller members' and mouldings as a means for tracing its development.

Do for ancient sculpture what has been done for Medieval architecture – make a museum of casts of legs, and arms, and heads, and such other anatomical details as can be conveniently arranged in a series of transition specimens. Lay together, for instance, side-by-side the leg of one of the Aigenetan statues, of the Elgin Theseus, of the Dying Gladiator, the Laocoon, the Farnese Hercules; compare the head of one of the Centaurs of the Parthenon with such later types as you have in the two Centaurs of the Capitol at Rome.

Then, again, Newton makes the fashionable comparison with the practice of natural scientists: 'Class your specimens as a naturalist classes his types: then you will be in a condition to state the characteristics of successive styles in clear concise formularies, and to recognize them everywhere in collections of sculpture, in spite of unscientific arrangement.'[44]

Hawkins's austere policy with regard to the inclusion of casts in the galleries of the Museum has already been mentioned, and not until the end of the century did the British Museum acquire a representative cast collection such as that envisaged by Newton and of the kind then being assembled in other European cities, notably in the university towns of Germany.[45] The necessity for such a series of casts was somewhat alleviated by the opening in 1854 of the Greek and Roman Cast Courts of the Crystal Palace at Sydenham,[46] although these never achieved the 'scientific' arrangement called for by more serious-minded archaeologists like Newton and his German counterpart Adolf Michaelis. The latter was later to write of the importance of a 'laboratory' of casts for tracing every nuance in the great development of antique sculpture.[47]

The Chain of Being

The progress that had been made in archaeological taxonomy by the middle of the nineteenth century ran parallel in many respects with that of the natural sciences. We have already remarked upon the fact that archaeological and natural curiosities were indivisible in the seventeenth- and eighteenth-century *Wunderkammer*, by virtue of their mutual status as 'specimen' objects. Moreover, the same ancient authors were read by those enquiring into both antiquity and the world of natural science. Pliny's *Natural History* had long served the pursuit of both interests.

In the early days of the Museum's history archaeology had been of secondary importance. Gradually the new discipline asserted itself until it succeeded in physically ousting the Natural History collections from the Museum altogether. For most of the nineteenth century, however, the two were exhibited within the same building, a fact which by the 1850s was causing concern in some quarters. Thus Pulsky complained of how 'We go from the masterworks of the Parthenon straight up to the stuffed seal and buffalo; and two monster giraffes stand as sentinels before the gallery of vases.'[48]

The officers of the respective departments will have had daily contact, and it is not surprising, therefore, that the thinking of one should have influenced the other. There were, as it has already been remarked, strong bonds linking the two disciplines, but perhaps the most important of all were Plato and Aristotle. Just how close were the disciplines of archaeology and natural science is shown in a memorial submitted to the Chancellor of the Exchequer in 1858 and signed by over 120 petitioners. Their intention was to impress upon the Government the desire for maintaining the Natural History collections intact in the Museum at Bloomsbury, against the growing assertion that they should be removed to some other site. Here 'the chief end and aim of natural history' was stated as 'to demonstrate the harmony which pervades the whole and the unity of principle, which bespeaks the unity of the Creative Cause.' It was, therefore, essential that the different classes of natural objects should be 'preserved in juxtaposition under the roof of one great building'.[49] *Mutatis mutandis* this could have been just as easily said of the collection of antiquities, as indeed it was in the citation given above from Newton's report to the Parliamentary Commission. The harmony of parts in relation to the whole was, after all, the fundamental Platonic premise of neo-classical theory.

Another related premise of both Plato's and Aristotle's philosophy was the

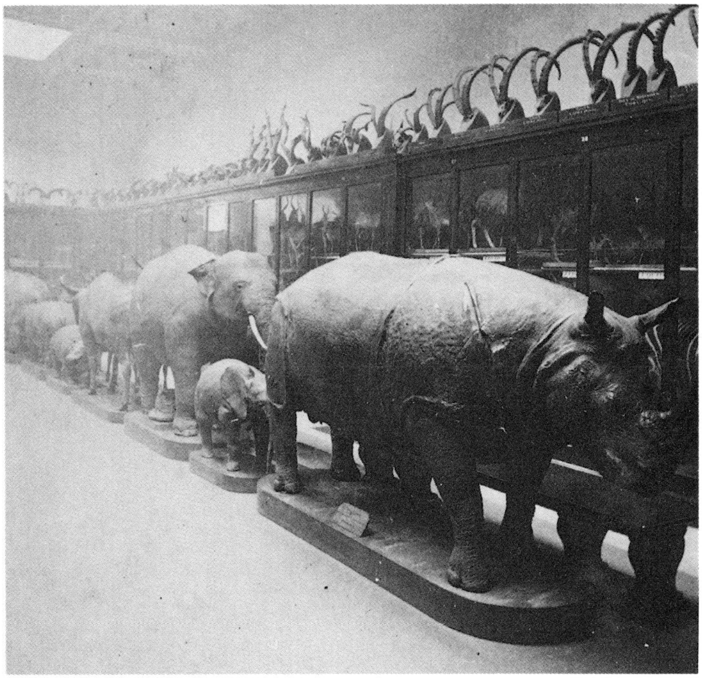

17 The 'Chain of Being': the Natural History collections in Bloomsbury, *c.*1875. Photo by F. York. British Museum, Central Archive.

Theory of Forms with its set of pre-existing immutable models. Manufactured artefacts, political institutions and biological entities could be created only in approximation to ideal models. Aristotle's treatment of the Forms, which was generally less austere and pessimistic than Plato's, allowed the potential for the realisation of a Form in nature, but not for any progress beyond it. In E.R. Dodds's words: 'In nature his [Aristotle's] doctrine of immutable Forms excluded any concept of biological progress: in the absence of any concept of evolution, his *Scala Naturae* is a static sequence not a ladder of ascent.'[50]

It was Darwin who would break the domination of the Theory of Forms over natural science by affording mankind a new status in his universe, not as a fallen angel, but as a risen ape. Darwin, however, was a radical thinker of a kind not usually found within the conservative British Museum. The presiding genius of the Natural History collections from 1856 until 1884 was Richard Owen, who took up a new 18
position as Superintendent of all the Scientific Departments, having previously been Conservator of the Hunterian Museum at the Royal College of Surgeons in Lincoln's Inn Fields.[51] Adrian Desmond describes Owen as 'personally quirky and disliked by the young bloods'.[52] In particular, it was his opposition to natural

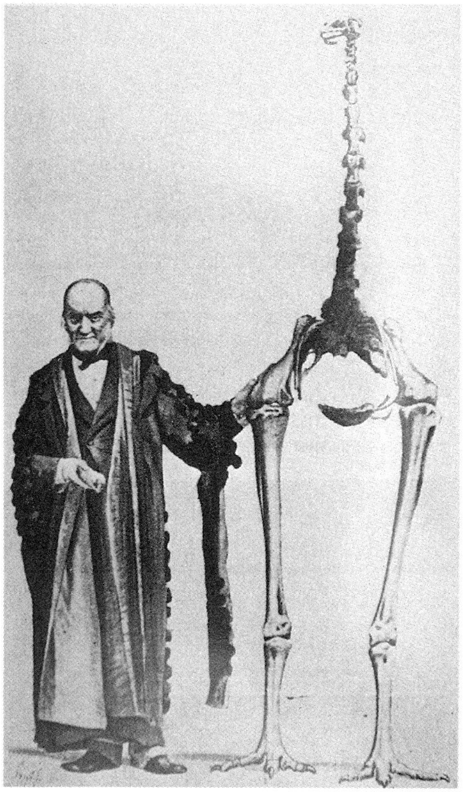

18 Richard Owen (1804–92) photographed about 1877 with a skeleton of the Giant Moa. From Stearn.

selection that brought him into conflict with 'Darwin's Bulldogs'. Owen was a religious believer who struggled like others of his age to reconcile his scientific profession with belief in divine creation. Like many Christian humanists, he adopted the course offered by Aristotle of measuring transformation and transmutation of living things in relation to the divine archetype. For the new Natural History Museum at Brompton Road he conceived the idea of the Index Museum, 'to show how the mammalian type is progressively modified from the form of the fish or lizard'.[53] This cathedral of the natural sciences, Alfred Waterhouse's Gothic response to Smirke's classical temple of the Muses, was to be equipped accordingly with a central nave and twelve side-chapels, 'devoted to specimens selected to show the type-characters of the principal groups of organized beings'. We find an archaeological equivalent of Owen's Index Museum in proposals put forward to the
19 Parliamentary Commission of 1852–3 by Edmund Oldfield, perhaps the most progressive of all the Museum archaeologists. He conceived of a new archaeological Museum comprising a series of parallel lines linked by a central corridor.[54]

In the museological aspirations of Newton and Oldfield, on the one hand, and Owen on the other, we seem to be witnessing parallel attempts at reconciling traditional beliefs with a progressive developmental vision. The metaphorical chain of art is adapted from the eighteenth-century Chain of Being, itself deriving from Aristotle's *Scala Naturae* as employed by natural scientists to describe the diversification of organisms from the transcendent archetypal form created by God. The idea gains full and eloquent expression in Pope's *Essay on Man*:

> Vast chain of being! which from God began,
> Natures aethereal, human, angel, man,
> Beast, bird, fish, insect, what no eye can see,
> No glass can reach; from infinite to thee,
> From thee to nothing. – On superior pow'rs
> Were we to press, inferior might on ours;
> Or in the full creation leave a void,
> Where, one step broken, the great scale's destroy'd;
> From Nature's chain whatever link you strike,
> Tenth, or ten thousandth, breaks the chain alike.

Applied to art, the chain is a potentially progressive image capable of describing the transformation of primitive Egyptian, Assyrian and Etruscan art into the archaic and classical forms of Greek art. It is, however, prevented from developing into a full-blown image of Darwinian evolution by the fixed standard of the Elgin Marbles, against which all progress in the arts, ancient or modern, was measured. To the nineteenth century the Elgin Marbles are the paradigms of ancient art and, as such, serve in the same inhibiting capacity as Plato's immutable Forms. Glyn Daniel, in his treatment of the rise of archaeology, locates the birth of the discipline as an

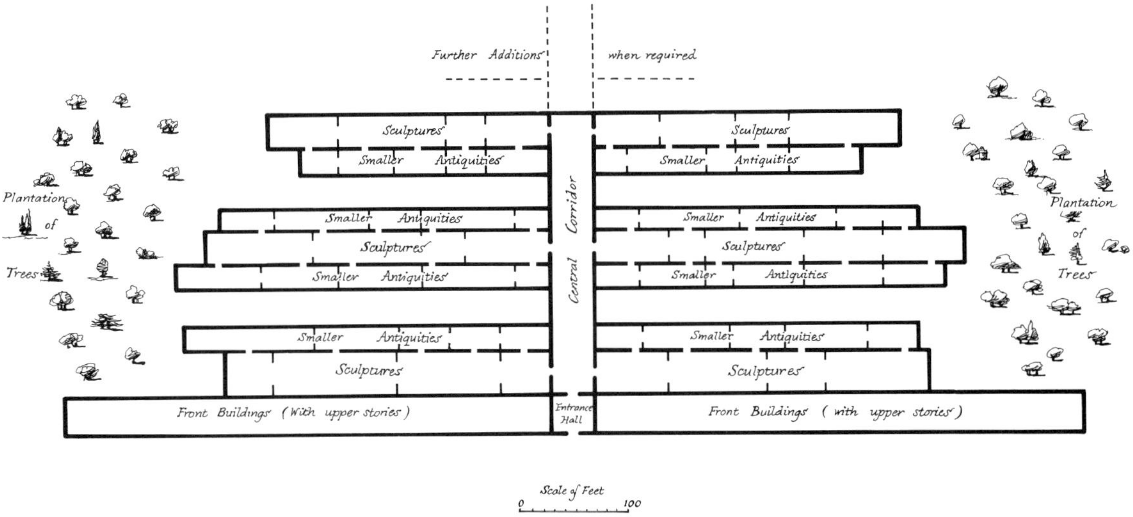

19 Edmund Oldfield's scheme for an ideal Museum in which to illustrate the 'Chain of Art'. P.P. (N.G. 1853), 8359.

independent science in the inspiration provided for prehistory by Darwin and by Charles Lyell's *Principles of Geology*.[55] Later, those who carried the torch of British Hellenism into the twentieth century would regret the pursuit of prehistory as an end in itself, rightly perceiving it as a threat to the old Platonically inspired vision that had motivated generations of classical scholars since Winckelmann's day. In his preface to the translation of Michaelis's summing up of 150 years of classical archaeology, Percy Gardner wrote: 'It is a Darwinian age, when the search for origins seems to fascinate men more than the search for what is good in itself.'[56]

Gardner's is one of the last attempts to defend that spirit of prescriptive Hellenism so eloquently dissected in Frank Turner's *Greek Heritage in Victorian Britain*.[57] This had striven to reconcile a double, sometimes self-contradictory impulse, namely the desire, on the one hand, for absolute standards and, on the other, the belief in moral and material progress. In the twentieth century the classical belief in ideal paradigms has given way to the Romantic spirit of cultural relativism, while the classically inspired doctrine of teleological progress has been replaced by amoral evolutionism. The Darwinian search for origins and its effect upon the views of traditional Hellenists gains no clearer expression than in Leonard Woolley's eulogy of the Sumerians:[58]

> We have outgrown the phase when all the arts were traced to Greece, and Greece was thought to have sprung, like Pallas, full grown from the brain of Olympian Zeus; we have learnt how that flower of genius drew the sap from Lydians and Hittites, from Phoenecia and Crete, from Babylon and Egypt, but the roots go farther back; behind all these lies Sumer.

PART II

5 Arcadia in Bloomsbury: The Elgin and Phigaleian Marbles

All previous accounts of the reception of the Elgin Marbles in England have treated the year 1816 as marking the end of the story.[1] It was then that the purchase was made for the Nation, and in 1817 the sculptures went on show in the British Museum. Through the efforts of a number of scholars we now have a detailed record of the rite of passage by which the Elgin Marbles were transformed from architectural ornament into museum art-object. Their removal from the Acropolis, transmission from Greece to England and eventual incorporation took at most sixteen years. Those momentous events were followed by almost 200 years of residence in England about which there is a near total silence.

This is not so remarkable, when we consider the tendency to think that placing an object in a museum somehow freezes it. Objects taken out of circulation and deposited in a public museum are seen to have completed their history. This assumption neglects the museum life these objects continue to enjoy, and the following account will therefore attempt to tell the story of the Elgin Marbles in the British Museum.

The Temporary Elgin Room

The Trustees received the keys of the Elgin collection, delivered to them by the Principal Librarian Joseph Planta, at their General Meeting of 12 August 1816.[2] Robert Smirke was directed to proceed with the building of temporary accommodation, while Richard Westmacott was appointed to oversee the removal of the sculptures from Elgin's property at Burlington House. Fair progress was made, and on 8 February 1817 Combe records that his time had been wholly occupied in the arrangement of the Elgin Marbles and that the new room was opened on 'Monday last'. Upon the opening of the Elgin Room it was found necessary to employ a person in the capacity of labourer, 'for the purpose of lighting and attending the fires, cleaning the Marbles etc'. A certain John Garrett was appointed, who had been employed in similar work during the removal of the Marbles by Westmacott. He was considered to be 'decent, well-behaved and sufficiently intelligent'.[3]

The Temporary Elgin Room had been tacked onto the west side of Saunders's Townley Gallery (an account of which will be given in the next chapter). It consisted of a large brick-built room with a pine floor. The roof was pierced with skylights and tied together with iron girders. At the western end Smirke had designed a small apse; at the eastern end a doorway led into the smaller room designed to house the so-called Phigaleian Marbles from the temple of Apollo Epicurius at Bassae. The colour of the walls of the temporary gallery, despite the evidence of Archibald Archer's painting (Colour Plate II), was blue.[4]

The building was constructed at ground level without a basement and was reached by a stair that led down from the second rotunda of the Townley Gallery
(Room IV). The plan is reproduced by J. Britton in his *Illustrations of the Public* 5
Buildings of London of 1825. There are also three views of the interior of the Elgin Room and a more fanciful watercolour by James Stephanoff of the Phigaleian Room.

The most evocative depiction of the gallery is Archibald Archer's oil-painting of 1819, once owned by Edward Hawkins and presented to the Museum by Dr J. E. Gray in 1872.[5] It now hangs in the ante-room to the Trustees' Boardroom at the British Museum. The picture was discussed by Arthur Hamilton Smith, who based the identification of the persons in it on a letter from 'Gray', one of the people
represented in the picture.[6] Smith's prosopographical key lists a number of promi- 9
nent members of the staff of the British Museum, but the most important figures, shown seated together in the foreground, are (7) Benjamin West, President of the Royal Academy, and (8) Joseph Planta, Principal Librarian of the British Museum. In these two persons the painting appears to celebrate the close association of the two institutions most responsible for the state of the arts in England at this time: the Royal Academy as chief practitioner, and the British Museum as custodian of the highest exemplars of antique art.

The other person worthy of special notice is Benjamin Robert Haydon (1), chief advocate for the 'commencement of real art', which he hoped public exhibition of the Elgin Marbles would arouse in England.[7] Shunned by the artistic establishment, he appears here isolated from the rest of the group, and yet seemingly at home among his beloved Marbles.

As we see from this painting and from an engraving by Charles Heath after a
drawing by Frederick Mackenzie, the arrangement of the sculptures in the 20
Temporary Elgin Gallery was aesthetic, so far as that modest room allowed.[8] The metopes and frieze lined the long walls, while in front was placed an 'avenue' of sculptures, inscriptions and architectural fragments leading to the apse at the western end of the room. Here, like some cult-statue seated at the innermost recess of a temple, was placed the colossal figure of Dionysus from the choragic monument of Thrasyllus. The figure was raised up on the massive column capital from the Parthenon, while to the left and right, separating this 'chancel' from its 'nave', were placed the reclining male nudes from the west and east pediments of the Parthenon.

Archer's painting well illustrates the rotating bases on which these figures rested,

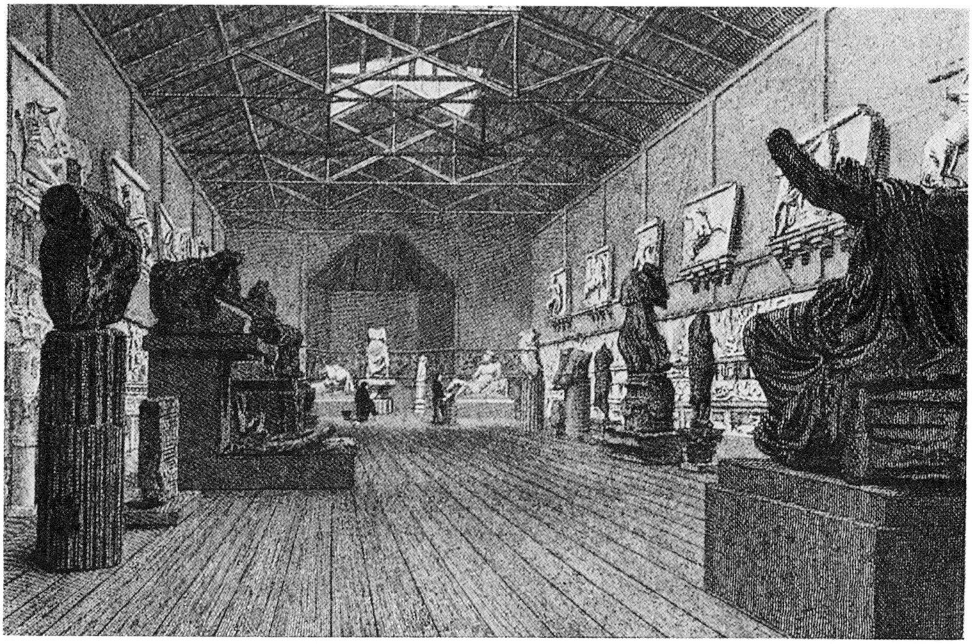

20 The Temporary Elgin Room, looking west. The arrangement was aesthetic in so far as the modest interior allowed. Engraving by C. Heath after F. Mackenzie, for *Views of London* (1825).

allowing them to be turned so as to take advantage of the light. The depiction of the sculptures is more picturesque, however, than it was in the actual arrangement, the bronze bowl and its stone casing being imported, to add extra interest, from the middle of the room, together with the horse's head and the Elgin 'Eros'.[9] The metope on the end wall, morever, was never there in reality, being added merely to fill this otherwise empty space.

In a drawing by W. H. Prior, we turn to face in the opposite direction, looking
21 east towards the doorway leading into the Phigaleian Room. Immediately in front of the doorway on the right, as one faced it, were placed two of the three female figures from the east pediment of the Parthenon thought at that time to represent the Fates,[10] and on the left two balancing figures also from the east pediment thought then, as now, to represent Demeter and her daughter Persephone.

No accurate representation is available of the smaller room on the other side of the doorway, but it is fancifully reproduced in a watercolour drawing by James
Col. Pl. V Stephanoff.[11] Here the artist has transformed the makeshift apartment of real life into a splendid interior, although the proportions of the room are about right in relation to the Elgin Room, visible in the drawing through the doorway beyond. The position of the staircase descending into the room from the Townley Gallery is also
5 just where it should be according to Britton's plan.

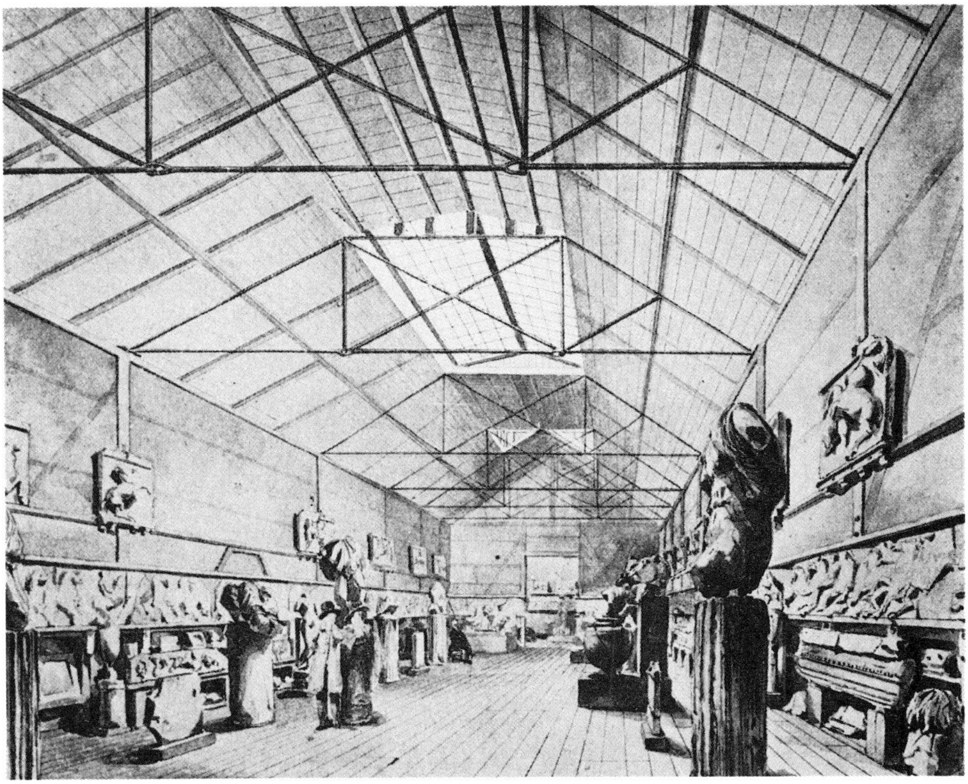

21 The Temporary Elgin Room, looking east. Undated drawing by W. H. Prior. British Museum, PD 1838–1–13–1.

The primary purpose of the smaller room in Smirke's Temporary Gallery was to accommodate the frieze from the Temple of Apollo at Bassae (Phigaleia). It was excavated in 1811–12 by the same team of travellers responsible for the discovery of the Aegina marbles, which the British Museum failed to acquire.[12] C. R. Cockerell, one of the original party of four who visited the site of ancient Bassae in 1811,[13] gives a full but belated account of their discoveries; the others were Baron Karl Haller von Hallerstein, James Linkh of Württemberg and John Foster. The first expedition was interrupted by Turkish officials and not resumed until the following year, when Cockerell himself had departed for Sicily. When excavations were permitted to be resumed, the party was joined by an English traveller, Thomas Legh, and George Christian Gropius, the Austrian Consul in Athens. Also in the party were Baron Otto Magnus von Stackelberg of Estonia and Peter Oluf Brönsted of Copenhagen.[14]

Cockerell gives an evocative account of the excavations amidst the ruins. Although absent from the second season of digging, he was well acquainted with the

Arcadian landscape and the hospitality of the local inhabitants. The temple itself is situated on a rocky spur, then densely wooded, beneath Mount Kotylion in south-west Arcadia. It was built around 430 BC in the Doric order, reputedly by Ictinus, one of the architects of the Parthenon, and dedicated to Apollo Epicurius (the Helper). The building was of limestone but its sculptured ornament was of marble.[15] Some very fragmentary metopes were excavated from the ruined temple,[16] but the most important discovery was the frieze that had surmounted the architrave above an inner colonnade.[17] It is carved with two mythical battles, showing Lapiths fighting Centaurs and Greeks fighting Amazons.

Like the Aegina marbles before them, the Phigaleian sculptures were packed up and transported to Zante (Zakynthos), thus narrowly escaping being impounded by the local Pasha. At Zante the sculptures were auctioned and sold to the British for 60,000 Spanish dollars, which, because of a bad conversion, worked out at £15,000. The proceeds were divided between the six proprietors, Cockerell, Linkh, Foster, Legh, Haller and Gropius.[18] In addition, as a condition of the sale, each was to receive a complete set of casts from the sculptures within twenty-four months of their safe arrival in England.[19]

The marbles arrived on 20 October 1815 and were deposited for safe-keeping in a room in the north-western corner of Montagu House.[20] An additional fragment arrived unexpectedly six months later, when John Spencer Stanhope presented a piece of the frieze he had purchased from a peasant in the neighbourhood of Phigaleia.[21] Further pieces were to be presented by Brönsted in 1824.[22]

A decision was taken, as with the Elgin Marbles, not to restore them, but some repairs were necessary and these were carried out by Westmacott.[23] The sculptures were fixed into the walls of the temporary apartment adjoining the Elgin Room, and were shown together with a number of casts and original pieces from the Elgin collection. The casts included those of the west frieze of the Parthenon, the frieze of the choragic monument of Lysicrates, and the metopes and friezes of the Hephaesteum.[24] Among the original sculptures and architectural members were the Caryatid from the Erechtheum, the Ionic column from the same building and the granite Egyptian scarab brought by Elgin from Constantinople.

Stephanoff's watercolour of the Phigaleian Room includes some of these but omits others, while adding some pieces that were never there. Among the latter we find the south metopes of the Parthenon, which were displayed in the larger adjoining room, the head of Perikles, which was in fact placed in Room III of the Townley Gallery, and the Elgin 'Eros' – providing so much interest for the group to the right of the doorway – which was placed in the Elgin Room itself.[25]

The Temporary Phigaleian Room, unlike the adjoining Elgin Gallery, was not
22 pulled down in 1831 but continued in use for a further ten years with a display of casts,[26] including those that had once belonged to Sir Thomas Lawrence[27] and the

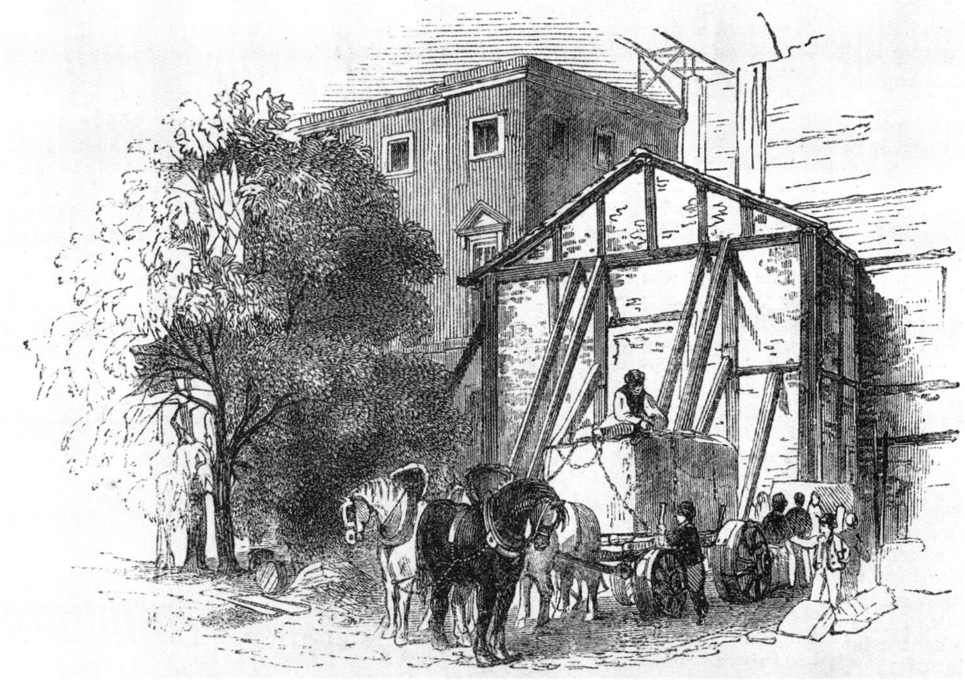

22 'Taking down the old exterior': the cart is parked in front of the last remains of the temporary shed, built 1816–17, in which the Phigaleian Marbles were first displayed. *Pictorial Times*, 1 April 1843. British Museum, PD 1936–5–11–97.

five casts of the metopes discovered at Selinus in Sicily by William Harris and Samuel Angell.[28]

The arrangement of the sculptures in the Elgin Room did not alter radically between its opening in 1817 and its dismantling in 1831. Some minor changes were made, however, including the removal by Elgin of some fragments of porphyry columns from Egypt.[29] There were besides a number of additions of both original fragments and casts. On 10 May 1817 the Trustees were informed by Sir Henry Englefield that the Society of Dilettanti had decided to present to the Museum two pieces of the Parthenon frieze that had previously been loaned to the Royal Academy.[30] On 14 March 1818 Combe reported that, in obedience to the direction of the Trustees, he had placed south metope 15 (now VI) in the Elgin Room 'so as to range with the other metopes'.[31] And, in order to balance the introduction of this on one side of the gallery, a cast of south metope 7 (now XXVII) was added, even though the original was already displayed, 'and a perfect symmetry thus obtained'.[32]

This desire to achieve an even number of metopes on each side of the Gallery was one of the reasons that prompted Combe to urge the Trustees to bid for south metope X at the sale of the Choiseul-Gouffier collection in Paris on 20 June 1818.[33]

The attempt failed and the metope went to the Louvre. A cast was subsequently acquired and this was incorporated into the 1832 arrangement.[34]

On 11 April 1818 Combe reported that he had recovered a piece of the frieze of the Parthenon, which had 'by some means been removed from among the Elgin Marbles during the time they were at Burlington House'.[35] On 9 December 1820 it was recorded that Francis Chantrey had presented a cast from a portion of the east
10 frieze (slab VII) which was in the Louvre. 'The restorations which this portion of the frieze has received', it was remarked, 'since it has been in the possession of the French, have by no means served to enhance the value of the marble.'[36]

In March 1830 C. R. Cockerell presented to the Trustees a fragment of the south frieze of the Parthenon (I 4).[37] In July 1828 Brönsted presented two casts of heads, which Combe's successor Edward Hawkins, with the assistance of Richard Westmacott, succeeded in joining to the 'eighth metope' (now south metope IV).[38] The originals of these heads were at the time of Hawkins's writing in the Royal Museum in Copenhagen, and Hawkins thought they might be transferred to the British Museum in exchange for a set of casts of all the metopes. A formal approach was made accordingly, but nothing came of it.[39]

The permanent gallery

Some ten years after it was built, the Temporary Elgin Room began to show signs of disrepair, and its safety was called into question.[40] Accordingly Robert Smirke was asked to alter the skylights and 'generally to do whatever may be deemed best calculated to maintain the strength of the building'. Two years later the construction of the West Wing, which was to include space for the permanent accommodation of the Elgin Marbles, was well advanced. Provision was made for linking the new building firstly to the Temporary Elgin Room, and then to the Townley Gallery.[41] The juxtaposition of the Townley Gallery and the new West Wing is shown in
6 George Scharf's drawing of July 1828, in which we can also see, extending westwards, the shell of the proposed new Elgin Room.

Smirke's original intention had been to provide permanent accommodation for the Elgin Marbles in a new gallery that was to project at right angles from the centre of the West Wing (occupying 12 on Fig. 1 and the central part of 8). As the building went up, however, the Trustees began to have serious doubts as to the utility of both this space and the main gallery (destined to become the Egyptian Sculpture Gallery) for the display of sculpture. On 14 June 1828 the Sub-Committee on Antiquities requested 'the immediate attention of the Trustees to Mr Smirke's design for the Western Wing, in which the walls on each side may very materially interfere with the deposition of statues and other works of art, and more particularly with any long and continued frieze, or series of bas-reliefs, if any such should be acquired in the future'. Westmacott was consulted and he confirmed the Trustees' premonitions of disaster.[42] The practical solution, however, came from Edward Hawkins.[43] This involved throwing down a portion of the side walls of the room Smirke had originally intended for the Elgin Marbles and extending it on each side to receive 'all the frieze and casts which the Museum possesses, and to allow of the figures of the pediment being placed in the relative positions which they occupied in the front of the Parthenon, which would probably have a grand effect when the spectator would enter immediately opposite to them in the centre of the room'. Hawkins proposed to light the room with a lantern extending the whole length of the gallery and to colour the walls and floors, 'so that the light which would fall upon the Marbles would not be generalised and counteracted by reflections in every possible direction'.

These last remarks are significant in view of the general dissatisfaction with the colour and distribution of light in the Elgin Room that were to be experienced in future years, and the Trustees would have done well to heed their servant's advice.

Although the tearing down of walls already built was a substantial waste of resources, Smirke's mistake was affordable since the rest of the Museum works had not cost as much as had originally been estimated. By the beginning of 1830 the East Wing of the Museum was complete except for the staircase at the north end, and the shell of the north division of the eventual Egyptian Sculpture Gallery was also standing as far as Saunders's Townley Gallery. The original estimate allowed by the Treasury for the completion of these works had been £215,000. An estimated expense of 'certain additions and of furniture as reported to the Lords of the Treasury' amounted to a further £12,770, making a grand total of £227,770. Parliament had already voted £184,192 of this and Smirke calculated that he would need a further £32,000 to complete all the galleries on the ground floor of the West Wing and to effect a temporary communication between them and the north end of the Townley Gallery (and also to finish the staircase in the East Wing).

Smirke's adoption of Hawkins's plan was approved on the express understanding that the expense would not exceed estimates already sanctioned by the Treasury.[44] The architect was called upon to prepare a section of the new room, particularly with a view to showing the 'lanthorn light', and at the same time he was requested to send a person whose accuracy could be relied upon to assist Hawkins in measuring the Parthenon frieze.[45]

On 9 March 1830 a Sub-Committee on Buildings consisting of Charles Long (Lord Farnborough), Henry Bankes and Alexander Baring MP (Lord Ashburton) met to discuss the arrangement of the Elgin Marbles in the new room that was about to be built for them.[46] Two resolutions were arrived at, the first sensible, the second not. In their opinion plaster casts (then in the Museum) of various missing parts of the frieze should be incorporated in the arrangement of the originals. Further, in

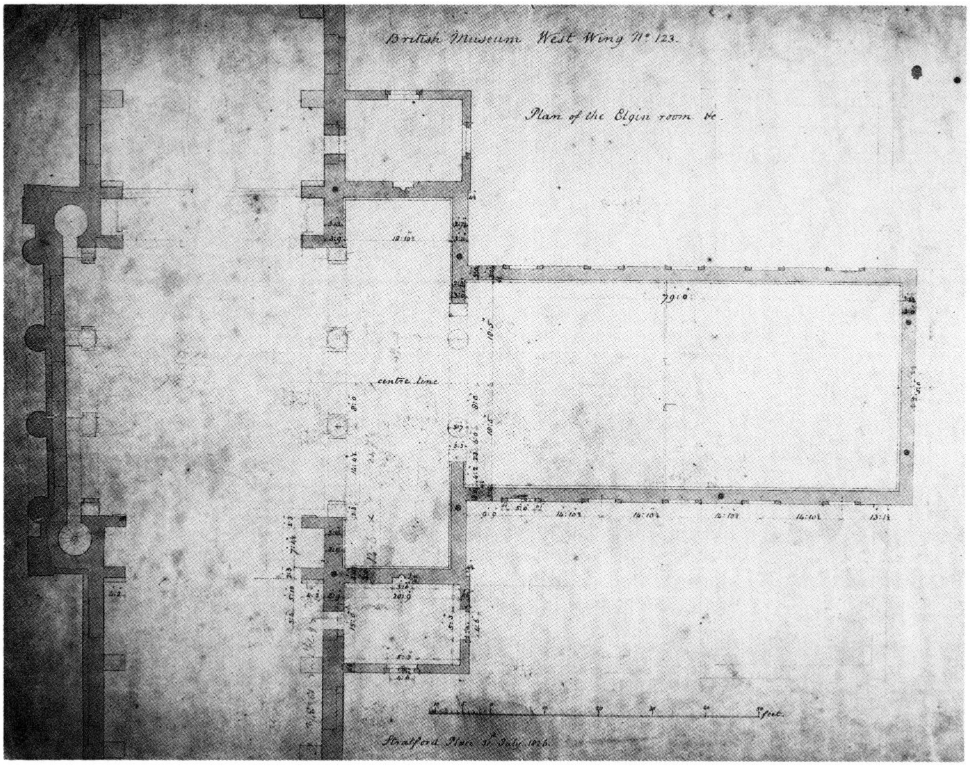

23 Plan of the 'permanent' Elgin Room as first begun, incorporating faint pencil alterations actually executed in 1830–31: the long walls of the gallery were built, only to be torn down, and the room redesigned to accommodate the Parthenon frieze (compare Fig. 6). Plan dated 31 July 1826. British Museum, Central Archive.

order to allow the centre of the procession (the gods of the east frieze) to be placed in the best possible position and in order to obviate the problem posed by the corner-blocks of the south-east and north-west angles of the frieze, it was proposed that these should be sawn through.

Happily the Trustees were advised by Westmacott against sawing through the corner-stones, and he was requested to prepare a model and a report detailing his views as to the best arrangement of the 'Athenian Marbles'.[47] In the event the model was made by Smirke, and Westmacott worked out his scheme by arranging within it drawings of the various parts of the frieze.[48] Two further models were then prepared by Smirke showing alternative methods of lighting the gallery and a decision was reached by the Sub-Committee on Buildings (22 May 1830), after consultation with the President of the Royal Academy, Westmacott and Smirke.

Meanwhile, discussions relating to the manner in which the sculptures were to be displayed were continuing. Hawkins wanted to surround the metopes in the new room 'with such architectural decorations as immediately accompanied them in the original building'. This he thought 'would increase considerably the general effect and display the marbles as nearly as possible under their original circumstances, enhancing their interest and value to artists and architects . . .'.[49] His proposal was referred to the Sub-Committee, however, and refused.[50] The metopes were to be mounted in the west wall of the gallery, opposite the entrance, with even less ancillary ornament than they had received in the Temporary Elgin Room. The frieze was to be placed in a continuous line around the room, while the Phigaleian frieze was similarly to occupy the ante-room (12 on Fig. 1).[51]

By November of 1831 the Elgin and Phigaleian Marbles had all been removed into the new rooms.[52] The metopes and friezes were fixed in their places and the temporary passage from the Townley to the Elgin Gallery was nearly complete. By February of the following year Westmacott had presented his bill for his part in the work.[53] His quotation had been for £1000, for both removing and installing the sculptures in their new locations.[54]

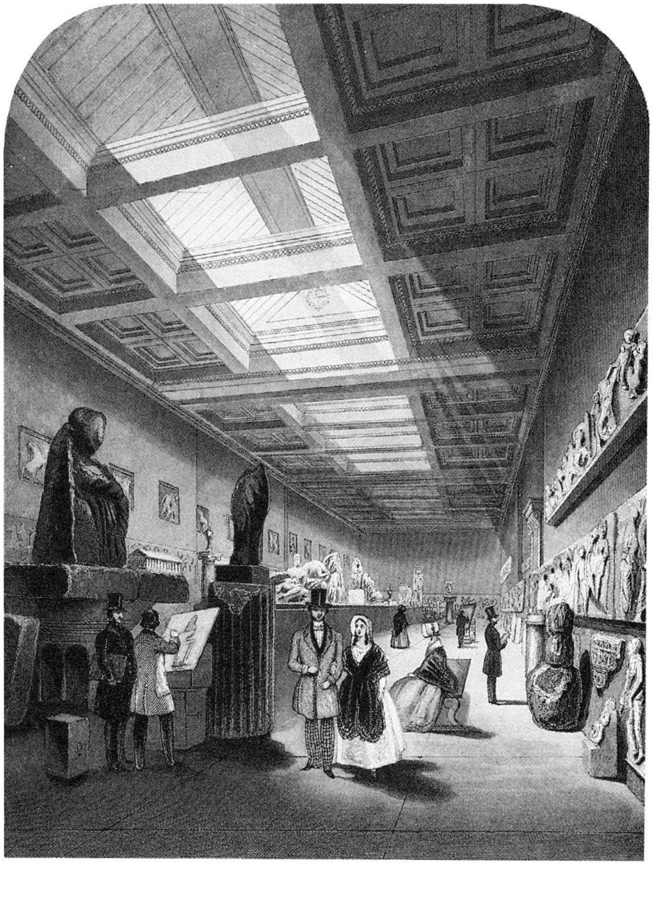

24 The Elgin Room (8 on Fig. 1), *c.*1846. This is now Room 7, where the Nereid Monument is displayed. Steel engraving. British Museum, PD 1912–8–22–3.

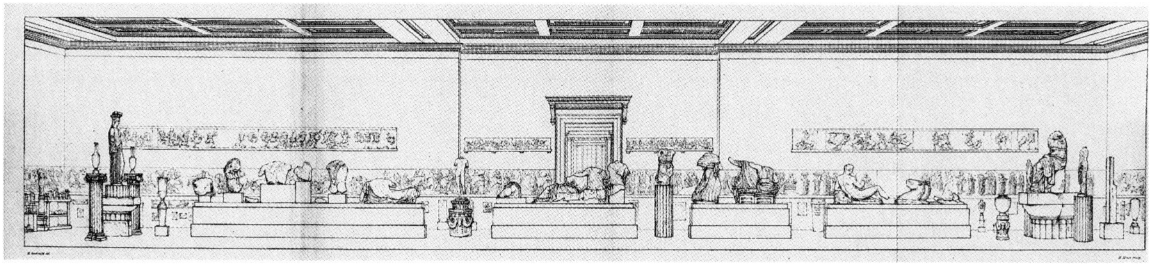

25 The Elgin Room looking east towards the door, *c.*1832. Engraving by H. Moses after a drawing by H. Corbould, *Ancient Marbles*, part VII, pl. 19.

In June 1832 the Trustees were at last in a position to determine the colour for the walls of the new Galleries.[55] On 14 July some last-minute adjustments to the arrangement in the Phigaleian Gallery were ordered.[56] At the same time, the Trustees ordered the new galleries to be opened to the public on the 23rd of that month.

The new Elgin Room contained virtually all the works in stone from the Elgin
25 collection, and their arrangement is mapped out in two engravings by Henry Moses after drawings by Henry Corbould. The Parthenon sculptures, dominating the centre of the gallery, were arranged with greater respect than before for their archaeological disposition, but much of the picturesque feeling of the Temporary Elgin Room was retained.

The pedimental sculptures were brought together and placed on four low wooden bases down the centre of the room. No allowance was made for the actual spacing of the sculptures on the building, and the better-preserved fragments from the east pediment occupied three of the long bases, while those from the west pediment were contained on a single plinth. This was done partly to allow the so-called 'Fates' to occupy the central position in the gallery and so to be seen first upon entering it. This group was flanked on one side by west pediment 'N' (which was then identified as Nike and believed to have come from the east pediment), while on the other side was placed the Elgin 'Eros'.[57] These two figures upon their extraordinary bases serve to divide up the central line of figures into three groups consisting of the 'Fates' and horse's head in the centre, with the west pedimental sculptures on one side and, on the other, the remainder of the east pediment. As picturesque elements within this arrangement, they echo the obviously picturesque groupings of sculpture and architectural fragments piled up at either end of the room.

At the southern end was the colossal Dionysus from the choragic monument of Thrasyllus, placed, as in the old gallery, upon the Parthenon capital;[58] around him, like dedications at a shrine, two lesser figures stood on column shafts,[59] while at his feet the bronze bowl in its marble casing rested on a votive altar.[60] Behind this image of the ancient god of wine was placed the inscribed archaic stele from Sigeum, recording the presentation of a wine-bowl and strainer for civic use in the Prytaneum at Sigeum.[61]

Balancing this group, at the northern end of the gallery, the Erechtheum Caryatid was raised up on a pile which included the drum of an Ionic column from the interior of the Propylaea,[62] resting on a capital from the east front of that same building. This was flanked by two marble funerary *lekythoi* on parts of Ionic columns and, in front, another *lekythos* mounted on an Attic columnar monument.[63]

Numerous other sculptures, casts, inscriptions and architectural fragments were arranged around the walls of the room. The principal monuments, namely the frieze and metopes of the Parthenon, were mounted on the walls. All fifteen metopes were placed on the west wall, to face the doorway, arranged in the order in which they had appeared on the Parthenon (II–IX;XXVI–XXXII). A cast of south metope X, the original being in Paris, was placed between IX and XXVI.

On the long wall opposite, in the recess on either side of the doorway, was placed the frieze of the Nike Temple, and on the main walls, Elgin's casts of the frieze and metopes of the Hephaesteum.

All around the lower walls of the gallery on a continuous plinth was placed the Parthenon frieze, incorporating casts of those portions, principally the west frieze, not removed by Elgin. The south and east frieze were mounted on the north and east walls, while the west and north friezes were placed on the west and south walls.

The adjoining Phigaleian Room, completed at the same time as the Elgin Gallery, contained the frieze of the Temple of Apollo Epicurius and a few other pieces besides, including the Elgin scarab, a giant granite beetle originating in Egypt but acquired by Lord Elgin in Constantinople.

Colour and light

It is not known from any contemporary description what shade the Elgin Room was painted when it first opened. The colour, however, seems to have been Westmacott's choice and was said at the time to be darkish in tone.[64] In discussing the question of colour for the walls of the Egyptian Sculpture Gallery, Robert Smirke remarked that these should be painted in a stone colour, 'for we have no superfluous quantity of light in the Centre Gallery, and any colour like that given to the Greek Rooms would be ruinously dark'.[65] The colour of the walls and the pedestals was, in fact, 'a mottled purplish gray' as we learn belatedly from a letter to *The Times* dated 26 June 1858 and signed Marmor. It was considered 'unobtrusive in character, harmonizing agreeably with the mellow tone of the statues'.

So it remained, until in August 1838 a periodic redecoration was contemplated.

Some discussion had already taken place when W.R. Hamilton was invited to comment upon the question of how this should be done.[66] Hamilton met Robert Smirke by appointment at the Museum and produced a drawing showing how the Elgin Room might be coloured. 'Mr Hamilton', we are told, made several suggestions as to the colouring of this gallery, including 'the darkening of the floor'. It was agreed that the architect would prepare portions of the wall as specimens and Hamilton would have the opportunity of commenting upon them before the walls were painted. The eventual result of all these deliberations was to colour the walls of the Elgin Room a bold and uncompromising red. The change was not welcomed in every quarter and the following letter was addressed to the Trustees in polite protest.[67]

My Lords and Gentlemen,

It is with great reluctance that I address myself to your honourable body; nor should I do so, did I not feel it a duty I owe to myself, to my fellow students, and the public in general. I have watched with considerable interest the colouring of the walls in the Elgin Room expecting daily to see a change, but there appears now no possibility of any such change taking place. The colour is of great beauty in itself, but I think quite out of place there. The expression of grief and joy cannot be represented in one face at the same time, nor can the breathing vitality of these fragments be felt when surrounded by inharmonious colours; consequently I have ventured to offer the following remarks with all due submission to my superior, and hope they will be received with the same kind spirit as given.

First then, as the Elgin Marbles are the most wonderful productions that man has yet produced, everything that can ought to be done to give them effect and all surrounding objects made wholly subservient. It appears to me that your object for using so much red on the walls was to give warmth to the figures; if so, I must beg widely to differ from you. Marble is cold in itself, and can only be warmed by surrounding it with colder colours still. Had you painted the walls a dark, invisible, transparent green, varying the plinth a few shades, I think you would not have altered it to the existing tint.

There is another obstacle to surmount of greater magnitude; the reflection of light, now reflected from side to side, from ceiling to floor and from floor to ceiling in the utmost confusion. The underparts of the figures receiving almost as much light from the floor as from the skylight above. The back of the Theseus on a sunny day will illustrate this to perfection. A darkened floor would, in some measure rectify this. If the glass of the skylight were ground also, I have no doubt it would; but as the expense would be more than your honourable body would feel justified in incurring, there is a method of simulating it at a fairly trifling cost. Common putty dabbed on the side of the glass would have the desired effect, stand for years and cleaned [*sic*] if desired.

Signed, Alfred Jeffrey

Jeffrey's letter was acknowledged, and copies passed to Smirke and Hawkins who, although they did not comment upon the criticisms of the new colour, were not unsympathetic to the grumbles about the light.[68] Hawkins suggested placing the sculptures from the pediments in two lines as near to the walls as possible so as to improve the lighting. He further urged the removal of some of the flagstones from the centre of the room and their replacement with slate or black marble in order to eliminate the reflection which threw so much light up onto the figures.[69]

No action was taken until the following spring, when the Trustees directed Smirke to colour the floor of the Elgin Gallery with 'different shades of a dark tint' in two or three places, and at the same time to consider whether the light in the gallery might be improved by means of blinds to the skylights.[70] Smirke agreed to prepare the colouring of the floor but, feeling defensive at the implied criticism of his design, he pointed out how very fully the position of the sculptures had been considered with the aid of a model, and that the objections that held then against separating the pediment sculptures into two lines would still now apply.[71] On the question of blinds over the skylights, he thought these would have some good effect in restricted places, but that it would be difficult to create any general improvement. The Trustees decided that the pediment sculptures would continue to be displayed in one line in the centre of the gallery, with some minor adjustments.[72]

In November 1843 dissatisfaction over the 'scattered and irregular light' in the Elgin Gallery was once more voiced, this time in the form of a petition signed by a body of artists.[73] Hawkins, whose attempts in the past to effect a thorough-going solution to the problem had been thwarted by the Trustees' sluggish response, found himself in rebellious sympathy with the signatories of the petition, or 'Students of Art', as they collectively called themselves. Using the petition as ammunition he once more requested the Trustees to attend to the problem of the light in the Elgin Gallery. He also asked that something might be done about the noise made by the hammers of the bookbinders who had their workshop in the basement of the gallery – a fact which was found to be 'a great impediment to artists and very disagreeable to visitors'.[74] Richard Westmacott was consulted and he too agreed that the lighting in the gallery was unsatisfactory from the point of view of an artist wishing to draw the sculpture.[75] He pointed out, however, that no complete remedy could be sought without disfiguring the room with curtains, and therefore suggested that the general diffusion of light might be modified by removing three sections of the paving from the centre of the floor and substituting Bremen paving, a darkish stone of purplish tint. He further suggested stretching canvas over the extremities of the two skylights furthest from the centre and removing the marbles from the centre to the sides of the room, which would weaken the reflection of light off the side walls. Finally he suggested lifting the pediment sculptures up to the level of the base-line of the frieze. In general Westmacott felt that the deficiencies of lighting derived not from any intrinsic fault of the gallery, but from the fact that the sculptures were displayed for general interest. The concentration of light necessary for study could not, he felt, be achieved in any gallery, whether lit from above or from the sides.

On the strength of these recommendations a number of experiments were conducted in the gallery: part of the floor was painted in purplish-brown watercolour and sheet lead was laid down to see what the effect of darkening the floor would be, but nothing seems to have come of these experiments.[76] Hawkins, however, seized his chance of reintroducing the problem to the Trustees, when at the beginning of 1846 he turned his attention to the question of incorporating into the gallery arrangement some recently acquired casts of sculptures in Athens. In particular he wished to place two figures from the west pediment among the Elgin pieces: the necessity of moving the sculptures, he suggested, would provide a good opportunity for placing the figures of both pediments much nearer to the walls of the room.[77] Shortly afterwards Hawkins submitted a plan of the Elgin Room showing the places to which he proposed to move the sculptures and, after conferring with Westmacott, the Trustees approved.[78] Hawkins had detailed the advantages he saw in his plan as follows:

> The eastern pediment will be detached from all other figures, and will be seen entire and uninterruptedly even before the spectator enters the room, at a distance of more than thirty feet. The space between the pediments and frieze will be greater than Mr H. has observed spectators to take for themselves when examining the frieze in detail. The oblique direction of the light will exhibit the figures of the pediments to greater advantage than they have ever yet been seen.

Hawkins's proposals were carried out in the following April, May, June and July.[79] They did not, it seems, please everybody, and James Fergusson, whose criticisms were not always reasonable, was especially scathing about the lighting in the Elgin Room which – even with the pedimental sculptures moved to one side – he regarded as far too high. He thought the artistic value of the sculpture could only be fully understood, 'by getting casts and lighting them properly', until such time as the sculptures themselves had been, 'placed in a light where they could be seen to advantage'.[80]

The frieze Fergusson thought tolerably well lit, but he complained it was difficult to get a good view of it owing to the narrowing of the gap between the pedimental groups and the western wall of the gallery. As for the metopes, he considered them 'destroyed' when built into such an 'expanse of flat, red wall'.

These complaints were perhaps justified, but less so was the charge that the room was unduly long and narrow and that the walls were too plain in comparison with the antae and panelling lavished upon the Egyptian Gallery. These were constraints forced upon the architect by the nature of the objects, and notably the frieze, for which the room was intended. Equally inappropriate is the suggestion that Smirke had committed 'a gross and unpardonable blunder' in running the gallery north and south, instead of east and west. Fergusson's argument here was that the most effective illumination a sculpture could receive was a steady light introduced from the very top of the north wall of a gallery. Again, we have seen how the architect had originally chosen an axis east and west, but had been forced to abandon it on account of the frieze. To have maintained the original axis and to have lengthened the gallery sufficiently westwards would have been to extend it beyond the boundary of the Museum grounds.

Fergusson had certainly identified the aesthetic shortcomings of the Elgin Room, but he was insensitive to, if not unaware of, the difficulties a fellow architect had encountered in attempting to reconcile tectonic aspirations with the particular needs of the Elgin Marbles.

The Elgin Room 1832–1860

Apart from these changes, the arrangement of the sculptures in the Elgin Room was to remain essentially the same for nearly two decades. There were during these years some additions to the body of material exhibited. A number of casts acquired from Athens were incorporated in the arrangement as well as some actual pieces. In 1840, for example, J.J. Dubois, Conservator of the Antiquities of the Louvre, wrote offering the Museum certain fragments of the Parthenon sculptures which had been acquired by the French from the Acropolis in 1814.[81]

Then in January 1842 W.R. Hamilton wrote with an extraordinary tale to tell.[82]

> You are of course aware that amongst the Elgin Marbles in the Museum are two blocks of limestone being some ornamental sculpture, which formerly belonged to the entrance of the very ancient building at Mycenae called the Treasury of Agamemnon. When these blocks were brought to England, they were accompanied by several others with sculpture of the same description, but when the great mass of the Elgin collection was removed from Burlington House, these last were most unaccountably left behind, and appear to have been soon after carried away as rubbish. Some years after, Mr Poynter the architect picked up two of them in the grounds of the Lodge in Marylebone Park, built for the Master of St. Catherine, where they were intended to form part of the rockwork in the garden.[83] Mr Poynter took them and had them cast. I accidentally saw impressions of them at Mr Scole's in Argyll Street, and immediately recognised them as old acquaintances. The originals have since been presented by Mr Poynter and suggesting to him the propriety of their finding their ultimate destination within the walls of the Museum, I was encouraged by that gentleman to make an application to the Institute of British Architects ... – who agreed.[84]

Less dramatic was the acquisition in 1850 of a fragment of the Parthenon frieze which George Scharf had discovered in the Smith Barry Collection at Marbury Hall.[85] The fragment which Scharf had identified as belonging to the North Frieze cavalcade was presented to the Museum by James H. Smith Barry.[86]

The major upheaval to the Elgin Marbles was to come as a consequence of Sydney Smirke's creation of a second Elgin Room where, it seems, he had originally intended to house the Assyrian sculptures, 'both those now temporarily displayed in the Museum and those expected shortly.'[87] The new gallery (7 on Fig. 1) was to be placed in line with the existing Elgin Room and to adjoin the Lycian Room. One of the advantages Smirke saw in this was the elimination of what he called the 'cul-de-sac effect' in those rooms, as they then were.

It was Hawkins who raised objections to Sydney Smirke's proposed new Assyrian Gallery which, he thought, would seriously interfere with the systematic chronological arrangement of the sculptures.[88] For, he argued, the collections should be instructive as well as entertaining. Besides, more space was needed for Greek sculpture, which would fit well in the space between the Lycian and Elgin Rooms. Hawkins proposed to place the newly acquired Nineveh sculptures in a slip room adjoining the west side of the northern section of the Egyptian Sculpture Gallery (16 on Fig. 1). The corresponding gallery to the south had already been erected.[89] The Trustees were persuaded by Hawkins's objections and wrote to the Treasury requesting that an addition be made to the estimates for the year 1850 to provide for a side gallery for the Assyrian sculptures.[90]

Work must have proceeded speedily on the new Greek Gallery, since early in 1851 Sydney Smirke was urging the Trustees to make the necessary arrangements for removing portions of the Parthenon frieze in order to allow for a doorway to be cut between the new gallery and the south end of the Elgin Room.[91] It was important that this be done before the redecoration of the Elgin Room was begun as part of the general repainting of the western wing at this time.[92]

Sydney Smirke's report on Works in Progress records that by May the 'New Gallery' between the Lycian and Elgin Rooms was nearly roofed in.[93] Although Smirke's original intention had been to house Assyrian sculptures in the new gallery, by the time it was nearly complete he was referring to it as 'the new Greek Gallery'. In February 1852 all that remained to be done was the decorative painting, which had to be delayed until the building work had thoroughly dried out.[94]

In June of that same year Sydney Smirke submitted some suggestions regarding the arrangement of the Parthenon sculptures, thus opening a debate that was to continue unresolved for many years to come.[95] Smirke thought it would be instructive to exhibit the metopes in an architectural context by constructing a full-size mock-up of the complete entablature, including the upper part of some of the columns. This proposal found willing support from Edmund Oldfield, whose own lengthy report upon the subject was submitted to the Trustees through Edward Hawkins.[96] Hawkins, however, raised a number of objections to Oldfield's scheme. In particular he declared that he would prefer to see the metopes in their present position on the west side of the Elgin Room, but set between casts of the triglyphs. He was also opposed to the suggestion that a representation of a pediment should be placed high up on the east side of the room, and found particular objection to Oldfield's suggestion that the casts within it should be coloured. Hawkins was on principle opposed to the painting of only partially surviving pieces on the basis of uncertain evidence and objected on these grounds to the architect's suggestion that the casts in the Phigaleian Room of the pediment and cornice of the Aegina Temple should be coloured.[97] Above all Hawkins objected to Oldfield's proposal for breaking up into individual pieces the groupings of the Parthenon pedimental sculptures. Hawkins would arrange them in the new room in two groups, leaving space between the figures to allow for the missing parts. By thus isolating the pediment sculptures from the rest of the Parthenon material, he proposed to alleviate the generally acknowledged nuisance in the 1832 arrangement of seeing these pieces against the broken line of the frieze mounted on the wall behind.

Hawkins conceived the utilisation of the new gallery in terms of a thinning out of the material into the additional space. Characteristically, Oldfield had a more radical rearrangement in mind, affecting the Elgin Room, the new gallery and the Phigaleian Room. In his view, the present crowding of Greek material into the Elgin Room was unscientific, and he proposed to appropriate this gallery exclusively for the remains of the Parthenon, forming the mid-part of a three-part chronological scheme. Thus the Phigaleian Room (12 on Fig. 1) would be reserved for Archaic sculpture (down to the Persian Wars), while the new gallery (7 on Fig. 1) would show the transition from the culmination of the Pheidian era to the 'effeminacy' of the Roman period.

Progress from here was very slow indeed. By the end of 1852 the new room was ready but still nothing was decided.[98] Only three years later did Oldfield submit a revised report to Hawkins upon the subject.[99] Obliged to abandon his former chronological scheme, Oldfield proposed a 'geographical arrangement', allocating the Elgin Room and the new room to Athenian sculpture; a small gallery connecting the latter with the Lycian Room he proposed to fill with antiquities from 'islands on the Asiatic coast of the Archipelago'. By this he meant a number of limestone figures from Cyprus and newly acquired sculptures procured through Charles Newton's activities in Rhodes.[100] In the Phigaleian Room, Oldfield proposed to place 'sculptures of all the remaining Hellenic localities, whether European or Asiatic', by which he meant, principally, the Phigaleian sculptures themselves and the Mausoleum frieze slabs acquired from Halicarnassus in 1846, together with a few stray pieces from Delos and elsewhere.

Oldfield's revised proposal for arranging the Elgin Marbles was approved in principle.[101] By the summer Hawkins was able to report that the sculptures of the western pediment of the Parthenon had been removed into the new room.[102] In the following month, however, when Hawkins was away for his annual holiday on the south coast, Oldfield wrote to Panizzi in a bid to reverse the decision taken by the Trustees and to persuade them once again to adopt his original plan.[103]

The Trustees made no order when Oldfield's letter was read to them, and at the

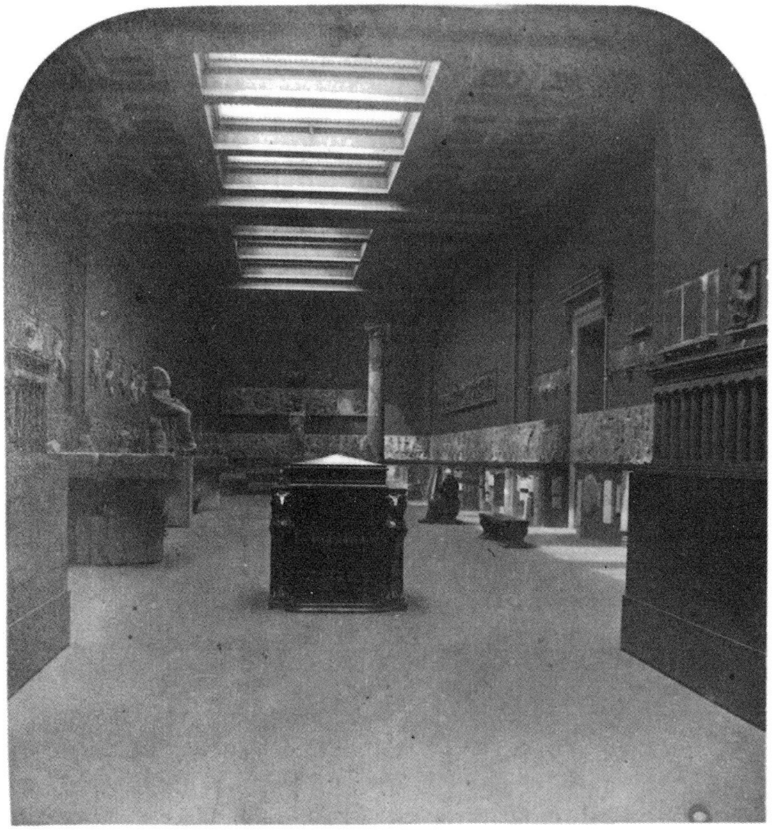

26 The Elgin Room (compare Fig. 24), renamed the Second Elgin Room, looking north, *c.*1857–9, after the removal of the pediment sculptures to the First Elgin Room (7 on Fig. 1). On the right is the fully restored model of the Parthenon by R. Lucas. The other Lucas model is seen on the left. Photo by R. Fenton for *The Stereoscopic Magazine*. British Museum, Central Archive.

26 beginning of the following year the work of thinning the Elgin Room and transferring sculptures into the new gallery began.[104] Thus by March 1857 part of the frieze of the Nike Temple had been transferred to the north wall of the smaller
27 room;[105] by June it had been joined by the pediment sculptures of the Parthenon, the Erechtheum column and Caryatid, and casts of the frieze of the Lysicrates Monument.[106] In December of the same year the Trustees were still debating the height of the plinth on which the pediment sculptures were to be set and experimenting with coloured paper in order to determine what colour the plinth should be, and these deliberations continued into the new year.[107]

None of these experiments proved satisfactory, and by the summer of 1860 it was proposed, on the recommendation of Charles Eastlake, to substitute for the pedestals a reproduction of 'the ruined entablature' on which the pedimental sculptures had once stood.[108] Accordingly Sydney Smirke prepared a portion of 'the framing' for the temporary experiment and this was placed in what was now called the 'Second' Elgin Room.[109] The name Second Elgin Room was given to the original gallery (8 on Fig. 1), while the room adjoining it (7 on Fig. 1) was called the First Elgin

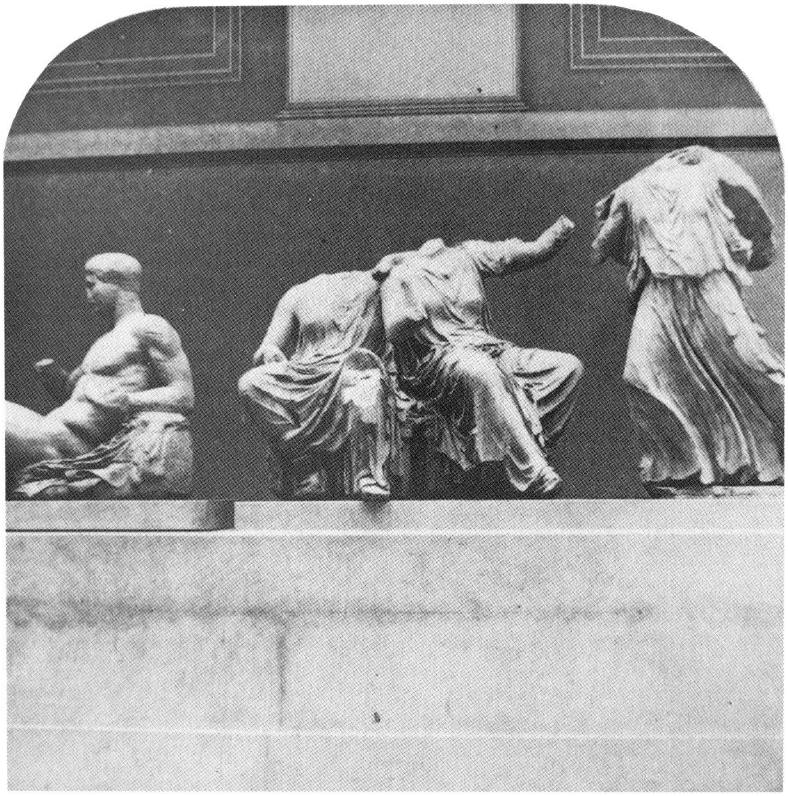

27 The east pediment sculptures exhibited in the so-called First Elgin Room (7 on Fig. 1), *c.*1857–9. This is Room 5 in the present scheme. Photo by R. Fenton for *The Stereoscopic Magazine*. British Museum, Central Archive.

Room. This nomenclature readily gives rise to confusion, since the so-called Second Elgin Room was built before the first. It reflects, however, the position of the two galleries in relation to the South Front of the building. The visitor was assumed to proceed in a northerly direction on entering the Greek Sculpture Galleries and so would encounter the 'First' Elgin Room before the 'Second'.

Comment was invited from a number of interested parties upon the tentative rearrangement of the sculptures from the eastern pediment, and their opinions are preserved in a series of lengthy reports, many of which were ordered to be privately printed by the Trustees.[110] The essential problem under review was one that still concerns the custodians of these sculptures today, namely how best to accommodate at ground level in a museum gallery sculptures originally intended to be seen in a triangular pediment from a great distance below. Richard Westmacott the younger took the view that a virtue should be made of necessity, displaying the sculpture to its best advantage in what would inevitably be 'a very false field of exhibition'. He readily accepted that the true view of the sculpture was to see it in its architectural setting, and that in a museum the sculpture is inevitably denied, as he put it, 'association with architecture except, unfortunately, with that of the rooms in which it may happen to be placed and which, usually, must be injurious to it'.

Accordingly, Westmacott urged against attempting to reconstruct a pediment in the gallery where he felt the setting and, in particular, the lighting would be all wrong. Instead his proposal allowed for the fact that we now view the sculpture primarily as isolated art, rather than as a decorative part of a greater architectural ensemble. He suggested that only a limited indication of the shape of the original pediment should be used in the gallery, with the aid of 'cords'.

In agreement with all those who were asked to comment, Westmacott felt the scale of the sculptures of the eastern pediment demanded that they should be displayed in the larger of the two galleries (8 on Fig. 1), together with the so-called Ilissus, which alone of the remnants of the west pediment was considered worthy of comparison with the sculptures of the east. (At this time the figure from the west pediment now identified as Iris was attributed to the east.) A cast of the Ilissus was to be left with the rest of the sculptures of the western pediment in the lesser Elgin Room.

Again in keeping with general opinion, Westmacott advocated raising the sculptures of the east pediment to a height at which they could be admired from below. To the objection that this would deny young artists the opportunity of viewing the sculptures at close quarters, Westmacott contested that they were there not for the benefit of artists alone; he then went on to make what some might regard as a surprising observation, for, he remarked, 'it may be stated that these are works which are scarcely adapted for the study of mere beginners in drawing – that very few students do make them the objects of their study – and that scarcely any even advanced artist is ever seen in the gallery making these admirable productions the standard of his practice.'

For general purposes, Westmacott contended, 'good plaster casts are preferable to original marble works', and this by virtue of a more 'uniform colour and determined contour'.

In this opinion he had the support of the classical scholar William Watkiss Lloyd, who pointed out that there were no restrictions on the times when casts could be viewed and that they could be easily moved to gain better lighting. He was all in favour of raising the sculptures of the east pediment: 'It is not many years', he recalled, 'since a learned German connoisseur, in desperation, and as a last resource, lay down on his back to look at the statues, to the alarm of visitors and the admiration of the custodes.'

Watkiss Lloyd, however, favoured more extensive reconstruction of the pediment architecture. The angles where the horizontal and the raking cornice met should be modelled, as they were in the temporary reconstruction, and the line of the rest of the raking cornice was to be indicated by a 'flat lath of painted iron'.

In a second report (22 February 1861) Watkiss Lloyd developed and refined his ideas: 'I proceed', he wrote, 'upon the understanding that the two saloons are to be thrown into one by the removal of the cross-wall that at present divides them.' The sculptures should be placed on bases simulating the pedimental cornice, and should be brought into the longer room, on the west side, facing the door from the Phigaleian Saloon. The eye of the visitor would therefore alight first upon these sculptures as he approached the gallery from what was considered the principal entrance.

The west pediment sculptures were to be left where they were in the smaller of the two rooms, but on the opposite side of the gallery from where they were then standing: 'A collection of antiquities is naturally a collection of fragments, and apt to be distracting enough in any case. The task lies upon the arranger to harmonize their distribution with the plan and space provided, without infringing higher proprieties and connections. Unless this can to some extent be done, his collection will be simply lying about ....'

Charles Newton, newly appointed as Keeper of Greek and Roman Antiquities, offered an alternative scheme. He too would restore the sculptures of the east pediment to the larger gallery, but preferred to locate them in front of the east wall, on either side of the doorway; the gap represented by the entrance would serve to indicate the area occupied by the lost sculptures. His objection to Watkiss Lloyd's suggestion of placing the sculptures from the east pediment against the west wall opposite the entrance was that this would break up the view of the frieze located behind. Otherwise Newton was in accord with Watkiss Lloyd in approving the 'mock-up' of the east pediment. He thought, however, that the 'Theseus' and the horse's head merited separate display on individual revolving bases, with casts of them mounted on the pediment.

Before we turn to consider proposals for the frieze, one further report is worthy of mention, even though it was not deemed worthy of printing. This is given in a letter by Edward Falkener to Samuel Birch, the Museum's Orientalist, dated 16 July 1860. The author began by lamenting the fact that the larger Elgin Room was too narrow to accommodate the pedimental groups, one at either end of the gallery. He proposed, therefore, to place the sculptures of the east and west pediments on the west and east walls respectively, high up under the ceiling. In order to allow for greater light to fall upon the sculptures he proposed raising the coffered ceiling at the sides of the room and inserting two slanting skylights.

In addition to the pedimental sculptures, most commentators had something to say upon the display of the frieze. The most detailed reports were those of Newton and Watkiss Lloyd. The former records that some ten feet of actual frieze and around forty feet of casts were at the time of his writing 'scattered about' in the Second Elgin Room. The casts were those recently acquired from Athens, and the actual frieze was that displaced from the south wall of the room when the doorway was opened into the First Elgin Room. Both Newton's and Watkiss Lloyd's proposals for rearranging the frieze depended upon taking down the partition wall between the greater and the lesser Elgin Rooms and utilising the entire length of wall space available.

The sequel

In spite, or perhaps because, of these many deliberations, the Trustees seemed incapable of reaching a decision. At a meeting of the Sub-Committee on Antiquities the possibility was raised of extending the Second Elgin Room northwards for the exhibition of casts from the east pediment of the Parthenon, and Sydney Smirke was instructed to draw up provisional plans.[111] When next the same committee met, however, it was decided to postpone further consideration of the arrangement of the Elgin Marbles until the results of Smith and Porcher's excavations in the Cyrenaica were fully known.[112] An appeal against this decision was made by Earl Stanhope, but the attempt was unsuccessful.[113]

By summer 1864 the rearrangement of the Second Elgin Room had still not been resolved. Newton complained that he thought its unsightly condition discreditable to the Museum: 'Portions of the frieze of the Parthenon are lying about, and of the architecture of the Erechtheum, on the floor. The walls are full of holes and patches marking the places from which reliefs have been removed.' The relatively empty space was deemed 'barn-like' in appearance and contrasted strangely with the crowded Lycian and Graeco-Roman rooms.[114]

Newton had a particular motive in making these criticisms, for it was he who had discovered and excavated the site of the Mausoleum of Halicarnassus. The sculptures from that expedition were still unplaced in the Museum, being given only temporary shelter within the colonnade. Newton hoped to remove the pedimental sculptures to the larger of the two Elgin Rooms in order to create a home for the Mausoleum sculptures in the smaller or First Elgin Room. Nothing came of this plan until autumn 1868, when, the sheds housing the Mausoleum sculptures under the colonnade being in need of substantial repairs, Newton proposed that one of them could be done away with altogether if the most important pieces were brought into the Museum. At last the Trustees agreed, ordering that the pediment sculptures of the west pediment of the Parthenon be restored to the Second Elgin Room. At
26 the same time Richard Lucas's restored model of the Parthenon was removed from the Second Elgin Room to the basement. Newton had always despised it (he also disliked the man) for 'the coarseness of its execution and the restored portions being quite unworthy of the original remains'.[115] The other unrestored model by Lucas was allowed to remain. Early in the following year the rearrangement was

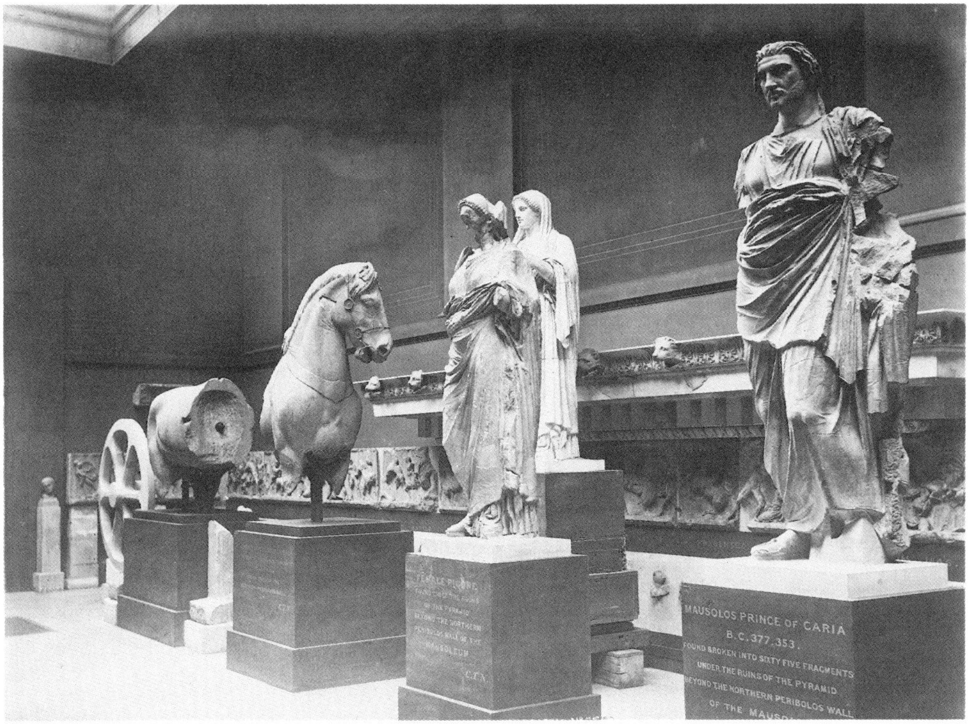

28 Mausoleum sculptures in the vacated 'First' Elgin Room (7 on Fig. 1), looking south-west, *c.*1872 (compare Fig. 27). Photo by C. Bernieri for Caldesi at Colnaghi's. British Museum, Department of Greek and Roman Antiquities.

completed and the name of the First Elgin Room (7 on Fig. 1) was officially 28–9
changed to Mausoleum Room.[116]

Now that Newton had had his way with the First Elgin Room, he set about improving the Second Elgin Room (8 on Fig. 1). In December 1868 he had submitted draft proposals to the Trustees for improving the accommodation of the Museum sculptures generally. These included a restatement of a proposal first made in 1861 for extending the Second Elgin Room northwards to provide additional space for the proper arrangement of the frieze, which could not all be accommodated on the walls of the present gallery.[117] The Treasury was approached with a view to funds being made available for work to begin on the extension, and the sum of £12,000 was allocated accordingly.[118]

Work on the Elgin Room extension proceeded remarkably quickly: by spring
1873 the gallery (9 on Fig. 1) was finished and the installation of the sculpture well 30–32
advanced.[119] The frieze was rearranged and for the first time put behind glass, so as to keep out the dirt of the London atmosphere. Newton had first proposed glazing the frieze in 1867.[120] The Trustees eventually approved the scheme and it was

completed in the autumn of 1873.[121] Newton reports that the experiment had met with general approval, 'and it is thought the effect of the sculpture has been in no way impaired, but rather enhanced by being seen under glass.' Comprehensive glazing, although contemplated, could not be undertaken since the heavy metal framing needed for supporting the glass would be too conspicuous.[122] Even so, at least one pedimental sculpture was actually glazed.

The extension of the Elgin Room allowed for a radical rearrangement of the frieze and for the incorporation of the now extensive collection of casts of the frieze. These had been lovingly assembled ever since excavations on the Acropolis following Greek independence had started to turn up new fragments of the Parthenon sculpture overlooked by Elgin. They now represented an important body of material in their own right and the understanding of the frieze, in particular, depended upon the proper arrangement of all the slabs in sequence.[123]

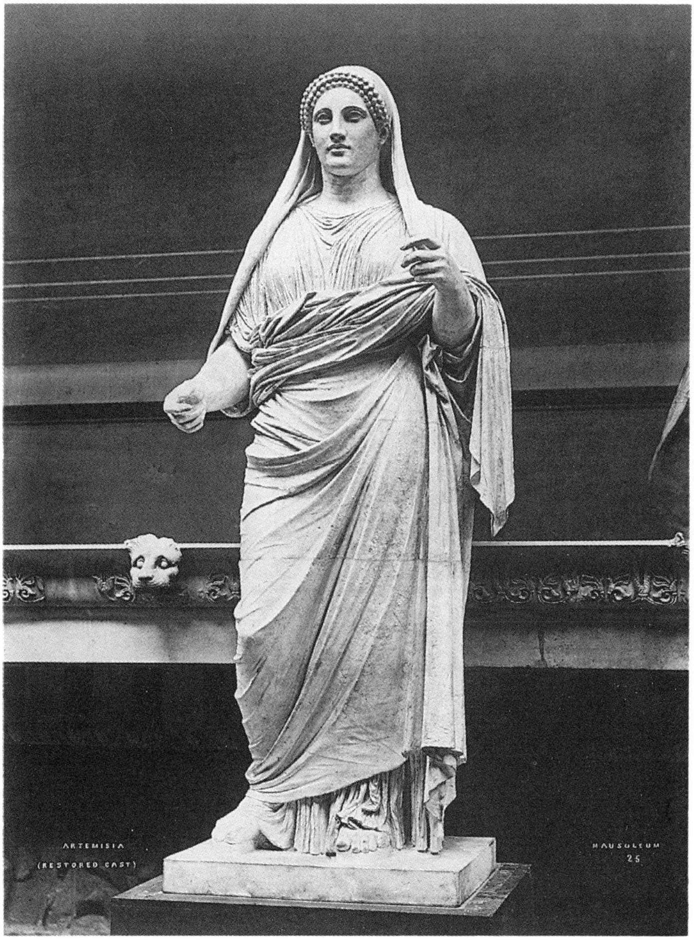

29 W.W. Story's cast reconstruction of the 'Artemisia', *c.*1872. Photo by C. Bernieri for Caldesi at Colnaghi's. British Museum, Department of Greek and Roman Antiquities.

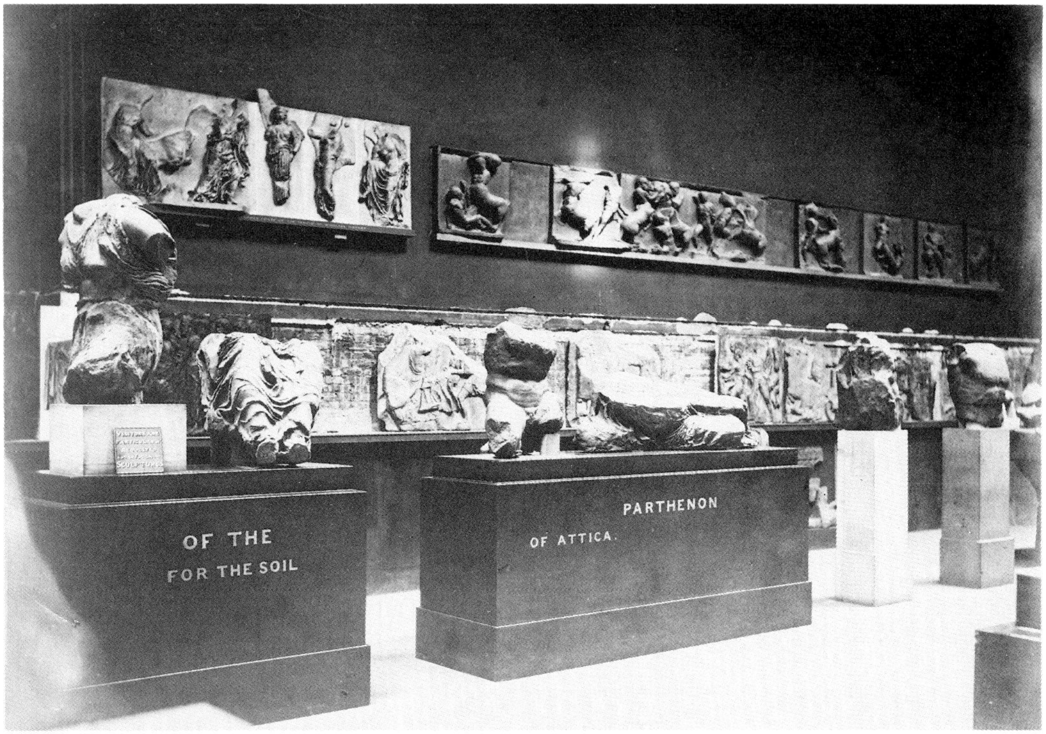
OF THE
FOR THE SOIL
PARTHENON
OF ATTICA.

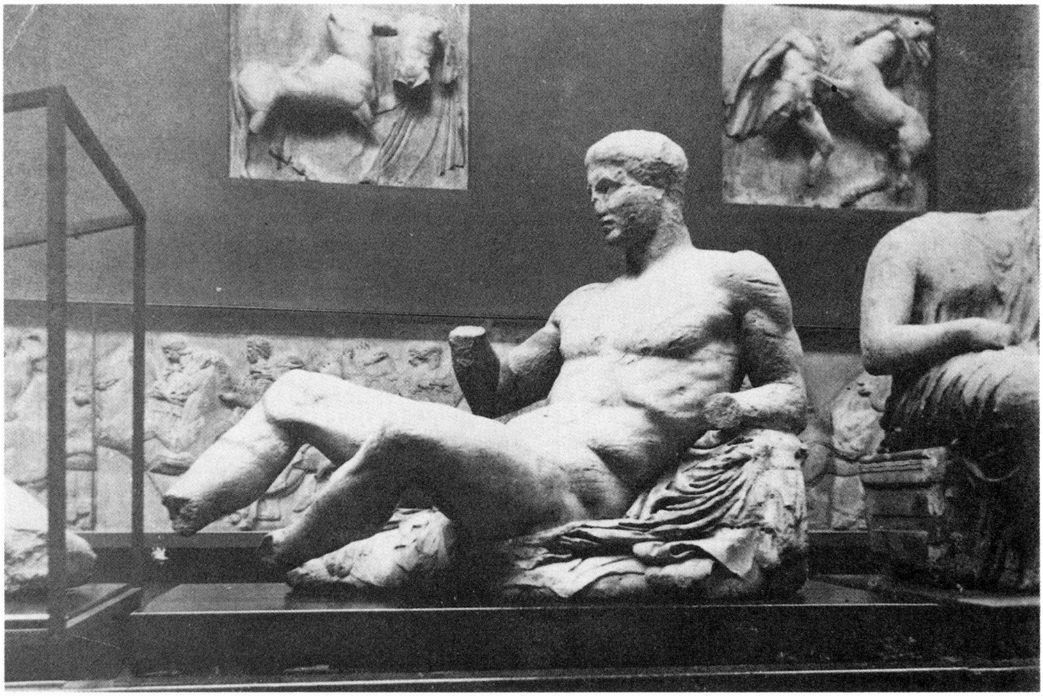

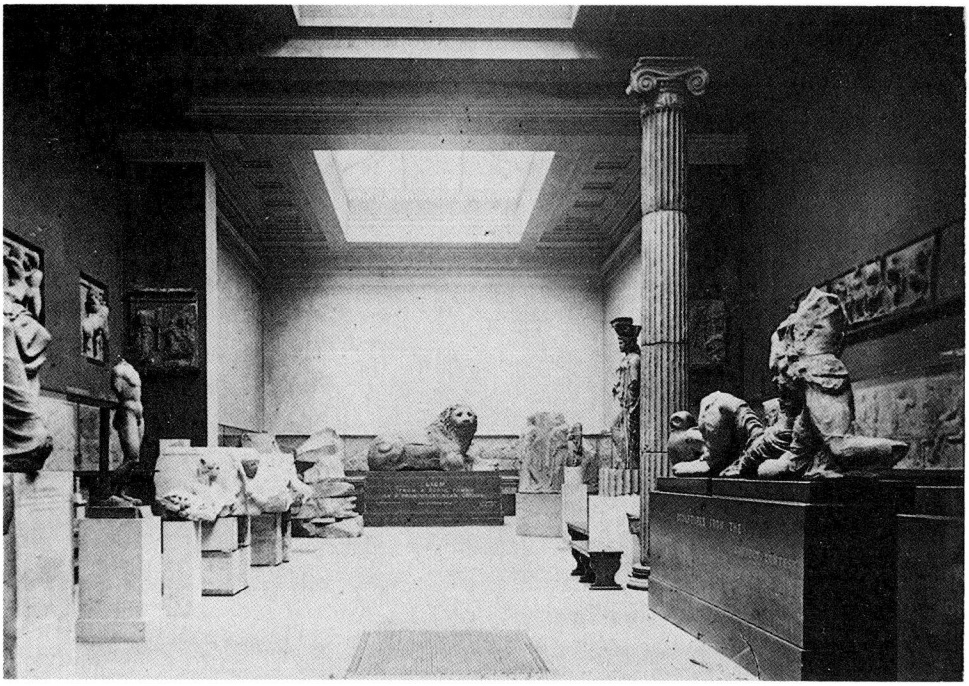

32 The northern extension to the Elgin Room (9 on Fig. 1), containing the Cnidus lion and Ephesus drum, *c.*1875. This space is today occupied by Room 9, where the Caryatid still stands. Photo by F. York. British Museum, Department of Greek and Roman Antiquities.

The new area was not restricted to the Elgin Marbles, for Newton took the liberty of placing in it other sculptures and architectural members, including the colossal
32 lion from Cnidus and the sculptured column-drum from Ephesus.[124]

Thus the protracted controversy over the arrangement of the Elgin Marbles was resolved, at least for the time being. After Newton's eventual retirement in 1886 his successors were to conduct experiments of their own. We shall return to these in the final chapter, but now it is time to look at how other parts of the Museum sculpture collections were accommodated. To do this we must return to the beginning of the nineteenth century and the early years of the Museum's history, when old Montagu House had not yet been replaced by Smirke's great classical building.

30 (*Opposite, top*) The Elgin Room (8 on Fig. 1) under rearrangement, *c.*1872 (compare Fig. 24). Photo by C. Bernieri for Caldesi at Colnaghi's. British Museum, Department of Greek and Roman Antiquities.

31 (*Opposite, bottom*) 'Theseus' from the east pediment, and (almost out of the picture to the left) Helios, put under glass, *c.*1875. The frieze and even the smaller pediment sculptures were glazed so as to keep out the dirt of London's polluted atmosphere. Photo by F. York. British Museum, Department of Greek and Roman Antiquities.

6 The Townley Gallery: Egypt and Rome

In the traditional eighteenth- and nineteenth-century hierarchy of ancient art, Egypt represents the primitive forerunner of Greece, while Rome is seen as the manifestation of an inevitable decline. Egyptian sculptures and the Graeco-Roman Townley Marbles were among the Museum's earliest acquisitions. The destinies of these two extremes of ancient artistic accomplishment became closely bound together when in 1808 a new gallery to house them was tacked onto the corner of old Montagu House. As Robert Smirke's new classical building gradually replaced the Townley Gallery, as it became known, the Egyptian and Graeco-Roman sculptures maintained a close relationship, sometimes even competing for the same space. They will therefore be treated together here.

French spoils

The arrival in summer 1802 of Egyptian sculptures captured from Napoleon's army at Alexandria in the previous year effectively founded the Museum's Egyptian collection. It made ever more urgent the need for the Museum to expand beyond the inadequate confines of old Montagu House. A list of some thirty individual pieces was transmitted ahead of their delivery,[1] but the best accommodation that could be provided was temporary cover in the courtyard.[2] Among the items listed was 'A stone with three inscriptions', this being the celebrated Rosetta Stone that was to provide the vital clue to the decipherment of Egyptian hieroglyphics. It was not sent immediately to the Museum with the rest of the sculpture, for its exceptional interest caused it to be conveyed first to the Society of Antiquaries.[3]

The lack of available space for such a large collection necessitated the planning of an extension to the existing Museum. A sub-committee consisting of Joseph Banks (President of the Royal Society), Thomas Astle (Antiquary at the Tower) and Charles Townley, the famous eighteenth-century collector of classical sculpture, was set up to consider a new building for the Egyptian antiquities.[4] The committee delivered its final report in the following May and declared that its members had met repeatedly in the house of Charles Townley, 'where they had abundant opportunities of studying the most approved methods of exhibiting works of sculpture to advantage, and with the assistance of Sir William Hamilton unfortunately deceased, whose taste the public have always allowed to be excellent, they have been enabled to lay before the Trustees the following opinions.'[5]

The report went on to say that the committee had consulted with the Museum's architect George Saunders and, having considered the plans drawn up by him, they had reached the conclusion that a building of 90 × 45 feet with a 'principal room' of 50 × 33 feet and 25 feet high would be appropriate for the Egyptian sculpture.

The new gallery was to be built projecting from the north-west corner of old
5 Montagu House. Before plans were drawn up by Robert Smirke in 1823 for a new Museum, doing away with the old building altogether, this extension was conceived as part of a much larger scheme. The intention was to extend the western galleries of Montagu House northwards, with a parallel extension on the eastern side. The north-west extension, or Townley Gallery, as it became known, was the only part of this plan to be carried out. It was to be linked to the main building by two passages which would provide fashionably top-lit areas for display, leading to two even more fashionable circular tribunes, also lit from above:

> Thus, with very small addition to the necessary expense of passages, two admirable places for exhibiting statues of prime workmanship will be provided; and ample room also on the walls for fixing up to advantage the numerous and very valuable ancient inscriptions which are now huddled together on the back of the stairs of the great House, as well as such bas reliefs as are now in the Collection, or may hereafter be added to it.[6]

The proportions of the main gallery in the new complex were dictated by the Egyptian sculpture intended for it, and plans and cross-sections were prepared into which sculptures were plotted.[7] The gallery was to be raised on strong brick arches designed to take the great weight of the sculpture to the level of the main floor of Montagu House. Over it would be built an upper room, 12 feet high, where Hamilton's vase collection would be displayed 'in a strong light'. This had been the especial request of the late Sir William Hamilton, whose collection had been acquired by the Museum in 1772.

As for the style of the new building, the design favoured by the committee was a
33 restrained Palladian, intended to blend with the old-fashioned look of Montagu House but without imitating what the committee considered 'the style of the worst period of French architecture in a house erected in 1676'. A petition was submitted to Parliament on 2 July 1804 for £16,000, and a few days later £8,000 was granted in order to permit the work to begin. The foundations were laid by the following November and Saunders predicted that the new building would be finished by the autumn of 1806.

The Museum was now growing too fast, however, even for the relative speed with which these events had taken place. For, following the death of Charles Townley in January 1805, it was decided to buy his celebrated collection of ancient, mainly Roman, sculpture.[8] The matter was resolved by the summer of the same

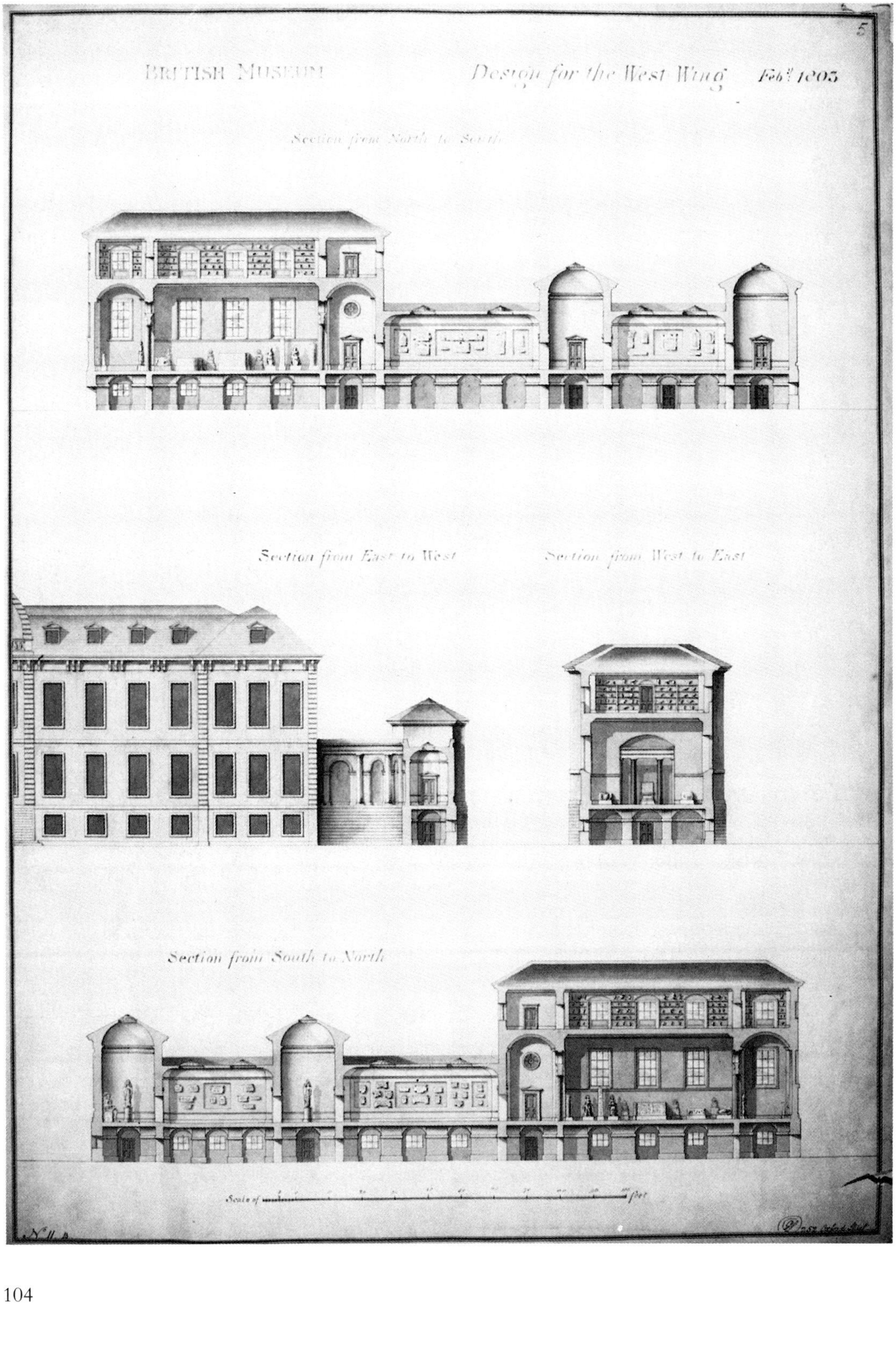
5
BRITISH MUSEUM
Design for the West Wing
Feby 1803
Section from North to South
Section from East to West
Section from West to East
Section from South to North
Scale of
feet

33 (*Opposite*) Sections through the design for an extension to Montagu House, February 1803. British Museum, Central Archive.

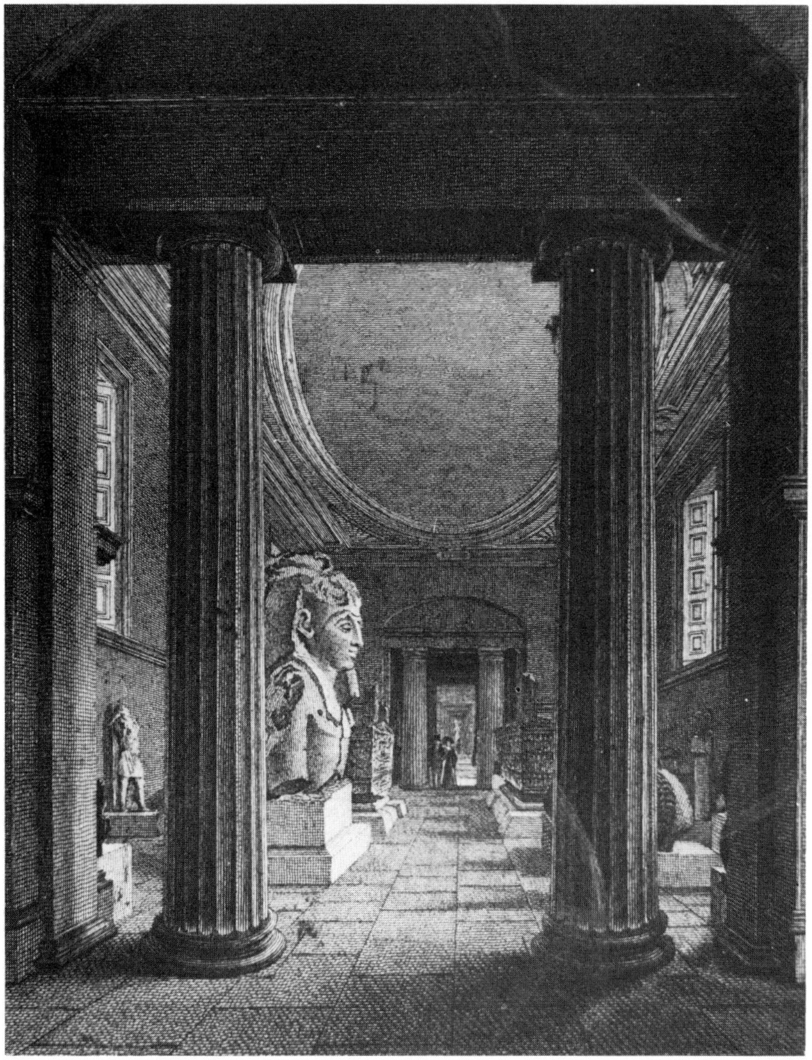

34 The head of Ramesses II installed in the Egyptian sculpture room of the Townley Gallery. Engraving by C. Heath after F. Mackenzie, for *Views of London* (1825).

year, and while discussions were held as to how the marbles would be accommodated, work on the new building was suspended. It was resolved that, rather than adopt a new scheme altogether and so as not to lose the advantage of the summer season, Saunders's original plan would be adapted and enlarged, and a new plan was approved.[9] The same basic format was retained and, with the help of the Navy, the Egyptian sculptures were placed in the principal gallery,[10] while the Townley
34–7 Marbles filled the rest of the ground-floor suite. The Egyptian Sculpture Gallery, which opened in June 1808, principally contained objects acquired through the capitulation of the French at Alexandria in 1801. There were, however, other pieces in the collection: for example, the earliest acquisitions were those presented

by King George III in 1766; then there were the small sculptures presented by the Earl of Bute in 1767;[11] pieces given by Earl Spencer in 1805;[12] the standing figure and Egyptian head that were acquired with the Townley sculptures in the same year; and the colossal hawk presented by T. Philipe, the auctioneer, also in 1805.[13]

The Townley Marbles

The story of the acquisition and display of the body of miscellaneous marbles that came to be known as the Graeco-Roman sculptures is different in kind from that of the other sculptures of the British Museum. The collection was formed in large part through the purchase in 1805 of Charles Townley's marbles which, displayed in his house in Park Street, Westminster, had been one of the great sights of late eighteenth-century London.[14] Townley's collection was assembled piecemeal from around 1767, mainly through his agents in Rome, Thomas Jenkins and Gavin Hamilton.[15] In this respect it differed from the great corpus of Egyptian, Assyrian and Greek sculptures that were brought into the national repository straight from their countries of origin. No other large group of sculptures in the Museum was ever a *collection* in the sense that the Townley Marbles had been in their day. The Elgin Marbles were never absorbed into the seventh Earl's *ménage*, in the manner in which Townley's collection became part of the furniture of his household.[16] Zoffany's famous portrait of Townley and his circle of cognoscenti nicely captures the spirit of the age in which the house-museum flourished.[17]

The Townley Marbles would, with some notable additions, continue through the century to form the major part of the so-called Graeco-Roman sculptures. The wish expressed by some nineteenth-century scholars that the scattered treasures of English country-house collections might one day be gathered into the national repository never materialised. Adolph Michaelis's Winckelmannesque image of 'the several brooklets' discharging themselves into this 'mighty stream' was a vain hope, for reasons that he knew only too well.[18] The British Museum prided itself on possessing the greatest collection of original Greek works in the world and had, therefore, no need of the inferior class of later imitations that filled the sculpture galleries of the seventeenth- and eighteenth-century English collections.

The Townley Marbles remained the first and only acquisition of a major private collection of Graeco-Roman works. The only comparable addition to the Museum's collections occurred in 1864, when several sculptures were bought from the Farnese collection at Rome. In the successive editions of the summary guide or *Synopsis*, first published in 1808, the convention was to list the Graeco-Roman sculptures as all coming from the Townley collection unless otherwise specified. In these lists, therefore, we can pick out at a glance those pieces acquired from other collectors besides Townley. They include, for example, the small collection of

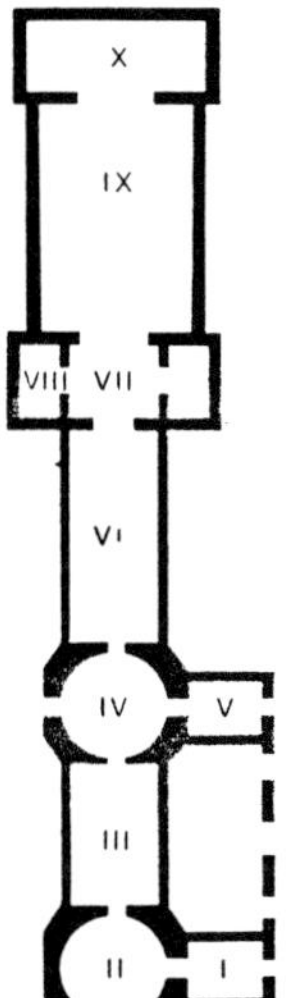

35 Plan of the Townley Gallery (after Cook).

marbles that came into the Museum with the founding collection of Sir Hans Sloane. There were also those presented by Thomas Hollis in 1757.[19] Sir William Hamilton is remembered more for his collection of vases purchased for the British Museum in 1772 and, once the Townley Gallery was built, displayed on the upper floor, but the Museum also aquired from Hamilton, whether by gift or purchase, a number of sculptures.[20]

The arrangement of the interior of the Townley Gallery was at first entrusted to Joseph Nollekens, but owing to the sculptor's ill health the commission was subsequently offered to Henry Tresham and the young Richard Westmacott. This was Westmacott's first service for the Museum, and he continued to act in a similar capacity until his death in 1856.[21] The collection was conveyed to the Museum in September 1806.[22] By 12 April 1808, the sculptures had, with a few exceptions, been placed in the galleries.[23] The exhibition rooms were opened, following a royal preview by Queen Charlotte accompanied by the Prince of Wales and the Dukes of Cumberland and Cambridge, on 3 June 1808. It seems the Royal path through Montagu House was lined with temporary displays of 'numerous cuttings in paper framed, and pictures of little interest hanging against the cases and walls of the old Rooms'. The visitors were not impressed, and the Prince of Wales ridiculed such, what he called, 'colifichets'. This Royal scorn precipitated a hasty dismantling of the exhibition, and all the papers were consigned to the garret of Montagu House.

Egyptian sculptures were placed, as we have seen, in the principal room, while
36–7 the Townley Marbles and terracotta bas-reliefs occupied the rest. Two passages linking the new suite of rooms to Montagu House (Rooms I and V) contained the so-called Campana terracotta reliefs and Roman funerary monuments. These last were displayed in wall-niches echoing the *columbaria* of the catacombs of ancient Rome. Such a setting became a standard device for accommodating sepulchral antiquities in fashionable Regency interiors, but the first such use goes back to the eighteenth century.[24] Indeed, as a watercolour drawing of the Hall in Townley's house-museum at Park Street shows, Townley had himself employed this feature in the exhibition of his funerary *cippi*.[25] In a published account of his arrangement Westmacott describes Room V as 'an apartment, fitted up in imitation of a Roman Mausoleum, or Columbarium, for the reception of Sepulchral Antiquities'.[26] A review of the Townley Gallery signed *Ambulator* and published in *The Gentleman's Magazine* two years after its completion objected to the placement of the Egyptian sculptures, 'consisting chiefly of large stone coffins, and massive uncouth figures', on the same floor as the 'elegant Greek and Roman sculptures'. The author recommended their removal to 'the solemn recess of a catacomb ... fitted up in the Egyptian style'.[27]

Another feature of Saunders's Townley Gallery that had its origin in English picturesque interiors was the top-lit tribune (Rooms II and IV), in which busts and

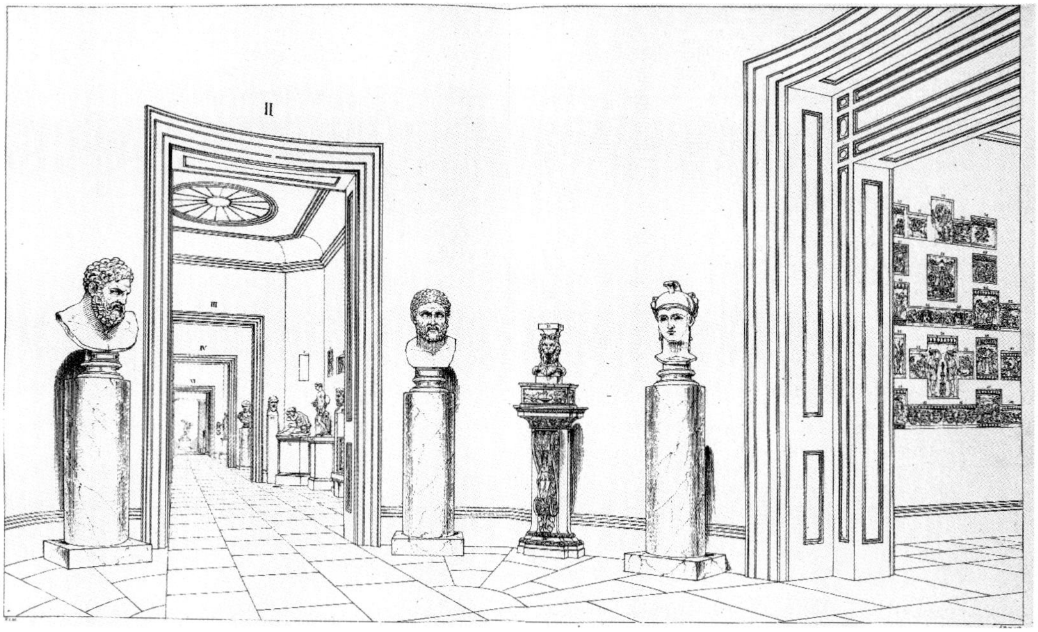

36 Interior of the Townley Gallery, looking north from Room II and east into Room I. *Ancient Marbles*, part I (1812), plate preceding pl. I.

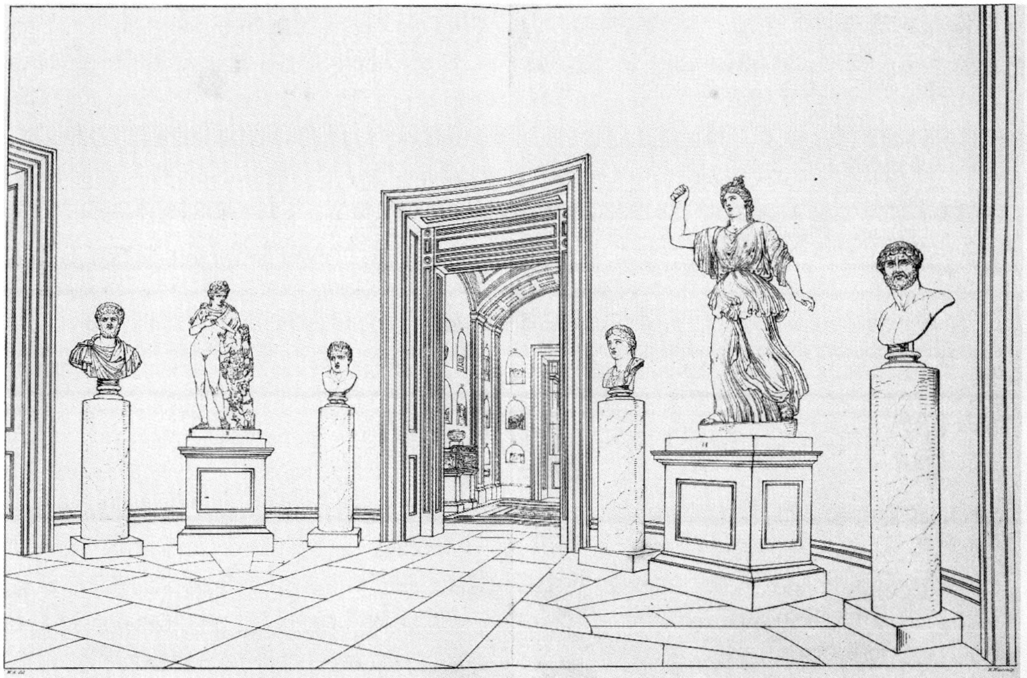

37 Interior of the Townley Gallery, Room IV, with a view looking east into the columbarium (Room V). *Ancient Marbles*, part III (1818), plate preceding pl. I.

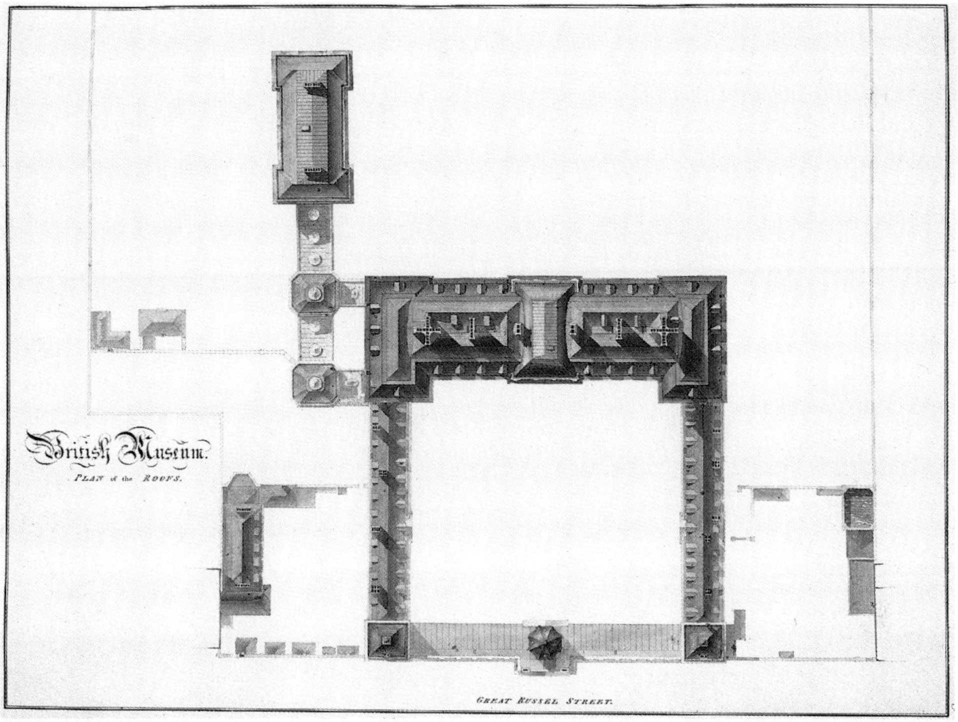

38 The Townley Gallery, showing the skylights, 9 July 1810. Plan for Saunders's presentation volume. British Museum, Central Archive.

full-figure sculpture were arranged on bases and pedestals. Susan Feinberg illuminates our understanding of the contemporary context of Saunders's design, distinguishing two parallel uses of the device in eighteenth-century forerunners: 'the tribune as a circulatory vestibule in the English country house and the tribune associated with the collector's cabinet (a small exhibition room) lit from above'.[28] Feinberg considers Soane's tribune for his house-museum in Lincoln's Inn Fields as a fusion of these two traditions; one that enjoys all the architectural benefits of the connecting vestibule but celebrates in its own way the Uffizi Tribuna's 'visionary profusion of curiosities'.[29]

Something similar may be said of Saunders's tribune, but here there is clearly less by way of 'visionary profusion'. Significantly, although the outer walls were octagonal, the inner chambers themselves were circular, an arrangement that precluded the fixing of bas-reliefs to the walls in sculptural imitation of the scatter-effect of paintings in the octagon of the Uffizi. A sober simplicity distinguishes Saunders's tribune from Soane's picturesque clutter and, while Soane's soared up through several levels of his museum from the the lowest crypt to the topmost lantern, Saunders's circular rooms served only to connect horizontally. Even so, the tribunes of the Townley Gallery enjoyed all the natural benefits of circular lantern light illuminating all the wall space below.

Top-lighting was provided in all rooms that did not support an upper story, 38
except Rooms VII through to X.[30] The decision to deprive the principal room containing the Egyptian sculptures of top-lighting would be repeated in Smirke's 34
new building, where it would be argued that the less noble forms of Egyptian sculpture would tolerate the confusion of crossing side-lights, thought undesirable for the pure outlines of classical works.

The top-lighting in Saunders's classical galleries was one of the earliest examples of this manner of lighting sculptures. Its immediate forerunners, from which Saunders's design perhaps took inspiration, were the sculpture galleries of Thomas Hope's Duchess Street mansion, laid out in the new Greek style around 1800.[31] Top-lighting became the approved manner of illuminating sculpture for the rest of the century.

More Egyptian sculpture and Robert Smirke's new gallery

The next major acquisition of Egyptian sculpture took place a decade after the opening of the Townley Gallery. In the early spring of 1818 the Admiralty informed the Trustees that 'several specimens of architecture and statuary from Libya, as also the head called that of the younger Memnon from Egypt are arrived at Spithead in HM Storeship *Weymouth* . . .'.[32] The architectural specimens comprised some 150 tons of marble and granite columns, bases and capitals that had been presented to the British monarch by the Bey of Tripoli. They were removed by Captain Dansey to Windsor Park for the folly at Virginia Water, between 28 August and 12 October 1826.[33] The so-called head of the Younger Memnon was, in fact, the great bust of Ramesses II presented to the British Museum in 1817 by Henry Salt, British Consul-General in Cairo, and the Swiss explorer and orientalist Jean-Louis Burckhardt.[34] These two succeeded in removing the colossal bust from the ruins of Ramesses's mortuary temple at Thebes with the assistance of the Italian adventurer Giovanni Battista Belzoni, who went on to make further extensive excavations.[35]
The head was brought to the Museum in 1818 and finally mounted upon a pedestal 39
in the Egyptian Room of the Townley Gallery at the beginning of the following year.[36] The introduction of so large a sculpture upset the arrangement in the room, and Taylor Combe was obliged to make radical changes in order to re-establish the mandatory symmetry that prevailed in all the other galleries.[37]

The success of this major undertaking encouraged Salt to further exertions and, with the indispensable assistance of Belzoni, he was soon sending to England yet more sculptures which he hoped the Trustees would readily purchase. The negotiations were protracted, however, and painful to the British Consul, for he was eventually paid only £2,000 early in 1823. This sum hardly represented the true value of the twenty or so pieces of sculpture and many other Egyptian antiquities that Salt had added to the national collection. There was not enough room for all the sculptures and, as before, temporary shelter was provided in the courtyard for those that could not be brought inside the Museum.[38]

The growth of the Egyptian sculpture collection added urgency to the already pressing question of how best to provide new permanent accommodation for the collections of the British Museum. In the same year as the purchase of Salt's collection, a Parliamentary Committee was set up to deliberate on the decision of George IV to present the King's Library to the Museum. Already on 10 February 1821 the

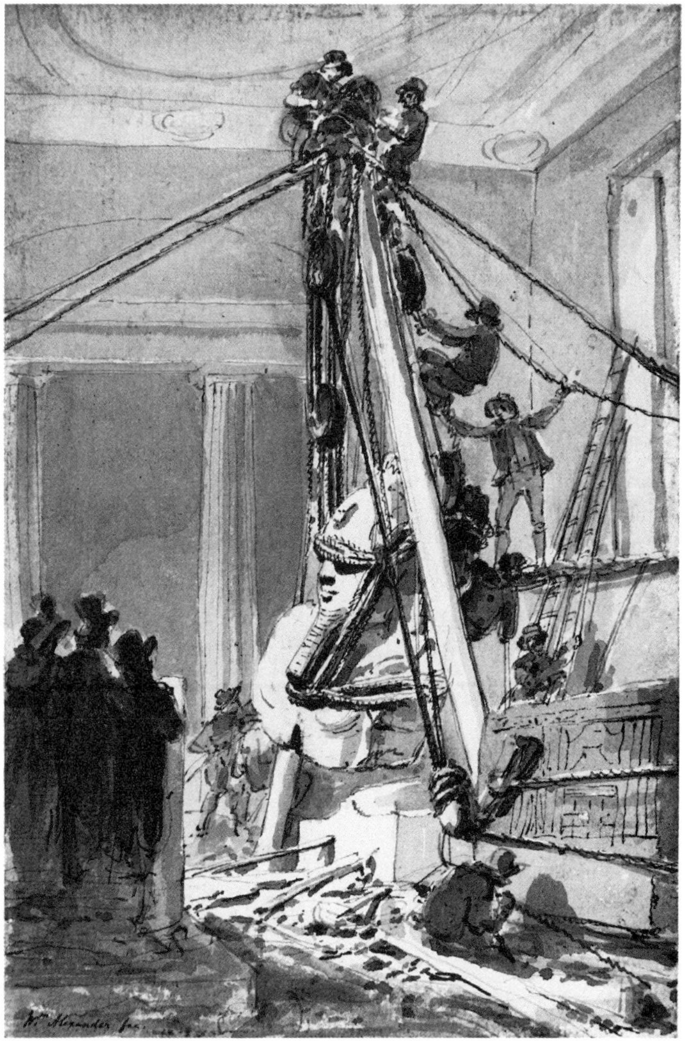

39 Installing the bust of Ramesses II. Watercolour, inscribed *Wm. Alexander fecit*, *c.*1819. British Museum, Central Archive.

Trustees had decided to request that the Government make provision for the early construction of additional buildings for the manuscripts and the ancient marbles.[39] Two years later Robert Smirke produced his plans for continuing the Townley Gallery northwards, and also for the construction of a north-east wing.[40] The wording of this minute suggests that Smirke had no more in mind than a scheme approximating to Saunders's plan of 1803 for extending old Montagu House, but this was in fact only part of a much more radical masterplan for a new quadrangular museum, which would lead to the progressive replacement of the old building.

When work on the new buildings began, the King's Library on the east wing of the Museum took priority, so that another decade passed before the building destined to become the new Egyptian Sculpture Gallery (17 on Fig. 1) was completed to the west. The main structure of the building was up, however, by July 1828, the date of a watercolour drawing by G. Scharf. It shows the Central Saloon open to the 6
south, with the Townley Gallery beyond. It was some years before the Townley Gallery itself was pulled down to make way for the southward extension of Smirke's new western wing.[41]

Meanwhile, not all the Egyptian antiquities that had been brought to the Museum were destined to remain there. Among the discoveries made by Belzoni was the Tomb of Sethos I, from which he had removed the great alabaster sarcophagus in which the Pharaoh had been laid to rest. The tomb had been pillaged long before by tomb-robbers, but the empty sarcophagus was itself considered a great prize. It was accordingly brought to England and deposited in the British Museum, but it was not included among the items listed in the 1823 settlement. Instead the sarcophagus became the object of a separate and lengthy wrangle resulting in its private purchase by Sir John Soane for £2,000.[42]

A few years later W.R. Hamilton wrote notifying the Trustees of his intention to remove a second sarcophagus given to him by Henry Salt, which had remained all this time in the courtyard of the Museum.[43] Hamilton was no doubt concerned that when Smirke's new Egyptian Sculpture Gallery was ready to receive the contents, his sarcophagus would become confounded with the rest of the collection. Hawkins was considering the arrangement of the sculptures in the new gallery by the summer of 1833, when he proposed to place the colossal bust of the 'Younger Memnon' (Ramesses II) in the centre of the north end of the room.[44] The rest of the larger objects he wanted to exhibit 'in two lines along the room in the same manner as at present, and the smaller objects in the recesses at the sides'. In the Central Saloon he intended 'to place all the statues at present in the Townley Gallery which did not originally belong to the Townley Collection'.

Nothing, however, had been decided by spring of the following year, when the Trustees inspected a model prepared by Richard Westmacott for the arrangement of the Egyptian sculptures and, in particular, the disposition of not only the colossal

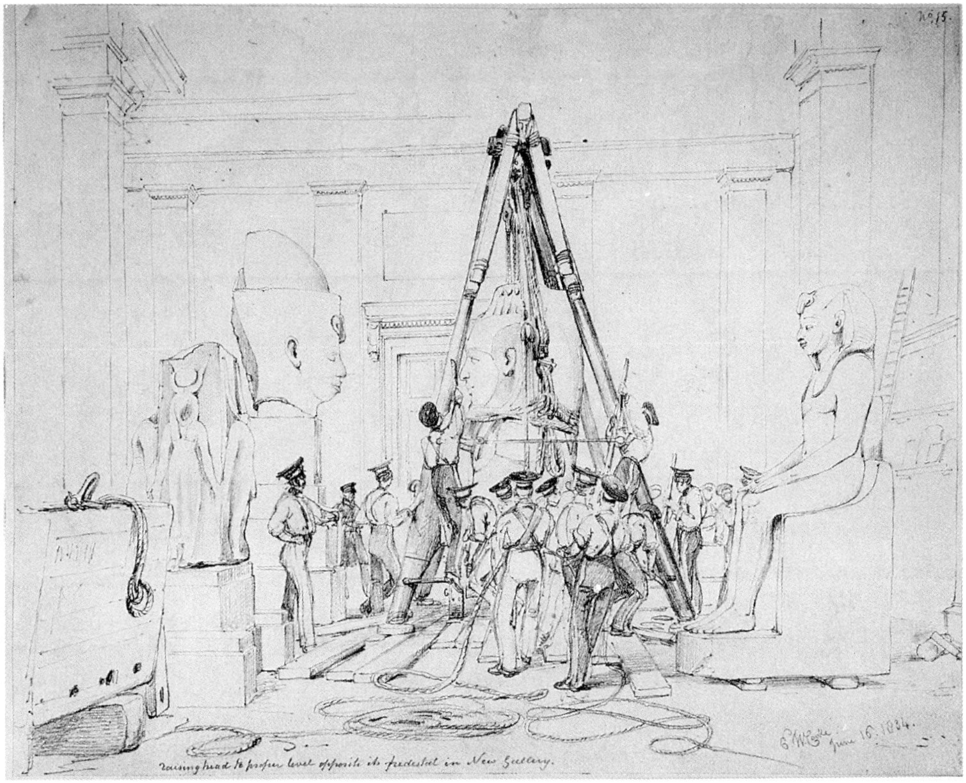

40 Gunners installing the Egyptian sculptures at the north end of Robert Smirke's new gallery (17 on Fig. 1). Drawing signed E. W. Cooke, 16 June 1834, from a sketchbook in the British Museum, PD 1914–2–6–21.

bust, but also the great head of Amenophis III.[45] The Trustees determined that they should be placed 'in the same relative position and elevation', which they currently held in the old gallery.

The position of the sculptures was not, however, the only consideration. Some weeks later Westmacott was to write:

> I am in some difficulty and quite at a standstill with the head of the Memnon. There is no private source on which I can rely for its removal with safety either to the men or to the object itself. I calculate the weight at about 14 tons., but this could be effected with care by the Government tackle and three or four of their men.[46]

In the event, a whole detachment of Gunners was supplied to move the
40 Egyptian sculptures into the new gallery with tackle capable of lifting two tons
more than the estimated weight of the bust. The floors in the temporary passage
connecting the Townley Gallery to the new building were strengthened to take
the great weight, and the work proceeded until June, when the Trustees wrote

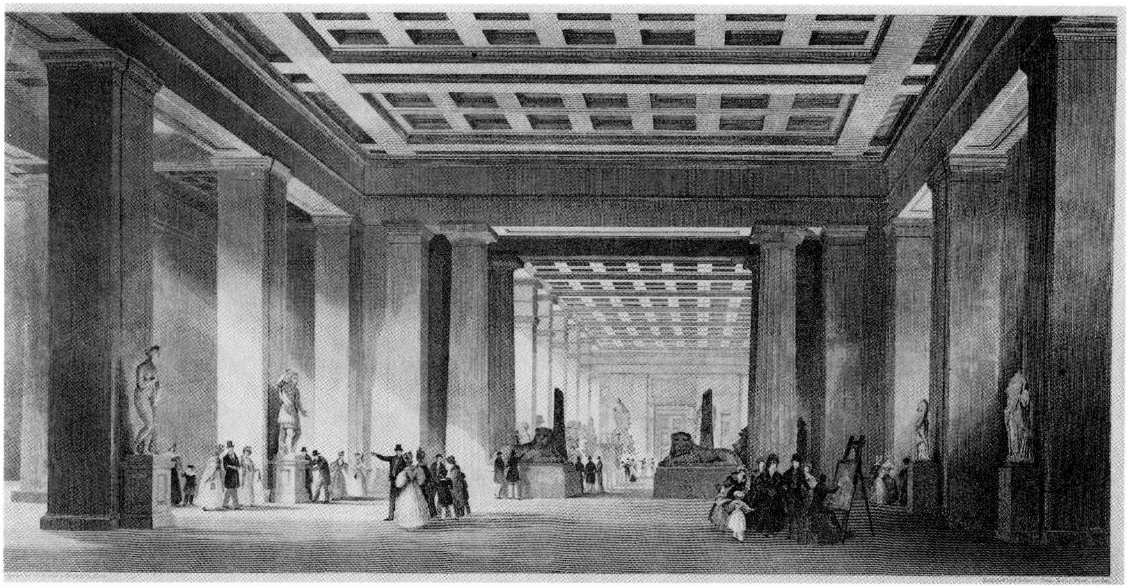

41 The Central Saloon and north division of the Egyptian Sculpture Gallery (17 and 18 on Fig. 1). Engraving, 1836. British Museum, PD 1944–7–4–2.

to the Office of Ordnance expressing approbation of the manner in which the Egyptian sculpture had been moved under the command of Major, formerly Captain, Dansey.[47]

The Egyptian sculpture occupied the northern division of the new gallery, while in the Grand Central Saloon, as it became known, Roman sculptures were placed 41
against the columns and pilasters, while in the recesses were to be found sculptures and casts of sculptures from Persepolis.[48]

Meanwhile, the Trustees were in the process of bargaining for another collection of Egyptian antiquities, including some important pieces of sculpture. In 1833 Joseph Sams, bookseller and antiquarian, wrote repeatedly to the Museum offering the collection he had compiled during a visit to Egypt in 1832–3.[49] Sams eventually succumbed to an offer of £2,500, which was £1,500 less than the sum he had originally demanded.[50]

Additions were not only made through new acquisitions, however, for in July 1834 Richard Westmacott wrote to say that, while he was arranging the Egyptian sculptures in the new gallery, he had discovered that a number of fragments housed in the basement of the Townley Gallery could be joined to form several 'nearly entire statues'.[51]

Such new acquisitions and discoveries delayed the final completion of the arrangement for some months. By the end of the year the room was still not quite

ready, but Hawkins advised the Trustees that it was sufficiently complete to admit the public.[52] This was done, as Hawkins's next report informs us, but in this same memorandum he has occasion to mention that two further sculptures only recently acquired had been placed in the gallery.[53] These were the Prudhoe lions, brought back by Lord Prudhoe, afterwards 4th Duke of Northumberland, from his journey to the Sudan in 1828. This pair of couchant lions provided an important decorative feature for the new gallery. They were placed on high pedestals, as an engraving of
41 1836 shows, guarding the entrance to the Egyptian Sculpture Gallery from the Central Saloon.[54]

Some extraordinary gains and losses

Following the 1834 rearrangement further small collections of Egyptian sculpture were acquired including those of W.R.Hamilton (1840) and that of Giovanni Anastasi, an Armenian merchant settled in Alexandria whose collection was sold in 1839. It is often the individual pieces, however, that have the most interesting stories attached to them. There is, for example, the black basalt kneeling figure of Wahibre which had stood in the premises of Messrs Fletcher, Shaw and Co., merchants of Iron Monger Lane, London, since about 1790. The statue was later said to have been found in 1785 in the vicinity of Lake Mareotis, some fifty miles from Rosetta.[55] But when the Trustees first made a bid to acquire it, the provenance was unknown, as, indeed, was its true ownership. Its custodians agreed to release it, therefore, only on condition that if ever a just claim be proven, the Museum would relinquish its possession.[56] This first attempt failed, however, as did a second in 1829.[57] Only in 1844 did Edward Fletcher finally sign the order allowing the statue to be brought into the Museum.[58]

Almost as curious was a letter received in the autumn of 1836 from the Admiralty authorities at Woolwich notifying the Trustees that in the Arsenal there was deposited 'a figure in relief of what appears to be a warrior in a mixed Roman and Egyptian costume'.[59] The letter went on:

> ... it is on grey granite, the work is extremely rude and I think was never finished; it is about 6 feet high, it was found among some ruins near Alexandria, when the first fortifications were constructed before that place, after the Battle of the 21st March, and it was stuck up in one of the works, when the soldiers used to amuse themselves by pelting it with stones ... there are besides three fragments of columns, two of red and one of grey granite. When the army quitted Egypt, these things were embarked as ballast, and were landed in the Arsenal, where they have remained since, and as for saying who they belong to, I suppose it would be impossible ....

The sculpture, which is in fact the black basalt lid of a sarcophagus dated to around 340 BC, today stands against the north wall at the very end of the Egyptian Sculpture

Gallery. Its history has not been recorded previously, and the damage wrought by the soldiers' stone-throwing is clearly visible.[60]

Among other sculptures with singular histories are two that were destroyed before they could reach the safety of the Museum. One was the finely carved sarcophagus removed by Colonel Howard Vyse from the Pyramid of Mycerinus and lost at sea in transit to England.[61] Again, in May 1842 the Admiralty forwarded a letter from Captain Mends stating that a Sphinx brought via Malta in HMS *Talavera* had been landed at Plymouth dockyard, only to be consumed by fire.[62] It seems that the arrival of the statue, which was probably that sent by Dr Bowring from Alexandria some years earlier, had never been reported to the Museum.[63]

Other objects, on account of their sheer size, failed to leave Egypt at all. One such was the colossal statue of Ramesses II that lay at Mitrahina, ancient Memphis. It was Charles Hoare, Chancellor of the British Consulate, who in a letter from Alexandria dated 11 July 1835, first suggested that the Museum acquire the statue, which measured 35 feet 2 inches in height.[64] Hoare claimed to have discovered the statue and to be its sole proprietor, since the Genoese mariner Giovanni Battista Caviglia had sold him his share.[65]

J. G. Wilkinson, the Egyptologist, wrote to the Trustees again a year later requesting that they send out an engineer to assist Hoare in moving the statue.[66] In February of the following year Joseph Bonomi, the sculptor and traveller, wrote to suggest that it might be sawn up. His letter was accompanied by a drawing indicating where it might be cut, but he acknowledged that this would be difficult without a steam-engine.[67] In May of 1838 Wilkinson wrote again to say that if the Trustees intended to do something about the Memphis Ramesses, they had better get on with it: if they did not, the French probably would. There was, moreover, an engineer by the name of Perring, employed in building the rail-road from Mokattum Mountain to Cairo, who would embark the statue at Alexandria for a sum not exceeding £600, subject to a firman being provided by the Pasha.[68] Hawkins felt that this brought the proposed removal within the bounds of possibility, and Robert Smirke was consulted as to whether the figure could be accommodated 'in any part of the existing or proposed buildings' of the Museum. The reply was in the negative even though Hawkins had advocated sawing off the legs below the drapery.[69]

Two years later a cast made by Bonomi of the head only was acquired from the 45
explorer Robert Hay, and here the matter rested until some years later Bonomi wrote again to suggest ways in which the statue might be raised. Portions of his letter, more detailed than any previous communication, are worth quoting in full.[70]

At the village of Metrehenah situated 12 miles south of Cairo and one mile and a quarter from the margin of the river, on the west bank of the Nile lies on its face a statue of admirable workmanship and believed to represent one of the greatest monarchs of antiquity. This statue was discovered by Capt. Caviglia [who in 1817 had endowed the Museum with a number of Egyptian sculptures] about the year 1826, by whom as it is currently reported, it was (with the consent of the Viceroy) given to the English nation, in virtue of which transaction it is said to be transferred from Consul to Consul as national property ... The material of the statue is a compact hard and flinty limestone commonly called churt ... Calculating the weight of this material at 14 feet cube per ton, the whole mass would weigh 96 ton. The front of this statue, or, as it lies, the lower surface is in perfect preservation as far as can be seen ... but the obelisk at the back is entirely defaced, and the left arm considerably injured.

Since its discovery the preservation of the face is mainly attributable to the circumstance of a deep hole immediately under the head, which is filled for more than half the year with putrid water; nevertheless, it is constantly exposed to Mohammedan fanaticism and to the much dreaded European propensity for breaking off pieces for private collections. Besides that, being of limestone it may be entirely demolished any moment that material might be wanted for the construction of a granary or factory ....[71]

The Trustees once more declined,[72] as they also did when C.A. Murry, as HM Consul General in Egypt, recommended sawing off the head and shoulders and the cartouches from the body, which gave the name and date.[73] The matter would be raised again, but the colossus of Metrahina was destined to remain where it lay, although it now rests on its back instead of its front.[74]

Another object of great size which failed to reach the British Museum, although it did at least reach England, was the obelisk known as Cleopatra's Needle. An attempt had been made to remove it as early as 1802, shortly after the defeat of the French at Alexandria. The Earl of Cavan made preparations for bringing it to England to serve as a memorial to the British victories in Egypt, but an eleventh-hour order was given for him to desist and the plan was abandoned.[75] In 1820, however, Muhammad Ali formally presented the obelisk to the Prince Regent (later George IV) and the matter was raised again, but to no avail; nor, when Muhammad Ali repeated his offer in 1831, was anything else done. In 1839 Robert George Kelly wrote from Stranraer with proposals for removing and re-erecting the obelisk, but this offer was declined by the Trustees.[76]

The question was much discussed over the next few years until, at last, on 15 April 1849, the Government resolved to acquire the obelisk and discussions ensued as to where it should be erected.[77] The Trustees of the British Museum expressed their hope that it might be placed either in the forecourt or in the quadrangle of the Museum. They then learned of a rival claim from the Crystal Palace Company, which desired the object as an embellishment for the Egyptian Court at Sydenham.[78] The Crystal Palace Company was granted permission by the Government to remove the obelisk at its own expense. When they were informed, however, that even then the object could only be considered as on loan to them, the Directors thought better of it.

Fifteen years later, when the question was raised again, the Treasury was informed by the Trustees of the Museum that owing to 'the nearly obliterated state of the hieroglyphics, the removal of the obelisk to England would not afford an adequate requital for the large expense which such removal would render necessary'.[79] Only in 1878 through the generosity of one man, Sir William James Erasmus Wilson (1809–84), and the courage and engineering ingenuity of several others was the obelisk finally brought to England. The dramatic story of its remarkable voyage in a cylinder made of boiler plates, its loss, salvage and eventual erection at the foot of the Adelphi steps on the Victoria Embankment of the Thames, lies beyond the scope of this book. Suffice it to say that before this site was finally resolved upon, the British Museum was deemed, seemingly undeservedly, as the best place for the obelisk. As E. A. Budge remarks, however, 'it was feared that the great weight of the obelisk would, in passing through the streets, crush the water pipes and gaspipes laid under them and damage the sewers.' One might think that the notoriously narrow streets of Bloomsbury would have provided an even greater obstacle to the progress of so long a thing as Cleopatra's Needle.[80]

The Townley Gallery 1831–1846

As a series of small low rooms, favourably lit, Saunders's gallery provided an ideal environment in which to display the Townley Marbles, and later, when it was pulled down to make way for Robert Smirke's new building, Hawkins referred to it wistfully as 'one of the most beautiful we had'.[81] The southern extension of the main west wing of the Museum beyond the Grand Central Saloon (19–20 on Fig. 1) and
the erection of the south front in its western limits (1–3 on Fig. 1) squeezed the 6
Townley Gallery until it was finally completely demolished in the winter of 1846. In 1831 the Discobolus was removed from its position at the northern end of Room
X, so that a door linking the old and new buildings might be broken through the 35
wall behind it.[82] Then, the migration of the Egyptian sculptures northwards into the new Egyptian Gallery occasioned substantial rearrangement of the classical sculpture in order to fill the gap left behind, and the entire suite of rooms was redecorated at this time.[83] Westmacott, who was given the task of reorganisation, observed that, since the floor space of the room vacated by the Egyptian sculptures amounted to more than one half of the total area occupied by the Townley Marbles, the existing exhibition of sculptures in the classical rooms would be seriously impoverished if the remaining sculptures alone were used. He proposed, instead, to introduce other objects, 'as may produce harmony of arrangement throughout the whole'.[84] In the *Synopsis* for 1835 there appear a number of pieces not previously listed, presumably brought out of the basement.[85]

The *Synopsis* is a useful tool for the modern museologist in recording the contents of each room of the Museum year by year. In its day, however, it was not to everybody's taste: in 1837 an anonymous reviewer of Henry Ellis's *Townley Gallery*, published in two volumes for the Library of Entertaining Knowledge, took the British Museum to task for the dullness of its guides. Comparing them unfavourably with the Comte de Clarac's publication of the Louvre sculptures, he reflected, 'We cannot help thinking its catalogue (viz. the British Museum *Synopsis*) should now be made out with a little more gusto and eye to dulcet utility and elucidation of relative subjects than a lumber-merchant's stock-book ... This very year there has been a new edition and lo! the improvements – Rooms IX and X are called XI and XII ....'[86]

It was while the Townley Gallery was in course of rearrangement that a 'mummy' was discovered in the basement of the building. The occasion is recorded in an amusing anecdote by Henry Ellis as follows.[87]

> Mr Barber and Mr Hawkins accompanied me this morning to Hatton Garden Police Office, on account of a lad of eighteen or twenty years old, who was found at six o'clock this morning by Young (when he came to his work) hid in a box of shavings in the basement of the Townley Gallery, and who stated himself to have been locked in between the doors at four o'clock yesterday. How he could have got there is something of a mystery because his dress and appearance were too wretched for him not to have been refused admittance to the hall. There he was and nobody could tell how else he got in. Young saw something black among the shavings in the box, and put his hand upon it and found it warm, when a face turned up and grinned at him. Young said, 'what are you?' The fellow answered, 'A Mummy!' Young started back some yards and sought Dodd's help and so finally the living Mummy was conducted to the Station house ....

The story loses some of its appeal when we hear that the miscreant 'mummy' suffered three months' hard labour in the House of Correction. Meanwhile the rearrangement of the Townley Gallery continued into the following spring and was not completed until May 1835.[88] The building would continue in service for some years to come, while the new works were erected around it. Then, early in 1842, Smirke drew the attention of the Trustees to the fact that the galleries soon to rise in the south-west corner of the new Museum building would occupy the site of the southern end of the Townley Gallery. The latter would therefore need to come down before the new building could commence.[89] The excavations for the new south front of the Museum had already begun in September 1841.[90] A year passed, however, before anything was done.

In January the urgency of the matter was once more pressed by Robert Smirke
42 and the demolition of Rooms I, II, III and parts of IV and V was carried out soon
afterwards.[91] Hawkins rearranged the sculptures thus displaced in the Grand Central
Saloon (18 on Fig. 1) and in the ante-room (15 on Fig. 1) to the Phigaleian Saloon.[92]
It may be noted in passing that up till now there still stood, adjoining Room V, the
5,22 eastern end of the old Temporary Elgin Room, in which the Phigaleian sculptures

were once placed and which now housed Sir Thomas Lawrence's collection of casts.[93] The Campana reliefs evicted from Room V of the Townley Gallery were taken down into a basement and there remained for some years to come.

The adjoining portions of old Montagu House were pulled down at the same time, or soon after, and the south-west and southern parts of the new building went up accordingly. The remaining vestiges of the old mansion disappeared in the course of 1846, and by the end of that year the south front and colonnade were almost finished. All that remained to complete the quadrangle of Robert Smirke's new building was to erect the gallery connecting the south-west corner (the present Assyrian Transept – 20 on Fig. 1) with the Grand Central Saloon. Before this could 43
be done, however, the remaining portion of the Townley Gallery had to come down, which it did at the very end of 1846.

Robert Smirke's new 'Townley Gallery'

In July 1846 the plans for the southern extension of the western wing of the Museum were presented to the Trustees for discussion. The main talking point was whether the pilasters of the northern division should be repeated in the south. Robert Smirke thought they should, but the Keeper of Antiquities, Edward Hawkins, warned that they would be an inconvenience to the arrangement of sculpture. It was assumed at this time that the Townley Marbles would be exhibited in the new room but, as Hawkins pointed out, no provision had been made for the smaller monuments, terracotta reliefs and cinerary urns of the Townley collection. These would naturally appear lost in the vast space of the new room, whereas in the old Townley Gallery they had been accommodated in a series of smaller rooms.[94]

The Keeper of Antiquities was overruled on the question of the pilasters, but it was no doubt due to his intervention that the next set of plans included a lower gallery to the west of the main room (14 on Fig. 1). This slip room would eventually provide much-needed space for the Assyrian sculptures from Layard's excavations.[95] Hawkins was permitted further minor changes in the plans for the new buildings,[96] but soon his energy was concentrated on the removal of the Townley Marbles out of what remained of the old gallery.[97] The building itself came down in the latter part of December.[98]

The Townley Marbles displaced by the impending demolition of the old gallery were either added to those already placed in the Grand Central Saloon and the ante-room to the Phigaleian Gallery, or were displayed in the long gallery (1 on Fig. 1) that had only just become available to the west of the Front Hall. Here, the Townley Marbles were arrayed in front of and between the pilasters on the north side of the room, where they caught the light from the windows in the south wall opposite. Along the ill-lit south wall, under the windows, were temporarily deposited Assyrian reliefs from Layard's excavations at Nimrud and Hector's excavations at Khorsabad.[99] Also in this room, under the windows, were placed the British antiquities that had formerly been housed in Room VII of the old Townley Gallery.[100]

Once the Townley Gallery was pulled down, the southern part of the main west wing (later the southern Egyptian Saloon – 19 on Fig. 1) was erected on the vacant
43 ground. A temporary passage linking the southern and northern part of the Museum was constructed to provide a way round the building works, and here were deposited a miscellany of Romano-British, Mexican, Hindu, Islamic and Chinese antiquities.[101]

By the time the 1851 *Synopsis* was published, the area to the south of what is now the Assyrian Transept had become accessible (2 on Fig. 1) and a new arrangement of the Graeco-Roman sculptures therefore became possible. The Grand Central Saloon was accordingly emptied of classical pieces in order to fill this new space. Virtually all that remained there for the time being were the Achaemenid sculptures and casts. At the same time, the new southern part of the main west wing (19 on Fig. 1) became available for the temporary storage of a variety of objects including the contents of the old Townley columbarium and the Etruscan cinerary urns.[102] Also placed here were the Indian and Mexican sculptures from the now demolished temporary passage.

Once the Assyrian sculptures had been removed from the long gallery to the west of the Front Hall, both the north and south walls were given over to the Townley Marbles, although the Romano-British antiquities remained as well. Indeed, this was their rightful place, since the intention was to create here a gallery of British antiquities, which was felt by some to be sadly lacking in the national repository.[103]

All the while that Robert Smirke's Townley Gallery was being completed, doubts were expressed about its suitability. The grand scale, as exhibited in the northern division of the west wing, might be appropriate for the colossal size of some Egyptian sculptures, but not, it was argued, for the Graeco-Roman sculptures, whose proportions were mostly life-size or less. One of its fiercest critics was J. Fergusson, who devoted two paragraphs of vitriol to the subject:

> It may be asked if this gallery is so manifestly bad and absurd, how came any man in his senses to design it, and any board of trustees to tolerate such a design? The explanation of the anomalies is unfortunately easy. When Sir Robert Smirke made the design, the Grecian fever was at its height and among other dogmas inherent in this absurdity, was the idea that perfect symmetrical regularity was a necessary and fundamental principle of this style. Never was doctrine so false or slanderous; but so it stood then: so Sir Robert believed and, consequently, because the royal library was built after one design, therefore, the sculpture gallery must be built exactly like it! If there are two classes of buildings in the whole world

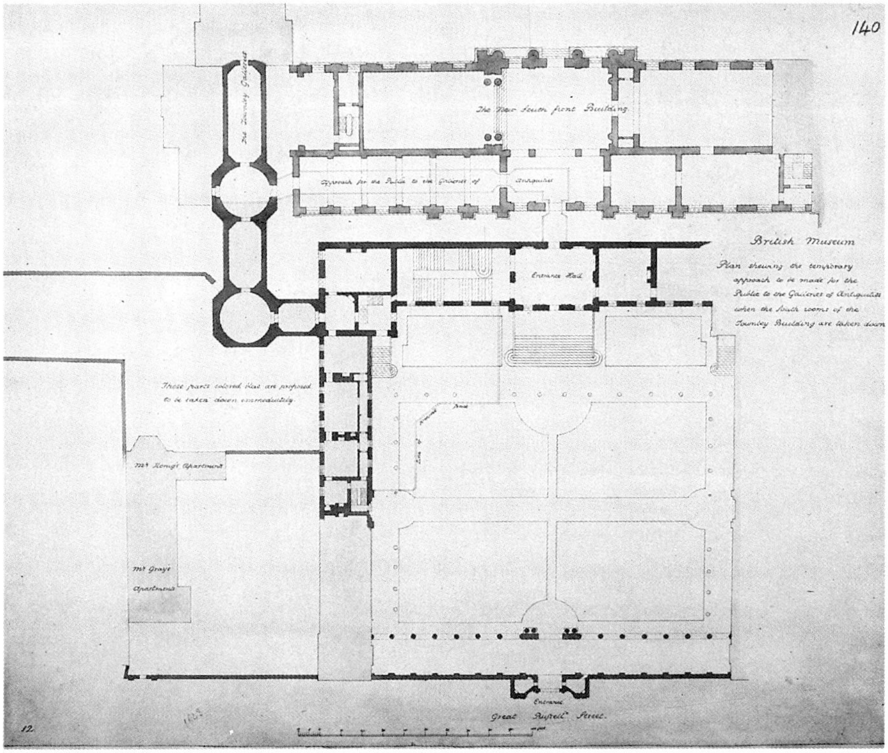
140
The Townley Galleries
The New South front Building
Approach for the Public to the Galleries of Antiquities
British Museum
Plan shewing the temporary approach to be made for the Public to the Galleries of Antiquities when the South rooms of the Townley Building are taken down
Entrance Hall
Those parts colored blue are proposed to be taken down immediately
Mr. Konig's Apartment
Mr. Gray's Apartments
Entrance
Great Russell Street.
12.

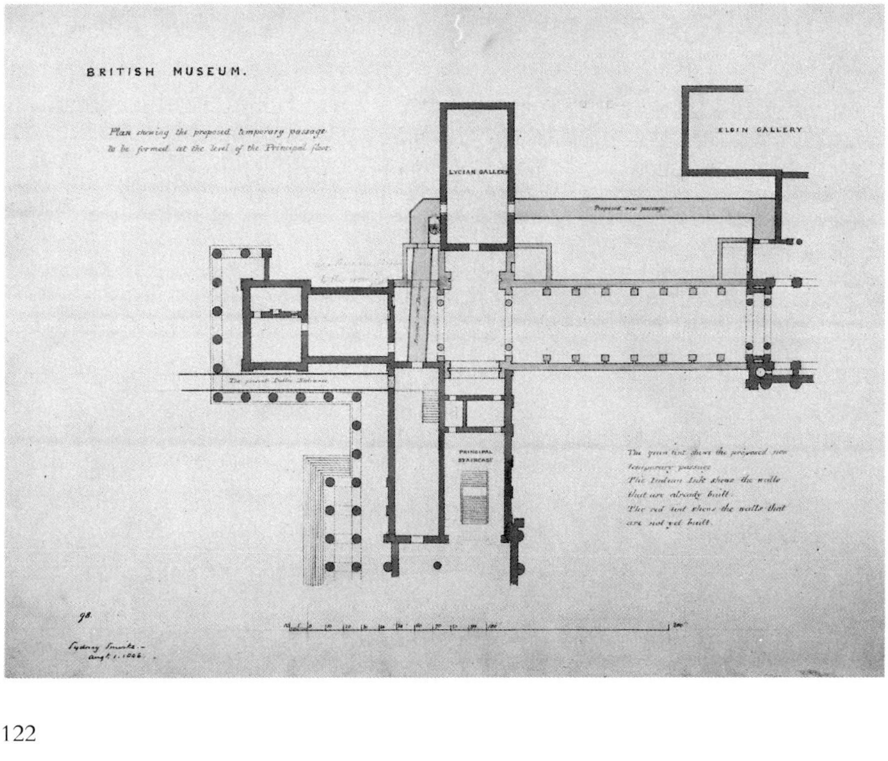
BRITISH MUSEUM.
Plan showing the proposed temporary passage to be formed at the level of the Principal floor.
ELGIN GALLERY
LYCIAN GALLERY
Proposed new passage.
PRINCIPAL STAIRCASE
The green tint shews the proposed new temporary passage
The Indian Ink shews the walls that are already built.
The red tint shews the walls that are not yet built.
98.
Sydney Smirke –
Augt. 1. 1846.

requiring treatment more essentially differing from one another, it is these two; yet to satisfy the requirements of this empirically assumed absurdity, the gallery was erected to match the library, and the statues are doomed to be caricatured, as they will be.

Twenty-five years ago this might have been excused; but after having a quarter of a century to reflect on the subject – after having seen all that has been done on the continent, and having all the means of information and observation we now possess, to set to work in the year 1848 to erect such a building, is a piece of gratuitous wickedness I scarcely know how to characterize.[104]

The ferocity of this attack was excessive but the criticisms were well founded. The Townley Marbles were indeed dwarfed by the building intended for them, as the German scholar G. Waagen pointed out in the publication describing his travels

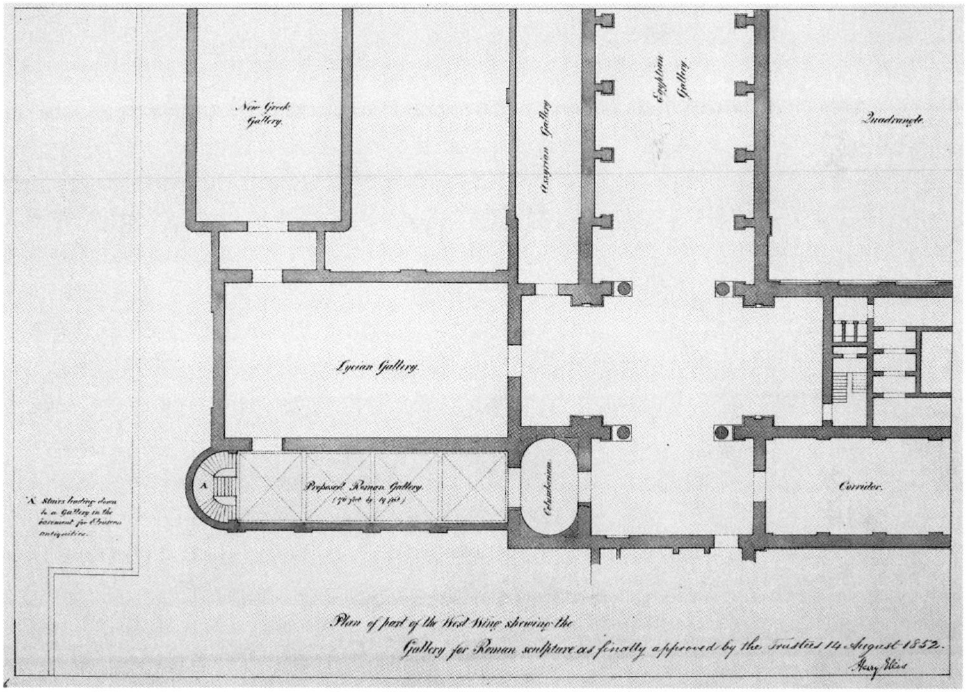

44 (*Above*) General plan of the south-west area, showing the proposed Graeco-Roman Galleries (1–2 on Fig. 1), 14 August 1852. British Museum, Central Archive.

42 (*Opposite, top*) Plan showing a temporary approach way to carry the public through the western wing of the Museum, pending the dismantling of the southernmost rooms of the Townley Gallery. The plan is particularly interesting in showing the relationship between the plans of Montagu House and the new South Front, *c.*1841–2. British Museum, Central Archive.

43 (*Opposite, bottom*) Plan showing the proposed temporary passage to carry the public round the works proceeding on the site of the demolished Townley Gallery, leading from the south entrance of the Museum into the principal galleries of the west wing, 1 August 1846. British Museum, Central Archive.

through England at this time.[105] Nobody felt the awkwardness of the situation more than the officers of the Department of Antiquities. The solution was one which had been resorted to more than once before, namely to tack on to the west side of the Museum an extra portion projecting beyond the main western side of the quadrangle (4 on Fig. 1). Here, along the south wall of the Lycian Gallery (5 on Fig. 1) would be erected a long, low, narrow room on an east-west axis which, together 44
with a basement and ante-room, would provide space of the appropriate dimensions for the Graeco-Roman sculptures.

The completion of the west wing

In the spring of 1848 Sydney Smirke reported on the progress made in completing the west wing: the roof was on, except at the south end, and orders had been given for work to begin on the 'low building to the west'. This last was a reference to the slip room designed to house the Assyrian sculptures (14 on Fig. 1).[106]

It was to be some time before serious consideration could be given to arranging sculptures in the new gallery. The original intention had been to place the Townley sculptures in this room (19 on Fig. 1). Only in autumn 1851 did Hawkins write to say that he thought the Egyptian sculptures should occupy both the northern and southern divisions of the western wing as well as a portion of the Central Saloon (18 on Fig. 1).[107]

By the following summer nothing had been done, but the space had been temporarily occupied by the Etruscan sarcophagi and Roman sepulchral monuments intended for the basement. In November 1852 Hawkins reported that the workmen were proceeding with putting up shelves in the southern division of the Egyptian Gallery, on which it was proposed to place the tablets and smaller sculptures. Meanwhile, thought was being given to the arrangement of the larger sculptures. The theme would be chronological, but Hawkins insisted that as much attention as possible should be paid to preserving a symmetrical and decorative arrangement.

At last in November 1852 Hawkins submitted to the Trustees Edmund Oldfield's report and detailed plan for the rearrangement of the Egyptian sculptures.[108] Hawkins agreed with the broad lines of the proposal, which had been drawn up in consultation with Samuel Birch, the Egyptologist in the Department of Antiquities. He was, however, nervous of moving the two great heads, the so-called bust of the Younger Memnon, by this time recognised as Ramesses II, and the head of Amenophis III, then thought to represent Tuthmosis III. Hawkins remembered the difficulty experienced in moving the heads out of the Townley Gallery in 1834. He doubted whether it mattered if objects of such scale were seen out of the chronological sequence Oldfield had devised for the two galleries.

Hawkins's brash lieutenant had anticipated this objection and was emphatic that his scheme could not be properly carried out without these two monuments, which 'most fully and forcibly exemplify the art of their respective periods'. Surely, with all the improvements that had been made in the science of engineering since they were first brought from Egypt, they could now be moved a few yards along the gallery. Then Oldfield, certain in the knowledge that Anglo-French antagonism would be sure to act as a goad to the Trustees, remarked upon how the French had very recently arranged their entire sculpture collection in a new room, with at least one figure considerably larger and weightier than those of the British Museum.

Oldfield's proposal was to arrange the sculptures in strict chronological sequence, with the earliest sculptures deposited in the northern division of the gallery. Here was to be placed everything ranging from the fourth to the eighteenth dynasty. In the Central Saloon would be placed the works of the nineteenth dynasty, which also spilled over into the southern division. This descended through the Ptolemaic to the Roman Imperial period.

Each piece was plotted on the plan in its appropriate place, numbered and colour-coded according to period. These numbers were then cross-referenced to a complete table of contents. The principal sculptures in each division were to be placed in front of the pilasters, with the less significant in the intervening recesses. In addition Oldfield created what he called 'the central avenue', which consisted of four 'isolated' objects, three in the southern division and one in the northern. The latter, placed centrally and facing south, was to be the head of Amenophis III. Facing each other at the northerly end of the northern division, Oldfield felt the colossal head and the bust were not seen to best advantage. They were an imperfect match and neither could be seen frontally from a sufficient distance. Together, moreover, they presented an asymmetrical outline that interfered with the architrave of the northern door. By placing the head in the centre of the gallery, on a plinth somewhat lower than the existing one, Oldfield hoped to avoid any conflict with the line of the door, and to provide a point of interest which could be enjoyed along the length of the room by the visitor approaching from the south.

The bust of Ramesses, meanwhile, was to be removed to the Central Saloon, where it would stand, together with the cast that had now been acquired of the head of the colossus at Memphis, on the western side, facing east. Oldfield did not place any sculptures under the windows on the east side of the transept, for it was dark there, as it also was in the northern division generally. He thought, however, that having windows on both sides of the room in the northern and southern divisions was an advantage, since Egyptian sculptures were frequently inscribed at the back and sides. In the Greek galleries lighting on both sides would be considered a disadvantage, whereas here 'the inartistic treatment of the human form renders the absence of shadow of less importance'.

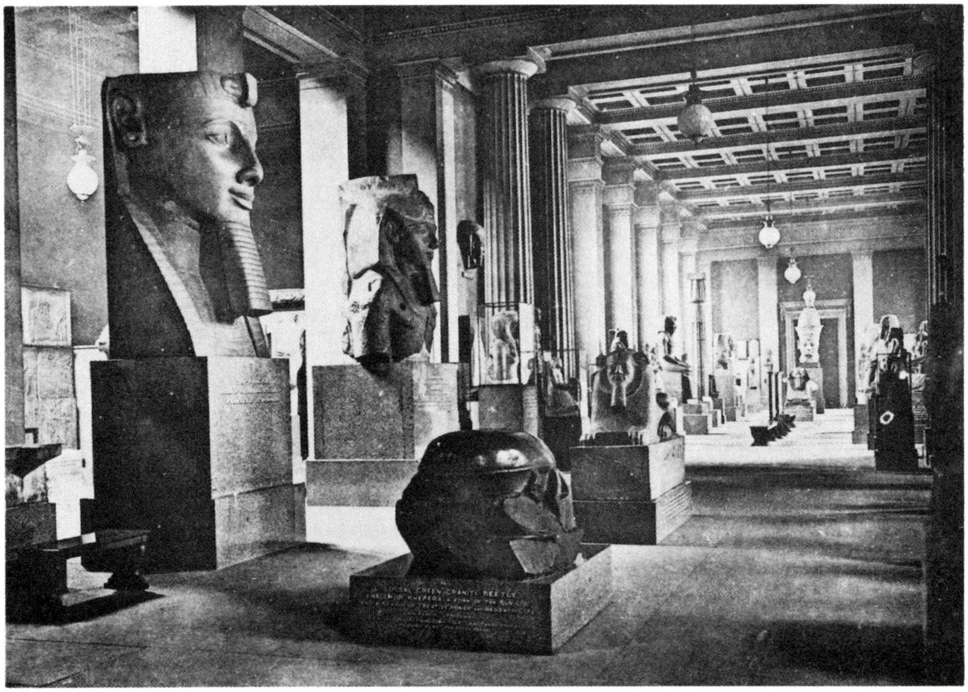

45 The Egyptian Sculpture Gallery, looking north from the Central Transept, *c.*1900–1908. In the foreground is the cast of the head of the colossal Ramesses at Memphis. Photo British Museum, Department of Prints and Drawings.

Oldfield's chronological sequence was approved at a special meeting of the Sub-Committee of Antiquities.[109] The removal began in the following month, but it was not completed until February 1854, by which time all the sculptures had been relocated, although some were still awaiting bases.[110] The rearrangement did not pass without mishap, and in spite of Oldfield's faith in 'modern' scientific engineering, one statue fell over early in the proceedings and sustained some damage.[111]

The preface to the *Synopsis* drawn up for the new arrangement is of some interest. Great stress was placed on chronological sequence, not only in the Egyptian Gallery but throughout the sculpture galleries of the western wing. Thus a 'vertical' chronology was seen to run from the southern to the northern end of the Egyptian Gallery, while another sequence ran laterally through the parallel suites of Egyptian, Assyrian and Greek rooms.[112]

The larger sculptures of the Egyptian Gallery were arranged strictly according to the divisions of Manetho's Egyptian dynasties. (The inscribed tablets and smaller sculptures presented greater difficulties and could not be classified in the same order.) The visitor approaching from the front entrance to the Museum and moving from south to north, first encountered monuments from the period of the Roman

Empire, ranging in date from the capture of Alexandria by Augustus in 30 BC to the Muslim invasion of AD 640. Then came the monuments from the period of the Ptolemies, which led in turn to the dynastic period, extending in the southern division of the gallery as far back as the nineteenth dynasty. The Central Egyptian Saloon, as it was now called, was given over to Ramesses II, the greatest of the kings of the nineteenth dynasty, while in the northern division of the gallery were to be found the great sculptures of the eighteenth dynasty, 'which comprehends the most splendid epoch of Egyptian history'. Finally, in the hallway at the foot of the north-west stairs leading to the upper galleries, were placed the very earliest objects from the period prior to the eighteenth dynasty.

Hay's casts

As a postscript to the history of the Egyptian sculptures something must be said of the cast collection of Robert Hay (1799–1863). The story of Hay's two expeditions to Egypt in 1824–8 and 1829–34 has been told by Selwyn Tillett,[113] who also records the protracted negotiations conducted between the British Museum and Hay for his casts of Egyptian sculptures. Hay had brought back from Egypt the moulds made during his travels, and towards the end of 1836 casts were being struck from these.[114] The British Museum first became interested in the prospect of acquiring casts from Hay's moulds in November of that year, when Hawkins expressed a desire to see a cast of the Abu Simbel head.[115] In January 1838 Hay made a formal approach to the Museum offering his casts for the cost of the work.[116] The matter dragged on, however, and it was not until December of the following year that he submitted a figure for the cost of his casts, namely £1001 7s. 8d.[117] In the event Hay presented his casts to the Museum, on condition that he be allowed to withdraw certain items and that Joseph Bonomi, who had acted as his agent, be compensated for his time and trouble to the tune of £100.[118] Before the casts were brought to the Museum the Trustees deliberated on where they could be accommodated and, in particular, where a place might be found for the casts of the Abu Simbel head and the colossal head of Ramesses II from Memphis.[119] Hawkins suggested that the two heads might find a place in the Central Saloon, near the entrance from the wooden passage connecting this part of the Smirke building with the old Townley Gallery.

The casts were all in the Museum by July.[120] The head from Abu Simbel was placed over the entrance to the temporary passage, the great cast having been sawn into four pieces for the purpose.[121] The Memphis head was, however, to occupy a different place. At the beginning of 1841 Hawkins consulted with Robert Smirke as to the possibility of placing the colossal cast over a doorway in the vestibule at the northern end of the Egyptian Sculpture Gallery.[122] This plan was subsequently approved by the Trustees.[123] Other casts were placed above the showcases in the upper Egyptian Gallery, namely those from the two friezes of the small temple of Beit-oually near Kalabshe.[124] Shortly afterwards, at his own suggestion, Bonomi supervised the restoration of the 'original' colours to these casts.[125] The work was completed by the early summer of 1842.[126]

Encouraged by the success of this experiment, Bonomi offered his services for painting other Hay casts with 'lost' colours.[127] This offer was not accepted, however, until 1845, when Hawkins arranged the casts intended to be so coloured on the landing of the north-west staircase outside the upper Egyptian Room.[128] The painting took longer than Bonomi had anticipated and was not finished until spring the following year.[129] The coloured casts remained in place until 1857–8, when they were removed to make way for glass showcases. This was made possible by the insertion of a skylight over the north-west staircase, introducing a great deal more light into this previously gloomy spot.[130]

The Townley Marbles in the Graeco-Roman Rooms

The Graeco-Roman Gallery represents one of those rare instances in the history of 44
the sculpture galleries where the eventual purpose was fixed at the outset. For the architect, however, architectural considerations remained ultimately the most important in determining the final proportions of the room: the height was measured in relation to the windows of the adjacent Lycian Room, below the line of which the roof of the new gallery must fall; the width was fixed by the alignment of doorways throughout the southern rooms. On being asked why the new gallery could not be wider, Robert Smirke protested:

> The position of the new door into the Gallery is determined by the present door from the Hall and corridor [meaning the room immediately to the west of the Front Hall – 1 on Fig. 1]; with which it must necessarily be central, and if this new door were not in the centre of the new Gallery the appearance would be most offensive. It would be an architectural blot that would strike the eye of every observer. The central line therefore fixed, the width of the Gallery became fixed.[131]

By the end of the 1854 the new room had been built. Meanwhile, work continued on the basement story, which would be reached by a staircase at the western end of the gallery, while at the eastern end a small ante-room (3 on Fig. 1) was formed between the new building and the south-west corner of the main Museum, this

46 (*Opposite, top*) The Roman Gallery (1 on Fig. 1), looking east, *c.*1875. Photo by F. York. British Museum, Department of Greek and Roman Antiquities.

47 (*Opposite, bottom*) Victorian gloom: the Roman Gallery looking west, *c.*1905. The serried ranks of dark bases were to be swept away by inter-war modernism: compare Fig. 90. Photo by D. Macbeth. British Museum, Central Archive.

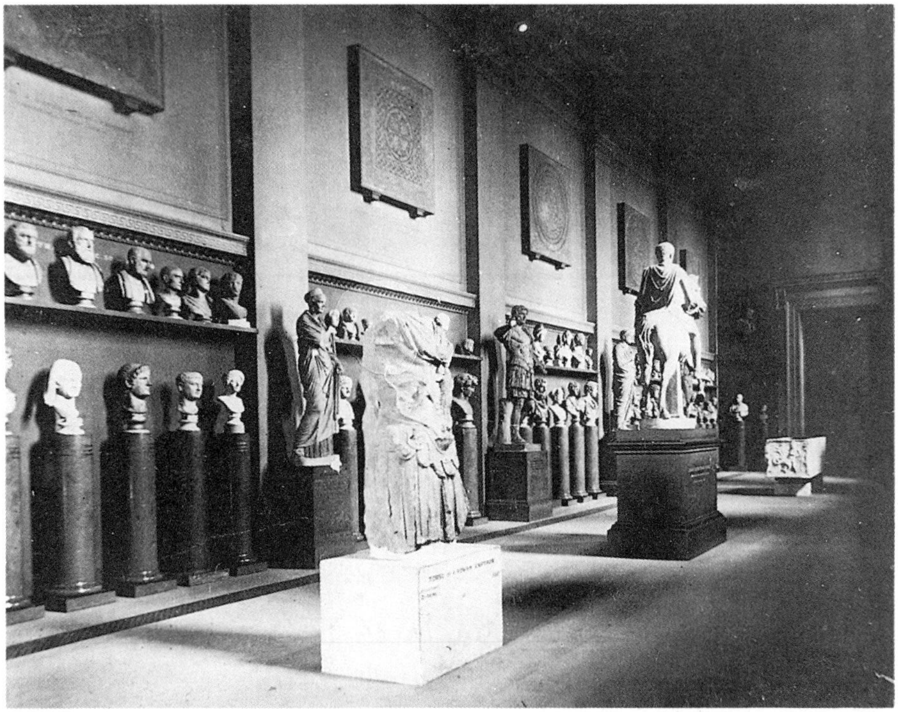

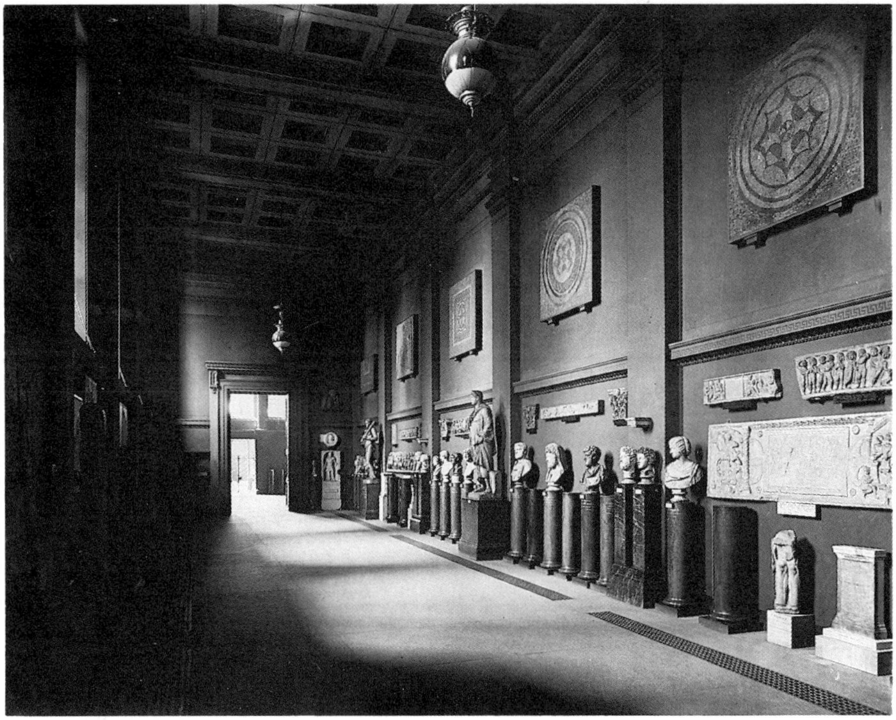

being the aforementioned landing of the staircase that had once led down to the Lycian Room.[132] The staircase at the western end would give access into the basement below the Graeco-Roman Room and from here a doorway led into the basement of the Lycian Gallery. A corresponding doorway was broken through the south wall of the Lycian Gallery at ground floor level, causing a certain amount of rearrangement of the sculptures in that room.[133]

By the beginning of 1855 the new rooms were completed, including the 'encaustic painting' designed to match the ornamental decoration of the rest of the sculpture galleries, and the Graeco-Roman sculptures were being arranged.[134] Hawkins's annual report submitted a year later declared, 'The arrangement of Graeco-Roman and Roman portrait sculpture in the new Gallery and basement has been completed.'[135] 46–56

The arrangement by Oldfield was as follows: the sculpture was displayed in four rooms; first, the area to the south of what is now the Assyrian Transept; second, the ante-room between it and the third or main room, which ran parallel with the southern side of the Lycian Room; fourth, the basement under the main room. In addition, in the room immediately to the west of the Front Hall (1 on Fig. 1) were

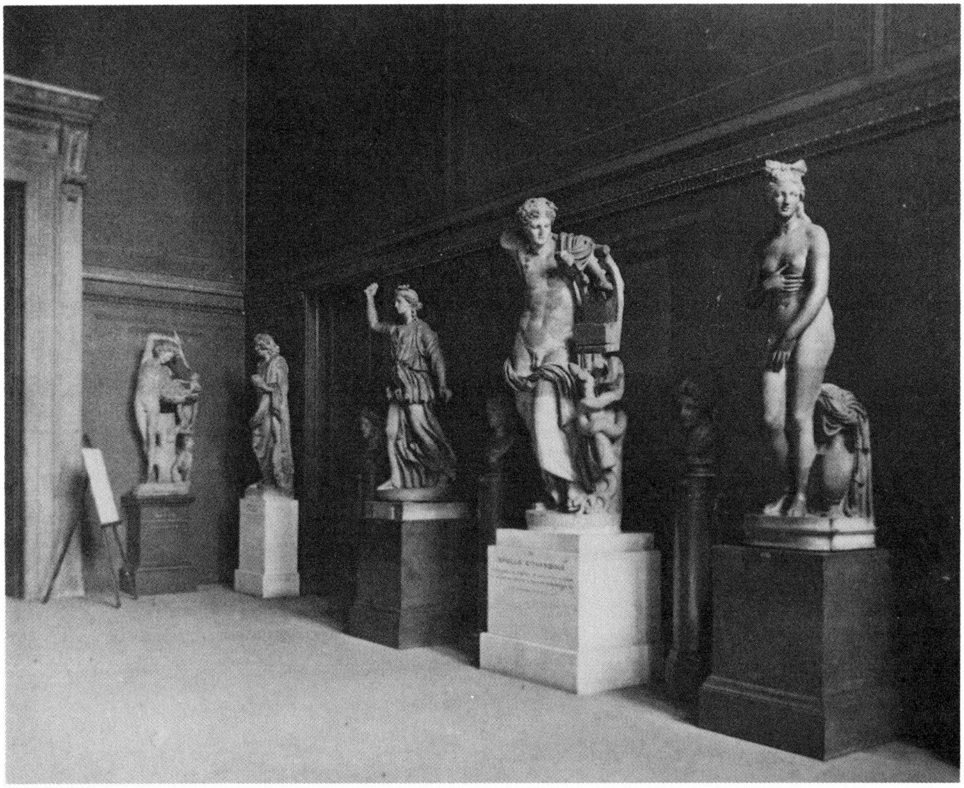

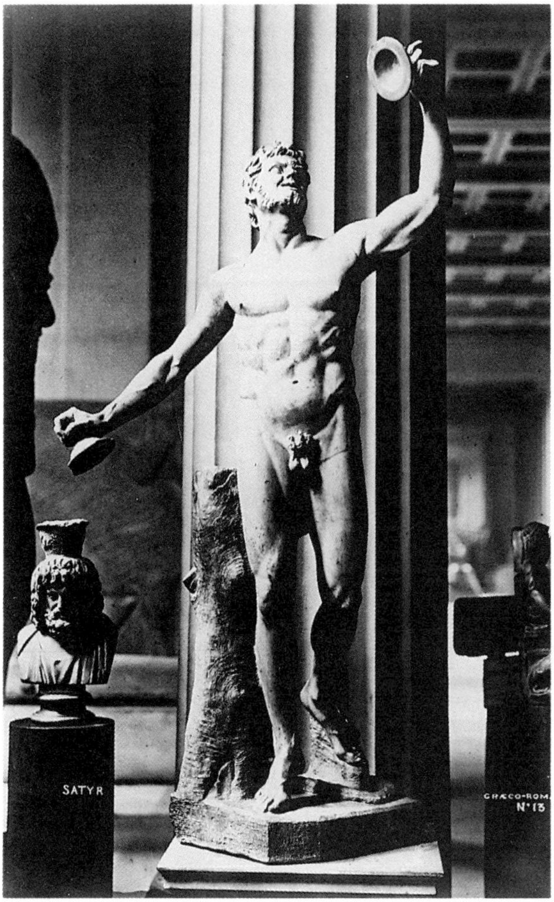

49 (*Left*) The Rondanini Faun in the First Graeco-Roman Room (2 on Fig. 1), *c.*1872. Photo by C. Bernieri for Caldesi at Colnaghi's. British Museum, Department of Greek and Roman Antiquities.

48 (*Opposite*) The south wall of the First Graeco-Roman Room (2 on Fig. 1) given over to gods and lesser deities, *c.*1875. The doorway today leads to the special exhibition gallery. Photo by F. York. British Museum, Department of Greek and Roman Antiquities.

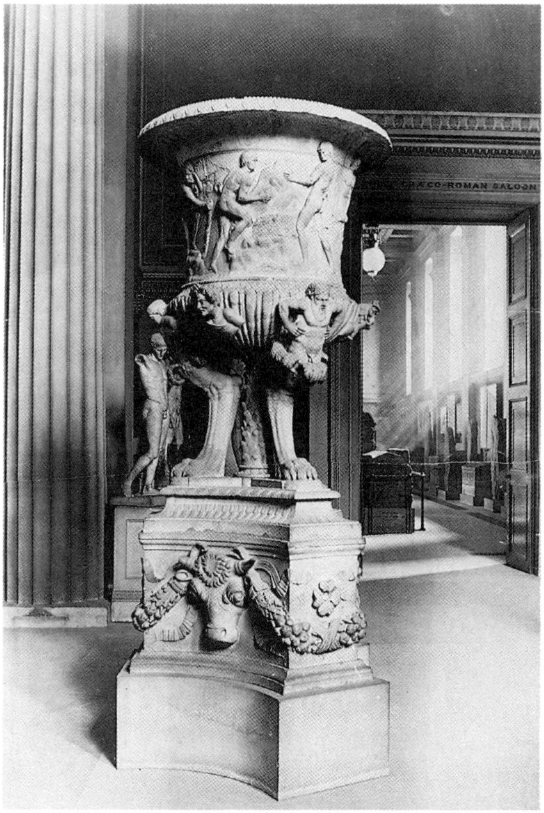

50 (*Right*) The Piranesi Vase in the First Graeco-Roman Room, *c.*1890. Photo The London Stereoscopic and Photographic Company. British Museum, Department of Greek and Roman Antiquities.

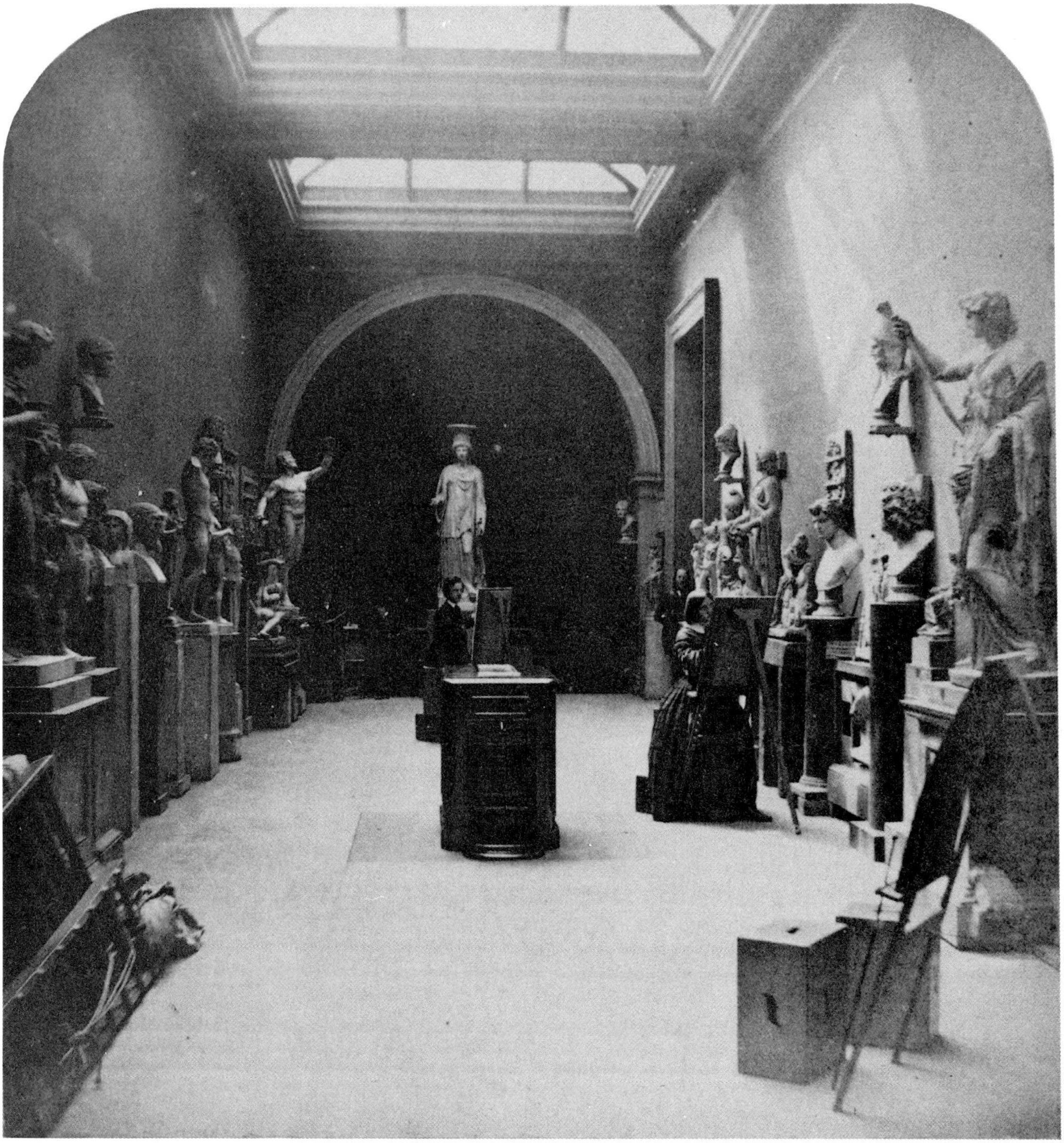

51 'Students' Day' in the Third Graeco-Roman Room (4 on Fig. 1), looking west, *c.*1857–9. Easels for use by artists had only just been reinstated after a ban of some twenty years. Photo by R. Fenton for *The Stereoscopic Magazine*. British Museum, Central Archive.

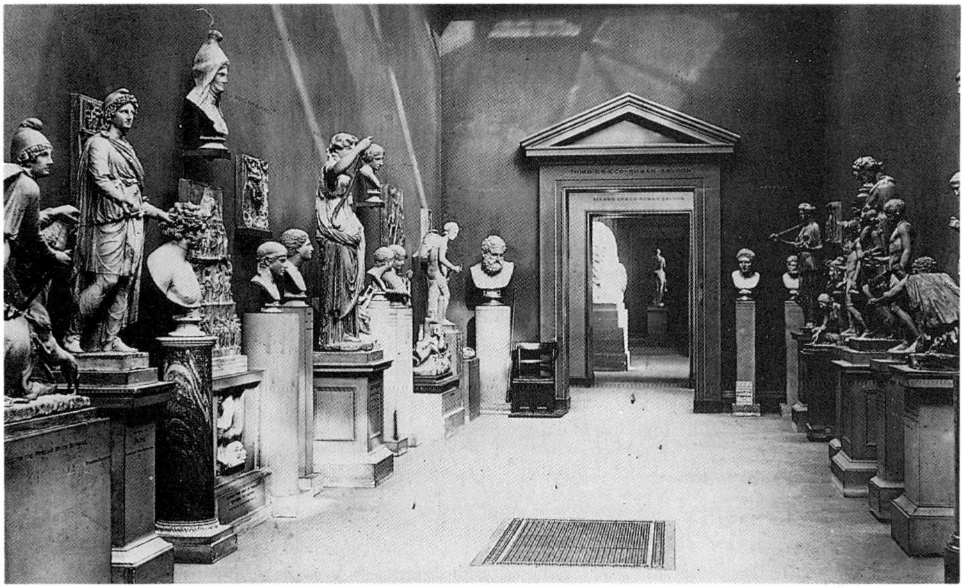

52 (*Above*) The Third Graeco-Roman Room, looking east across the main west wing (First Graeco-Roman Room) and into the Roman Gallery, *c.*1872. For the equestrian statue, compare Fig. 46. Photo by S. Thompson for Mansell. British Museum, Department of Greek and Roman Antiquities.

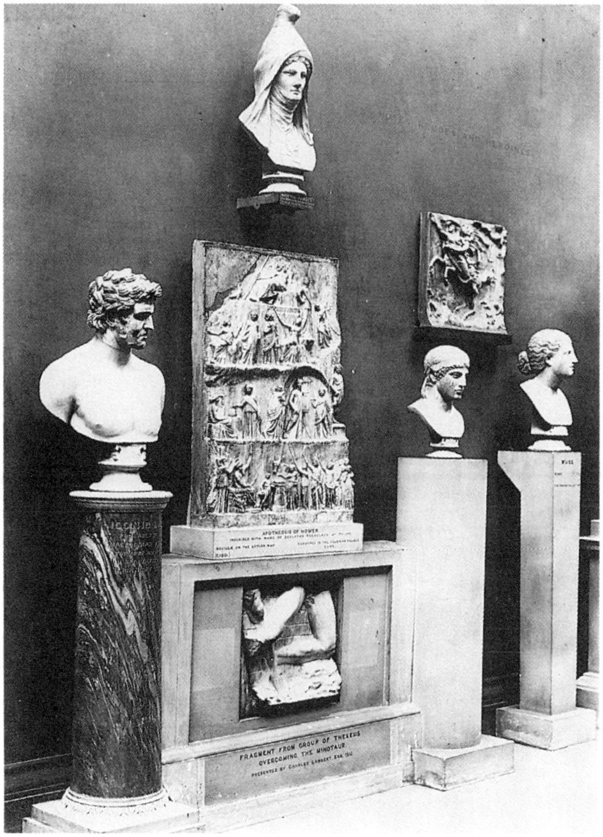

53 Third Graeco-Roman Room: part of the north wall, *c.*1872. Photo by S. Thompson for Mansell. British Museum, Department of Greek and Roman Antiquities.

placed against the north wall, facing the windows, a series of Roman portrait busts and statues arranged in chronological series. It had been hoped to place the Townley and other Graeco-Roman marbles in chronological order but, not surprisingly, it was soon realised that this would be extremely difficult, given the nature of the material.

At this time it was thought the Graeco-Roman sculptures might include some 'original monuments of the autonomous or ante-Roman period of Greece, afterwards transported by the conquerors to their own country'.[136] In general, however, the Townley Marbles were regarded as Roman copies of Greek originals. There were therefore two choices: either to arrange the sculptures in chronological arrangement in respect of the date of the Greek originals they were thought to copy, or to arrange them by subject. A third approach, which might appeal to the modern

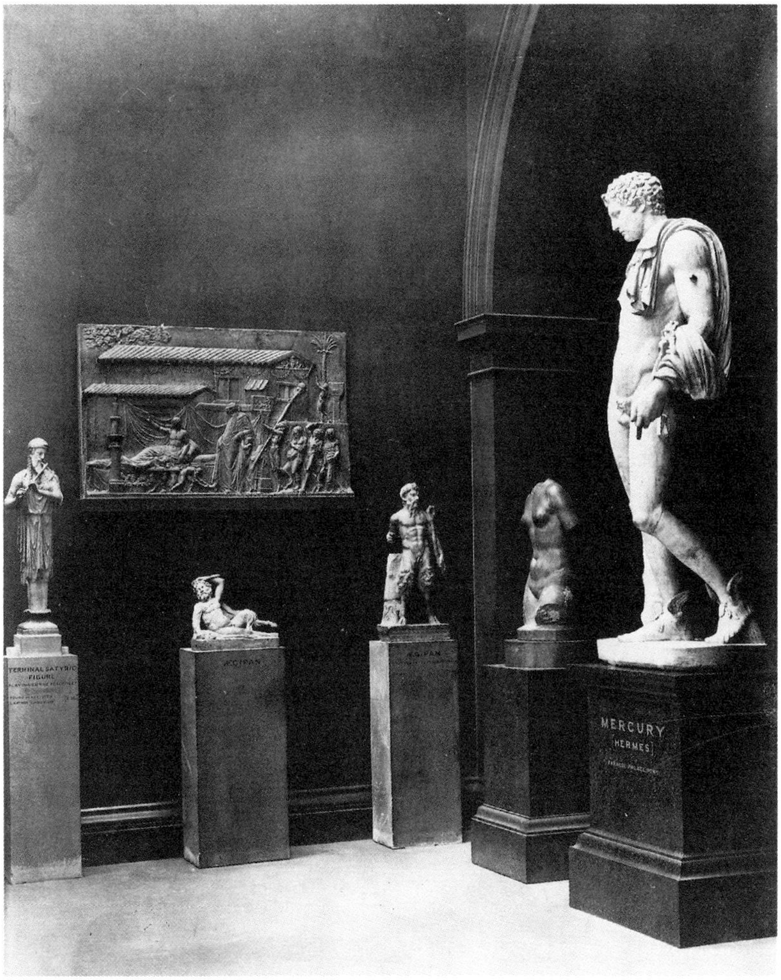

54 (*Left*) Third Graeco-Roman Room: the Farnese Hermes under the arch at the west end, *c.*1872. Photo by S. Thompson for Mansell. British Museum, Department of Greek and Roman Antiquities.

55 (*Opposite, top*) Third Graeco-Roman Room: north side, with view through the doorway into the Archaic Room, *c.*1900–1908. We catch a glimpse of the cast of the Nike of Paionios from Olympia: compare Fig. 16. Photo British Museum, Department of Greek and Roman Antiquities.

56 (*Opposite, bottom*) The newly opened Graeco-Roman Basement. This was reserved for miscellaneous sculptures 'of subordinate rank', such as figures of animals and architectural and decorative pieces. *The Illustrated London News*, 26 May 1855.

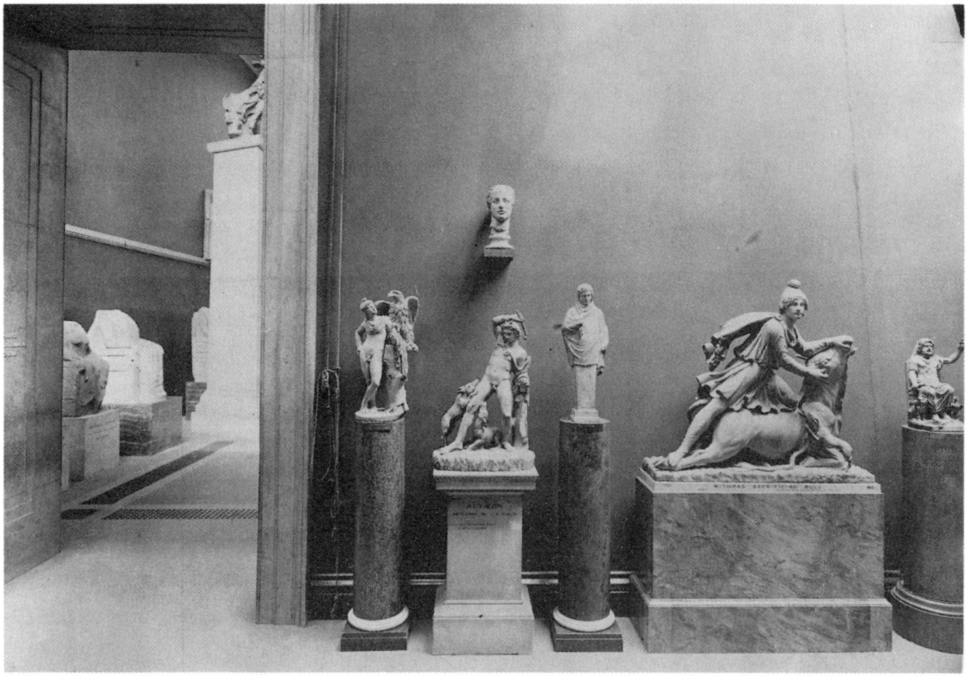

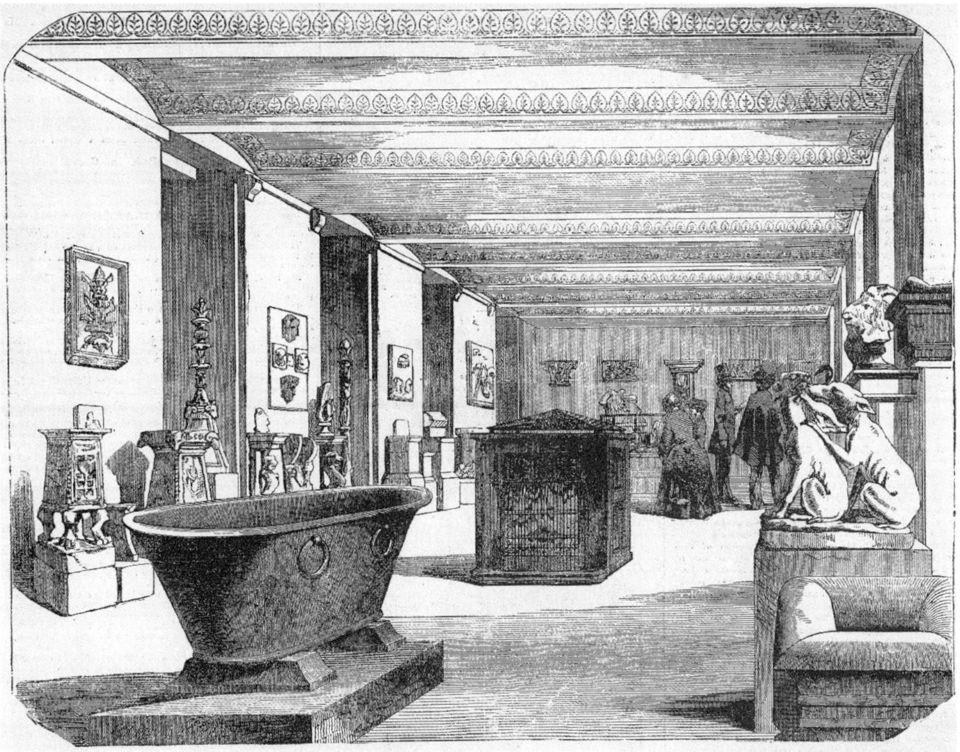

scholar, namely to attempt a chronology based on the supposed date of the copy, rather than the work it was copying, did not occur to connoisseurs of ancient sculpture at this date. The emphasis was always on Greek art, and the Graeco-Roman sculptures were seen as a decadent form placed vaguely in the Roman period.

For want of a better system, therefore, the sculptures were arranged by subject: in the First Graeco-Roman Saloon (2 on Fig. 1) were placed examples of all twelve Olympian deities 'and their several modifications in the Greek and Roman Pantheon';[137] in the second compartment were placed representations of human personages (3 on Fig. 1); in the third (4 on Fig. 1), heroic figures; and in the fourth or basement room, miscellaneous sculptures 'of subordinate rank', such as animals, architectural and decorative pieces.

Although the basic arrangement was to remain unchanged until the period between the two world wars, alterations were made. Soon after the reorganisation of the Graeco-Roman galleries was completed, there began a process, which would continue for some years to come, of remounting the sculptures on new, uniform marble bases. In the spring of 1857 an improvement was suggested for the placement of the Townley Venus and the Discobolus. It was proposed to position these two gems of the Townley collection facing each other on opposite sides of the Second Graeco-Roman Saloon (3 on Fig. 1), in newly constructed alcoves.[138] This involved removing the roof of the room, which had been created out of the former stairwell down to the basement of the Lycian Gallery, and reconstructing it two or three feet higher, and building two large alcoves in the north and south walls at an estimated cost of £320.[139] The recesses were completed towards the end of 1858 and the two statues were placed therein.[140] Some time afterwards, they were remounted on revolving bases.

The effect of this change, combining divine and human subjects in the same room, was to break up the strict division between divine, human and heroic subjects and to create a pictorial hiatus in the series, focusing more upon the concept of ideal male and female beauty. In this it may be fancied that we detect something of a return to the decorative effects for which the display of English private collections had become justly famous.[141] Certainly, the use of semicircular niches offered an architectural setting worthy of a Holkham or a Newby Hall.

The Graeco-Roman galleries were to survive largely unchanged until the great upheaval in the sculpture galleries that took place between the wars. Then a new archaeological functionalism demanded a more 'scientific' order, and the classification 'Graeco-Roman' was eventually abandoned altogether.

The Townley terracottas

One salient omission from the rooms replacing the old Townley Gallery was the
36 fine series of terracotta reliefs, now known as Campana reliefs, which had occupied one of the two connecting vestibules of the former building. The fact of their not being exhibited came to the attention of the committee set up to enquire into the future of the national collections. Faced with the possibility of finding these precious objects transferred to some other repository, the Trustees ordered a special arrangement to be made for the Townley terracottas. Accommodation was found by Hawkins for them in the Second Vase Room.[142]

Columbaria and the Sepulchral Basement

Another body of material formerly displayed in the old Townley Gallery and for
37 which special provision was now needed, was the sepulchral antiquities. Even before Room V in the old building had been demolished, Hawkins was demanding that some new arrangement be made. He suggested that the side gallery adjoining the south-west wing of the Museum should contain a smaller room at its southern end designated as a columbarium.[143] His proposal was accepted by the architect who considered it an interesting feature.[144]

Shortly before demolition the contents of Room V in the Townley Gallery were removed to the south recess of the ante-room of the Phigaleian Saloon.[145] A re-
57 placement columbarium was subsequently built at the southern end of what is now the Nimrud Gallery, but it seems never to have been used for its intended purpose, or, if it was, then for only a short period. In 1852 the Assyrian bas-reliefs from Layard's excavations were installed in the southern slip room (14 on Fig. 1) to the Egyptian Gallery and the partition wall that had been erected to separate the columbarium compartment from the rest of this narrow room was pulled down to provide the maximum possible accommodation for the reliefs from Nimrud.

The sepulchral antiquities, having been displaced for a second time, were temporarily stored in the southern division of the main west wing while Hawkins deliberated upon the best means of providing permanent accommodation for them.[146] It was resolved that they should be exhibited in a basement that would be adapted for the purpose and which was to become known as the Sepulchral Basement. This ran under the new southern extension of the west wing and below the Assyrian side gallery (basement under 19 and 14 on Fig. 1).[147] Three years later the necessary architectural alterations had been made but the 'crypt', as Hawkins now liked to call it, still needed painting and the columbarium itself was not yet made.[148] Only in 1860, in the annual report for that year, did Hawkins's assistant Samuel Birch notify the Trustees that, 'the arrangement of the Etruscan sarcophagi and

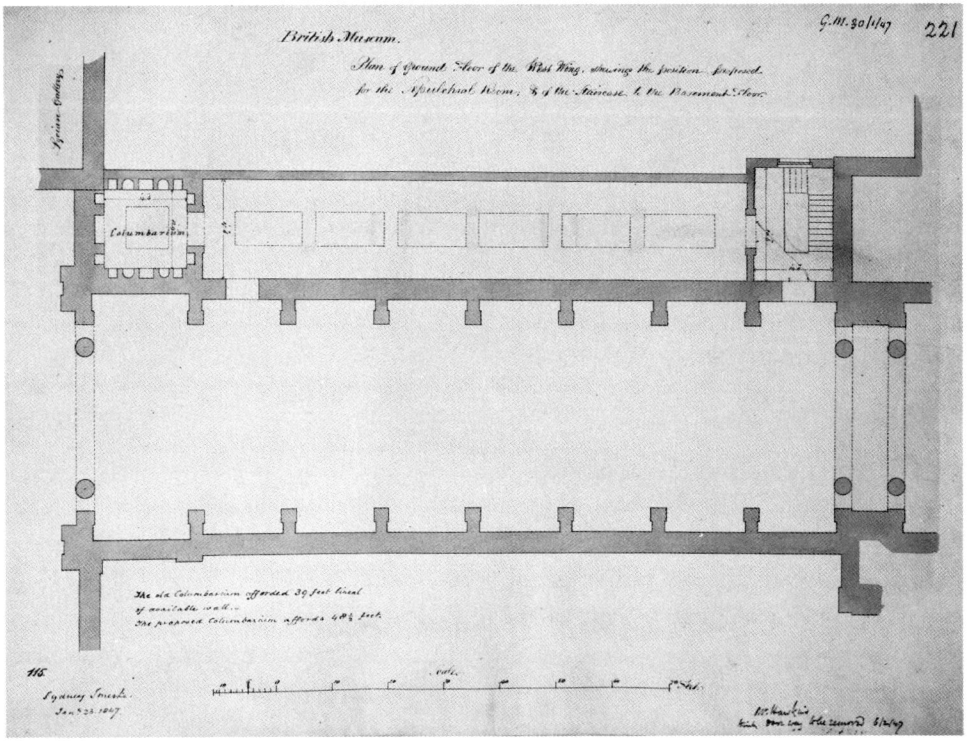

57 Ground-floor plan of the southern division of the Egyptian Sculpture Gallery and side room (14 and 19 on Fig. 1), incorporating a columbarium at the southern end and, at the northern, a stairway into the basement, 23 January 1847. The columbarium became a casualty of the need for space to display the Assyrian sculptures, and was removed to the sepulchral gloom of the basement. British Museum, Central Archive.

cinerary urns on the west side of the sepulchral basement room, and the fixing of the facsimiles of the wall paintings from the tombs in which these monuments were discovered have been completed.'[149] These copies of Etruscan tomb-paintings had been displayed upstairs in the Vase Rooms, above the showcases, where other similar paintings that could not be accommodated in the basement remained. They were purchased in 1838 from Campanari, having previously been displayed in a special exhibition at Piccadilly.[150] Birch's report went on to add that, 'on the east side of the same room the collection of Roman sarcophagi and other sepulchral monuments have been arranged and a recess in the room has been fitted up as a columbarium in the walls of which have been placed cinerary urns to illustrate the ancient Roman method of sepulture.'

The contents of the Sepulchral Basement were much more extensive than those previously housed in Room V of the old Townley Gallery. Among things acquired since the fitting up of the first columbarium was a series of crudely carved grave stelae rescued from the ruins of the museum at Kertch on the Black Sea by, among others, Robert Westmacott, son of the sculptor, who was serving in the British army in the Crimea.[151] Other important additions were the Etruscan cinerary urns, for which the copies of Etruscan wall-paintings provided a pictorial setting.[152]

The Sepulchral Basement has today surrendered its holdings of funerary sculpture to the public galleries, although the name persists and the columbarium still survives, albeit stripped of its funerary remains. At the time of writing it has a picturesque appearance evoking an eighteenth-century fantasy of a museum in ruin.[153] This twentieth-century survival of a nineteenth-century installation has its roots in the picturesque eighteenth-century reuse of the ruins of ancient Rome. In the modern scientifically minded Museum, however, there is no place for such romantic conceits. Indeed, while the new room was in course of arrangement Charles Newton, who was in many respects a pioneer of modern archaeology, complained in a private letter to Antonio Panizzi, Principal Librarian, of what he regarded as an inappropriate manner of displaying funerary art. Such monuments as those then being gathered together by Hawkins should not, he argued, be grouped merely on account of their sepulchral associations. Rather, he preferred to see them placed in chronological sequence among the main series of ancient sculpture, according to their place in the general development of art.[154]

Such, then, was the history of the Graeco-Roman and Egyptian sculptures from the setting up of Saunders's Townley Gallery in 1808 until its eventual replacement by the new Smirke buildings. The later history of these sculptures will be treated in the last chapter, but now we may turn to two other cultures whose discovery in the mid-nineteenth century provided two new and unexpected links in the great chain of art.

7 Lycian Tombs and Assyrian Palaces

At the outset of the nineteenth century Egyptian, Greek and Roman antiquities were the usual stock of museum collections. The art of Greece was thought to have been nurtured in the lap of Egypt, while Greece in her turn was seen as the mentor of Rome. The archaeological sculpture of the Orient and of Meso-America was known in the eighteenth century but was little understood. It seemed, in any case, too remote from Greece to be of any importance. The art of Achaemenid Persia, on the one hand, and of the Etruscans, on the other, enjoyed a certain place in the 'chain of art' as archaic forerunners to Greece and Rome. As for the biblical Assyrians and the Lycians of Asia Minor, the existence of their art was virtually unknown until the 1830s and 1840s.

As so often, the Museum was to owe its massive acquisitions from these new cultures to the energy and vision of remarkable individuals, namely Charles Fellows, as the champion of Lycia, and Austen Henry Layard, that of Assyria. Their achievement marked a turning point in the aesthetic doctrine of the Museum and prepared the way for the eventual shift away from the domination of narrow Hellenism towards the more open aesthetic and cultural pluralism of the modern Museum.

Charles Fellows in Lycia

Charles Fellows was, in the words of Adolph Michaelis, 'the son of a wealthy banker 58
without any vocation' – that is, until he discovered it in Asia Minor. The journal of his first excursion there in the spring of 1838 begins simply with an entry dated 12 February: 'I am now in the Frank town of Smyrna, having this evening set foot for the first time in Asia Minor.' From here he embarked upon a journey that took him first north-east through Mysia to Constantinople, and then south again through Bithynia and again southwards through Phrygia, Pisidia and Pamphylia until he reached Lycia on the most southerly part of his travels. Here he made his way up the valley of the River Xanthos discovering and noting as he went the ruins of the ancient towns of Lycia.[1]

Upon his return to England and the publication of his adventures in the following year, Fellows's discoveries attracted the interest of Edward Hawkins.[2] In March 1839 Hawkins submitted to the Board of Trustees engravings of some of the sculptures and inscriptions newly discovered at Xanthos.[3] Thomas Graves, conducting the hydrographic survey, was then in command of a vessel in the Mediterranean, and Hawkins requested that the Admiralty be asked to give the necessary orders for making good use of the opportunity.[4] The Admiralty, however, felt unable to act without referring the matter to Lord Palmerston, who advised against any action without a firman from the Sultan.[5]

In his anxiety not to lose the chance of acquiring the sculptures, Hawkins took the rash and unprecedented step of himself writing to the Treasury, which duly pledged £300–400 towards the cost of an expedition.[6] For this Hawkins was called to account by the Trustees and severely reprimanded.[7] The Treasury also punished his unauthorised act by withdrawing the offer of money 'because Hawkins's letter had not been sanctioned by the Trustees'.[8]

Meanwhile, in the autumn of 1839 Fellows had returned to Lycia, taking with him George Scharf the younger to assist in recording the monuments. Upon his

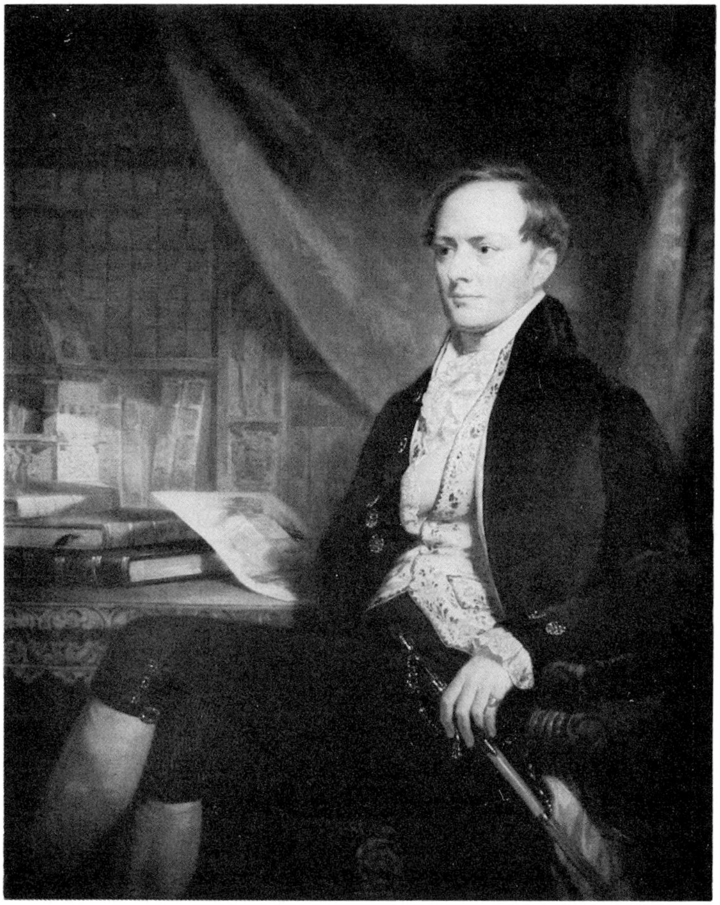

58 Sir Charles Fellows (1799–1860) by John Wood. Oil on canvas, 1850. British Museum.

arrival at Smyrna, Fellows wrote to Lord Ponsonby, British Ambassador at Constantinople, urging the need for a firman by the following spring.[9] No authorisation was forthcoming, however, and once more Fellows returned to England to advertise his most recent discoveries by again publishing his journal.[10]

In the early summer of 1841 he wrote to say that if the Trustees really intended to procure the Lycian sculptures, then they had better do something about it. Fellows warned that he had so far managed to prevent the French and Austrian governments from claiming them but that, 'within the last few months two expeditions have been sent from Prussia expressly to seek further into the remains of Ancient Lycia, one from the Academy at Berlin, the other from the University of Bonn.'[11] Shortly afterwards W. R. Hamilton wrote urging the Trustees to pay the fees necessary to obtain a firman from the Porte.[12] There follows a second memorandum from Hamilton giving precise instructions as to the terms in which the firman request should be framed.[13]

In expectation of the Turkish permit Fellows departed for the Mediterranean. He sent ahead 'Instructions for finding the monuments in the ruins of the ancient city of Xanthus and Lycia . . . ', addressed to Captain Graves who, as officer in charge of the *Beacon*, was engaged in a survey of the eastern Mediterranean coast.[14] Fellows reached Xanthos in December 1841, the later stages of his journey being recorded in a series of letters from Paros, Constantinople and Smyrna.[15]

When all seemed to be going well, however, Canning wrote from the Foreign Office enclosing a quantity of correspondence concerning the proposed expedition and explaining that what had been supposed a firman received from the Porte was, in fact, no more than a vizierial letter giving agreement in principle but asking for more details.[16] It seems this difficulty had arisen because the Trustees had failed to heed Hamilton's advice that in the wording of their request they should make a clear distinction between the Xanthian sculptures and those built into the castle at Bodrum (ancient Halicarnassus).[17] The Turkish authorities were anxious about these last, since their removal would incur the partial dismantlement of a military building.[18] Exasperated, Fellows himself set out for Constantinople, intent upon securing the consent of Riouf Pasha: 'To assume an appearance of authority, of which I had but little in reality, I requested Captain Graves to accompany me in the steam-packet, leaving his ship at Smyrna.' With the assistance of the British Minister Plenipotentiary, Bankhead, Fellows secured his firman.

Fellows and the team of British sailors laboured in the valley of the River Xanthos until the beginning of March 1842. The story of his activities and the many discoveries he made is told in a third monograph, *The Xanthian Marbles, their Acquisition and Transmission to England*, published in 1843.

The *Beacon* sailed for Rhodes on 3 March 1842, leaving behind eighty-two cases of sculpture. Fellows himself returned to England, but the sculptures did not arrive until the following December, aboard HMS *Cambridge*.[19] Fellows was in England by May and entrusted to Hawkins's care a notebook 'for his guidance when the marbles should be under arrangement'.[20] The question of the arrangement of the Lycian sculptures would, as we shall see, give rise to a bitter controversy that soured the relationship between Fellows and the Museum. For the time being, however, Fellows was a celebrity, and the Museum eagerly awaited the arrival of his much publicised discoveries.[21] In October, W.R. Hamilton wrote to say that he had received a letter from Benjamin Robert Haydon, the painter, whose son sailing aboard *Impregnable* in the Mediterranean had seen the Xanthian marbles aboard *Phoenix* bound for England. Haydon's son paid the Lycian sculptures the greatest compliment imaginable in recalling that they had reminded him of the plaster casts of the Elgin Marbles he had seen in his father's studio.[22] Meanwhile other reports of the imminent arrival of the sculptures from Xanthos had reached the Museum, and the Trustees had ordered arrangements to be made for their temporary storage in the basement of the Townley Gallery.[23] It is doubtful whether the sculptures were there for very long, since in January 1842, shortly after their arrival in the Museum, Hawkins reported: '... one interesting monument from the Xanthian marbles has been brought into the Phigaleian Saloon for exhibition and preparations are making for the temporary arrangement of the whole in the same room.'[24]

The Xanthian sculptures did not arrive until very late in 1842. On Christmas Eve Hawkins reported their arrival and stated that they were being cleaned and prepared for exhibition. He requested permission to saw off the superfluous marble and to engage the services of Richard Westmacott to supervise the repair work.[25]

Even before the arrival of the sculptures in the Museum, Hawkins was urging the Trustees not to delay in making the necessary preparations for bringing to England the sculptures left behind at Xanthos.[26] The Trustees duly appealed to the Treasury, which in its turn asked for confirmation that there was something to be gained by adding to the eighty cases of sculptures already received.[27] For their part, the Trustees needed no reassurance of the value of the sculptures, 'as illustrative of the progress of art among the Greeks'. Hawkins, therefore, was asked to draw up a summary of those sculptures that were still outstanding, which included the so-called Lion and Horse Tombs (the latter now known as the Tomb of Payava).[28] Becoming overzealous, however, in his eagerness to acquire as much as possible of this important new body of material, Hawkins not only included sculptures that could be deemed 'lying about' at Xanthos, but also advocated employing a team of sawyers to cut away certain painted, rock-cut reliefs, both at Xanthos and in the other Lycian towns discovered by Fellows. Hawkins was probably acting here at Fellows's behest and it seems that in some quarters, at least, Fellows's domineering temperament was already beginning to grate. A letter from W.R. Hamilton to Sir Robert Peel is revealing and worth quoting in full:

I trust you will excuse my having deferred writing to you respecting Mr Fellows until I had ascertained from him what were his real intentions respecting the monuments in Lycia which he should be unable to remove entire. I find on enquiring that he has not decided what steps to pursue but contemplates the possibility of sawing up the obelisk at Xanthos, having an inscription in Lycian characters on its four sides, if there should be any difficulty in removing it, giving as his excuse that if he did not, the French would soon remove it entire to Paris. My object in troubling you with this application is to express the hope that some means be adopted to prevent such a stigma from being cast on our national character as that of wantonly destroying works of art which we could not remove in order that others might not have the merit of possessing a monument which we were unable to carry off. As I understand that Mr Fellows goes out under the orders of Government, I hope some instructions may be given to him as to his conduct in the matter and he may be told not to mutilate works of art merely for the purpose of facilitating their transport, so as to destroy their integrity or their value, as would undoubtedly be the case in the instance to which I am alluding. Of course, the same objection does not apply to sawing off the back of a bas-relief where the merit does not consist in the mere thickness of the block of the marble as has been recently done at the British Museum. If the French when removing the Obelisk of Luxor had found the difficulties so great, as to compel them to desist from their attempt unless they had cut it in two, and they had carried such a measure with execution, they would have richly deserved and would surely have met with the indignant reproaches of every lover of antiquity in Europe.

I ought, however, in candour to add that my views are not shared by all to whom I have spoken on the subject, and that there are some, whose love and zeal for antiquity is undoubted, who would prefer the mutilated monument in this country, to the risk of leaving it to fall into the hands of the French. I cannot think such motives creditable or worthy of this country and I, therefore, hope the Government will not sanction such a proceedings ....[29]

Robert Peel let it be known in a private communication to the Museum Secretary that he disapproved of such a practice.[30] Fellows was consulted and he agreed that his first object would be to carry on his researches on the ground at Xanthos: '... to continue to pull down the walls built with fragments of ancient art upon the Acropolis by the Romans, to search around an inscribed monument, and to turn over other stones which might lead to further discoveries.'[31] The Trustees ordered that it would be improper to remove any sculpture if there was a reasonable probability that it might remain intact in its original position and free of injury.

On his fourth and last expedition to Asia Minor, Fellows proposed to take George Scharf again as his draughtsman and also this time Rohde Hawkins, a trained architect and son of Edward Hawkins.[32] Their drawings were destined to become the property of the Trustees – having been commissioned by them – although executed under the direction of Fellows.[33]

Towards the end of 1843 Fellows and his team were again labouring on the banks of the River Xanthos, whence the Trustees received periodic reports. A plan of the camp and excavations dated 1 December 1843 was sent, together with a drawing by George Scharf of one side of the monument now called the Payava Tomb.[34] The

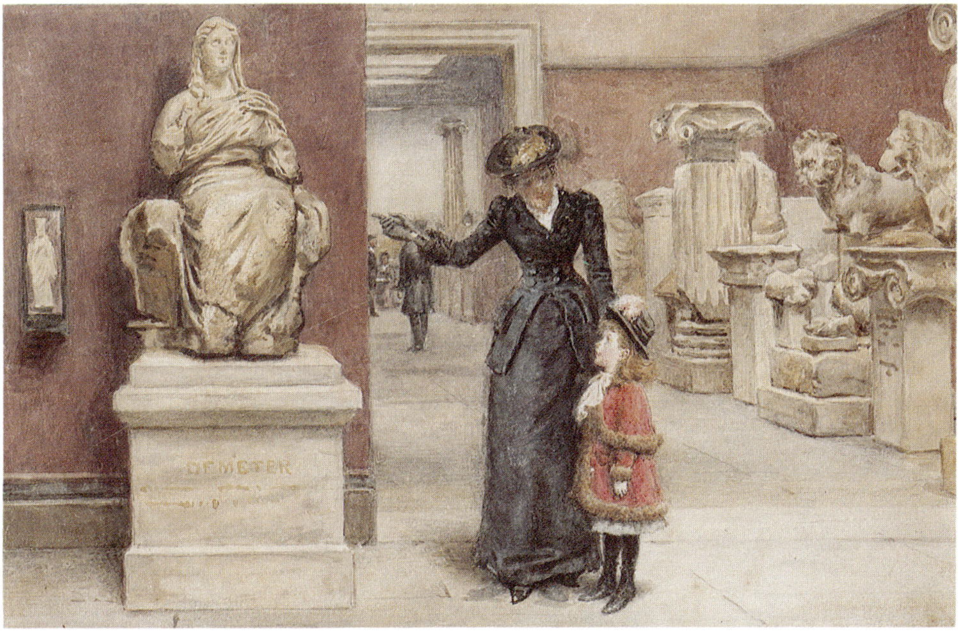

Plate VII The Demeter of Cnidus in the Mausoleum Room (7 on Fig. 1). Watercolour by George Goodwin Kilburne, *c.* 1880. British Museum, Department of Prints and Drawings.

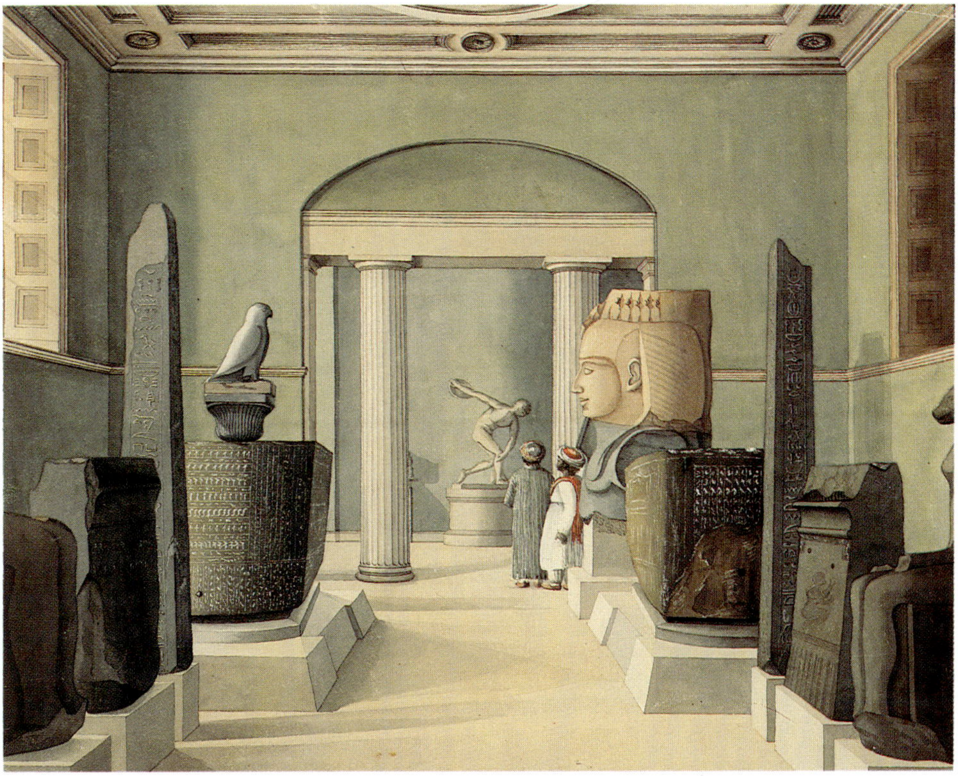

Plate VIII 'A Room in the Sculpture Gallery of the British Museum, February 1820. From a sketch taken on the spot, September 1819': Egyptian sculpture in the old Townley Gallery. Anonymous watercolour. British Museum, PD 1881–11–12–137.

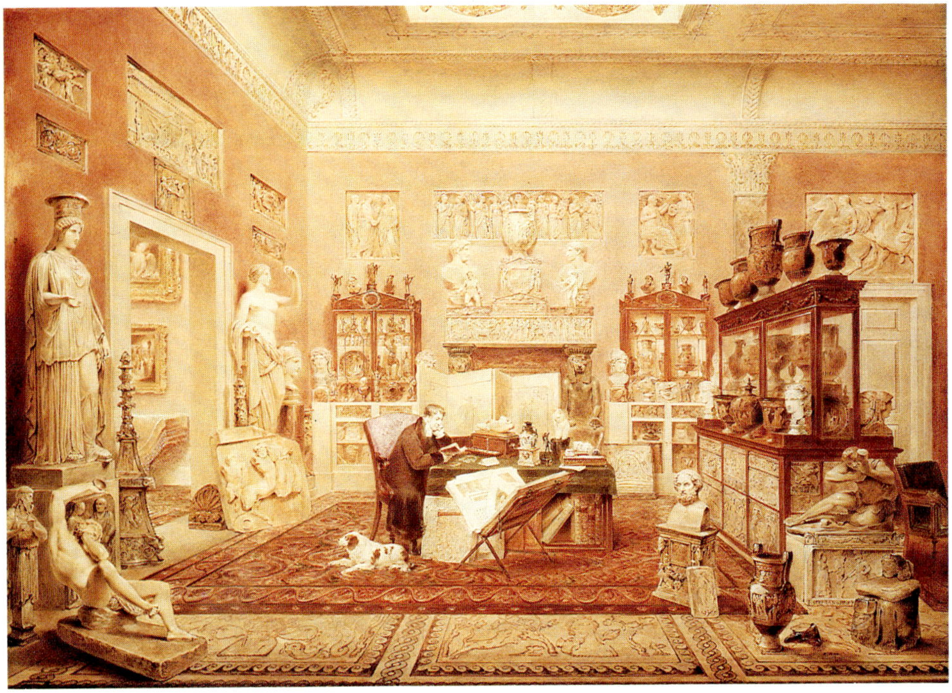

Plate IX 'The Connoisseur', by James Stephanoff, an imaginative rendering of a room in the Townley Gallery, featuring the Townley Marbles and Hamilton's vases. Watercolour, exhibited 1817. Private collection.

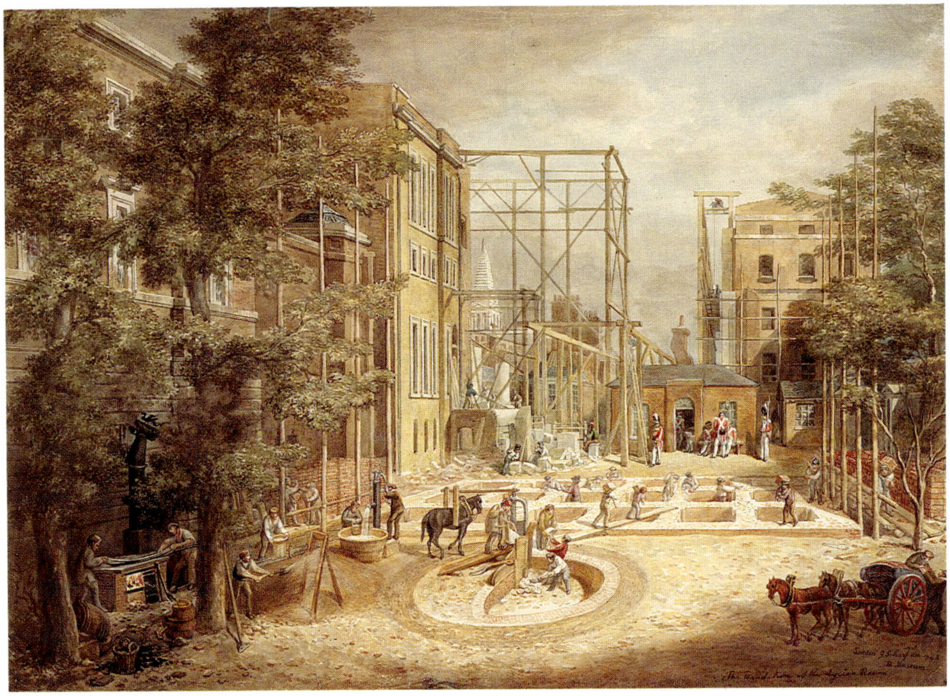

Plate X 'Laying the foundations of the Lycian Gallery'. The room (5 on Fig. 1) was tacked onto the side of the main west wing of the new Museum. Through the trees on the left can be seen the last vestige of the old Townley Gallery. Watercolour signed G. Scharf, 1845. British Museum, PD 1862–4–14–617.

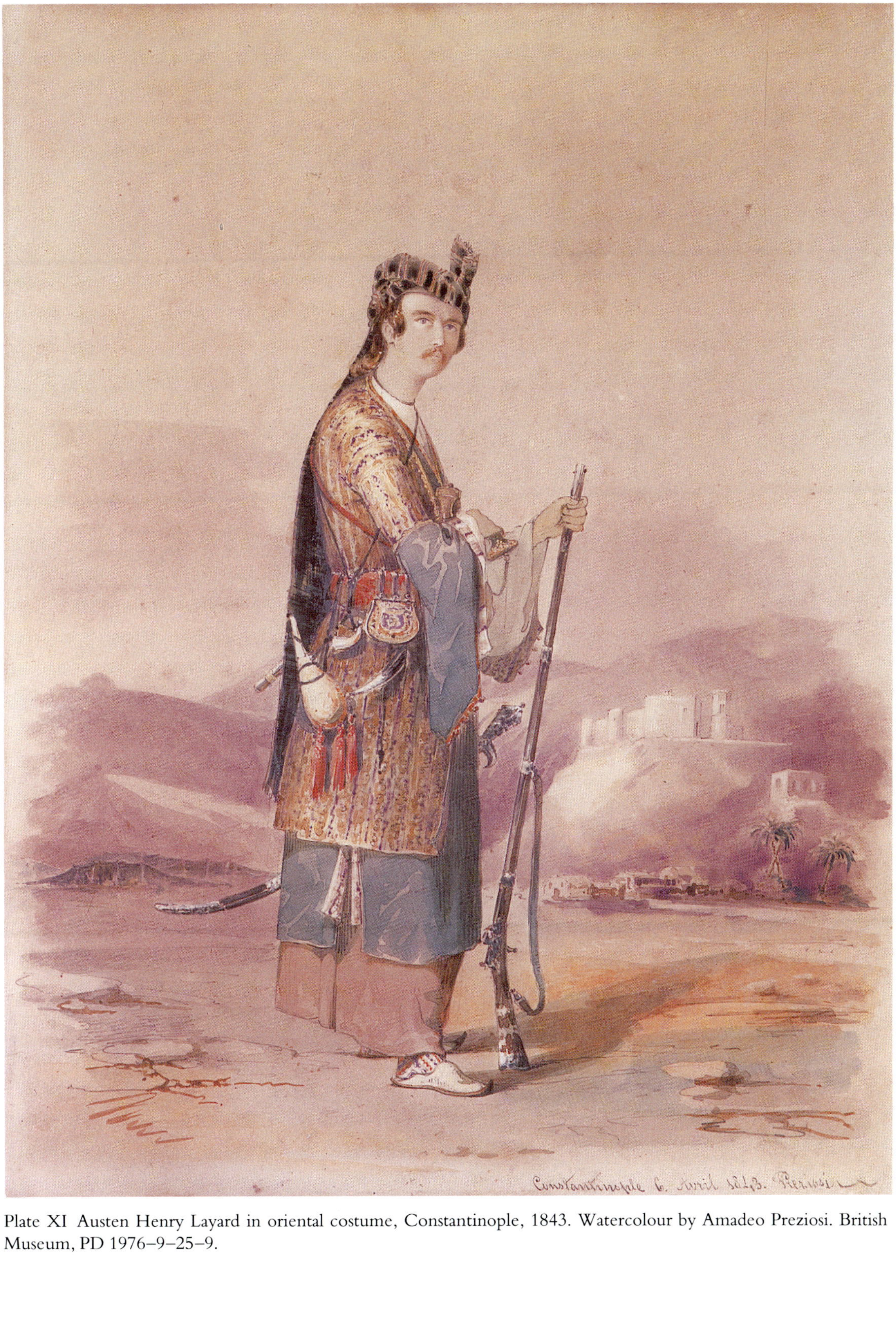

Plate XI Austen Henry Layard in oriental costume, Constantinople, 1843. Watercolour by Amadeo Preziosi. British Museum, PD 1976–9–25–9.

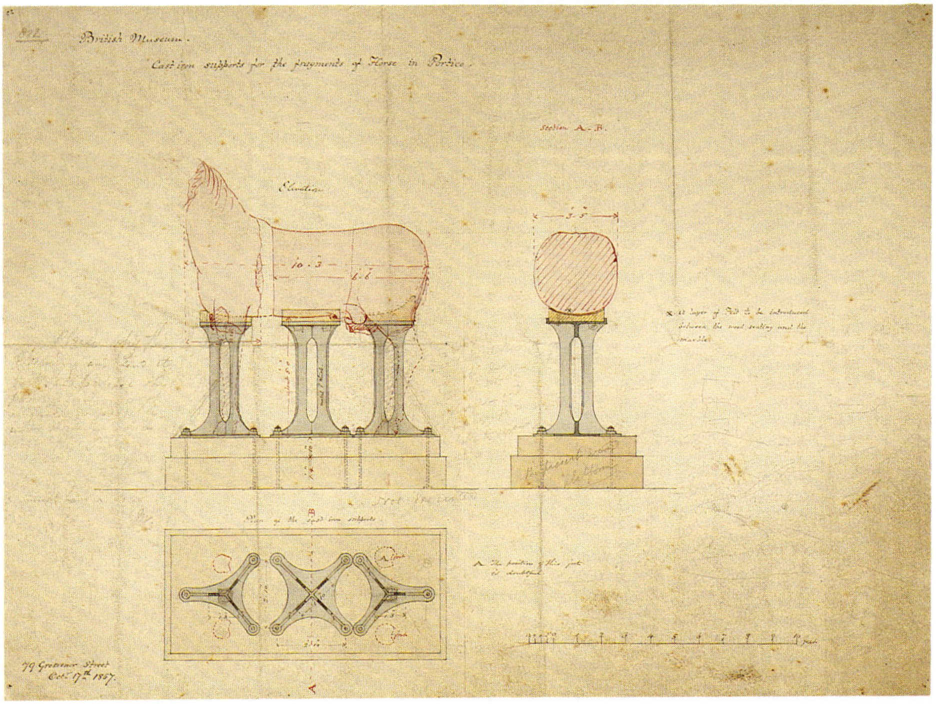

Plate XII Design for cast-iron supports to mount fragments of the colossal horses from the Mausoleum of Halicarnassus, 17 October 1857 (compare Fig. 80). British Museum, Central Archive.

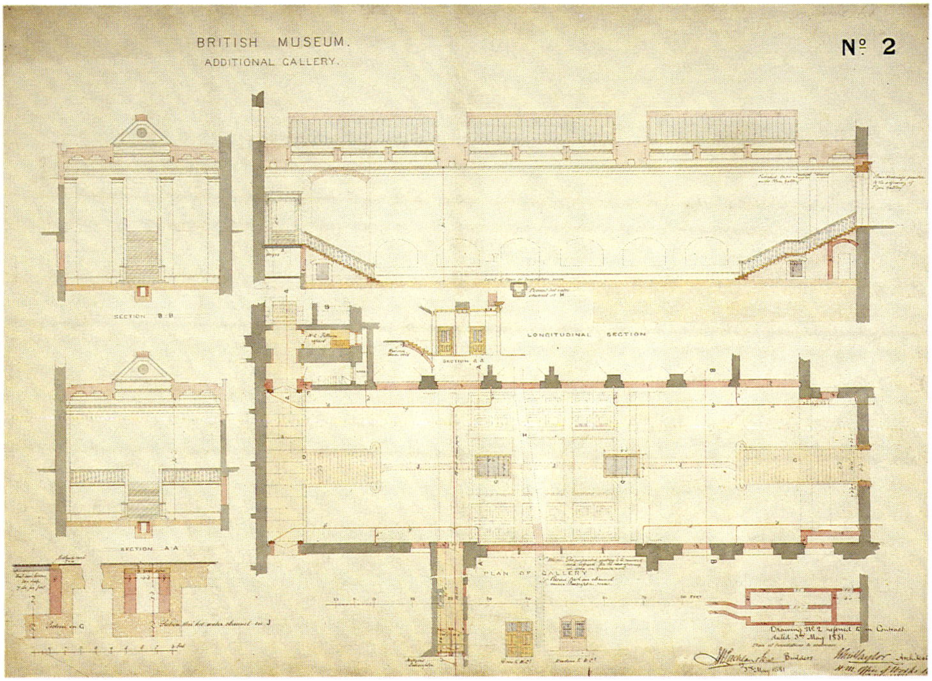

Plate XIII Plans for the design of the Mausoleum Room (11 on Fig. 1), 3 May 1881. British Museum, Central Archive.

season lasted until March, when Fellows and Scharf embarked for Malta, while Rohde Hawkins took a longer route back through mainland Greece, Italy and the Rhine. A number of sketches made on this homeward journey have recently been acquired by the Department of Greek and Roman Antiquities and by the British Library, Department of Manuscripts. The Trustees received a long report from Fellows, dated 30 March 1844, detailing what had been accomplished and stating that all the marbles and casts removed from Xanthos were safe at Malta except for seven crates that had been left behind at the river mouth. HMS *Warspite* had been despatched to fetch them.[35] At the end of June Sir John Barrow wrote from the Admiralty to say that the Xanthian marbles, consisting of sixty cases of sculpture and forty-seven of casts, were arrived at Portsmouth Dockyard aboard *Queen*.[36] Some months later the seven outstanding cases arrived at Woolwich.[37]

The sculptures in the Museum

While plans were being drawn up for a permanent gallery in which to display the Lycian sculptures, a number were temporarily placed in the Phigaleian Room (12 on Fig. 1).[38] The *Synopsis* for 1844[39] lists friezes and architectural elements from what is now called the Nereid Monument and, in the centre of the room, eight of the so-called Nereids. Yet more sculptures were temporarily mounted in the Grand Central Saloon.[40]

A fanciful view of the sculptures in the Phigaleian Room was executed by James 59 Stephanoff as part of his Museum series.[41] This watercolour drawing was exhibited at the Old Watercolour Society in 1843. The arrangement of the sculptures in Stephanoff's drawing is certainly more picturesque and more cohesive than it would have been in real life, bearing in mind that the individual pieces had been scattered about the Phigaleian Room and the adjoining Central Saloon. He has arranged the various reliefs in three horizontal bands topped by a third frieze supporting a pediment. This temple-like structure is flanked by free-standing figures on imaginary bases. The pediment of Stephanoff's construction is crowned by an acroterion modelled on those of the pediments of the temple of Aphaia on Aegina, casts of which were mounted on opposite sides of the Phigaleian Room.

The floor of the room, with its lozenge-shaped inset of coloured stone at the corner of each slab, is very like that of the Front Hall of the Museum . The colour of the walls is the same pink that appears in all Stephanoff's Museum drawings. It is, therefore, a convention of his own, but is perhaps not so very different from the true colour of the walls of the Phigaleian Saloon at this time.

Stephanoff's view of the Lycian sculptures displayed in their temporary setting owes as much to his own imagination as it does to reality. It is almost uncanny, however, how very similar it was to the scheme devised by Richard Westmacott for

the west wall of the eventual Lycian Room. It is probable that the sculptor knew Stephanoff's drawing and was inspired by it. Westmacott's taste for the picturesque 60, 61
was to bring him into conflict with the more archaeologically minded Fellows.

Plans for the permanent gallery were submitted in March 1844. They showed it connecting with those rooms recently erected to form the south front and the southern division of the west wing, yet to be built (20 and 2 on Fig. 1). A gallery in this position (5 on Fig. 1) had been marked on the plan dated 14 July 1836, which the House of Commons had ordered to be printed.[42] It was to be 41 feet wide, the same as the west wing, and 73 feet long. The height was to match that of the Elgin Room. Robert Smirke envisaged the room as being lit by a high lantern, instead of a flat skylight, with vertical windows on both sides of the recess. Thus he hoped to reduce the amount of diffused light, which was an acknowledged nuisance in the Elgin Room, and to create a more controlled and concentrated lighting for the sculptures, which would be arranged in two lines along the sides of the long walls.[43] Robert Smirke changed his mind, however, about the manner of lighting the gallery, when news reached him of the scale of some of the monuments that Fellows was in the process of transporting to England. The only place appropriate for these would be down the centre of the gallery. That being the case, the architect felt it

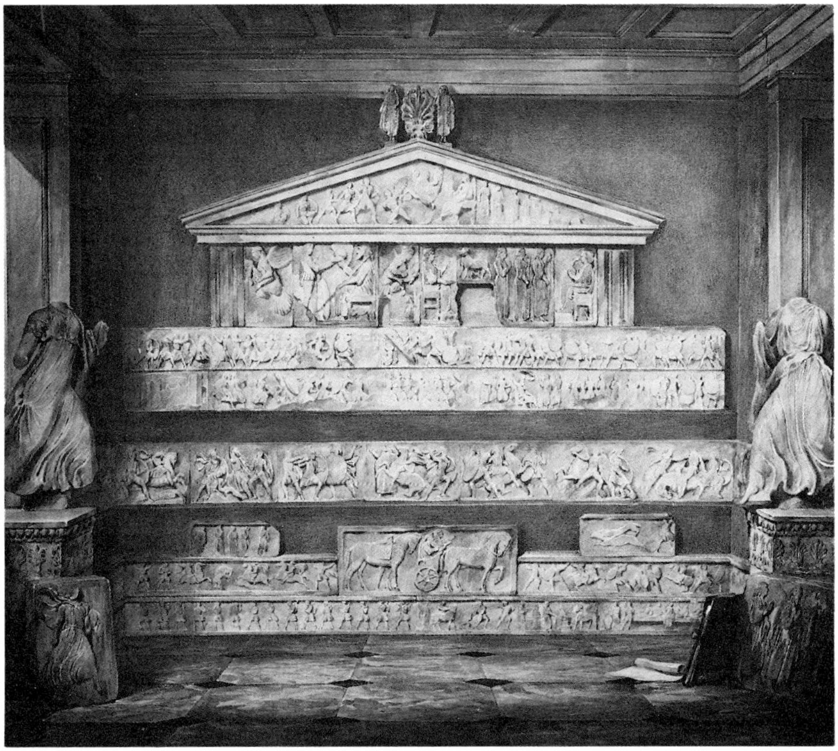

59 James Stephanoff's idealised display of the Lycian sculptures. Watercolour, exhibited 1843. British Museum, PD 1984–12–15–10.

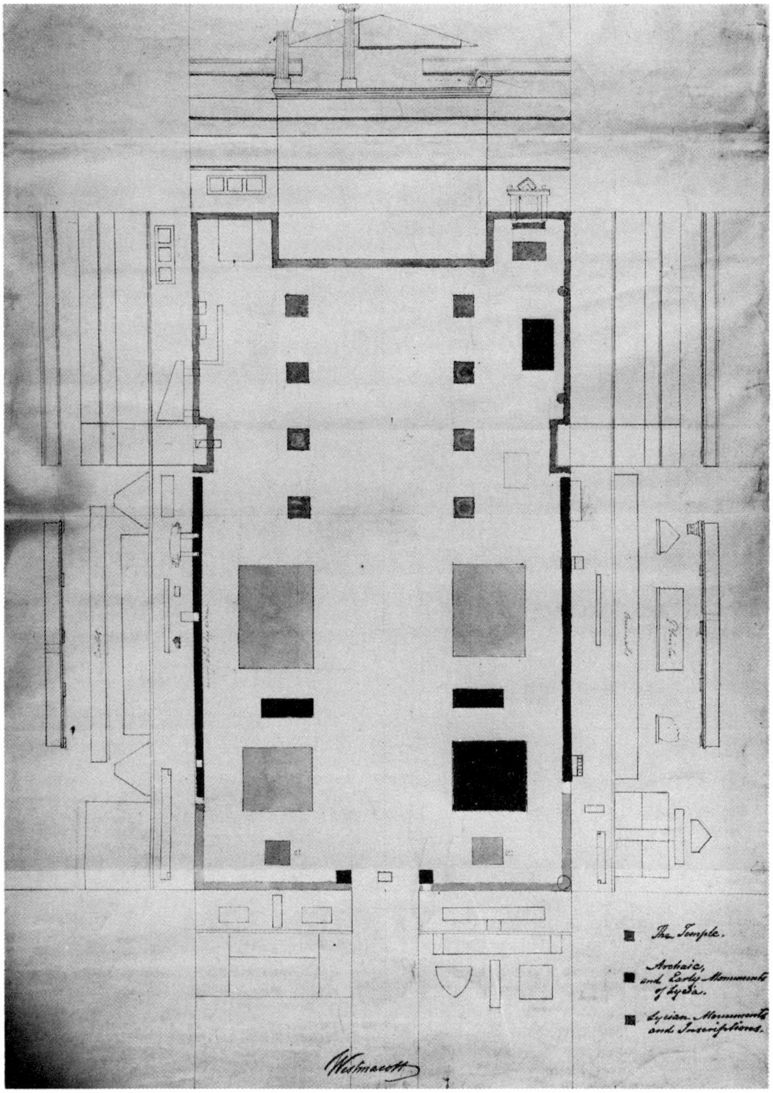

60 Richard Westmacott's plan for displaying the Lycian sculptures, *c.*1846. British Museum, Department of Greek and Roman Antiquities.

would be better if the windows were let into the walls on each side and not set within a lantern above the gallery. In order to avoid the cross-light that would inevitably occur from such an arrangement, he proposed that down one side of the room blinds should be kept permanently drawn.[44]

Already by April 1844 the ground was being prepared for the erection of the new Lycian Gallery. In the course of excavating a cesspool on the site, the remarkable discovery was made of a large quantity of miscellaneous small antiquities, including a number of bronzes. How they got there no one knows, but they are now listed in the Register of the Department of Greek and Roman Antiquities.[45]

A watercolour drawing by George Scharf the elder shows the foundations of the Lycian Gallery under construction, projecting westwards from Room V of the old Townley Gallery, roughly on the site of the former Temporary Elgin Room. The southernmost parts of the Townley Gallery, Rooms I-III, had already been demolished to make way for the south-west corner of Robert Smirke's new building. In Scharf's drawing this can be clearly seen, connected with the scaffolding occupying the centre of the picture, while to the left – partly hidden by the trees – are the last vestiges of Saunders's Townley Gallery, destined to be demolished at the end of 1846.[46] Col. Pl. X

In June 1845 Robert Smirke reported that the ceiling of the new Lycian Gallery was finished, and asked what was to be done about arranging the sculptures.[47] The Trustees conferred and requested Hawkins, Westmacott and Fellows to submit their proposals.[48] Fellows was later to complain that he should have been consulted earlier about the gallery, when the plans were first submitted.[49]

Fellows was most concerned that the sculptures should be displayed with due regard for the original construction of the monuments to which they belonged, and that those which he reckoned to be of native Lycian manufacture should be kept separate from the various parts of the Nereid Monument, which he thought to be Greek. In November 1844 he had presented to the Trustees a paper and a number of drawings detailing the archaeological context and his own classification of the Xanthian sculptures.[50] He later reproduced this document in an Appendix to his *Travels and Researches* (1852), where it is dated April 1844.

Fellows's preference was for seeing the Lycian sculptures collected together in one room and the Greek-style Nereid monument displayed in another: 're-erected as high as the top of the pedestal upon which might be placed the statues and fragments of columns, and within this pedestal might be deposited the frieze, pediments and architectural fragments of the superstructure'.[51] Hawkins also favoured a separation of the Lycian and Greek elements. The latter, he suggested, should occupy the new gallery, while the Lycian monuments might be placed in the Grand Central Saloon.[52] He submitted a plan of the new Lycian Gallery with the Lycian monuments tentatively arranged within it so as to demonstrate the impracticability of accommodating them all in so confined a space as that proposed.[53] The Trustees conferred again, but their eventual decision went contrary to the wishes of Fellows and Hawkins. It was therefore determined that all the Xanthian marbles, whether of Lycian or Greek origin, were to be exhibited in the new Lycian Gallery. The great weight of the sculptures and of the 'chariot' (Payava) tomb, in particular, was to necessitate the strengthening of the floors. This was the origin of the extraordinary cast-iron Doric columns visible today in the basement gallery below the current Room 3.[54] Westmacott was requested to prepare a rough model, as he had done in the case of the Elgin Marbles, showing how he would arrange the sculptures.[55] This was submitted a fortnight later.[56] Fellows was consulted, but there was disagreement and he was invited to submit an alternative scheme. The two models were then compared and Westmacott's was generally approved. Fellows was bitterly to resent the fact that he was not even allowed to see the Trustees on this occasion, but was kept waiting in an ante-room, only to learn of their decision afterwards from Westmacott:

He came out and said that his model was adopted, and that he should do a great many things – alter the monuments to make them perfectly Greek; and that he should put inscriptions from one monument on to another, and asked me if I would help him. I said, 'Decidedly I will not be a party to misplacing anything I have seen in the country;' and from that day to this we have never spoken on the subject of the Lycian sculptures.'[57]

The conflict between Fellows and Westmacott had arisen from two major differences of opinion: first there was Westmacott's insistence on giving greater prominence in the Lycian Gallery to the Nereid Monument at the expense of what Fellows considered to be the Lycian sculptures proper; and second there was Westmacott's tendency towards a picturesque arrangement at the expense of 'the facts'. Fellows had wanted to see the Nereid Monument friezes mounted in four lines on the east wall of the Lycian Gallery, either side of the doorway. Thus, upon entering, the visitor would be aware first of the freestanding Lycian monuments in the centre of the room, the friezes mounted as a backdrop to them upon the west wall.[58] Westmacott effectively reversed the importance of the Greek and Lycian monuments by setting the sculptures and architectural members of the Nereid Monument against the west wall. When, in 1856, the formation of two doorways, one in the south and one in the north wall of the Lycian Gallery, necessitated the displacement of some of the sculptures as arranged by Westmacott ten years previously, Fellows wrote:

I am obliged by your drawing my attention to the rearrangement about to take place of the sculpture in the Lycian Saloon. I have never sanctioned the detail of the arrangement of the Greek friezes, which have now been necessarily broken through by the mutilation of two large doors . . . My idea has always been when I considered that the art of Lycia is strongly marked in its architecture, sculpture, mythology and language, and that the British Museum alone contained specimens of Lycian art, that this character should be all prominent in the Saloon appropriate for its display.

The character of the Room is now marked by an Ionic Trophy monument with its sculptures, an isolated work of Greek art found at Xanthos, and as foreign to the country as the Egyptian obelisk in Paris is to the art of France . . . .[59]

Fellows then added a postscript: 'I perhaps need not remind you that the portfolios of the Lycian expedition contain artistic views, architectural drawings, measurements and that the Museum have the moulds of all sculptured portions of rock tombs, which are the chief feature in Lycian art and that these were collected with great trouble and cost for the purpose of illustrating the art of these early people by reconstructing the tombs in the British Museum – these materials have never been used.'[60]

Clearly it was as the discoverer and champion of ancient Lycia that Fellows wished to be remembered, and not as the person responsible for having recovered the remains of a Greek monument which, for all its historical interest, must be held inferior to the Elgin Marbles displayed nearby. Fellows was at pains to emphasise the relatively early date of the Lycian monuments, which he regarded as evidence for the exquisite artistry of a people who occupied the region of Xanthos before the sixth century BC and prior to the Greeks. In particular, he had in mind the Harpy Tomb, which, ironically, is now thought to be Greek.

In this, the heyday of Pugin's Gothic Revival, when the virtues of pure Gothic were being extolled over those of Regency Greek, it is worth reflecting upon the appeal Fellows's 'Gothic-formed' Lycian tombs may have had in some aesthetic quarters, but – alas! – not in this hallowed temple of the Muses. Fellows's Lycians were to fall foul of Bloomsbury's Greeks, and pride of place was given in the new Lycian Gallery to the single monument that he felt least typical and representative of what had been found.

Westmacott was a Hellenist who considered the Lycian sculptures artistically unimportant. Fellows tended to see things differently. Of the model he made to illustrate his proposal for the display of the sculpture he wrote: 'Mine was a collection of facts which I was tied to; I could not help their being ugly.'[61] Edward Hawkins was by no means afraid of 'ugly facts', and had the arrangement been entrusted to him the result would certainly have been more in keeping with Fellows's ideas. The matter was, however, entirely taken out of his hands, and after preliminary consultation he had no more say in it.[62] 'Sir Richard Westmacott', he later remarked with obvious grievance 'has always been disposed rather to attend to the picturesque effect, than the scientific arrangement.'[63]

When in 1848, during one of the periodic investigations into the management of the British Museum, Westmacott saw which way the wind was blowing, he parried Fellows's accusations of incompetence by questioning his accuser's own claim to science: '... he should bear in mind he is not a professional man, nor an archaeologist. He simply discovered the marbles in his travels ....'[64] This was a mean attempt to discredit his opponent, and the question put subsequently to W.R. Hamilton by the Commissioners suggests they were unconvinced by the argument: 'On what ground do you consider that the services of Sir Richard Westmacott are taken into the employment of the Trustees ... artistic eminence or archaeological science?' Hamilton's reply was as tactful as possible: 'Artistic eminence in the first instance, and as being the best archaeologist among the sculptors.'[65]

There were a number of niggling points of difference between Fellows and

Westmacott, but the main objections were Westmacott's failure to reconstitute the rock-tombs from the casts supplied by Fellows's expedition and the refusal to reconstruct the Nereid Monument. Of the casts, Fellows complained to the Commissioners: 'They are built into the wall, conveying no idea whatever of the tombs from which they were taken. In order to illustrate the art of the Lycians as well as to understand the monuments that we now possess, I think a reconstruction of the rock tombs, introducing these ornaments, is quite necessary; for this purpose I had casts made of all the ornamental parts, and detailed architectural measurements made by the architect who went out, and drawings by the artist.'[66]

A drawing, probably by Fellows himself, shows his suggestion for the disposition of the Lycian sculptures in the new Lycian Gallery. It is clear from this that he envisaged the casts of the rock-tombs as a sort of pictorial backdrop to the free-standing monuments which would suggest in microcosm something of the feel of the landscape from which the sculptures had been removed. The place reserved by Fellows for the rock-tomb casts Westmacott assigned to the remains of the Nereid Monument.

Already in November 1844,[67] before the arrival of the second consignment of sculpture from Xanthos, Fellows had submitted four drawings illustrating his reconstruction of the placement of the sculptures on the Nereid Monument, while in the following month Rohde Hawkins sent in his version.[68] In May 1845 Fellows, only recently knighted, presented a model and plans of the monument.[69] A paper to explain it was requested by the Trustees and subsequently received.[70]

Shortly after the Trustees' meeting took place – effectively removing the arrangement of the sculptures from the hands of the archaeologists Fellows and Hawkins, and putting it into the hands of Westmacott – Fellows despatched his letter of protest, but the important decisions had already been made and the Nereid Monument was not to be reconstructed.[71]

Fellows left England for the Mediterranean in the following October. When he returned a year later he found much to displease him in the arrangement of the sculpture in the Lycian Gallery, and he wrote a barrage of letters to the Trustees in protest.[72] The chief problems lay with the arrangement of the friezes from the Nereid Monument and the manner in which this differed from Fellows's own model. He stated that his authority for constructing the model had been derived from the various positions in which he had found the several parts. Westmacott submitted a long memorandum in his own defence with plans,[73] but the effect of Fellows's outburst was to revive the debate as to whether the Nereid Monument should be reconstructed, and some Trustees were won over to the notion.[74]

Westmacott resisted it and produced an elevation of the building showing the quantity of material that was deficient in the Museum. In particular, he remarked upon the anomaly of there being no architrave between the column capitals and the

Ionic frieze. Westmacott liked his architecture Greek, but he also liked it to be pure Greek, and 'he was disposed to think that some accident must have prevented the discovery of any fragments of its architrave, and that until this extraordinary omission could be accounted for by professional men' (remember Fellows was not one of these!) 'he was inclined to recommend the reconstruction being deferred.'[75] There was also the difficulty, of which Westmacott was to make much in the Commissioners' enquiry, that while Fellows calculated the width of the facade at 19 feet 6 inches, Westmacott – and here he was supported by Rohde Hawkins – found it to be 22 feet.[76]

Westmacott submitted on behalf of his own case a letter from C. R. Cockerell, also remarking upon the lack of an architrave.[77] The Trustees decided to seek the opinion of another architect and called upon Sydney Smirke to comment. He came down against reconstruction, on the grounds of insufficient evidence.[78]

The decision not to reconstruct the monument was therefore upheld, but still a stream of correspondence came in from Fellows insisting on the changes necessary to correct the errors he saw in the arrangement of the friezes.[79] At last a change in the arrangement of the siege frieze was made, but, not satisfied with the simple fact of the 'improvement', Fellows, now seemingly bordering upon the manic, pressed the Trustees to admit that this was done in recognition of himself.[80] The only statement Westmacott would make, however, was the ironic comment that it was done 'simply out of courtesy' to Fellows.[81]

The Lycian Gallery was opened to the public in December 1847.[82] Fellows never recovered from the bitterness that had arisen over the arrangement of the Lycian sculptures and when in 1852 he published an abridgement of his Journals he included a note making his dissatisfaction public, as he had threatened to do in his correspondence of 1847.[83] In an Appendix reproducing a paper he had presented to the Trustees in 1844 he wrote:

> The following Document was a Paper given to the Trustees of the British Museum, together with the portfolio of drawings, plans, and architectural measurements, the result of the Lycian Expedition, sent out to remove the announced discoveries to the British Museum.
>
> As no use has hitherto been made of the information contained in this paper, or of the portfolio of drawings, either in the arrangement of the objects in the Museum, or in making the public aware of their existence as a part of the Lycian Collection, I have, after waiting more than eight years, thought right to offer them to the public in an Appendix to this edition of my Journals.

Thus ended the controversy over the arrangement of the Lycian antiquities. Fellows had lost the battle and was to remain embittered all the rest of his days. The outcome was, no doubt, inevitable, since the Lycian sculptures were too like the Greek for them not to be compared unfavourably and so to be treated as a minor backwater of Hellenic art. The incident would, however, have long-term impli-

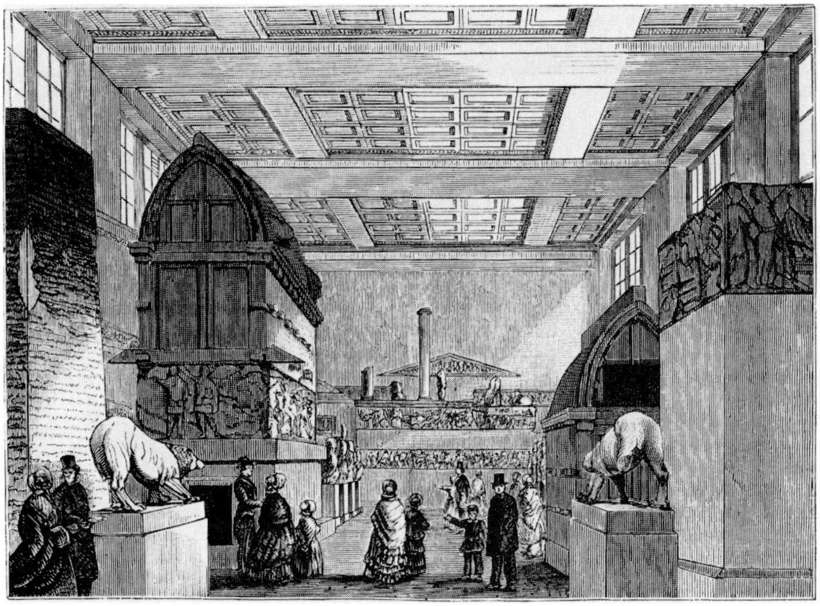

61 The newly opened Lycian Gallery (5 on Fig. 1). Journal cutting, *c.*1848. British Museum, PD 1939–1–16–8.

cations, marking, as it did, the watershed between incompatible attitudes in the display of the Museum sculptures. Westmacott had won, but his victory was Pyrrhic. In a subsequent Parliamentary Commission on national museums his behaviour over the Lycian marbles was called into question, and the pro-Fellows camp in the Department of Antiquities at last had their revenge. Westmacott emerged from the enquiry as a somewhat old-fashioned aesthete unable to grasp the principles of the new science of archaeology.

When it came to evaluating the Assyrian sculptures, however, even Westmacott could not deny their importance. Although they remained aesthetically repugnant to him, as pictorial records of biblical events they suggested a new value for archaeological sculptures as visual history.

Layard in Assyria

On 6 March 1821 Claudius James Rich, English Resident of the East India Company at Baghdad, was floating down the Tigris on a *kelek* from Mosul to Baghdad. Passing the mound of Kalah Sharkat and being unable to make a landing he peered through his glasses at 'a protruding piece of stone carved like the fragment of a statue'. This was probably the headless, seated figure of an Assyrian god – previously thought to be Shalmaneser III – later excavated and brought to the Museum.[84]

Rich's collections bought for the Museum in 1825 contained only two small fragments of carved stone,[85] but his account of the topography of Nineveh, published posthumously by his widow in 1836, is acknowledged to have paved the way for the great French and British expeditions of the 1840s.[86] Having earlier mapped the ruins of ancient Babylon,[87] he was well equipped to sketch and plan the great mounds of Nineveh.[88]

Rich died prematurely in 1821 and was therefore denied the satisfaction of seeing the resurrection of the great sculptures that lay entombed within the mounds. Some twenty years later the French Government appointed Paul Émile Botta as Consul in Mosul. Botta left France early in 1842, determined to take advantage of his diplomatic appointment to investigate the antiquities of the region. In December of that year he began excavating at Kuyunjik, the largest of the mounds of Nineveh. His first efforts were fruitless, however, and in March of the following year he moved his workmen to Khorsabad, fourteen miles to the north-east. Here in a concentrated effort, which lasted until October 1844, Botta excavated a complex series of rooms lined with carved and inscribed gypsum slabs, later recognised to be a palace of Sargon II, erected around 710 BC.

The French Government was quick to realise the importance of Botta's discoveries and equally swift in providing funds. They also sent out an artist, Eugène Flandrin, who recorded the finds at Khorsabad between May and November 1844. These drawings were subsequently published together with Botta's description in five volumes entitled *Monuments de Ninive*.[89] Some of the sculptures themselves reached France by December 1846, and today they are among the great treasures of the Louvre.

While Botta was making his dramatic discoveries on behalf of the French Government, the British remained inactive. The British Vice-Consul at Mosul, Christian Rassam, wrote urging the Trustees of the British Museum to conduct similar excavations at the mound known as Nimrud situated on the banks of the Tigris some twenty miles below Mosul, but his exhortations came to nothing.[90] In the following year Samuel Birch, orientalist in the Department of Antiquities, forwarded to the Trustees two copies of the *Malta Times* reporting Botta's discoveries at Khorsabad in the hope that, 'we shall have some of these Median sculptures, as they are a new feature in the history of art. The remains of these people are most intimately connected with biblical learning and tend to prove the truth of many passages in scripture and elucidate the customs of the Hebrews and other oriental peoples.'[91] The Trustees remained unmoved, however, and it was left to the enterprise and vision of a single individual and his patron to initiate the excavation of the great mound of Nimrud, namely Austen Henry Layard and Sir Stratford Canning, British Consul at Constantinople. Col. Pl. XI

Layard, a qualified attorney, had set out on his eastward journey from England in 1839 in the company of his friend Edward Ledwich Mitford. He had intended to practise as a barrister in Ceylon but failed to reach that island, becoming instead 'a roving agent attached to the embassy at Constantinople'.[92] Already in 1840, in the company of W. Ainsworth, E. Mitford and C. Rassam,[93] Layard had visited Nineveh and had approached an English merchant by the name of Stirling[94] with a view to funding an excavation. Nothing came of this plan, and Layard had departed for Baghdad before any answer was received. On his return journey from that city to Constantinople he once more passed through Mosul and in June 1842 he met Botta, who had yet to begin his momentous excavations. At Constantinople Layard would meet Canning, who was to play a vital role in shaping the younger man's destiny.[95]

From 1842 to 1845 Layard was employed as the unofficial agent of the British Ambassador, Stratford Canning, better known to Hellenists for having removed the frieze slabs of the Mausoleum at Halicarnassus from the Crusader Castle of St Peter at Bodrum.[96] He is less renowned for his role in Assyrian archaeology, having been overshadowed by his celebrated protégé, but he was among the earliest to bring fragments of Assyrian sculptures to England. At the beginning of 1846 it was announced that certain 'marbles' belonging to Canning had arrived at Whitehall and instructions had been sent by the British Ambassador that, if the Trustees so wished, the marbles should be loaned for inspection to the British Museum. Canning believed these pieces to be the first Assyrian sculptures to reach England.[97]

Already before the end of 1845 Canning had commissioned Layard to begin his own excavations into the mound of Nimrud with the aid of local tribesmen. From the very first the excavations were fruitful and were to continue until the middle of 1847. During this time Layard was to work principally at Nimrud, but he also excavated the palace of Sennacherib in the mound of Kuyunjik at Nineveh and conducted small-scale excavations at Kalah Sharkat. The story of Layard's discovery of the sculptures at Nimrud and elsewhere is told in his own remarkable chronicle *Nineveh and its Remains* and in numerous popular accounts deriving from it.[98]

By early spring 1846 many of Layard's first finds had reached Baghdad and from there a list was transmitted to London and submitted to the Trustees by Hawkins in the hope that the sculptures might be purchased for the Museum. The list of fourteen cases and their contents is headed 'Antiquities brought from Nineveh packed in cases now at Baghdad'.[99] In the event twelve cases were transmitted to England, arriving aboard HMS *Grecian* in May 1847. The cases were duly transferred to the British Museum in June and deposited in the room only just completed to the west of the Front Hall (now the Museum Bookshop).[100]

The Museum's claim to these first fruits of Layard's labours had been made possible by the agreement of the Treasury in the previous summer to sanction £2,000 for purchasing 'certain antiquities discovered by persons acting under his [i.e. Stratford Canning's] direction in Kurdistan'.[101] This facility effectively relieved Canning of the burden of financing Layard's activities, for the money was to be divided between compensating him for his expenses to date and financing further excavations. Earlier, in a letter dated 4 June 1846, Canning had expressed to Sir

Robert Inglis his anxieties over the disastrous effect further subvention of Layard's excavations would have on his personal finances:[102]

The sculptures will soon, I trust, be on their way to England . . . Mr Layard my agent continues his operations with good success and by this time is in possession of a firman for exporting as well as excavating. Export, however, he cannot I presume, before Autumn or Spring of next year, and he has no other funds but what I supply at my own charge . . . By the Oriental packet I intend to send some more correspondence and a very interesting sketch of a colossal winged lion with a man's head received by the last post, together with a line from Maj. Rawlinson saying that he can read the cuneiform . . . If the Museum or Government does not come to my assistance, I shall be tempted to club with Maj. Rawlinson and secure the prize, at the risk of utterly ruining the young ladies . . . [i.e. his daughters].

As Consul-General at Baghdad Henry Rawlinson played a key role in the transmission of the Nimrud marbles from there to England. In the summer of 1846 he wrote to Canning at Constantinople notifying him of the despatch of his marbles to Bussorah (Basra) at the Persian Gulf, whence they would be transported to Bombay. This same letter carries a remarkable statement by Rawlinson as to the relative importance he ascribed to the Nimrud marbles in the comparative study of antiquity. He also attempted to allay anxieties in Canning's mind, which he had himself raised by questioning the value of the sculptures as works of art. Canning was not unreasonably concerned, both on his own behalf and Layard's, as to the reception that this entirely new style of sculpture would be given when it reached London.

In a remarkable memorandum, Rawlinson explained:[103]

My criticisms referred exclusively to a supposed comparison of the slabs with the Elgin or Halicarnassian Marbles. I still think the design in general crude and stiff, the execution careless, the grouping confused and fantastic. I am sure, in fact, that modern art cannot desire instruction from the marbles of Nineveh, and that the mere connoisseur in statuary will be offended at the inelegant (sometimes even grotesque) forms. But far be it from me to declare the marbles valueless on this account. I am rather afraid of erring on the other side – afraid that my antiquarian predilections may cause me to overestimate their importance, to regard them with an undue reservation.

The case appears to me to stand simply thus:- of the Assyrian Empire, one of the earliest established after the primitive settlement of mankind, we have at present absolutely nothing. Its history, theology, arts, manners, civilization, language, military skill, political relations are all equally obscure to us. In these marbles we have an index to the whole. They fill up an enormous blank in our knowledge and it is hazardous to say how far they may enable us to carry authentic history. It would be absurd it appears to me, to quarrel with the Assyrians merely because they had not reached in the eighth century BC, as high a degree of art and civilization as the Greeks in the time of Perikles . . . The marbles of Nimrud will be, in my opinion, an honour to England, not in the exclusive department of art, but in that more worthy field, a general knowledge of the early world; and I should indeed be disappointed to find after your Excellency's zealous exertions in the cause that a mere inferiority in their design and execution had led to an abandonment of such extraordinary relics . . . .

Layard was under no illusions himself and had written to Canning to say that he evaluated the sculptures as 'undoubtedly inferior to the most secondary works of Greece or Rome'. But he went on to say that what mattered was the interest they had for the study of literature, philology and history.[104] Even Layard could not predict, however, what the reception of the sculptures would be when they were first seen in England. Soon after their arrival in the Museum he wrote from Constantinople expressing his gratification that the impression made was a favourable one and, 'As they are on the whole the least interesting and important of the sculptures from Nimrud, I feel less uneasy as to the reception of the remainder.'[105]

Layard sailed for England shortly after writing this and proceeded to crown the success of his achievements and to secure his instant fame by publishing his discoveries. In November 1848 he saw a second consignment of his sculptures conveyed to Chatham dock aboard HMS *Jumna* and received into the Museum.[106] The most important piece was the black obelisk of Shalmaneser III, which Hawkins wanted to set up in the centre of the Front Hall. Henry Ellis objected, however, clearly thinking its unaesthetic appearance inappropriate for Sydney Smirke's newly completed Grecian hall.[107]

A third consignment arrived aboard a privately owned schooner, *Apprentice*, in mid-January 1849.[108] These and all further arrivals were to be placed in the basement under the newly built Lycian Gallery (5 on Fig. 1), where they were said to be of such unrivalled interest that an attendant was fully occupied in escorting visitors down to view them.[109] The *Apprentice* brought seventeen cases of sculptures and the headless seated statue from Kalah Sharkat.[110] HMS *Meeanee* reached Chatham in August 1849 with a further twenty-three cases,[111] while the merchantman *Urania* brought a small delivery to England in the following November.[112]

Still there were sculptures remaining at Basra, including the colossal winged and human-headed lion and bull from Ashurnasirpal's palace at Nimrud. These great statues had been floated down the Tigris to Basra on rafts specially constructed with skin bladders in the spring of 1847.[113] They had been dragged to the river on carts drawn, in the case of the bull, by 300 men. Imaginative reconstructions of the scene were featured in the frontispieces of *Nineveh and its Remains*. As C.J. Gadd remarks, 'the closest parallel for the frontispiece of Layard's second volume is the scene depicted on slabs of Sennacherib's palace at Nineveh, showing these same huge stones being hauled into their place by the enslaved enemies of the Assyrians; the wheels of the cart and some details of costume are almost the only difference in twenty-six centuries.'[114]

Since their removal the sculptures had remained at Basra, awaiting transport capable of carrying their great size and weight. Now, at last, *Apprentice*, specially fitted out for the purpose, was despatched from Southampton in August 1849 to fetch them, and returned with her cargo a year later. The lion and bull were set up in

the Front Hall and others placed in the gallery leading westwards (1 on Fig. 1), 62
intended for British antiquities.[115] The other sculptures brought by the *Apprentice* were stored with the rest in the basement of the Lycian Gallery.[116]

Before the end of 1848 Layard had left for the Bosphorus, and from there he sent an outline of a second campaign. Now, however, he had become a rather different figure from Canning's young and unknown protégé. His communication concluded, therefore, with a demand that if the Trustees wished him to conduct these new researches on behalf of the Museum his position in the Porte would have to be established on some official footing. Thus it was agreed that Layard should be appointed Attaché to HM Embassy at Constantinople and paid the sum of £250 per annum.[117] At the same time the Government agreed to furnish £3,000 towards a two-year campaign of research.[118] Part of this was to cover the cost of a draughtsman, Frederick Charles Cooper, appointed as the British Museum's artist at Nineveh from 1 October 1849 until mid-July 1850.[119]

Layard's activities during October 1849 and April of 1851 included the further exploration of Nimrud and of Sennacherib's South-West Palace at Kuyunjik. At the end of this period and on Layard's departure for a new career in England, a number of rival bodies moved in to fill the vacuum left by his exit from the scene. The post-Layard era of excavation in Assyria saw the renewal of French interest in the ill-fated expedition of Victor Place, and applications to remove 'unwanted' sculptures were submitted by a number of European nations as well as from America.[120] British interest was itself represented by more than one camp: the British Museum continued to conduct its activities under the general management of Henry Rawlinson, while in July 1853 the short-lived Assyrian Exploration Fund was set up and represented in the field by William Loftus. Again, early in 1853 the Crystal Palace Company had gained a permit to acquire, at its own expense, sculptures not otherwise claimed. A number of these are now in Berlin.

Further discoveries were made and sculptures too numerous to mention acquired for the Museum, until the outbreak of the Crimean War diverted the resources of the French and British Governments in this part of the world towards other more pressing concerns. Thus ended the great age of Assyrian exploration.

The Assyrian sculptures in the Museum

By the end of 1851, the year in which Layard's activities came to an end, the British Museum had already acquired Assyrian sculptures far in excess of the physical space available for their exhibition. During that year the Museum had received no fewer than four colossal statues including, largest of all, the great human-headed winged bulls procured by Rawlinson from Khorsabad.[121] In a letter dated 16 May 1849,[122] Rawlinson had written to announce that he had recently obtained the two bulls, which had been excavated by Botta but then left exposed by him for want of the means of removing them. Rawlinson had reserved the right to first refusal of these sculptures by arrangement with the French consular agent Guillois. He then resolved the problem of transportation by having each of the bulls sawn into four pieces and each of the attendant figures into two, and so they were brought at last to Basra. He now offered the sculptures to the Museum for the amount of his expenses, which Rawlinson estimated at around £250–300, and the Trustees agreed. When they were at last brought to the Museum they had to be left outside, partially exposed to the weather under the Museum colonnade, owing to the lack of available space inside the building.[123]

In order to understand fully the sequence of events by which the chronic want of space was resolved in order to accommodate the Assyrian sculptures, it is necessary to go back to the year 1846, when Layard's excavations were in full swing but none of the proceeds had yet reached England. Already before the arrival of the first consignment of Assyrian sculptures the Sub-Committee on Antiquities had conceived of a side-gallery (14 on Fig. 1) to the southern division of the great Egyptian Sculpture Gallery, which was then in the course of erection. Such a gallery, it was thought, would be 'extremely desirable for the arrangement of smaller antiquities, if not essentially necessary to the present moment'.[124] In the event the long narrow room destined to be built to the west of the Egyptian Gallery was to prove absolutely necessary, but not for the imagined purpose. Sydney Smirke drew up a plan, estimating the cost at £4,000.[125]

Smirke's original plan was later modified, at the suggestion of Hawkins, to
57 include a 'columbarium' at the south end of the new gallery, south of a doorway in the west wall of the Egyptian Sculpture Gallery. A staircase was to be built in the corresponding space at the north end of the gallery, leading down to the basement.[126]

The southern side-gallery was still not complete when, at the end of 1848, the Trustees requested Sydney Smirke to prepare an estimate for an equivalent room to the north (16 on Fig. 1). He calculated the cost at £3,300.[127] The Treasury was not, however, prepared to sanction the additional expense in the forthcoming year and so the work was postponed.[128] Already before their answer had been received Hawkins complained bitterly of the 'unsatisfactory and disarranged state' of the sculptures in the Museum, and in particular of the fact that the Assyrian sculptures remained invisible and inaccessible for want of a proper room. In light of the Treasury decision he resolved that it would be advisable to place all those sculptures not already displayed in the long room (1 on Fig. 1) leading westwards from the Front Hall in the basement under the Lycian Gallery (5 on Fig. 1). Visitors were to be admitted through the great door at the end of the room, and for this purpose a broad temporary staircase of one flight was to be made from the temporary wooden passage linking the southern part of the new Smirke building with the Central Egyptian Saloon (18 on Fig. 1).[129]

The situation was generally acknowledged to be unsatisfactory, but Hawkins reacted strongly when Sydney Smirke proposed to remedy it by accommodating the Assyrian sculpture permanently in the room then under construction between the Lycian and Elgin Rooms (7 on Fig. 1).[130] The Keeper was determined that this space be set aside for the Greek sculptures, since any intrusion here would seriously disturb his chronological scheme.[131]

Such intransigence in one quarter did not prevent Hawkins from pressing upon the Trustees the necessity for some substantial provision of accommodation elsewhere, and the year 1850 opened with his perennial complaint as to the generally unsatisfactory state of the sculptures, and of the Assyrian sculptures in particular.[132] Sydney Smirke had not yet given up his scheme, however, and it must have been his influence that persuaded the Trustees that, as and when a northern side-gallery was built (16 on Fig. 1), it should be appropriated to the display of prints and drawings. Hawkins discovered this plan only by accident and earnestly beseeched the Trustees to reconsider, since: '... in that situation alone can the Assyrian Antiquities be placed with any degree of propriety, and if that space is appropriated to any other purpose, it will be in vain for the officers of the Department to attempt that consistent, systematic and instructive arrangement of the Museum sculptures which they have been so anxious to accomplish.'[133]

In spite of these objections, the Trustees continued to confide in Carpenter, the Keeper of the prints and drawings collection, that they intended to appropriate the side-gallery for the exhibition of prints,[134] and to reassure the architect that the gallery between the Lycian and Elgin Galleries would be assigned to the Assyrian sculptures.[135] The cost of completing the latter was estimated at £14,000.[136]

At the beginning of the following year the Assyrian sculptures remained in their basement store under the Lycian Gallery, all except the colossal bull and lion which had arrived during the previous summer and, being too great to accommodate elsewhere, had been placed in the Front Hall and the new gallery leading westwards from it (1 on Fig. 1).[137] The southern side-gallery (14 on Fig. 1) was nearing completion, however, and Hawkins sought final approval for his plans. He proposed to place in it the Assyrian sculptures, reserving the new gallery between the Lycian and Elgin Rooms for Greek sculptures. Thus the Egyptian, Assyrian and Greek galleries would be seen in a concerted sequence approached through the British and Roman monuments, and so a 'systematic and chronological arrangement' would be effected, at least so far as circumstances would allow.[138]

Hawkins drew up the general outline of his scheme in consultation with Sydney Smirke,[139] but the details were worked out by Edmund Oldfield who had been appointed as Assistant in the Department of Antiquities in October 1848 and who was to concentrate much of his energy over the next ten years in devising arrangements for the ancient sculptures.[140] A sub-committee was appointed in a supervisory capacity, consisting of Sir Robert Inglis, Sir David Dundas and W. R. Hamilton.[141]

In December 1851 Oldfield submitted through Hawkins two lengthy reports. The first, dated 5 December 1851, accompanied a detailed plan which has happily survived.[142] The plan and Oldfield's explanation seem designed to demonstrate the impossibility of cramming all the Assyrian sculptures into the available space, limited as this was to the southern side-gallery (14 on Fig. 1) and the central transept to the north of it (15 on Fig. 1). Oldfield set out to show the folly of the Trustees' insistence on reserving the northern side-gallery (16 on Fig. 1) for prints, when this would provide the only likely resting place for the Kuyunjik sculptures. As for the Grand Central Saloon (18 on Fig. 1), Oldfield refused to utilise this space for Assyrian sculpture on the grounds that it would incur an unnatural break in the line of the Egyptian sculptures, which were shortly to be rearranged.

He feared the Trustees would insist on placing the great Khorsabad bulls against the east wall of the Central Saloon for aesthetic rather than 'scientific' reasons. To introduce such a solecism would, he argued, be in keeping with the mere magnificence of a palace, but would be unworthy of the 'intellectual dignity' of the Museum. After all, the Assyrian sculptures were 'generally wanting in artistic beauty', and if it was visual effect that was desired, then something more beautiful might be found for the purpose. He proposed to place the bulls against the pillars and

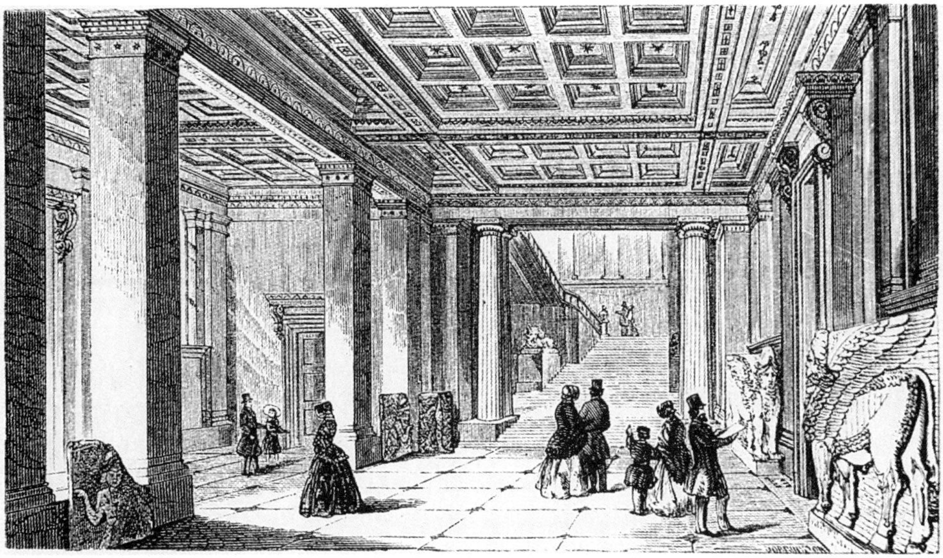

62 Assyrian sculptures in the Front Hall, *c.*1850. *Illustrations of the British Museum*, vol. II. British Museum, Central Archive.

pilasters on the west side of the Central Saloon, where they would flank the entrance to the central transept.

Hawkins put his weight behind Oldfield's recommendations. Wherever possible, he explained, the aim was to keep the sculptures together in the order they were found. Occasionally, it had been necessary to disregard the architectural features of the Museum galleries concerned, 'but as the rooms were made for the purpose of exhibiting the sculptures, and as the sculptures were not collected for merely architectural decorations, where the two come into collision the architecture must give way'.[143]

Oldfield's first Report met with only partial success: it succeeded in impressing upon the sub-committee of Trustees the need to acquiesce where the northern side-gallery was concerned, but failed in respect of the Khorsabad colossi. Otherwise, they largely approved the scheme.[144]

Hardly had their resolution been made, however, when the resourceful and energetic Oldfield submitted a second report offering an alternative.[145] In this he brilliantly countered the committee's determination to use the Grand Central Saloon by offering instead the transept at the southern end of the newly built extension to the Egyptian Sculpture Gallery – the area in front of the Lycian Gallery and known today as the Assyrian Transept.

On this basis Hawkins and Oldfield went to work fixing the Assyrian sculptures in their allotted places.[146] In the course of arranging the southern side-gallery (14 on Fig. 1) Oldfield expressed dissatisfaction with the lighting and persuaded Sydney Smirke of the virtue of glazing the side panels on either side of the existing skylights so as to render the lighting more vertical. This, it was agreed, would be more appropriate for tall slabs of sculpture carved in very flat relief.[147]

At the beginning of the following year Hawkins was able to report: 'The southern side-gallery has been completed and the roof adapted to alter the light for Assyrian bas-reliefs. The sculptures from Nimrud and Khorsabad have been arranged in this side-gallery and in the two adjoining saloons. The sculptures from Kuyunjik intended to be placed in the northern side-gallery are undergoing the repairs rendered necessary by the calcined state in which they were discovered by Mr Layard.'[148] A year later the arrangement of the Assyrian sculptures was complete.[149]

The *Synopsis* for 1856 describes the arrangement in detail,[150] explaining that the sculptures had been placed according to where they had been found and that this sequence also happened to correspond, broadly speaking, with the chronological relationship between the different mounds of Nimrud, Khorsabad and Kuyunjik. It was, however, admitted with some embarrassement that the Khorsabad sculptures, seen as chronologically intermediate between those of Nimrud and Kuyunjik, had necessarily been placed out of sequence in the Assyrian Transept to the south of the main galleries.

No less awkward is the instruction to the visitor that he should enter from the Greek galleries and, finding himself in the Nimrud Central Saloon (15 on Fig. 1), he should ignore the sculptures there until he had first turned left and perused the sculpture in the Kuyunjik Gallery to the north (16 on Fig. 1).[151] Then, retracing his steps, the visitor should re-enter the Nimrud Central Saloon and from there go on to the Nimrud side-gallery (14 on Fig. 1), so that the later Assyrian sculptures were seen before those of the 'earlier' kings in a manner consistent with the guiding principle of the *Synopsis* as a whole. Thus the visitor was led backwards through time, first to the Roman and later Greek sculptures and then to the classical Greek; from there he was directed through the sequence of Assyrian sculptures which terminated in the Assyrian Transept (20 on Fig. 1). Here, turning north again, were to be found the Egyptian sculptures, recently rearranged to run from the Roman and Ptolemaic at the near end of the gallery through to the early dynastic at the far end.

Following the *Synopsis*, therefore, the visitor to the Assyrian Galleries first entered into the northern or Kuyunjik side-gallery (16 on Fig. 1) where the relief

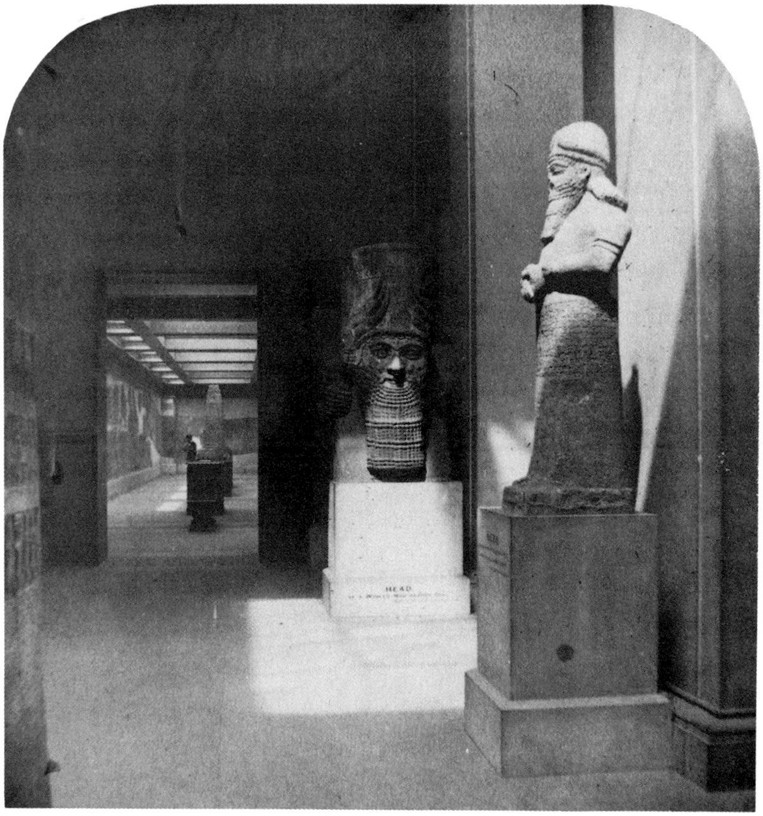

63 The Assyrian Central Saloon (15 on Fig. 1), looking north into the Assyrian side-gallery, *c*.1857–9. Photo by R. Fenton for *The Stereoscopic Magazine*. British Museum, Central Archive.

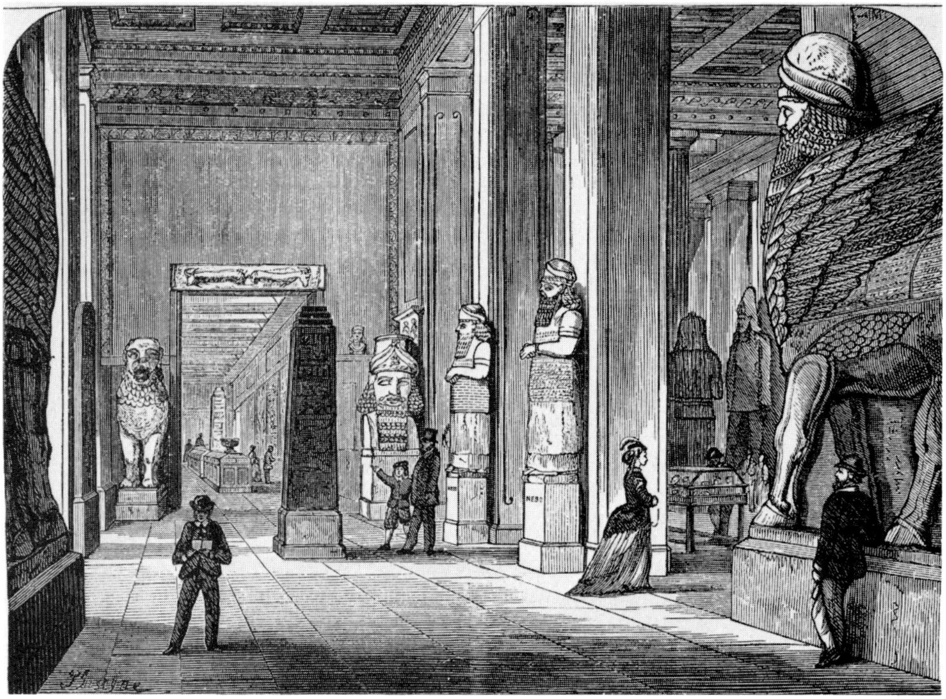

64 The Assyrian Central Saloon (15 on Fig. 1), looking north. Journal cutting, *c.*1854. British Museum, PD 1939–1–16–10.

sculptures lining the walls were chiefly those excavated by Layard in 1849–50 from the palaces of Sennacherib and his grandson Ashurbanipal. At this time the dates of Sennacherib's reign were calculated as 716–698 BC, while Ashurbanipal was dated to around the middle of the seventh century BC. They are now dated more accurately to 704–681 BC and 668–627 BC, respectively.

In the middle of the room was placed the White Obelisk,[152] showing the exploits of one of the early Assyrian kings, perhaps Ashurnasirpal I (1049–1031 BC), whom Rawlinson called Sardanapalus the Great.[153] At the northern end of the room was placed the Broken Obelisk;[154] to the south was placed the so-called Circular Bowl.[155]

On the walls of the adjoining transept, the so-called Nimrud Central Saloon (15 on Fig. 1), were mounted relief sculptures excavated by Layard in 1847 and 1850

65 (*Opposite, top*) The Assyrian Transept (20 on Fig. 1): moving the colossal human-headed and winged lions into place. Bonomi (1852), frontispiece.

66 (*Opposite, bottom*) The Assyrian Transept, *c.*1854. *Illustrations of the British Museum*, vol. II. British Museum, Central Archive.

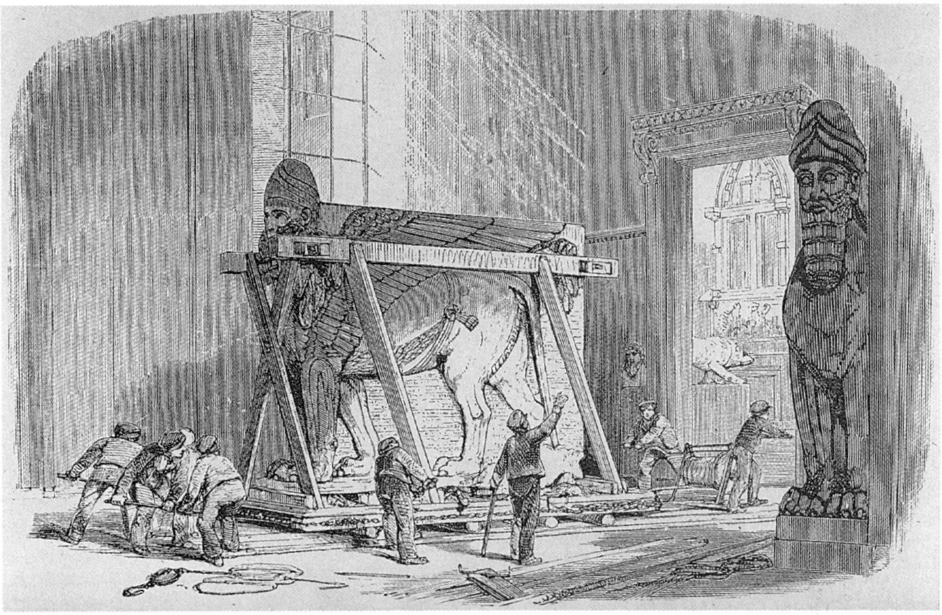

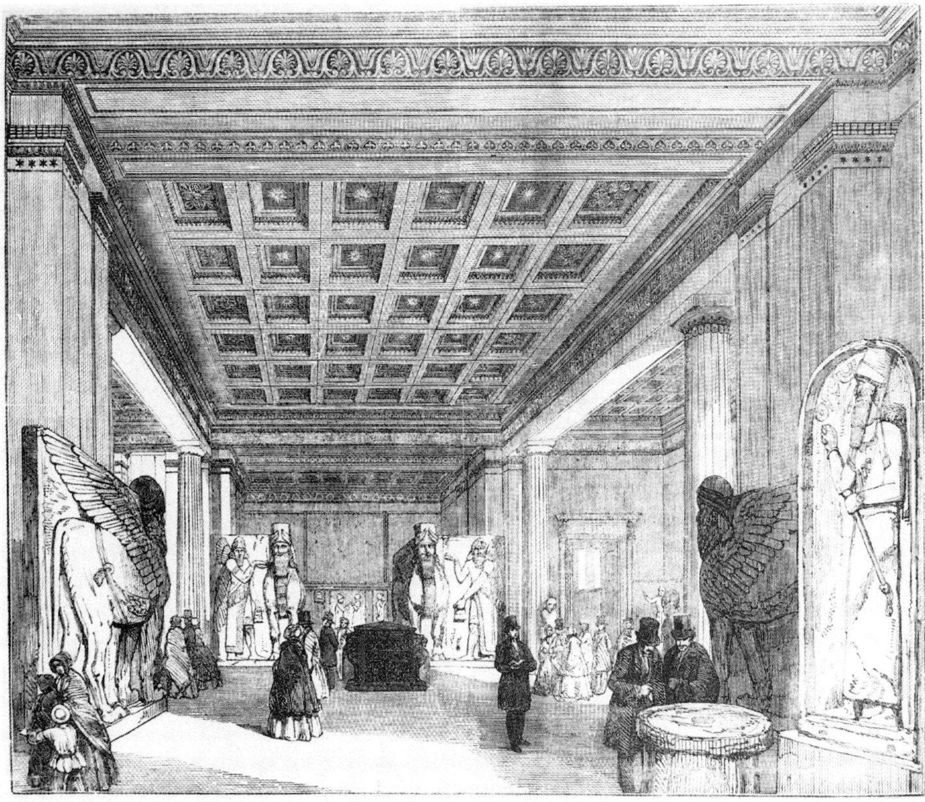

from the great mound at Nimrud. To the west of the doorway leading from the Kuyunjik Gallery was placed the colossal lion, originally one of a pair that had stood at the entrance to the shrine of Ishtar at Nimrud, while on either side of the corresponding doorway on the southern side of the room were placed, as today, the colossal human-headed winged bull and lion from the ruins of the North-West Palace. In the centre of the room stood the Black Obelisk of Shalmaneser III.[156]

Through the door on the south side of this room the visitor reached the southern or Nimrud Side-Gallery (14 on Fig. 1). On the west wall were placed the bas-reliefs from the North-West Palace of Ashurnasirpal II, which continued onto the east wall.

The south doorway led into the Assyrian Transept (20 on Fig. 1). Against the pilasters on the western side of the room stood the two colossal human-headed and 65–6
winged lions that originally flanked the entrances to one of the rooms of the North-West Palace. Against the pilasters on the opposite side of the room were to be found the great Khorsabad bulls and their attendant figures. On the east wall were placed the bas-reliefs from Khorsabad acquired by Mr Hector, a merchant at Mosul.[157]

Such, then, was the arrangement of the Assyrian Sculpture Galleries, which had been almost a decade in the making. Hardly a year passed, however, after their completion before yet more sculptures began to arrive, the fruit of excavations conducted by Hormuzd Rassam and W. Loftus under Rawlinson's superintendence at Nimrud and Kuyunjik.[158] No provision had been made for exhibiting these, and Hawkins complained that there was not even a convenient place for their unpacking.[159] Still more sculptures arrived in the following year,[160] and the problem of accommodation became acute. Three months later Loftus announced that another consignment of Assyrian sculptures[161] had been disembarked at Le Havre for conveyance to England aboard the British steamship *Soho*.[162] The French had conveyed these sculptures from Basra (via Bombay and the Cape) in exchange for a share in the wealth of material unearthed by the British excavations at Nimrud and Kuyunjik. The *Manuel* had been chartered by the French in the first instance to bring home the great collection of sculptures and other antiquities from Victor Place's renewed excavations at Khorsabad. As it turned out, however, the ship sailed from Basra with a greater proportion of antiquities for Britain than for France, since much of Place's sculpture was wrecked and lost in the course of being floated down the river.

The British consignment reached London Bridge docks on, or around, 16 June. Gadd reports that upon being transferred to the Museum the sculptures had to be stored in cellars for want of space. They did go into a basement, but by way of a temporary exhibition, since the public were, in fact, admitted to see them.[163]

As early as December 1855, an estimate was submitted to the Building Committee for glazing over the open area between the 'main building and the Greek

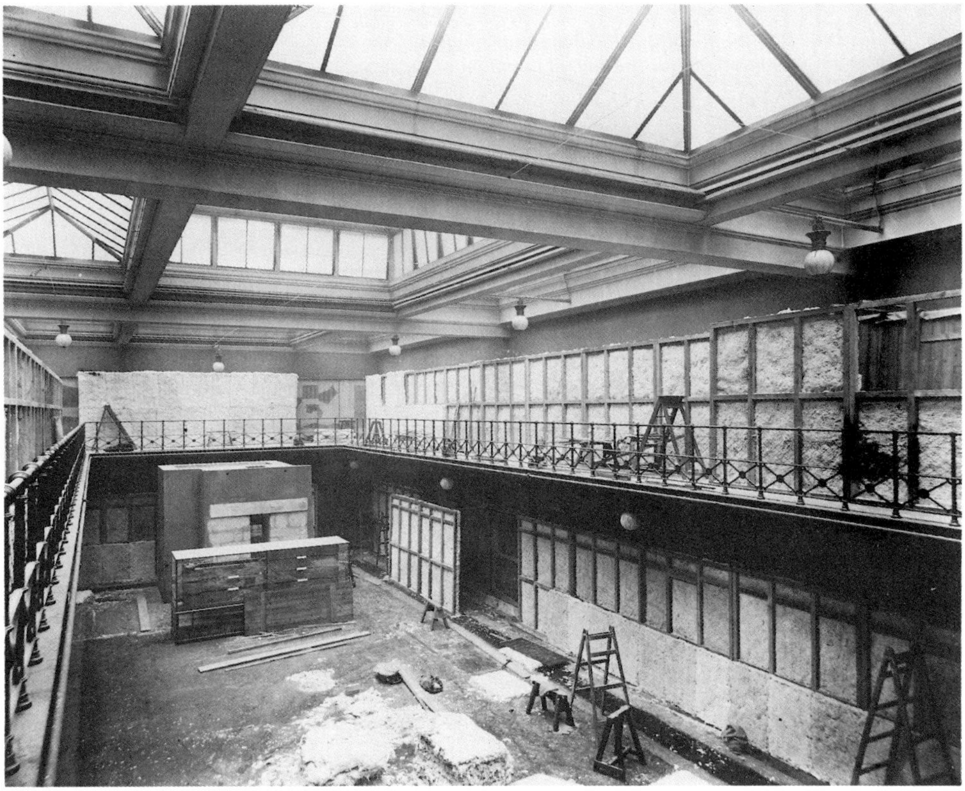

67 The Assyrian Basement Room (13 on Fig. 1) protected against bombing, *c.*1915. Today this space is divided by a mezzanine floor and internal cross walls. Photo by D. Macbeth. British Museum, Central Archive.

Gallery' and converting it into a place for the exhibition of the new sculptures.[164]
67 This gallery, to become known as the Assyrian Basement Room, was constructed in 1857–8 to the west of the Nimrud Gallery (13 on Fig. 1). The building was completed towards the end of 1859 and by the beginning of the next year the sculptures had been installed.[165] In the main room were placed the reliefs from the South-West Palace of Sennacherib at Kuyunjik, together with the hunting reliefs from Ashurbanipal's Palace. In the passage at the foot of the stairs that led down to the Assyrian Basement Room were placed the reliefs illustrating the military campaigns of Tiglath-Pileser III, removed by Rassam from Nimrud.

Since the nineteenth century the Assyrian Basement Room has undergone considerable alteration. It now comprises an upper and a lower floor, with internal divisions of a labyrinthine complexity worthy of the Assyrian palaces themselves. In general, however, of all the sculpture galleries of the Museum, the Assyrian have most retained their nineteenth-century character.

8 Charles Newton and the Sculptures from Asia Minor

The 'Canning Marbles'

Early in 1844 Charles Somers (Lord Eastnor), acting on behalf of Stratford Canning (later Lord 1st Viscount de Redcliffe), HM Ambassador at Constantinople, was granted the rare privilege of entering the gates of the old Crusader Castle of St Peter at Bodrum. The firman obtained by Canning allowed him to view, but not on this occasion to remove, the classical bas-reliefs and other sculptures that had been incorporated into the walls of the castle by the Hospitaller Knights of St John, probably at the very end of the fifteenth and in the early part of the sixteenth century.[1] These sculptures were believed to have originated from the Mausoleum of Halicarnassus constructed around 350 BC to house the remains of King Mausolos and other members of the Hekatominid dynasty of ancient Caria. The tomb was designated in antiquity as one of the seven wonders of the world. It was probably in 1494 that the Christian community occupying the Castle of Bodrum uncovered the remains of the Mausoleum during the repair and extension of their defences.[2] Sculptures and architectural members from the site of the Mausoleum were either burnt for lime to make mortar, or reused as building blocks. In addition, in an age of burgeoning classical sensibilities, they were used to decorate the external and internal walls of the castle. Thus, as A. Luttrell remarks, 'the Amazon frieze slabs . . . must have created a unique and impressive gallery of classical sculptures.'[3] Some sculptures, indeed, found their way into actual galleries. Fr. Constanzo de Opertis, Captain of the castle from 1505 to 1507, may have been the Hospitaller responsible for the export to Italy of a well-preserved piece of Amazon frieze later purchased by the British Museum from the collection of the Marchese di Negro at Genoa.[4]

We gain an inexact impression of the effect of the sculptures displayed on the castle walls from Luigi Mayer's composite view of the interior published in 1797.[5] It was difficult for European visitors to obtain permission to see the sculptures once the castle had passed into Turkish hands. Among the earliest and the most important of the eighteenth-century visitors was Richard Dalton who, while accompanying Lord Charlemont's tour of Greece and Italy in 1749, gained access to the interior of the castle and so made a number of detailed drawings of the sculptured friezes.[6] These were subsequently published as engravings.[7] Some of the original drawings survive in the Department of Greek and Roman Antiquities at the British Museum, while others have recently come to light in the library of Sir John Soane's Museum. Other visitors had to content themselves with viewing only those sculptures visible on the external wall of the castle overlooking the harbour. These, it seems, were three pieces of the Amazon frieze arranged around a Crusader shield and one slab of the centaur frieze.[8]

Previous attempts to secure the marbles are recorded in a letter addressed by Captain James Mangles to Captain Beaufort of the Admiralty, dated 1 December 1840:

> ... In 1816 Mr. Bankes obtained a firman to have the sculpted marbles removed from the castle walls ... The order, however, was so vaguely worded that the Pasha who commanded at Bodroume refused to permit the marbles to be removed. In 1818 Capt. Irby and I, being at Constantinople, offered to Sir Robert Listor, our ambassador (provided he provide a firman) to remove those marbles at our own expense and to present them gratuitously to the British Museum. We could not, however, persuade Sir Robert to comply ....[9]

Now, it was thought, was the time for a third attempt. And, indeed, never since the acquisition of the Elgin Marbles had there been a more propitious moment. After years of estrangement, British foreign policy was again drawing the British and Ottoman empires closer together. In 1838 the Anglo-Turkish commercial convention opened up the eastern Mediterranean to British merchants, and in prohibiting all monopolies allowed Britain to trade anywhere in the Ottoman empire. In 1840 a convention was drawn up between Austria, Prussia, Russia, Britain and Turkey for the pacification of the Levant, and the above-mentioned Captain Mangles saw the recent capture of Acre by the British as an event offering an advantage as great as that given to Lord Elgin by the capture of Egypt. The archaeological opportunities provided by improved Anglo-Turkish relations were not lost on Sir Stratford Canning, Britain's able ambassador to the Sublime Porte.[10] Canning has already been mentioned for his patronage of Layard in the early stages of his Assyrian excavations, but he also deserves to be remembered for his own efforts to enhance the classical collections of the British Museum. His involvement with the Amazon frieze of the Mausoleum was direct and personal.

Canning's attempts to acquire the sculptures from the castle began in 1844, but were not successful until two years later. On 19 February he wrote to Sir R. H. Inglis from Constantinople informing him that he had at last been able to secure the long-coveted Bodrum Marbles and that he had placed them on board HMS *Siren* bound for Malta. His intention was to present the sculptures to the British Museum.[11] Some months later Inglis sent to the Museum a portfolio of drawings he had received illustrating both the Bodrum, or Canning Marbles as they were now known (in spite of the fact that they had been presented in the name of the Sultan), and the Assyrian sculptures excavated at his expense by Layard.[12]

In late July or early August the Canning Marbles were transmitted from Malta to

Portsmouth aboard HM Steamship *Acheron*, and from there to Woolwich.[13] The sculptures were brought into the Museum from the Thames between 5 and 9 September and the Trustees despatched to Canning their thanks for this present. In the same letter they sanctioned Layard's activities in Kurdistan to the sum of £2,000.[14]

Once in the Museum, the twelve slabs from the Mausoleum frieze were temporarily arranged in the Phigaleian Room. Permission was first given and then withdrawn for the backs of the sculptures to be sawn away, so as to reduce their weight.[15] In 1848 the Prussian Consul General had written enclosing a request for casts of the marbles.[16] There were none then available but it was resolved in the following April that the frieze should be moulded and that twelve sets be put at the disposal of Canning.[17] These were not ready, however, until the summer of 1851.[18]

Acquisition of so large a part of the Mausoleum frieze prompted the Trustees to attempt to buy a stray piece known to be in the so-called Villetta of the Marchese di Negro at Genoa.[19] How and when this piece reached Italy is not known, but it was probably removed from Bodrum by one of the Hospitallers of St John in the fifteenth or early sixteenth century.[20]

An offer of £200 for the piece, made through Émile Braun, Secretary of the Archaeological Institute of Rome, failed to interest the owner.[21] Nearly a decade later Sir Charles Eastlake suggested that the attempt should be renewed, and the Sub-Committee on Antiquities recommended to the General Meeting of Trustees that £500 should be pledged for the purpose.[22] All that was offered, however, was a £40 increase on the sum of the previous attempt and, once again, the project failed.[23] Six years later, when Charles Newton was at the helm of the Department of Antiquities, a more determined effort was made, and the Genoa slab was purchased through Consul Brown for £720.[24] It arrived safely in the Museum later that same summer.[25]

This was, however, among the least of Newton's achievements, for in the decade preceding this purchase, during the course of diplomatic service in the eastern Mediterranean, he was largely responsible for the acquisition by the British Museum of huge quantities of excavated sculpture, inscriptions and other antiquities from Halicarnassus, Cnidus, Didyma and elsewhere. Newton's personality and career is so inextricably bound up with the major sculpture acquisitions of the 1850s and 1860s that a brief biographical sketch must be given as a necessary prelude to the story of the acquisitions themselves.

C. T. Newton KCB

68 Charles Newton, destined to become one of the great figures of nineteenth-century British archaeology, was born in the year in which the British Museum acquired the Elgin Marbles, 1816.[26] He was educated at Shrewsbury School and in 1833 went up to Christ Church, Oxford, where Ruskin was a fellow undergraduate. Later, in his *Praeterita*, Ruskin remarked upon Newton's 'intense and curious way of looking into things'.[27] His apparent suitability for a career in the new and growing science of archaeology was eventually brought to the attention of the British Museum at a time when new men were being recruited into the Museum service to cope with an ever-increasing work-load in the Department of Antiquities.

In January 1840 Edward Hawkins had written to the Trustees requesting two additional subordinate officers:

> There is more than fully sufficient employment for two such persons in arranging, cataloguing and illustrating the various coins and antiquities. If young men were appointed to such situations, they would gradually become well-acquainted with the history of our various acquisitions and familiar with the peculiar business of this institution; the Depart-

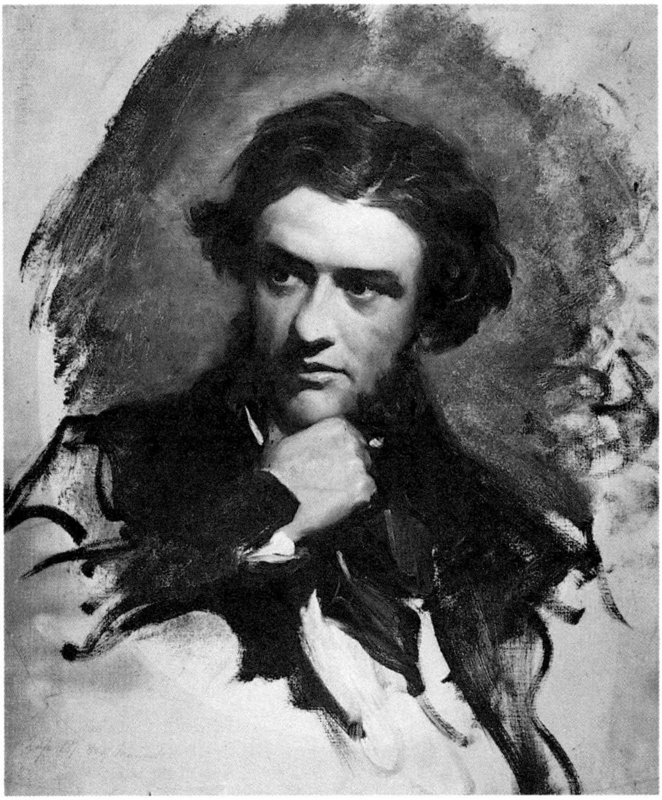

68 Charles Newton (1816–94), Keeper of Greek and Roman Antiquities 1860–86, by Henry Wyndham Phillips. Oil on canvas, *c.*1850. British Museum, Department of Greek and Roman Antiquities.

ment would become a sort of school of archaeology; and the young men would be qualifying themselves to succeed in due time to the higher stations, or to undertake management of some of the numerous Museums which are rising up in all our own great towns.[28]

Two Reverend gentlemen were to secure Newton's selection as one of Hawkins's new 'young men'. The Rev. Dr Philip Bliss at Oxford recommended Newton to Rev. William Cureton, Assistant Keeper in the Department of Manuscripts at the British Museum.[29] Newton was appointed on 10 March 1840, and William Vaux on 13 April 1841. Three years after he had first submitted his request, and well pleased at the diligence of his young protégés, Hawkins wrote again expressing his satisfaction at the

excellence of the system adopted by the Trustees of introducing as assistants into the higher departments of the Museum young men possessing a liberal and classical education, a taste for the particular branch of art and literature in which they are engaged, and early habits of diligent application to study, qualifications absolutely necessary to take full advantage of the great and unrivalled opportunities of practical acquaintance with the subjects of their investigations, by which alone they can become accomplished Archaeologists and hope to acquire that distinguished reputation which ought to belong to the British Museum.[30]

The discipline was indeed a rigorous one and poorly paid. In 1851, after ten years' service, Newton's annual income was £215.[31] To reach a modern equivalent this may be multiplied by sixty, giving a sum hardly designed to add incentive beyond the employee's love of scholarship, as Hawkins was himself to complain to the 1848 Select Committee appointed to investigate the management of the Museum. Newton had therefore been obliged to supplement his income from private means.

The work itself was often tedious, and Hawkins's monthly reports to the Trustees record with regular monotony the years of toil Newton spent in the routine writing of tickets for the seemingly inexhaustible coin collection. Newton saw the necessity of this work and valued the skills that so much concentrated effort brought him, especially in the fields of numismatics and epigraphy. More to his liking, however, were the periods of detachment from the Medal Room spent editing for the press several Museum publications, namely the ninth and tenth parts of *Museum Marbles*, the preface to the *Select Papyri*, the first volume of the *Catalogue of Vases* published in 1851 and the second volume, not published until 1870. In 1856 when Newton was about to begin his campaign of excavation at Bodrum, he wrote to Panizzi a long letter detailing his prescription for an 'ideal Keepership', if and when the post should become vacant at the Museum. He confessed that in the study of archaeology it had always been what he called its 'literary interest' that had most attracted him. By that he meant the quiet activities of research and publication as opposed to the many administrative tasks which tend to fragment the working day of the Museum curator.[32]

In the summer of 1848, Newton had enjoyed a rare respite from his Museum duties when he was allowed three months' special leave to visit Naples, Rome and Athens 'to examine antiquities in situ'.[33] His subsequent report is still preserved in manuscript in the library of the Department of Greek and Roman Antiquities. It was much praised by the Keeper.[34]

Newton returned to the Museum for a little over three years more, before leaving for the adventure of a post in the Foreign Service as Vice-Consul at Mytilene on the island of Lesbos. His departure did not, however, remove him from Museum service, and through this relatively minor diplomatic appointment he was to achieve far more in the interests of the Museum, and indeed of his own career advancement, than would have been possible had he remained at home. From many hours spent listing the harvest of their labours, he knew how much the fame of the Museum's collections depended upon the efforts of a long and distinguished line of archaeologically minded envoys: men who had exploited the political advantages of the country they represented to endow its national repository of the arts. He had done well, therefore, in gaining through his friend General Fox what he coyly described in a letter to his old patron Dr Bliss as 'a small Consulship'. In fact, Newton was fully aware of the advantage his new post afforded him and in another letter to Bliss wrote of 'a small coup d'état' in the Museum hierarchy.[35]

If he felt any disappointment at the limited opportunities Museum life had given him so far, he showed no outward sign of it. In his letter of resignation he wrote of his 'sense of the peculiar advantages which the Museum offers as a training-school to those who wish to combine the cultivations of literature with the duties of active life'. He then went on to state in no uncertain terms his intention to pursue his archaeological interests in his new career and in this he received sanction and limited financial support from the British Museum.[36]

The first years of Newton's consulship are chronicled in *Travels and Discoveries* where he describes several excursions from his residence at Mytilene to the Greek islands and the Turkish mainland. Newton recorded the numerous inscriptions he encountered upon his travels,[37] and wherever possible procured the original stones along with other antiquities, including some sculptures. He was, however, kept painfully short of funds and complained in a private letter to Panizzi of the apparent half-heartedness of the Trustees in their commissioning of his services.[38] Nevertheless, he was able to exploit his office to the full, and on 10 January 1855, the Keeper of Antiquities at the Museum reported that in the last year there had arrived 'an extensive collection of marbles, inscriptions, vases and other antiquities from Greek islands procured by C. T. Newton'.[39] A further consignment of four cases of inscriptions arrived in the following summer.[40] Like Layard before him, Newton received help and support from Lord Stratford de Redcliffe. Through him he received both a firman and funds for conducting excavations on the island of Calymnos between

November 1854 and the following March.[41] The first fruits of his labours reached the Museum in the following summer.[42]

As his operations on Calymnos were coming to an end, he took the opportunity of crossing over to Bodrum: 'The steamer took us rapidly across to the Asiatic shore; and after having been so long accustomed to the noisy streets of Calymnos, thronged with Greeks and pigs, it seemed strange to find myself in the stillness of the picturesque old Turkish town, which stands on the site of Halicarnassus.' Upon his arrival Newton was permitted to see the interior of the castle, experiencing none of the difficulties that had frustrated so many European visitors before him. While there, he was astonished to see in various places a number of fine white marble lions ornamenting the walls, which he instantly recognised as Greek and as coming originally from the Mausoleum of ancient Halicarnassus. He was not, in fact, the first to make this observation since Ludwig Ross had already published the fact, but it seems the lions had been little noticed, if at all, by English visitors to the castle, and Newton became determined one day to secure their removal and to transport them to the British Museum.[43]

At the outset of the following year he was once more in Bodrum, having sailed there under the expectation of a firman promised by Lord Stratford to excavate in the town.[44] The firman never materialised, in fact, but this did not deter Newton from conducting some minor excavations, principally in the field of Mehemet Chaoux, described by Newton as a very intelligent old Turk, on whose property were found hundreds of terracotta figurines.[45] His funds exhausted, Newton determined to return to the field, intent as he was upon his real objective, the discovery of the site of the Mausoleum of Halicarnassus.[46] Upon his return to Mytilene, he found an instruction to go to Rome, where he was to value the Campana collection. This he eventually did, enlisting the help of his former colleague Samuel Birch in the colossal task.[47]

In the late summer of 1856 Newton was back in London, and there wrote a long letter to Panizzi describing his visits in the preceding spring aboard HMS *Medusa* to Bodrum and Cnidus and offering proposals for further operations in those places.[48] The archaeological importance of Cnidus was already well documented through the expedition of the Dilettanti Society.[49] Newton had more than one reason, however, for wishing to excavate the site of ancient Halicarnassus. It was the birth-place of Herodotus and had been the capital of the Carian kings, but chiefly it was the site of the Mausoleum from which the British nation already possessed a portion of the sculptures. He enclosed a copy of the chart of the site prepared by Captain T. Spratt, which had been made as a part of a survey of the area commissioned by Sir Francis Beaufort, then in charge of the Hydrographical Department. Beaufort's own survey, an account of which may be read in his *Karamania*, was later said by Newton to have provided the inspiration for his search for the Mausoleum.[50]

In 1847–8 Thomas Spratt, then a lieutenant of the survey branch of the Royal Navy, provided a detailed ground plan of Bodrum and afterwards published a memoir arguing his choice of location for the site of the Mausoleum.[51] Spratt chose a site to the east of a hypothetical placement already published by Newton and C. R. Cockerell, who were working from literary sources and the old Admiralty Chart.[52]

During his second visit in 1856, as has already been noted, Newton had attempted some small-scale experimental excavations.[53] It was here that he resumed excavations in the following December.[54] By the time he was writing to Panizzi, Newton had secured the firman and the matter was therefore referred by the Principal Librarian to the Foreign Secretary, the Earl of Clarendon.[55] In a memorandum Newton submitted a list of his requirements, including the services of a ship of war for at least six months.[56] This was 'absolutely necessary' for conducting excavations at Cnidus, since there was no local habitation, and all food and, as he thought, water would have to be imported.[57] In fact, a natural spring was later located and made use of.[58] Newton also needed a firman giving permission to remove the lions from the walls of the castle. He also requested £2,000, a lieutenant of the Royal Engineers and a party of four Sappers, one of whom should be a photographer – the first time a photographer would accompany an expedition of this kind.[59]

All Newton's requests were granted by the Government, and *Gorgon*, a steam corvette, was put at his disposal by the Admiralty under the command of Captain Towsey. With the crew of 150 men were Lieutenant Robert Murdoch Smith of the Royal Engineers, Corporal William Jenkins and, as photographer, Corporal Benjamin Spackman. The two other non-commissioned officers were Lance-Corporals Patrick and Francis Nelles, who served as smith and mason respectively. Also accompanying the party were the young painters Roderick Stanhope and Val' Prinsep, and Newton's life-long friend George Frederic Watts.[60]

Newton had strengthened his case for securing a ship for his own expedition by suggesting to the Trustees that it might serve a double purpose. In a letter dated 8 August 1856 he had responded, at the Trustees' request, to an application from the Rev. Nathan Davis, an American attached to the consulate in Tunis, to excavate on the site of ancient Carthage. 'If a ship of war be placed at my disposal for excavations at Halicarnassus and Cnidus', wrote Newton, 'I could from there visit periodically the excavations at Carthage and report progress.'

In recent years the Trustees had received through the Foreign Office periodic reports upon the scope for collecting classical antiquities along the north coast of Africa. In 1848 it was reported that the French Vice-Consul of Benghazi was already collecting antiquities from the cities of the Cyrenaica.[61] A year later a report was received from the British Vice-Consul at Benghazi, Lt. Col. G. F. Herman, urging the Trustees to take some action.[62] Then, only days before Newton made proposals for his expedition to Asia Minor, the Trustees received a copy of a memorandum addressed to the Foreign Secretary by Nathan Davis.[63]

I take the liberty of soliciting your attention and aid on behalf of a field of antiquities which has hitherto been almost entirely neglected. No museum can boast of any important specimens illustrative of the once famous north African Republic. The plough now passes over a fertile soil, which is supported by the remains of architecture reared in the days of Hanno, Amilcar, Asdrubal and Hannibal – and yet Carthage is not inferior in interest either to Herculaneum, Pompeii or even Nineveh. It is to enable me to resuscitate this ancient city that I now appeal to you.

The attention of the scientific world has at different periods been directed to the city of Dido; but religious and political prejudices have hitherto been a barrier, and hence every application to obtain permission for systematic excavation has been met, either by a positive, or an evasive refusal. I have, however, now the honour to inform you that his highness the reigning Pasha of Tunis, has granted to me that permission and my desire is to employ it for the public benefit, by handing over all the antiquities that may be found to the Trustees of the British Museum . . . .

The letter went on to outline Davis's proposals for proceeding with the expedition.[64] In the event, Newton played no part in the excavations at Carthage, being more than fully occupied with his own venture. In the summer of 1858, however, HMS *Supply*, conveying a second consignment of antiquities from Bodrum and elsewhere, called at Carthage to pick up a further cargo of mosaics and sculptures from Davis's excavations.

The Mausoleum

Gorgon sailed out of Spithead in October 1856, reaching Smyrna on the 11th of the following month. Newton went separately and reached Constantinople by 4 November, where he was well received by the British Ambassador.[65] After the necessary preliminaries, the first excavations began on 24 November, where Newton had previously left off in the field of Chaoux. Here were discovered more terracotta figurines and lamps by the shovelful, and the foundations of a building later identified as a temple of Demeter and Persephone.[66]

After sending his first despatch to the Earl of Clarendon, Newton wrote a private letter to Panizzi in which he described the progress so far but also added his anxieties at Lord Stratford's not sending the firman from Constantinople authorising removal of the lions from the castle. He wrote of his fear that some 'indiscreet scribbler from the ship may send a report to *The Illustrated London News* and then the eyes of jealous and rival embassies will be attracted to my doings here.'[67]

Newton need not have worried, if all the letters from the English at Bodrum were as inaccurate as that which was later picked up, apparently lost, in a street in the town and handed over to him:[68]

Dear father and moter, with gods help i now take up my pen to right these few lines to you hopeing to find you in good health & sperits as thank god it leaves me at present. Dear father of all the drill that a seaman was put to i think the Supply's company have got the worst, for here we are at Boderumm a useing the peke madock & shovel. nevur was there such a change from a sea man to a navy; yes by George we are all turned naveys sumetimes a diging it up & sometimes a draging it down to the waters edge & then imbarking it. Dear father this is the finest mable that ever i saw; we get on so very slow that i fear we shall be hear a long time; the city of Ninevea as been sunk such a long time that we find nothing but mable; every thing els is compleatley roted away. what is most to be seen is the crockery ware that they used in those days.

Newton was inclined to invoke G. F. Watts from time to time as the presiding genius of his labours and aspirations, and he did so in respect of the lions in the castle, enclosing a copy of a memorandum from the painter for the eyes of Lord Clarendon. Watts extolled the virtues of the lions, observing that they were 'less severe than the sculpture of Pheidias' and, therefore, 'perhaps more beautiful in the popular sense of the word'. This was praise, indeed, from one who, more than any painter since Benjamin Robert Haydon, held the Elgin Marbles to be the highest artistic achievement known to man.[69] He went on to describe their 'Correggio-like grace and flow of outline' corresponding exactly with 'the style of Praxiteles as described by the ancient writers'. In this they would provide the 'links hitherto wanting between the art of Pheidias and that of the later and more conventional periods'. Watts, like most of his contemporaries, was inclined to see the progress of ancient art in terms of a developmental growth, and the prospect of discovering a 'missing link' in that chain was of obvious importance.

Disappointed at not finding the Mausoleum in Chaoux's field, Newton decided to transfer his team to the place marked 'Mausoleum' on Spratt's chart. Excavation began at the site which became known as Spratt's Platform, to the north-east of Chaoux's field, on 1 December. Here, however, confused with the foundations of a Byzantine monastery, all that belonged to the classical period were some mosaics mixed with fragments of painted stucco. Newton trenched the field in all directions, covering the greatest area in the shortest possible time by instructing his men to throw the earth behind them as they went, but still there was no sign of the elusive Seventh Wonder.[70] There followed on the 8th and 9th of the month a brief and fruitless excavation to the east of the theatre, and then on the 10th digging commenced to the south-west, in the field of Hadji Captan.

Newton had hoped to proceed with excavations on a site known as Ross's Platform, the place identified as the Mausoleum by the distinguished archaeologist Ludwig Ross. The local Turkish inhabitants, however, were understandably reluctant to have their houses pulled down and fields dug up, and every plot had to be bargained for before Newton could commence digging. This was a constant hindrance to the progress of the excavations. At this time the cost of Ross's Platform was considered too high, and Newton decided to delay, 'till their pretensions are somewhat abated'.

The field of Hadji Captan had been the find-place of a draped female figure removed by Stratford Canning's agents and transported to the British Museum at the same time as the frieze from the castle.[71] Newton found another female figure with flying drapery under the mosaic floor of a large Roman villa.[72] The mosaics of this villa were too extensive to be lifted entire, but a photographic record was made by Corporal Spackman from a camera mounted on a scaffold suspended above the site.[73]

Newton describes the fascination of the owner of this field with his activities. Hadji Captan is characterised as 'a jovial old Turk' who was so interested in the 'strange pictures which had lain concealed under the soil of his field for so many centuries' that he would watch the diggings for hours on end. Sadly, his interest cost him his life, for he caught cold from standing around too long on the wet ground and died.[74]

On 27 December Newton transferred to a site just north of the Aga's *Konak*, which served as the headquarters and residence of the excavation. Here, at last, were to be unearthed the ruins of the Mausoleum. The importance of this place became apparent soon after digging commenced. On Wednesday 7 January 1857, Towsey drily wrote in his diary: 'Newton in raptures thinks he has found the site of the Mausoleum and that his name will be immortalized among the number of antiquarians who delight in such things.' From this point on, Newton would claim the discovery as his own, and we should have no reason to doubt him if not for the posthumous publication in 1901 of the letters of Lieutenant Robert Murdoch Smith. These letters, written when Smith was just barely twenty-one years old, were addressed to Sir John Burgoyne from Bodrum. They present a remarkable account from the point of view of one of the key figures involved in the success of the expedition.

Robert Murdoch Smith (1835–1900) was one of those nineteenth-century giants who combined a pioneering spirit with diplomatic skill and technical know-how. He deserves to be remembered for three principal reasons: first, for his part in Newton's excavations at Bodrum and elsewhere; second, for his own dangerous and daring expedition to Cyrene with his friend Lieutenant Porcher in 1860–61, which brought a number of important sculptures to the British Museum;[75] third, for having organised the laying of a telegraph cable across Persia linking England with India.[76] Towards the end of his career he was able to combine his vast administrative experience with his earlier antiquarian interests to become Director of the Edinburgh Museum of Science and Art, now called the National Museum of Scotland.

Although he receives too infrequent a mention in the pages of Newton's chronicles, his own unselfconscious account makes clear how important a part he played in the success of the expedition to Halicarnassus. His biographer records a tribute paid to him by Sir Charles Wilson in an article published after his death in *Royal Engineers Journal* 30 (September 1, 1900), pp. 192–4:

> It is scarcely too much to say that the success of the excavations was largely due to the intelligent insight and skill with which they were conducted by Smith, and his friends have always felt that he received scant credit for his work in the elaborate publications of his chief.

On 1 January 1857 Murdoch Smith had himself written:

> On the 27th we commenced digging in another place. As I happened to point it out as the probable site of the Mausoleum it goes by the name of Smith's Platform. It lies on the rising ground a little to the north of the Pasha's palace, which you will see marked in the chart . . . .[77]

Towsey's diary similarly refers in the early days of the excavation to Smith's Platform. In his despatch sent on 12 January, Newton makes no mention of Smith's Platform or of his part in the discovery. He merely refers to it as the place where Thomas Leverton Donaldson had, many years before, noticed 'the ruins of a superb *Ionic edifice*'.[78] This place, it must be said, coincided roughly with the site of the Mausoleum, as worked out from the old Admiralty chart and from literary sources by Newton and Cockerell in their preliminary article of 1848. It is, however, surprising that Newton did not set his diggers immediately to the proper place. It may be that he did not have access to the ground because of the chronic difficulties experienced with the Turkish proprietors, but he does not say so. Indeed, he seems to imply that the problem of buying up the land dated from the first day of the discovery.[79]

There is, moreover, one circumstantial piece of evidence which suggests that Newton's claim to have anticipated the exact location of the Mausoleum was in fact made retrospectively. When he had set out for Halicarnassus in the previous autumn he had forgotten to take with him the text of his own article, and he wrote to Panizzi begging him to forward a copy.[80] Panizzi obliged, and in a following letter Newton thanked him with the following:

> I was rather pleased to find in referring to my memoir written ten years ago, that I had then, from the imperfect evidence before me, pointed out the most probable site for the Mausoleum in the very spot where I am now excavating its remains.[81]

In the published accounts of his travels Newton would proudly proclaim his having proved his theory. The fact that he had needed to refer back to his own 'memoir' for confirmation, however, suggests that he had not always been firm in this conviction. The theoretical site of the Mausoleum had been worked out using the old Admiralty chart drawn up by Graves and Brock, and had been challenged subsequently by Spratt and Ross, both of whom had – unlike Newton at that time –

actually visited the site. Ross identified the site of the Mausoleum with the foundations of a building later confirmed by Newton's excavations as the Temple of Mars; Spratt chose a location to the south-east of this place.[82] Newton's inspired guess was the most accurate by far, but when he did eventually have occasion to visit the site itself in 1855, as he gazed upon the remains of actual antiquity strewn across the hillsides above the harbour at Bodrum, he was confronted by a very different set of data. It was, perhaps, this new circumstance that distracted him from following his original, sound intuition and prevented him from going straight to the goal of his expedition. In due course other sharp-eyed observers would scout the hillside looking for signs of the lost 'wonder' and among them Murdoch Smith, charged with the task of planning anew the remains of ancient Halicarnassus. So it was that Newton's fellow explorer was able to discover what Newton had guessed at but not yet himself realised to be the site of the Mausoleum.

Once the realisation had been made, Newton quickly reasserted his claim as *protos heuretes*, and posterity would be none the wiser had Smith's son-in-law, in the early summer of 1900, not turned out the contents of a box in the Edinburgh Museum and there discovered a packet of letters long thought lost.

If the authenticity of Newton's claim may be questioned, there is no doubt about the single-mindedness of his will to pursue the discovery. Of particular note is his ruthless determination to countenance no refusal from the local inhabitants who still occupied the site. 'They tell me you are a man who, when once you get your foot into a field, contrive to get your whole body in after it', one local worthy is reported to have said to him on being approached.[83] By this method Newton succeeded in first tracing the outline of the building and then, as he explains, 'I proceeded to buy up and demolish everything which stood in my way – houses, garden walls, fig-trees, almond-trees, were all swept away before my band of workmen.'

The negotiations, however, did not always proceed without difficulty. The Turks were in the habit, once the idea had caught on, of staying put for the longest possible delay, in order to ask the highest possible price for their property. Newton and Murdoch Smith both describe the difficulties they had with the 'termagant wife' of one proprietor. The excavators had dug up to and around the house until, as Murdoch Smith remarks, it had the appearance of a 'fortress surrounded on all sides by a large ditch'.[84] From here the owner's wife made a 'spirited resistance'. Smith describes how, at times, she was given to 'firing from the windows solid shot in the shape of large stones, at others red-hot in the form of burning charcoal'. He goes on, 'By a well-directed shot she succeeded in hitting Corporal Jenkins on the back of the head and sending him very speedily to the bottom of the ditch.'[85]

Eventually, Newton decided the time was right for making an offer on the house:

After much parleying, the price was fixed at £20. I waited on old Suliman in his house with the money in my hand, and found myself in the awful presence of Mrs Suliman .... The poor old man gazed wistfully on this treasure as if he had never seen as much money in his life. 'It is not enough!' said the stern old hag. I immediately swept up my little heap of gold and withdrew. This prompt measure had more effect than hours of parleying, and I got the house two days afterwards.[86]

The reluctance of the local inhabitants to sell up their family houses, even at much inflated prices, was a source of great annoyance to Newton. In some instances the problem of local intransigence was overcome by tunnelling beneath a house or boundary wall. Sometimes the inhabitants would sell up for fear of being undermined. Corporal Jenkins, a six-foot giant of Welsh mining stock, found himself in his natural environment, below ground, and tunnelled relentlessly through the subterranean passages and chambers that belong to the Mausoleum complex. Newton describes how he would occasionally surface to escape the foul air of his underground world, poking his head up through the earth of a private garden or courtyard, much to the astonishment of the inhabitant. 'One day, on probing the roof of a gallery where the rock had been replaced by masonry, he detected a soft place, and his crowbar suddenly finding its way upwards, lifted up the hearthstone of a grave sententious Turk, who was sitting quietly smoking his chibouque in his own house.'[87]

In the course of these activities Newton's men opened up a vast area consisting of the quadrangular cutting in the native rock for the basement of the Mausoleum itself, and the north-east corner of the surrounding *temenos*. A mass of architectural and sculptural fragments were brought to light. 'The whole of the hollow Quadrangle' wrote Newton, 'was filled with remains of architecture and sculpture. The quantity of these fragments was so great that it would have been impossible to specify their exact position on the Plan, nor would such information be of any value in reference to the majority of the marbles, which had evidently been rolled and pitched out of the way by the spoilers of the tomb, as they removed successive courses of masonry.'[88] Newton did, however, go on to discuss the position of the most substantial pieces of sculpture with reference to the plan of the site drawn up by Smith.[89]

On the west side of the site was found the so-called Persian Rider,[90] and nearby the lower part[91] of a draped standing male figure wrongly marked as female on the plan.[92] Further east was found a colossal seated statue.[93] Further east still were found four well-preserved pieces of the Amazon frieze.[94] There were other sculptures, including fragments of the lions, but the most sensational discoveries were to be made on the northern reaches of the excavations, behind the *peribolos* wall that marked the boundary of the temenos on that side.[95] Here was discovered 'a mass of large marble slabs, lying piled one over the other in the earth, and intermixed with statues'.[96] The slabs were soon recognised as having once formed part of the stepped pyramid said by Pliny to have surmounted the building. The bronze clamps that were used to join the slabs together were sometimes still in place, and from this Newton concluded that the steps and the sculptures found with them were lying where they had fallen during the earthquake that toppled the Mausoleum in late antiquity. If the stones had been disturbed subsequently, then their clamps would certainly have been removed, being a valuable source of metal.[97]

The stepped pyramid of the Mausoleum was said by Pliny to have been topped with a *quadriga marmorea*, made by the sculptor 'Pythis' (Pytheos).[98] To the great delight of the excavators, along with the steps were found the forepart of one 80
colossal horse and the hinder part of another (thought at this time to be all parts of the Col. Pl. XII
same horse). Fragments of the spokes of a colossal wheel were found here.[99] The head of one of the two colossal horses was found in two parts, a portion of the bronze bridle attached to one and the bit in the mouth of the other fragment.

Other sculptures from the deposit north of the peribolos wall included a lion, whose gaping mouth still showed signs of the original red paint. This, the best preserved of all the lions found, was said by Newton to have been lying on the peribolos wall itself, while according to Murdoch Smith's diary it was located behind the wall.[100] The greatest prize, however, were the two great portrait statues that were to be identified as Mausolos and Artemisia. The grandeur of these sculp- 28–9
tures was not immediately apparent, particularly in the case of the Mausolos, which had to be reconstructed in the Museum from numerous fragments. Newton assigned these two figures to the chariot group, but today scholars prefer to place them in front of the cella of the Mausoleum among the other members of the Hekatominid dynasty who stood there.[101]

While engaged in the main object of his expedition, Newton did not neglect to explore other points of interest at Halicarnassus. Ludwig Ross had earlier dismissed Newton's theory of the location of the Mausoleum and had adopted instead the view put forward by W.J. Hamilton that a large platform to the north represented the real site. Newton had preferred Spratt's identification of 'Ross's Platform', namely that this was the site of the Temple of Ares mentioned by Vitruvius in his description of Halicarnassus and said to have housed a cult statue by Leochares, one of the named sculptors of the Mausoleum. A small detachment of sailors from the *Gorgon* was set to work under the command of Mr Royce on 2 February 1857,[102] and on 15 July Newton submitted a full report to the Foreign Secretary.[103] No sculptures were found, but Newton was able to establish that this was the likely site of the Temple of Ares and thus had the satisfaction of proving his German critic wrong on two counts.[104]

One of the principal aims of the expedition to Halicarnassus was the removal from the castle of the lions that Newton had identified during his first visit there in the spring of 1855.[105] As the weeks went by and no word came from Lord Stratford to say that the necessary firman was granted, Newton became increasingly anxious and even despondent. His anxiety was justified when the Turkish minister of war was found to have his own designs upon the lions. Newton's account of the circumstances concentrates more on his personal feelings of disappointment and upon his eventual revenge on the Turks, while Murdoch Smith is more matter of fact and, thereby, more informative:

> It would appear from the accounts brought to us, that when the firman was asked for by Lord Stratford the request was granted by the Porte, and as the lions were in the walls of the fortress, the firman was placed in the hands of Fethi Pasha, the War Minister. When the affair was still under consideration at Constantinople he sent a scientific man, Arakil Bey, to Bodrum, nominally to inspect some mines in this neighbourhood, but in fact to make a report on the lions and send them with the greatest despatch to Kos to wait a steamer for Constantinople. When at last he gave the firman to Lord Stratford he told him that some of the lions had been removed, but that firman gave us authority to take the remaining ones.[106]

When Newton saw what was happening he sent messages by sea and overland to inform the British Ambassador of the danger. On the very day that the lions were removed from the castle, Newton had to suffer the humiliation of a formal visit to his excavations from the Commandant of the castle and his entourage who, under orders from the War Minister, was responsible for the removal of four lions, including three of the best. Newton had photographs taken of two of them when, wrapped in raw sheepskins, they were waiting to be put aboard a caique that would take them to Cos before their eventual transport to Constantinople.

Early the next morning (18 March) *Swallow* arrived from Constantinople with the firman. It made quite explicit Newton's right to the lions in the castle, and he immediately conspired to delay the sailing of the caique and, confronting the Commandant with the text of the authorisation, laid claim to all the sculptures, both those waiting to sail and the three still remaining in the castle.[107] Newton handed back the most inferior of the four lions – in fact, a lioness – removed by the Commandant, and it was resolved that two more should be offered to the Museum at Constantinople. Newton conferred with Watts as to which of the lions could be spared.[108]

While the business of gathering the sculptures was going on ashore, Captain Towsey's assistance was particularly valuable aboard *Gorgon*, supervising the preparations for their eventual transport to England. Newton is full of praise for the man who was his 'mainstay and sheet anchor' during the excavations, both in practical matters and in the management of the men.[109] Towsey's entertaining journal of the expedition is preserved in the library of the Department of Greek and Roman Antiquities in the British Museum.

The Gorgon *arrives in England*

Gorgon eventually sailed from Bodrum for England on 24 June 1857 with a cargo of some 218 cases and packages, these being the fruits of the expedition so far. On board were the three artists, Watts, Prinsep and Stanhope. The two younger had not proved of any great service, and Newton later wrote privately to Panizzi that he was glad to see the back of them.[110] A full inventory of the cargo of sculptures and other antiquities was sent to Lord Clarendon, and Newton wrote separately to Panizzi of the despatch of *Gorgon* and her precious burden.[111] The arrival of *Gorgon* at Woolwich was announced on 22 July 1857, the ship having left Bodrum a month earlier. She was replaced at Bodrum by a large transport, HMS *Supply*, under the command of Captain Balliston, who had orders to remain with the expedition until all the marbles were shipped.[112] Newton would later describe Balliston in a private letter to Panizzi as 'an excellent officer with a large family and a precarious income'.[113]

The arrival of the Mausoleum sculptures placed an intolerable strain on the space in the Museum sculpture galleries. Every available inch had been given over to the sculptures only recently acquired from Assyria. Now all that could be done was to allow the Mausoleum sculpture to spill out of the Museum onto the colonnade, where a temporary shed constructed from timber and glass was erected to the west of the main doorway.[114] Here the various fragments of the principal sculptures from the Mausoleum were to be rejoined and arranged, while the lesser sculptures and fragments, along with the mosaics, were placed partly in basements under the North Library and partly in the room recently vacated by the removal of the moulds employed by the *formatore*.[115]

The pressure for space was rendered all the more acute by the arrival that same summer of *Curacao* from Tunis with her cargo of mosaics and sculptures excavated from the site of ancient Carthage by the Reverend Nathan Davis. Temporary storage was found for these in a basement room.[116]

The work of piecing together and arranging the Mausoleum sculpture took more than a year to complete.[117] A detailed summary of Newton's acquisitions and of the related works in the Museum was submitted by Hawkins to the Trustees some nine months after their arrival.[118] In April 1858 the Canning Marbles were incorporated into the arrangement of the Mausoleum sculptures under the colonnade, having been removed from their temporary home in the Phigaleian Room.

Once the Mausoleum sculptures had been unpacked, Newton was particularly anxious that a committee of 'competent persons' should examine them for traces of ancient polychromy:

> I have in my several despatches noted the more prominent cases, but I have never had the opportunity of examining the whole of the marbles at leisure. It is quite certain from the observations which I have made already that the columns, their bases and capitals were all

coloured, so were the cornice, frieze, subordinate and architectural mouldings. Traces of colour appear on the principal sculptures in the round ....[119]

Newton nominated Samuel Birch, Edmund Oldfield, Francis Penrose, Thomas Donaldson, George Scharf, Baron Marochetti, and William Watkiss Lloyd as all fit for the task. No doubt he had in mind the committee of savants who had gathered in the Elgin Room of the British Museum twenty years earlier to determine whether colour remained to be found upon the Elgin Marbles.[120] Unfortunately when the packing cases from the *Gorgon* were opened in the British Museum, the colours that had appeared so vivid to Newton and his co-workers in Bodrum had since faded. Newton expressed his disappointment to Panizzi and went on in the same letter to list those instances where he recalled distinct traces of colour.[121] In the published accounts of his discoveries, he would make much of the colour he knew once embellished the Mausoleum and its sculptures.[122]

Cnidus and Didyma

After *Gorgon* had sailed, Newton continued his exploration of the Mausoleum and its environs, making further discoveries of sculpture including a colossal ram, which he at first mistook for a leopard,[123] until by the end of 1857 progress was severely restricted by the determined refusal of the Turkish residents to budge from the site. Already by November of that year, Newton had decided to divert part of his force to Cnidus, calculating that if the Turks were made to realise that Bodrum was not the only object of the expedition, they might give up the waiting game of holding out for a higher price.[124] Newton landed with a work-force at Cnidus on 10 December 1857, leaving Murdoch Smith and Corporal Jenkins in charge at Bodrum to round things off.[125] Eventually they too would transfer to Cnidus.[126] Among the party was Richard Pullan, who had been sent out as architectural draughtsman to replace the ineffectual artists who had returned to England with *Gorgon*. He arrived at Bodrum on 28 August, some days after an additional Sapper photographer, one McCartney.[127] The latter was to prove unreliable, and following some breach of conduct was placed on a charge and imprisoned.[128]

The first month was mostly spent in putting up the huts that were to provide an inadequate protection against the cold, as Newton complained in a letter to Panizzi.

An exposed promontory like Cape Crio gathers round it all the tempests of the Archipelago. We have had this year a winter of extraordinary severity. A Crimean north wind blowing a hurricane in our huts and nothing but half-inch planks to keep the cold out. I had asked for stoves which usually accompany huts, but they had none at Malta.[129]

The second month was spent in excavations at the theatre, chosen because of its proximity to the sea. The southern harbour of Cnidus lacked a safe landing and, by shooting barrow-loads of earth and stones from the excavation of the theatre into the sea, Newton constructed a pier for the disembarkation of stores and, he hoped, the eventual shipment of sculptures.[130]

The theatre proved barren of sculpture and operations were transferred elsewhere. Newton next tried his luck at the platform marked out by the earlier expedition of the Dilettanti Society as the famed Temple of Venus, in which Praxiteles's celebrated Cnidian Aphrodite once stood. This temple was soon dismissed as 'Roman of a late period' and 'quite unworthy of the matchless work of Praxiteles'.[131] From here Newton proceeded to a platform to the north-east, lying beneath the towering Acropolis of Cnidus, which had been noted on the Admiralty plan as containing statues.[132] The platform, supported on three sides by well-formed polygonal masonry, is bounded on its northern limit by a sheer cliff rising 50 to 70 feet above the site at an angle of 79 degrees. Such is the regularity of the slope that Newton at first supposed the scarp to have been man-made. It was only later that, by blasting below the surface to a depth of 28 feet, he realised the cliff must have been caused by a natural land-slide along the line of a fissure in the rock.[133]

Nor was the nature of the site immediately apparent to Newton. At first he supposed it to be a cemetery and referred to the votive deposits from which he extracted numerous finds as 'graves'. It was only through decipherment of the inscriptions which he discovered and the proper identification of a number of sculptures that he learned to call this the Sanctuary of Demeter and Persephone.[134] The seated statue of Demeter which he found had already been noted by the Col. Pl. VII Dilettanti expedition, who supposed it to have fallen from one of the niches cut into the cliff above the sanctuary. Newton could not at first recognise the sculpture as a Demeter, nor fully appreciate its great beauty, owing to the fact that the head was missing and was only found some weeks later. Having already packed the body, Newton was unable to check his correct assumption that the two belonged together.[135]

Working their way from west to east, Newton's team of Sappers and locally employed Turkish labourers stripped the site, extracting from the shallow surface soil such finds as came to hand. In three places, at the western and eastern ends and just east of centre, Newton uncovered a series of underground enclosures bounded by rough masonry walls. The combined fills of these subterranean votive chambers yielded a rich harvest of finds including sculpture, inscriptions, inscribed bases, terracotta figures, numerous terracotta lamps, glass bottles, lead curse tablets and, in one instance, a series of curious marble weights in the form of female breasts.[136] The sanctuary yielded only two near-complete pieces of life-size sculpture, namely the seated Demeter and a standing figure thought by Newton to represent Demeter Achaea, but now believed to portray a priestess of the cult.[137] There were, however, numerous fragments of a variety of sculptures apparently destroyed by a violent shock, and among them some heads including that of a lost figure probably representing Persephone.[138] One of the deposits yielded curious marble pigs and calves, in some cases well preserved.[139]

Newton was pleased with these discoveries in the Demeter Sanctuary. Further sculptures and fragments would be retrieved from the site of a building identified by an inscription as a temple of the Muses,[140] and also from the Necropolis.[141] From a tomb situated on the Triopian peninsula overlooking the city of Cnidus came the portrait statue of a Roman lady,[142] but the most sensational discovery would be made outside the main site on a lofty promontory about three miles from Cape Crio. In *Travels and Discoveries* Newton records how, while at Bodrum, a Greek by the name of Nicholas Galloni, whom he had known at Calymnos, visited him and, on seeing the Mausoleum lions lying in the courtyard of the Aga's *konak*, declared that he had seen a much bigger lion lying on a promontory south of Cnidus.[143] When first he visited Cnidus with Captain Towsey, Newton enquired from the local Turks about the lion but with no result. Only half-believing the story, therefore, he pressed Galloni once more, who insisted on the existence of the lion and pointed out 'on Kiepert's map' the very promontory. Newton's private letter to Panizzi gives a livelier account of the eventual discovery than any version hitherto published.[144]

> Since my arrival at Cnidus I have from time to time instituted a search for this lion, but the winter was so intensely cold, that distant expeditions were most formidable undertakings and a Crimean north wind swept over all the promontories with such ferocity as to deter us from exploring them. Since the weather has been milder, Mr Pullan has occupied himself a good deal with excursions in the environs. I particularly pointed out to him this lion as an object to be sought for. On the 15th instant he presented himself to my astonished gaze in a state of most unusual excitement, for he is naturally of a most equable temperament. His hat was crowned with a large wreath of oleander flowers, his eyes had a wild expression like those of a person who had passed the night on Parnassus or Snowdon. 'I have found the lion', he said. Those words explained the discordant state of his nerves. No wonder that he was astounded. This noble animal is ten feet long from stem to stern. He is of Parian marble and in very fine condition. He is in a couchant attitude, his head turned round to the right. From the base to the top of his head he measures six feet. His weight I should imagine to be eight tons ....

The lion was found lying face down and, after being raised, it was lowered into a
69 reinforced packing case. The task of packing and transferring the lion to *Supply* fell to Murdoch Smith, and it is truly shameful that neither of Newton's published accounts of the episode makes a single reference to the lieutenant's extraordinary skill in achieving those ends. Fortunately Murdoch Smith's own account describes in full the process that went on for an entire month.[145] While the ship's carpenters and Nelles, the blacksmith, were making the case, Murdoch Smith constructed a road, eighteen to twenty feet wide, zig-zagging down the hill towards the point of embarkation: 'At some places I was obliged to cut off pieces of the rock, and at others

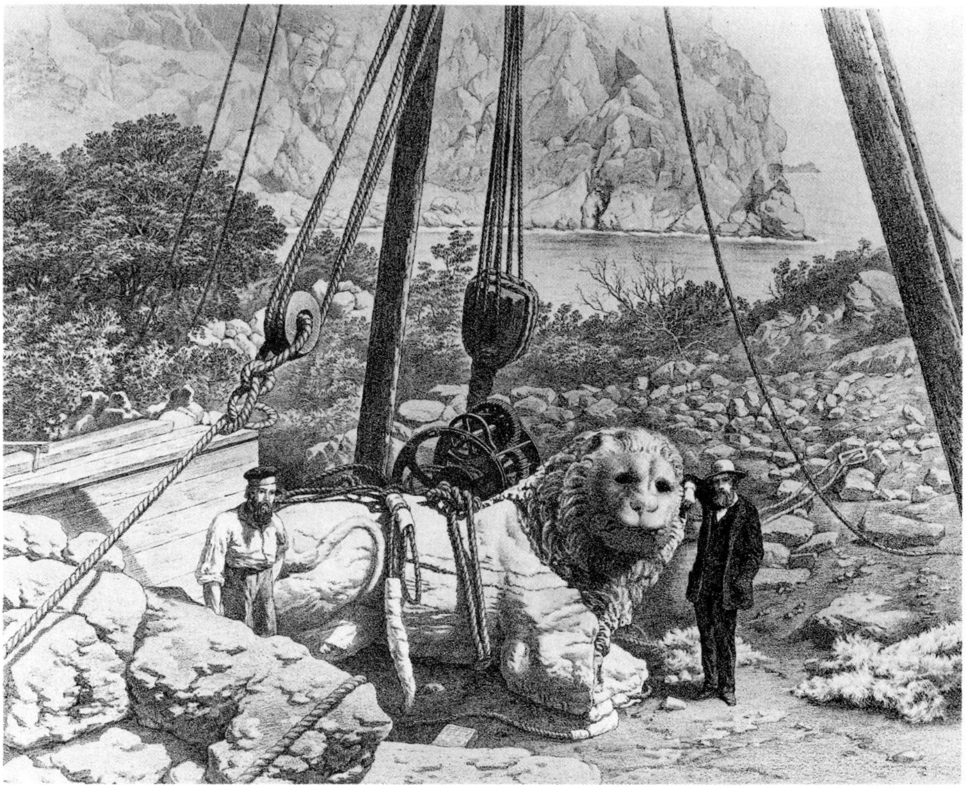

69 Charles Newton with the Cnidian lion. Newton (1862), vol. I, pl. LXI.

to raise the road eight or ten feet by embankment.' By this route the case was hauled on a sledge to the water's edge. Here it was to be winched onto a raft from a low but precipitous cliff. Murdoch Smith gives a dramatic, if highly technical account of his brilliant improvisation of the ship's tackle by which, after a near disaster, the lion was successfully lowered to the water.

Once the lion had been stowed aboard *Supply*, Newton and Pullan set about a thorough examination of the remains of the ruined tomb, from whose summit the beast had been toppled, probably by earthquake.[146] The result of their labours was a satisfyingly full reconstruction of the original appearance of the tomb, which Newton concluded was built in the first half of the fourth century BC. He suggested that it had been constructed to commemorate the defeat of the Spartans by the Athenian commander Conon in the great naval engagement that had taken place off Cnidus in 394 BC. Nowadays most scholars are content to date the tomb to the second century BC.[147]

The excavations at Cnidus would be continued in various parts of the site until May 1859, but apart from the lion and those sculptures already mentioned from the

Sanctuary of Demeter, no other major sculptures were discovered. Shortly after the colossal lion had been embarked, however, Newton set off with Corporal Jenkins and sixty Turkish workmen from Cnidus for the Greek village of Geronta (ancient Didyma). There, in the vicinity of the Temple of Apollo, he made short work of embarking ten archaic Greek seated statues together with a lion and a sphinx.[148]

The groundwork for this bold stroke had been laid a year earlier when Newton visited the site of the temple of Apollo in the company of the photographer Corporal Spackman.[149] To the north-west of the temple Newton had located the ancient Sacred Way that once linked Didyma with the Ionian city of Miletus. The Society of Dilettanti published their examination of the temple in the first volume of *Ionian Antiquities*, and in so doing had made passing reference to the statues and sarcophagi that lined both sides of the Sacred Way. Newton found the statues, as indicated by the Dilettanti, partially buried in the ground. With the aid of his Turkish workmen he cleared the earth from around the figures, which were then recorded in drawings, and photographs by Spackman. Once uncovered, the sculptures became vulnerable to the superstitions of the local Greeks. One night a marble lion, whose back carries a five-line inscription, was attacked and the inscription deeply scored. The marks are clearly visible to this day.

Once the work of recording the sculptures was complete Newton despatched to the Foreign Secretary, Lord Clarendon, a report which he considered to be the most carefully written to date. His purpose was to persuade the Foreign Secretary of the need for a firman facilitating the removal of the sculptures. 'If he takes up my suggestion', Newton wrote to Panizzi, 'we shall make a descent upon Geronta in April and whip the sculptures on board in no time. If they are not taken now there never will be another such opportunity because we have on board the *Supply* all the gear necessary. I wrote a long letter to W. Hamilton about them. Depend upon it they would be as you say unique in Museums, and to us who have so much from Egypt and Greece, it would be most valuable to exhibit sculpture which forms the connecting link ....'[150]

The Foreign Secretary complied with Newton's request, and in due course twelve sculptures were embarked shortly before *Supply* left for England with her cargo, which included all those antiquities collected since the departure of *Gorgon* in June 1857. On her way home *Supply* called at Carthage to take on board 57 cases of antiquities from Nathan Davis's excavations there.[151] At the very end of November, she arrived at Woolwich with these and, in addition, 111 cases from Newton's excavations, together with 106 blocks belonging to the north peribolos wall of the Mausoleum complex.[152] Also on board was a case containing a sarcophagus from Sidon, sent by Niven Moore and shipped at Malta.[153]

The temporary arrangement of the sculptures within the colonnade of the Museum had only just been completed[154] when the Trustees were obliged to

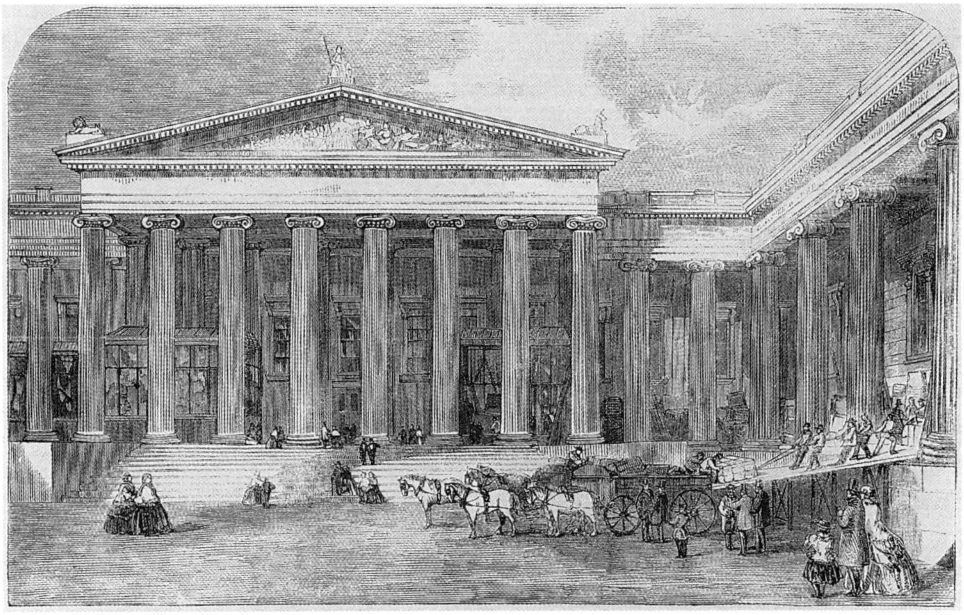

70 Mausoleum sculptures being taken to temporary sheds on the colonnade. *The Illustrated London News*, 22 January 1859.

deliberate upon this new arrival. They issued instructions for the 'eastern side of the deep part of the colonnade' to be enclosed, and ordered the blocks from the peribolos wall to be 'ranged along the inside but below the top of the granite plinth of the iron railing in front of the Museum'.[155] By early January the cases had been brought to the Museum and placed under the colonnade, but only partially unpacked.[156] As the month wore on, it became obvious that even more of the colonnade would have to be enclosed than was at first anticipated and it was determined that the eastern enclosure should be extended 'eastward and southward up to the centre of the last column but one facing the west'.[157] At the same time some authorities were questioning the need to retain the ashlar blocks from the peribolos wall for Museum purposes. Lord John Manners and Francis Penrose suggested that the blocks of marble might be offered to St Paul's Cathedral to be used in the works then being planned there.[158] The situation within the colonnade 70
is shown in an engraving published in *The Illustrated London News* dated 22 January 1859.

Meanwhile, Newton continued his operations at Cnidus but without the assistance of Murdoch Smith, who had returned to England with the *Supply*, and Pullan, who left at the same time. Smith returned some months later at Newton's special request.[159] His biographer says that he did not reach Cnidus before March 1859, but a letter from Newton to Panizzi makes it clear that he had returned already by the end of February:[160] 'The *Coquette* came in this evening bringing me back Smith whom I was right glad to see.' Corporal Jenkins had fallen dangerously ill with fever and, without his intimidating presence, Newton had detected a growing spirit of insurrection among the men.

All Newton's resources were now concentrated upon Cnidus, and for the time being at least he had given up hope of making further progress against the two resistant Turkish residents at Bodrum. Little had been done at the site since May 1858. Then on 10 May 1859 Newton received a telegraphic message from Smyrna notifying him of the imminent return of *Supply* and instructing him to begin preparations for his departure.[161] Before the month was out everything was aboard ship and *Supply* set sail for Malta early in June. On the way, however, at Newton's request Captain Balliston steered a course for Rhodes, where Newton negotiated the purchase of an important collection of vases and gold objects recently excavated by Salzmann and Biliotti from tombs on the island. These he brought with him to England together with the remaining antiquities from his own excavations and the plans, drawings, photographs and photographic negatives assembled over some three years of absence from England.[162] On 6 August 1859 the safe arrival of these objects in the Museum was reported to the Trustees.[163] Newton had himself arrived some weeks earlier, anticipating the cargo of *Supply*, which had been detained at Malta.

Newton's energies would soon be diverted elsewhere, but he never gave up hope of securing the properties covering the unexplored areas of the Mausoleum. In 1865 Biliotti and Salzmann returned to the site and, with the houses removed, conducted further excavations on behalf of the Trustees.[164] Numerous fragments of sculpture and architecture were found and conveyed to the British Museum in two consignments by HMS *Orontes*[165] and HMS *Chanticleer.*[166] A few years later great excitement was caused by a report from Biliotti that the Porte had decided to dismantle the castle at Bodrum.[167] Biliotti was asked to make enquiries on behalf of the Museum, but nothing came of the rumour.[168]

In 1865 the Museum had already purchased through Consul Brown the slab of the frieze formerly at Genoa. In 1876 two further fragments of frieze were obtained from a Turkish house in Rhodes, where it was thought they had been transported in the time of the Knights. In 1879 Layard wrote to Newton to say that the Sultan Abdul Hamed had decided to present to the British Museum a fragment of Amazon frieze, first noticed by Newton in the museum of the Seraglio in 1852.[169]

London and Rome

Upon his return from Bodrum, Newton set about making plans for the publication of his discoveries. He spent time in the British Museum reflecting upon the sculptures displayed in the temporary sheds under the colonnade. Much of what he saw there previously had been known to him only as fragments packed piecemeal. He had not, hitherto, seen the figure then identified as Mausolos in all his reconstructed glory; nor had he enjoyed the sight of the head of the Demeter reunited with the body. Much of the important work of reconstruction was done by the foreman of Masons, J. Sumsion. Later Newton was to pay tribute to the important role Sumsion played in rendering the sculptures fit for public inspection:

> Sumsion has been for thirty years employed in his capacity at the Museum, first in the service of Sir Richard Westmacott, and lately in that of the Trustees. During this period of service he has directed the repair, arrangement and setting up of the Lycian Marbles, the rearrangement of the entire Egyptian Gallery, the transfer of the pedimental figures of the Parthenon from the Second to the First Elgin Room, the arrangement of the Graeco-Roman sculptures, the repairs, setting up and arrangement of the entire collection of Assyrian sculpture, the repairs and setting up of the sculptures and mosaics from the Mausoleum, Carthage, Halicarnassus, Cnidus, Cyrene and Branchidae [Didyma], concluding the reconstruction of the statue of Apollo out of 123 fragments [the Cyrene Apollo]. These operations required the greatest care and no ordinary intelligence, and could not have been accomplished without considerable mechanical knowledge as well as familiarity with the characteristics of different styles of art.[170]

The purpose of this eulogy was to persuade the Trustees to grant Sumsion a special retirement gratuity. He had fallen ill at the age of seventy and, no longer able to work, he did not qualify for a pension. Sumsion was succeeded by Loxston and in his turn by William Pinker, who was to retire, without a pension, aged eighty-five.

Newton might delight in the practical skills of such men as these but he was to clash headlong with another dedicated craftsman, namely the irrepressible Richard Lucas. Hardly had the first consignment of marbles from Bodrum been unpacked before Lucas, a model-maker and sculptor, was writing to the Trustees requesting permission to examine them and to make a model of the Mausoleum. This request was refused, but it was repeated nearly two years later when Newton had himself just returned from Asia Minor.[171] This time the Trustees assented, but opposition came from another quarter.[172] On 19 August 1859, Newton wrote to Panizzi in protest:

> Mr Lucas called upon me three days ago at the Museum with proposals for a restoration of the Mausoleum. I referred him to you and said further that I did not think it desirable that the work of restoration should be given to him till an experienced architect had examined all the fragments. He is evidently mad but as he persuaded the late Sir R. Peel to buy his rubbishy restored model of the Parthenon contrary to every person qualified to judge in the matter, he may succeed in his present object if not watched ....[173]

The result was a fiery exchange between the two men in one of the temporary sheds, and Lucas was for a period suspended from working there.[174] His suspension was evidently short-lived, however, for in November he was demanding 'to have a barrier placed in the enclosure to prevent the principle of his restoration being seen before completed'.[175] In January of the following year he submitted a printed paper on the reconstruction of the Mausoleum.[176] In March of the same year, his confidence growing, Lucas applied with a recommendation from C. R. Cockerell to be sent out to Bodrum and there to purchase the remaining houses on the site of the Mausoleum with a view to completing Newton's excavations. Newton submitted a long report to the Trustees in response and successfully blocked Lucas's application.[177] Nothing daunted, he then offered to the Trustees for purchase his models and diagrams illustrating his reconstruction of the Mausoleum.[178] They declined, and poor Lucas was ordered to remove the models and all the paraphernalia of his art from the premises.[179]

Newton perhaps had the satisfaction of seeing the back of Lucas disappearing through the Museum gates before he himself departed to take up a new consulship in Rome. Before doing so, however, he made known his thoughts on the subject of a proper arrangement of the marbles. For the moment things had been arranged, as best they could, in the makeshift accommodation within the temporary sheds. The structure on the east side of the colonnade had been extended 'to the S.W. angle of the east wing' to receive the sculptures from Cnidus and Didyma, while that on the west side, which had been extended in the winter of 1858–9, accommodated the remainder of the sculptures from Bodrum.[180] The enclosure under the eastern part of the colonnade would be extended again in the summer of 1861 to receive the twenty-two cases of sculptures from Cyrene, fruits of the labours of Murdoch Smith's own expedition with his friend Lt. Porcher.[181]

Newton's prescription for a new arrangement of the Museum sculptures, incorporating those added by himself, divided the material into stylistic classes arranged chronologically. First would come the archaic sculptures and the casts of archaic sculpture, namely those of the Selinus metopes and the Aegina marbles; then the Parthenon sculptures arranged in a room of their own free of the other Elgin material; this would be followed by the remaining sculptural and architectural fragments 'from Athens or Greece ... known to belong to the period of Phidias', including the Phigaleian marbles; next in the series would be the Mausoleum sculptures which, like those of the Parthenon, would be exhibited by themselves; this would be followed by a 'Greek Room' containing the Lion of Cnidus as the principal feature along with the sculpture from the Sanctuary of Demeter and other miscellaneous pieces acquired by him from Halicarnassus, Cos, Rhodes, Mytilene and Smyrna, as well as two statues from Crete acquired by Spratt and a black marble statue from Davis's excavations at Carthage: 'All these sculptures, with the exception of that from Carthage are from Greek localities and the greater part of them are, I believe, work of Greek sculptors of a good period'.

The 'Lion Room' would be followed by a new Lycian Room, adequately proportioned to relieve the sculptures of the constriction universally felt in the existing apartment. Last and least would come the Graeco-Roman Room.[182]

This sequence of galleries tracing the rise of Greek art from its archaic beginnings, through its full flowering in the Parthenon, Phigaleian and Mausoleum marbles, to its relative decline in the Graeco-Roman era represented an ideal synthesis, never to be realised, even though Newton would devote much of the next quarter of a century to the attempt. In the light, however, of discussions that were then being held about the future of the British Museum and about the disposition in particular of its collections of ancient sculpture, Newton's speculations were by no means untimely or entirely theoretical.

For nearly a decade representations had been made to Parliament to relieve the serious want of space in the galleries of the British Museum. Much of this discussion had gone on while Newton was himself absent from the Department of Antiquities. He did, however, participate by post in the ensuing debate, and from January 1861 onwards, as Keeper of the newly formed Department of Greek and Roman Antiquities, he took an active part.

On 5 May 1860 Edward Hawkins, who had been Keeper of the Department of Antiquities since 1826, reached his eightieth birthday.[183] His inevitable retirement had been anticipated for some time. As early as 9 November 1856 Newton had written to Panizzi detailing a proposal for his own future role in the Museum, as and when Hawkins left the scene.[184] Newton, it seems, wished to assume none of the arduous responsibilities of administering the Department: 'I have no wish to undertake the duties of custody, acquisition and exhibition; such duties are foreign to the habits of my mind. My health will not bear the strain of constant interruption, hurry, anxiety and fatigue which these duties when efficiently discharged must produce.' Instead he put himself forward as a person ideally suited to some literary labour, by which he meant the task of either writing or editing the Department's publications. This office of 'Editor' he saw as distinct from that of Keeper. His proposal was repeated and developed two years later.[185] It was not, however, adopted, and as the day approached when Newton would have to declare his intention in respect of the soon to fall vacant post of Keeper, he privately expressed his reservations to Panizzi. When, therefore, in early summer 1860 he travelled out to Rome to take up a new diplomatic post, his future role in the running of the Museum was very much in the balance.

The prospect of Keepership was, however, rendered more attractive to Newton by Panizzi's proposal to divide the large and unwieldy Department of Antiquities into smaller, more manageable units. As a consequence three new Departments were created, namely Oriental Antiquities, including the Egyptian and Assyrian, as well as the British, Medieval and Ethnographical collections; Coins and Medals; and Greek and Roman Antiquities. A description of the break up of the old Department is given by Edward Miller, who remarks: 'It was now far too large and too cumbersome to be under the control of one man, however able. It was utterly illogical that Coins or Ethnography, for instance, should be under the same administration as Egyptian mummies, Greek marbles or Assyrian bulls.'[186]

In June 1860 Newton made his interest in the new post known to Panizzi.[187] In October of that year, after keeping everybody guessing for some months, Hawkins at last tendered his resignation.[188] On 17 January 1861, Newton was appointed Keeper of Greek and Roman Antiquities; his former colleague Samuel Birch would be in charge of Oriental Antiquities, and William Vaux became the first Keeper of Coins and Medals.[189]

Upon receipt of this news Edmund Oldfield, who had been designated Newton's Assistant, asked whether he might not be placed in 'some more independent position', suggesting that the new Department would best be divided into two sections under a senior and a junior Keeper.[190] Having laboured so long under Hawkins and having done much of the important work of drawing up and executing the considerable arrangement and rearrangement of sculpture throughout the preceding decade, Oldfield now found himself passed over in favour of one who had been absent from the Department for nearly the whole of this period. Rather than bow his neck to the yoke of Newton, he offered to assume the junior Keepership without salary. Oldfield was a conscientious and able man, but, as Edward Miller points out, he was somewhat opinionated and not a favourite of Panizzi. His counter-proposal failed and he was forced to resign his post.[191] Ruskin's eloquent pen portrait of Oldfield confirms his innate intelligence and early promise, 'not enough recognised by the public, and, I believe, further obscured by the ill humour or temper of Mr Panizzi'. Ruskin describes how, even as a schoolboy at Dale's on Denmark Hill, Oldfield was distinguished by his 'already almost middle-aged aspect of serene sagacity'.[192]

His going and Hawkins's own departure marked the end of an era that had seen the most remarkable growth in the extent and the importance of the Museum's collections. It coincided, however, with a a major public debate over the future of national museums that set at risk the very survival of the British Museum's sculpture collection as the one great 'chain of art' it had become.

PART III

9 The Contest for Attica

A mid-century crisis

While Newton was in Asia Minor, at home there was a growing controversy as to the future of the collections whose Keepership he was destined to assume. By 1851 the original Smirke conception of a great quadrangle with a classical front had been realised. Long before the completion of this scheme, however, it had become obvious that the Museum collections, particularly of sculpture, printed books and natural history, were growing faster than the building. As part of the original conception, it was intended that single-storey rooms with top-lighting would be tacked on to the western wing to receive the Elgin Marbles.[1] Already in 1832, therefore, the western wing had bulged outwards to provide adequate accommodation for the Elgin and Phigaleian Marbles, and further accretions were added throughout the 1840s and 1850s. The building could not keep pace with the needs of the collections, and among the first to warn of the eventual crisis was Edward Hawkins. As early as 1843 he was urging the Trustees to abandon the idea of a colonnade and to buy up the ground around the Museum to allow for natural growth. The colonnade, as he later complained, would restrict such expansion by effectively putting a strait-jacket around the Museum.[2]

Similar objections were expressed that same year by certain anonymous contributors to *The Builder*: 'We are not thoroughly pleased with the exterior character which Sir Robert Smirke has given to this building ... it is a mannerism of times recent and time present; it is a bastard product of classic fancy, a false face (though a fair one) put on a noble carcase ....'[3]

Hawkins became increasingly outspoken as the building and the collections grew. In 1846 he complained of additions to the original plan that were already inadequate to their purpose and would only serve as obstacles to the 'Ultimate Museum'.[4] Nor were his complaints entirely in vain, for in 1846 and again in 1848 the Trustees made approaches to the Treasury with a view to extending the boundaries of the Museum grounds.[5] In 1852–3 a Parliamentary enquiry was held to look into the question of the enlargement of the Museum. Hawkins was asked to give evidence, and submitted a biting attack upon the state of the Museum's galleries.[6] 'The present possessions of the Museum are in almost every room crowded together, and piled over each other, like goods in a warehouse; and it is almost impossible to attempt a correct classification or satisfactory arrangement which shall be instructive to visitors, or to isolate in any degree those objects to which it is desirable to direct particular attention.' He urged the immediate purchase of houses on the south and west sides of the Museum. Only then could all the collections be arranged in 'chronological and scientific order'.

Hawkins's report concluded with one final condemnation, so complete as to leave us in no doubt of his dissatisfaction: '. . . although the Building is not yet finished, scarcely a room remains as it was originally constructed, great alterations have been found necessary in almost all; the Building is surrounded by inconvenient and unsightly excrescences, and it may be asserted with truth, that Europe cannot show any Building so ill adapted for its internal purpose, as the British Museum.'

Hawkins was by no means alone in voicing such criticisms. Even W. R. Hamilton, that most thoroughly Greek of British Museum Trustees, had been condemnatory:

> The Building was made by an architect of very great eminence, but in this instance I fear that he was not a sufficiently severe critic of his own plans, or of the views and notions of others. I have been assured that when he received his instructions for this building, Mr Bankes told him that what was wanted was a simple quadrangle, with four rooms below and four rooms above, large long galleries; there is consequently a great want of small rooms, whether for working apartments, or for exhibitions. It was decided upon too hastily.[7]

According to Hamilton, a great deal more attention should have been paid to the construction of similar establishments on the Continent.[8]

Outside the Museum, one of the most articulate and damning critics, the architect James Fergusson, was not so sure that England had anything to gain by looking to the Continent for models. In a pamphlet published in 1849 he wrote: 'I am certain it is not either the Berlin Museum, nor the Munich Walhalla, or Glyptothek, nor the Paris Madelaine, or Bourse, which, considering the difficulties of the subject, either show more taste or more knowledge of the style.'[9] He does, however, go on to describe the Museum as 'bad' and 'extravagant' and to catalogue its faults: in short, Robert Smirke's sculpture galleries were wrongly lit, wrong in scale, wrongly proportioned and inappropriately arranged. Fergusson's remedy was to abandon the building as a repository for the 'arts', to remove the sculpture to some other site and then to unite it with the contents of the National Gallery; by thus combining the statues with the paintings he would seek to create 'one great national repository of fine art'. The Natural History collections he would have removed either to a separate new institution, or, combined with the minerals and fossils, to the Museum of Economic Geology in Piccadilly. Having thus emptied the galleries on the west and north sides of the quadrangle, he proposed to turn Smirke's sculpture rooms into 'depositories' of records taken from the Public Record Office which, combined with the Library, would make the British Museum 'the great repository of all the printed and written Treasures of the nation'.

This was not the first time that it had been proposed to combine the national collection of antique sculpture with the corresponding collection of Old Master paintings. Thus, when Robert Smirke first drew up his plans for the new British Museum, he allowed for the exhibition of paintings in the upper galleries,[10] while others had then proposed to transfer the Elgin Marbles to Pall Mall, to the newly created National Gallery.[11] Henry Ellis, the Principal Librarian of the day, wrote to Sir Charles Long (first Baron Farnborough) outlining his reasons for not wishing to see 'fine' as distinct from the 'coarse specimens of art' deposited with the Academicians. His argument was one that would be used again by the Museum, namely that to separate the collections was to break the 'chain of comparison'.[12]

The National Gallery enquiries of 1852–3 and 1857

During the 1850s the idea of combining the British Museum's sculptures with the National Gallery's pictures was revived and became a major debating point among persons who thought they knew better than those entrusted with the task how to accommodate and arrange the national collections. In 1852–3 a Parliamentary enquiry was held 'to consider how collective monuments of antiquity etc. possessed by the nation may be preserved, judiciously augmented and advantageously exhibited to the public'.[13] This enquiry focused upon the question of a new site for the already much criticised National Gallery; it was followed by another similar enquiry in 1857–8. In 1844 Charles Eastlake, as Keeper of the national collection of pictures, had published a pamphlet in the form of a letter to Sir Robert Peel on 'the unfitness of the present building for the purpose'. His criticisms were set out under five familiar headings: 'the inconvenient arrangement, or disposition, of some of the rooms; insufficient space for the due exhibition of even the present collection of paintings, insufficient room for the accommodation of those desirous of studying in the Gallery; want of offices; the imperfect system of ventilation and warming the rooms.'[14] All these defects had been discussed at frequent intervals during the life of the British Museum, both in respect of Montagu House and of Smirke's new building. Now the future of the two institutions was to be discussed in tandem.

The Great Exhibition of 1851 had given fresh impetus to the clamour for a new permanent national repository of the arts, and the site favoured by most was that owned by the Commissioners of the Great Exhibition at Kensington Gore. There the South Kensington Museum (now the Victoria and Albert) would later rise up, and there also the Natural History collections of the British Museum were destined to find a new home. One pressing advantage in such a location, situated as it was on the outskirts of the great smoky metropolis, was the relative relief it would afford the collections from the detrimental effects of the London atmosphere. There was, however, another major consideration, namely the advantages seen by some of combining in one location, perhaps under the same roof and possibly even in the same galleries, the public collection of Old Master paintings with that of the national corpus of antique marbles.

At this time, the Royal Academy drawing school was housed in the same building as the National Gallery in Trafalgar Square. Philip Hendy describes how the dome 'with its tall stone drum . . . housed on several days a week the shivering model and the life class . . .'.[15] An intimate relationship had always existed between the Royal Academy and the British Museum, where students would regularly gather to study the Townley and other sculptures. It was, therefore, a natural process of reasoning that led to the suggestion that the sculpture collections should be detached from the amalgam of the British Museum and married to the paintings in the National Gallery.

Richard Westmacott was in no doubt that the 'art collections' in the British Museum should be combined in one building with pictures. Painter and sculptor alike, as he explained, were trained to practise their art by first mastering form. These preliminary exercises would be even more important if it were not for the fact that there was insufficient employment in England for those who practised historical painting, where an understanding of form was paramount, as opposed to the more popular subject of landscape. It would be misleading, however, to suggest that Westmacott envisaged his students of painting and sculpture acquiring an understanding of form through the habitual drawing of sculpture. On the contrary, in accordance with contemporary practice, he could only think of this being done by copying casts. For what purpose, then, would he exhibit the sculptures of the British Museum with the paintings? It seems he envisaged them as exemplars, whose perfection might in some way, as it were, rub off on those students who studied in proximity to them. Clearly in this respect he had in mind the Elgin Marbles. To the question 'Are the Elgin Marbles as much the subject of interest and admiration now as they were in former years?', he replied, 'With all persons conversant with art they must be and will always, because these are the finest things in the world; we shall never see anything like them again.'[16]

It is difficult, however, to attribute the same reasoning to his desire to remove the non-classical sculptures. Asked whether the Assyrian and Egyptian sculptures, if exhibited as works of art, might not have the opposite effect and cause the public taste to deteriorate, Westmacott agreed that the Nineveh sculptures were objects of curiosity, certainly not of art, and, similarly, 'no man would think of studying Egyptian art'. As for cultures on the fringe even of Oriental barbarism, such as the Chinese, Westmacott felt that the fewer artists who looked at their art the better. In general, however, he thought that anyone who had gazed upon and understood the beauty of the Elgin Marbles would remain pure in his artistic sensibilities, no matter what barbarisms he might be exposed to.

In spite of these prejudices against 'inferior' forms of art, Westmacott could not take what for him would have seemed the logical step, and remove only the Elgin Marbles and works of approximate value. He had seen the great collection of sculptures brought into the British Museum piece by piece and assembled there culture by culture, and could not bring himself to sever a single link in this great chain of living history. It was, after all, in relation to what had gone before, and to what came after, that the Elgin Marbles were conceived as paramount. To detach them from the series would be to leave them without their aesthetic terms of reference.

Four years after Sir Richard Westmacott had given his evidence to the 1853 Committee, his son and namesake was called before the enquiry of 1857. The prospect of breaking up the collection was to him equally deplorable: as he put it, 'I think that any intelligent person who understands archaeology and sculpture might, in the course of the morning of one day, for instance, even in three or four hours give with existing monuments before him in the British Museum, a history of the progress of art and, therefore, of the progress of the human mind in civilisation, which could not be equalled or illustrated in any other collection in the world.'[17]

To even the most aesthetically minded, the Victorian veneration of the idea of Progress overrode any desire to achieve a merely grand or decorative effect in the arrangement of the Museum's sculptures. Even Baron Marochetti, who proposed a more decorative scheme combining pictures with sculpture, as in the Tribuna of the Uffizi, still wished to retain a chronological progression in the placement of the sculptures.[18] When we consider that the same men who advocated the artistic importance of a chronological series were the very ones who preferred to teach their students from casts rather than original sculptures, we see that their interest in a museum of paradigms was an academic one; Sir Richard's refusal to separate an object's value as a means of artistic instruction from its relative place in the progress of civilisation must be seen as a case of wanting both to have and to eat the cake. More straightforward was the testimony of John Ruskin. A decade earlier, in the controversy that had followed the cleaning of pictures at the National Gallery during the autumn of 1846, Ruskin had put forward firm views on the importance of establishing a historical collection, properly exhibited.[19] And yet he admitted to the 1857 Committee of enquiry that an archaeological, chronological and historical series was of little consequence for the course of study of a creative artist: 'The teaching of the future artist might be accomplished by very few pictures of the class that artist wished to study.'[20]

The drawing school and the museum were not, therefore, one and the same thing, and Ruskin, who described himself with affected modesty as 'Master of the

Elementary and Landscape School of Drawing at the Working Men's College in Great Ormond Street', could provide little reason for separating out the collections of the British Museum to that end. Indeed, he argued on the contrary that, since his ideal museum was a great body of reference for the history of art, he would include not only sculpture and painting but 'what may be called the handicrafts of a nation, down to the pots and pans'.

The conclusions to be drawn from the evidence of Ruskin, artist and aesthetician, were not very different from those arising from the views of the Museum staff and their sympathisers. For them the removal of the sculptures would be an act of desecration ruinous not only to the collections left behind but also to the sculptures themselves. The longest and most detailed protest came from Charles Newton in a missive forwarded from Rhodes and dated 28 May 1853. It was addressed in the first instance to Colonel Mure, the Chairman of the Select Committee on the National Gallery, and was printed in the form of an Appendix (XII) to the published Report.[21]

> I shall confine myself to the question, whether, in the event of an entirely new arrangement of our national collections, the antiquities now at the British Museum ought to be considered as one entire collection, or whether as has been recently proposed, the finest specimens only should be transported to a new Museum of Art, the rest of the antiquities being left where they are at present, or distributed in other Museums, of which the formation is now contemplated.

The antiquities of the British Museum he divided into three classes: monuments of art, inscribed monuments, and the products of handicraft. These collectively touched upon four principal races: the Egyptian, Assyrian, Greek and Roman. To remove the inscribed objects and the objects of minor art from the monumental sculpture was, to Newton, to remove the 'collateral evidence'. Greek sculptures, as he pointed out, do not explain themselves; in order to understand them we must study not only other sculptures, but other branches of antiquities, vases, coins, gems, bronzes, terracottas. Thus, for example, the east pediment of the Parthenon, as Pausanias informs us, showed the birth of Athena, but the figures themselves being missing must be restored with reference to other works of art, such as vases.

A museum of antiquities not restricted to one period or people, but comprising all races and times, 'exhibits a vast comparative scheme of the material productions of man.' Such a range of reference was essential, moreover, not merely for an archaeological understanding but also for the aesthetic appreciation of ancient art. The 'chronological sequence of sculpture [in the British Museum] is such as no other museum in Europe can boast of. Take away the Elgin Marbles and the continuity of the series is destroyed. It is as if the keystone had fallen out of the arch.' The brilliant choice of metaphor is expanded in a passage so essential to Newton's museological doctrine that it deserves to be quoted here in full:

But it may be said that I have dwelt too exclusively on archaeological considerations; that the question before the Committee of the House of Commons at this moment is the formation of a Museum of Art, by which the taste of the English people may be educated and elevated, not the arrangement of materials for the use of the historian and the scholar; that the accumulation of collections distracts the eye and confuses the uninformed judgement by simultaneous exhibition of heterogeneous objects and styles of art; that archaeological research and aesthetic culture do not go well together; and that it is better to make a kind of *florilegium*, or selection of specimens for a museum of art, so as to separate the beautiful from that which, being simply curious, is fit only to be studied through the spectacles of the antiquary.

To such arguments as these, I would reply that we cannot appreciate art aesthetically unless we first learn to interpret its meaning and motive, and in order to do this we must study it historically; that if a series of specimens be arranged in schools and periods, according to the time and place of their production, the merit of the more beautiful works of art will be enhanced, not diminished, by contrast and comparison with the rest.

The argument that to understand the aesthetic value of art we must view it historically would have found sympathy with the staff of the Museum and with a few of the more enlightened Trustees. There was, however, one curator in the Museum who took what stands out as an extreme view in defence of the Museum's collections. Edmund Oldfield argued that 'it is incorrect to view the British Museum as a collection of works of art; it is in its primary character a collection of antiquities of the highest value as illustrative of history.'[22] In this Oldfield anticipated the modern separation of art history from archaeology, but his was an exceptional view: 'I do not know', declared Panizzi, 'where art begins and archaeology ends.'[23] Hawkins even went so far as to describe the antiquities of the British Museum as 'essentially an art collection'; but then qualified that by adding, 'Our collection is a thing that would gratify the taste of a gentleman of taste, but it should particularly afford materials for the historian.'[24] When asked for a second time if he would make a distinction between the archaeological and historical value of the Elgin Marbles and their artistic and aesthetic value, he replied less ambiguously: 'Our collections are available for both purposes. They are for the instruction of artists, and for the gratification of men of taste, and they are also of great assistance to the historian.'[25]

W.R. Hamilton had taken a similar line. He was emphatically in favour of keeping the antiquities together: 'They are so intimately connected with each other that the study of one promotes a knowledge of the others.'[26] To separate one branch of the collection from another would be to break up the 'chain' now considered more or less complete. Hamilton was, however, prepared to make an exception of the Elgin Marbles; not because he thought they were any less integral to the main body of the collections but because 'being perfectly unique of their kind, and superior to anything existing in any part of Europe, they ought to be preserved for future times; and not to be allowed to be deteriorated by the dust and soot of a

London atmosphere, as they are now.' He proposed that they should be moved at least as far away as Hampton Court, leaving in their place casts 'which would have a much more striking appearance than the original marbles have in their present state'. He saw no advantage in taking them to Kensington, having himself lived for many years at Chelsea, 'where they certainly had plenty of soot'.

Hamilton, who had been a Trustee of the Museum since 1838 and who had, therefore, been in part responsible for the architectural development of its buildings, differed in one respect from Oldfield and Hawkins, whose opinion as servants of the Trustees had all too frequently been disregarded. Unlike the officers of the Antiquities Department, Hamilton claimed to be satisfied with the galleries of the British Museum, even though he had voiced criticisms in the past. Both Hawkins and Oldfield appeared to welcome the transfer *en bloc* of the antiquities to some new site. Hawkins favoured Hyde Park but had to admit that, even here, the sheep were blackened by smoke.[27]

Oldfield went so far as to draw up a plan of his ideal Museum. Unlike Hamilton, he considered the chain as far from 'complete'. More room would be needed not only for a proper accommodation of the existing collections but also for additions that would be made in the future. The progress of civilisation as represented in the collections of the British Museum could only be shown in a linear arrangement of
19 galleries running parallel to each other and linked by a central corridor. Like the branches of a tree, each gallery would constitute an offshoot from the main stem. There was therefore room for longitudinal and lateral growth or expansion. All galleries would be at ground level to allow the sculptures to be top-lit by sky-lights, 'which after many experiments, and much observation, I would say are indispensable to a well arranged gallery of sculptures.'[28] Slip-rooms running parallel to the main galleries would provide fitting accommodation for appropriate displays of smaller antiquities. This uncompromising sequence of parallel lines Oldfield proposed to front with an architectural façade, as to the style of which he did not greatly care. His Museum would be set in open ground, and therefore he proposed to obscure the raw ends of his galleries with trees.

What Oldfield had in mind was the very antithesis of Robert Smirke's museological conception. While Smirke had subordinated the needs of the collection to the building, Oldfield intended the reverse. Smirke had endeavoured to create a building that was in all its parts architectural. The colonnaded front provided the principal side of a Greek Revival quadrangle and court. Oldfield's façade would be the very opposite; namely an architectural screen of whatever style, which concealed behind it an uncompromising grid of low, shed-like rooms. Oldfield's proposal was never adopted, but it demonstrates the contemporary division between the practical concerns of the progressive archaeologist, on the one hand, and on the other the aesthetic approach of the neo-classical architect.

Both Robert and Sydney Smirke's designs for the British Museum were drawn up and executed with only a passing thought in the early stages for the collections they would contain. Robert Smirke rarely attempted to interfere in the arrangement of the collections; his brief was to create space, and often this was allocated a specific function only when the building work was well in hand or, indeed, actually finished. In the first instance the responsibility for arranging the marbles had been left in the hands of Westmacott, and the results were frequently criticised by the officers of the Department of Antiquities. By the early 1850s Westmacott, now in advanced old age, was losing his grip on the arrangement of the collections and the energetic and opinionated Oldfield assumed more and more responsibility, albeit acting through the no less ancient Keeper, Edward Hawkins.

The Commission of 1848 had been much concerned about the manner in which Westmacott had been able to impose his aesthetic prejudices upon the arrangement of the Lycian sculptures. At this time it became a commonplace to make open criticism of Westmacott's picturesque arrangements and at the same time to wonder how things had been managed abroad. It is symptomatic of the whole manner of planning and arranging the British Museum's sculpture galleries that, only when the building designed by Robert Smirke was complete and the sculpture placed within it, did attention turn to the question of how foreign institutions had treated similar problems. Of the building J. Mordaunt Crook has written:

> . . . the British Museum certainly formed part of a general European movement, that alliance between the cult of the antique and the question of organised *Kultur*, which engendered a rash of museum-building during the post-Napoleonic period. But a strict examination of the genesis and chronology of Smirke's scheme reveals that the design was almost certainly conceived with no more than indirect reference to its Continental counterparts, Klenze's Glyptothek in Munich (1800–30) and Schinkel's Altes Museum in Berlin (designed 1823, built 1825–28).[29]

And if that is true, as Crook convincingly shows it is, of the architecture of the British Museum, then it is certainly true of the arrangement of the sculpture. On the question of colouring of walls and lighting there seems to have been next to no direct reference to foreign museums.

One of the most interesting of the testimonies presented to the National Gallery inquiry was that of the architect Leo von Klenze who, with the assistance of the sculptor J. M. von Wagner, had laid out Ludwig of Bavaria's sculpture collection in a series of sumptuously decorated galleries arranged around a courtyard.[30] The arrangement was more or less chronological, leading from the Egyptian Room through Greek to Roman sculptures and including the early Greek Aegina marbles 12
which Haller von Hallerstein had acquired for the Bavarian king in 1812. Klenze's observations were mostly related to the question of lighting and other architectural matters. As for the sculptures themselves, he saw no advantage in placing them

under the same roof as paintings, not least because of the different lighting requirements. Klenze himself had avoided this by creating a separate Pinakothek for Ludwig's pictures. He had, it is true, placed pictures and sculptures together in the building commissioned from him by Nicholas I in 1839 (completed 1851) at St Petersburg, but, as Klenze was quick to point out, the sculpture collection there was not very great.

Klenze would have arranged the sculptures of the British Museum chronologically in schools, and on the basis that all Greek art 'rests' on the art of Asia and Africa (i.e. Assyrian and Egyptian), he would have begun with the Egyptian, followed by the Assyrian collection, the Athenian marbles, those of Asia Minor and finally the Roman. As for the style of the building, it was a choice between what he termed 'academic', on the one hand, and 'picturesque' on the other. This was in essence a distinction between regular and irregular styles of architecture; thus, the Pinakothek (and presumably also the Glyptothek) was an example of academic design, the Vatican picturesque. On this reasoning, although Klenze does not actually say so, the British Museum was an academic design forced by the sheer magnitude of the collections to stray into the picturesque. Klenze's recommendation was that nature should be allowed to take its course, and in England, where the collections were so vast, he considered the picturesque the best model, allowing, as it did, for natural growth.

Charles Barry's 'Hall of Antiquities'

Expansion offered one possible way to accommodate the Museum's sculptures; another idea was their wholesale transfer to another building; and a third was to extend the space allocated to the sculptures within the existing area of the Museum. As far back as 1836 a plan had been proposed for building over the inner quadrangle surrounded by the four wings of the Museum.[31] Edward Miller described the area at the time as a gloomy grass-covered plot where two small boys belonging to the difficult Keeper of Manuscripts played alone.[32] The proposal was to enhance the
71 growing Library, but in 1848–9 the architect William Hosking put forward his plan for what he described as a 'Pantheon structure in the central quadrangle, by way of providing a Grand Central Hall or Rotunda for the display of the finer and important works of sculpture'.[33] The plan was returned with the Trustees' refusal.[34]

Another major scheme for utilising the inner court for the display of sculpture was that of Sir Charles Barry. He was one of those to whom the archaeological integrity
72 of the Museum meant little, favouring as he did a grander, selective display. His proposal was put up, however, in competition with one from inside the Museum itself. On 5 May 1852 Antonio Panizzi had first laid before the Trustees his proposal for filling the central quadrangle with a round reading room.[35] The preliminary

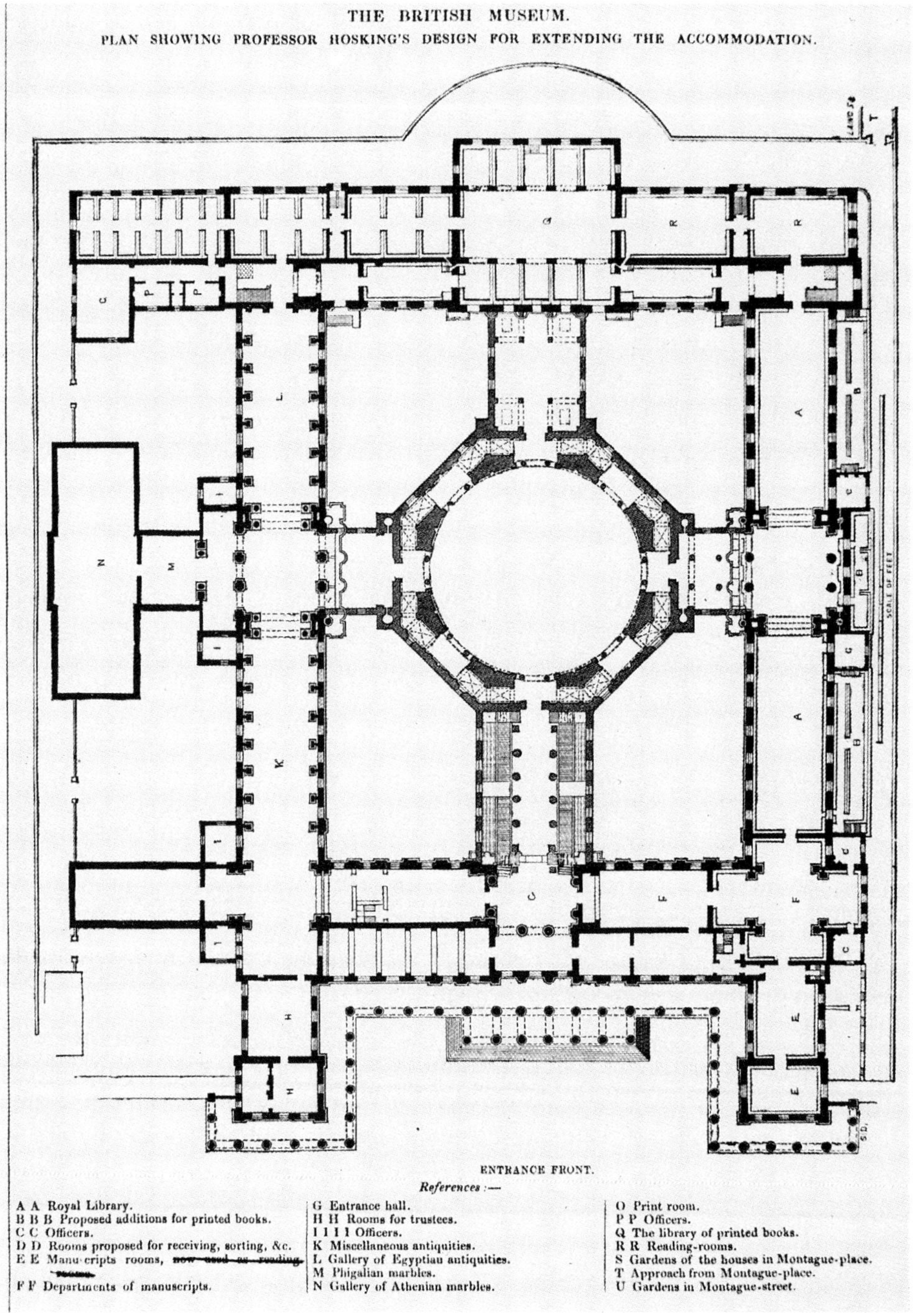

71 Plan showing W. Hosking's proposal for a 'Pantheon structure' in the central quadrangle, *c.*1848–9. The round Reading Room would later occupy this space. *The Builder* 8 (22 June 1850).

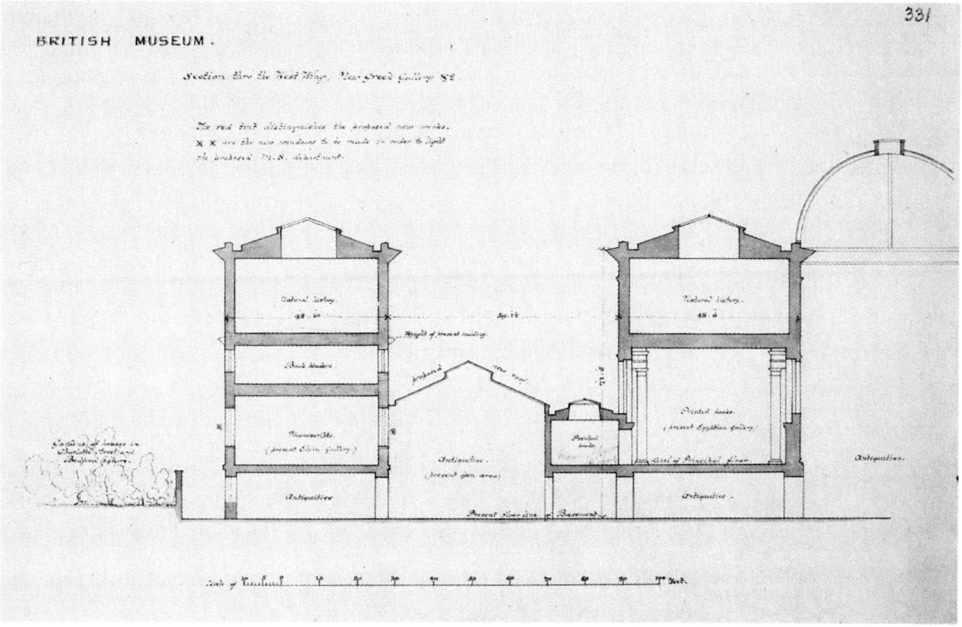

72 Section through the west side of the Museum to illustrate the implications of Charles Barry's proposed 'Hall of Antiquities', 28 October 1853. British Museum, Central Archive.

sketches, worked up into a formal architectural design by Sydney Smirke, were at first rejected by the Treasury but eventually carried into effect between 1854 and 1857.

Barry's proposal was published in the *Quarterly Review*.[36] In essence, the plan was to roof over the quadrangle with what would amount to nearly two acres of glass supported on forty or fifty iron pillars, and under this transparent canopy to exhibit the principal sculpture collections. The rooms vacated by the sculptures were to be given over to the Library. Barry, architect of the recently built Houses of Parliament, was a powerful threat to the success of Panizzi's own scheme and the Museum's independence. The Trustees did something they had done too little in the past, and took counsel, not only from the Museum Architect, but also from the heads of the various Departments concerned, so as to answer Barry's proposals point for point.[37]

Barry's scheme took inspiration from the contemporary vogue for exhibition glass and iron railing structures. Hawkins complained that as a showpiece of the modern style it would be eclipsed in splendour by the Crystal Palace at Sydenham. More importantly, he challenged the aesthetic premise on which 'a style of construction which is perfectly appropriate to an exhibition of modern industry and science' could be adapted for the relics of ancient art. He concluded: 'In truth, the entertainment of the eye by a spectacle of scenic magnificence, is not the legitimate object of such a Museum as this: it would be to degrade it from a school of intellectual teaching, to a medium of gratification to the outward sense.'

There was one proposal within Barry's scheme that was dismissed by both Hawkins and Panizzi as derisory, namely his suggestion for accommodating the frieze of the Parthenon. The intention was to provide the frieze with an architectural setting more in keeping with its original placement. On the south side of his Hall of Antiquities Barry would build a colonnade and high up on the wall within it place the frieze. In fact the wall was neither sufficiently long nor ideally constructed for such a fixture. 'By what Procrustean operation, this noble monument of art is to be accommodated to a space only two thirds of its own length, Sir C. Barry has abstained from communicating', wrote Hawkins, and on the general inaccessiblity of the frieze in that position and the lack of good lighting he added: 'The marble-pieces of Pheidias would then appear to have been brought from Athens for little other purpose than to form an architectural decoration to Sir C. Barry's colonnade.'

Barry's scheme failed, but a vestige of it was revived in 1857 when the imminent arrival of new acquisitions from Newton's excavations at Bodrum and Nathan Davis's activities at Carthage brought a new urgency to the problem of want of space. A suggestion was put forward for glazing over the remaining open space around the Reading Room.[38] The scheme was rejected, however, on the grounds that the area would be badly ventilated and would darken the surrounding basement of the main building. Attention was diverted, instead, to the possibility of connecting the southern side of the Insect Gallery and Print Room with the north wall of the Elgin Room to form a new sculpture gallery at the north-west corner of the Museum. This idea had been raised before, and would be again.[39]

Nature versus Art

By the end of 1857, the needs of the Library having been met for some years to come, attention focused upon the ever-growing needs of the Antiquities and Natural History collections. It was now clear that either the Museum must expand outward, or some part of the collections must go. All the while that discussions were going on with regard to the future of the collections, the officers of the Department of Antiquities maintained pressure from within for the enlargement of the present buildings. In 1856, Oldfield appended to his report to the Trustees on the rearrangement of the Greek sculptures a long list of faults to be found in the sculpture galleries.[40] His proposed remedy was to buy up the ground to the west of the Museum between the Museum and Charlotte Street, 'now occupied by second-class dwelling-houses and their gardens'. Here he saw the potential for achieving a near approximation to his ideal Museum based on the principle of parallel lines.

There would be ample space for at least four lines of galleries, parallel to the three now appropriated to the Egyptian, Assyrian, and Greek sculptures: and such lines might be carried in process of time to a length virtually unlimited, being intercepted in the north only by Montagu Place, and on the south by Great Russell Street, at a distance of 800ft from each other.

In May 1857 Newton had found time in the midst of his sensational discoveries at Bodrum to write a long letter to Panizzi detailing his prescription for the future of the British Museum's sculpture collections. The Commission set up in 1857 to enquire further into the future of the National Gallery was then sitting, and he wished to communicate his latest views upon the subject through Panizzi, who had recently been appointed as Principal Librarian. The question was whether it would be best to combine all the collections, pictures and antiquities in one great building, as in the Louvre, or to group several buildings together in 'suggestive juxtaposition', as in Munich's Pinakothek and Glyptothek. His final verdict was that the antiquities of the British Museum should stay put, except the recently developed collection of early Christian and medieval art, 'which has been struggling into existence at the British Museum', while a larger, more ambitious collection had been formed at the Museum of Christian Art in Marlborough House (afterwards transferred to the South Kensington Museum). These two collections Newton would combine with the pictures of the National Gallery to form one museum, while the British Museum would remain an exhibition of pagan art. In the latter the sculpture would naturally be the 'paramount point of interest, presenting the highest manifestation of the power of the ancient artist . . .'.[41]

There was, however, another possible solution to the need for space in the Museum, and this was the removal of the Natural History collections. As early as 1826 it was felt in some quarters that the Museum had strayed sufficiently from its original purpose, namely the 'advancement of the study of Natural History' to warrant the removal of the scientific collections to some other, independent repository.[42] In his evidence to the 1853 National Gallery Commission, this was the course of action that had been favoured by Panizzi. The Library was, he felt, more 'in rapport' with the antiquities than with the scientific objects: 'It is not necessary that there should be the first edition of Homer or of the Classics, and so on, for Zoology; it is only necessary to have good editions of Pliny or of Aristotle.'[43]

By the end of 1858, the very latest Commission on the National Gallery seemingly having failed to find a satisfactory solution to the overcrowding of the Antiquities collections at the British Museum, the Trustees were forced to find their own solution to the mounting problem. By December of that year the matter seemed resolved; the Natural History collections would go. Newton wrote from Cnidus to Panizzi: 'I was much interested in your account of the contest of Nature and Art for the territory of the Museum, and rejoice that Athena has ousted

Poseidon and his pickled and stuffed fishes.'[44] The contest had not been won without a struggle, and in July 1858 a body of petitioners calling themselves 'Promoters and Cultivators of Science' had lobbied the Government to preserve the Natural History collections in the main Museum.[45] One of the signatories was Richard Owen, the powerful Superintendent of the Natural History Departments. In December of that same year a comparable body of interested parties on the arts side submitted their petition to the Government.[46] The text itself, which merely rehearses the now familiar complaints, is perhaps less interesting than the names of the thirty-six signatories. Among them we find men who had argued on opposite sides of the debate over the proposed dismantlement of the collections in the earlier part of the decade. They were now united against a new breed of professional scientists who came to represent a common enemy in what Newton had wittily referred to as the 'Contest for Attica', evoking the mythical contest between Athena and Poseidon for the possession of Athens.[47]

The Trustees were persuaded of the expediency of removing the Natural History collections and in time even Richard Owen was himself brought round to the view that they would be better rehoused. He submitted a long report to the Trustees upon the subject, which they in turn forwarded to the Treasury.[48] A separation of the collections was resolved upon in the following year and is recorded in the Treasury Minute of 13 November 1861. Shortly afterwards a special committee of Trustees was set up to deliberate upon that decision. Their recommendations were privately printed and were to form the basis for all future discussion of the matter of accommodation.[49] The actual site of a new Museum of Natural History was not resolved until the beginning of the following decade, and the move, commenced in 1878, was completed in 1883.[50]

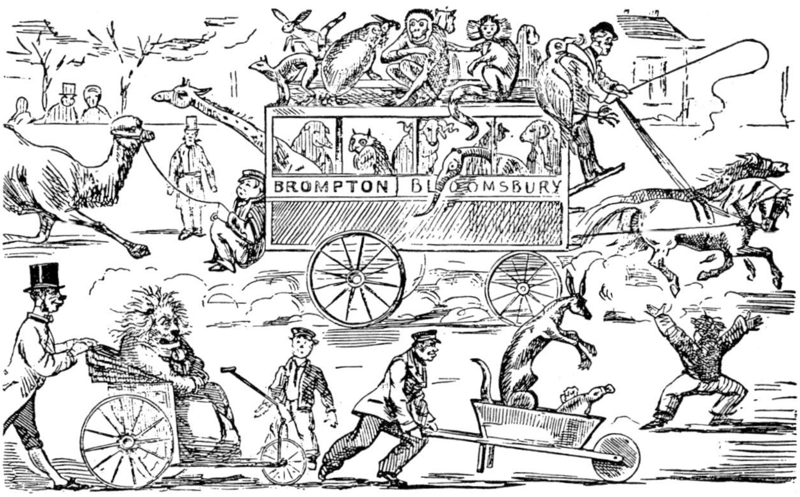

73 The *Comic News* heralds the transfer of the Natural History collections from Bloomsbury to Brompton.

10 The Chain is Broken

West and East

The preceding chapters have described the growth of the British Museum's sculpture collections during the first part of the nineteenth century. This was the period when activity was most intense, both in respect of the acquisition of antiquities and in the development of space to house them. Inevitably, attention is focused upon the great bodies of classical sculpture that were gathered in, and the Egyptian and Assyrian sculptures that accompanied them. Next to nothing has been said of the few sculptures that reached the Museum from Central America and the archaeological cultures of Sri Lanka, India, Pakistan and Afghanistan. Although never regarded by the Museum as art, they certainly had a place in the 'chain' that formed the metaphorical premise of nineteenth-century archaeological theory. And yet, little was done to afford them that place, either through a positive acquisitions policy or by a serious attempt to provide independent gallery space.

After the publication of John L. Stephens's travels in Central America, moves were made towards acquiring a representative collection of Mayan sculpture.[1] The attempt was, however, never more than half-hearted, and difficulties of terrain and local politics seemed always to conspire to prevent a wholesale gathering of sculptural remains on a scale comparable with those brought from Egypt, Assyria and the classical lands of the Mediterranean. Only with the transfer from the South Kensington Museum of Alfred Maudslay's collection of original sculptures and casts from Mayan sculpture, did the British Museum make up the deficiency. These casts have never been properly or fully displayed, however, and still today of all the great archaeological cultures the sculpture of the Mayan peoples is the least well known or understood.[2]

As regards the sculpture of the oriental Indian cultures, here too the Museum was sluggish in its response to a generally acknowledged need: 'It is something of a disgrace', wrote Hawkins in 1836, 'to have so few memorials of our Indian empire', yet he was hardly vigorous in pursuit of filling this lacuna.[3] The situation was only remedied by acts such as the transfer in 1879 of a considerable body of Gandharan and other sculptures, including those from the Amaravati stupa, from the India Museum. Already in 1872 the far-sighted A. W. Franks had secured an important collection from the Bridge family.[4] By the end of the nineteenth century, therefore, the Museum had substantial and important holdings of Indian sculpture, but these were not given the prominence they deserved until the years between the wars. So although in 1845 James Stephanoff incorporated such 'primitive' arts into the bottom register of his pictorial microcosm of the Museum's collections, even this lowly position implies they had greater importance than was in fact the case.[5] In reality the 'Much Maligned Monsters' of Partha Mitter's brilliant study of the reception of Indian art were imprisoned in basement chambers until liberated by the new age and new thinking of the twentieth century.[6]

Want of space

In the years following the retirement of Edward Hawkins and the three-way division of the old Department of Antiquities, the pace of acquisitions, so far as the sculptures were concerned, slowed down. The major acquisitions of classical sculpture in the course of Charles Newton's Keepership of the newly formed Department of Greek and Roman Antiquities were as follows: the collection formed by the 4th Earl of Aberdeen in 1801 and presented by the 5th Earl in 1861; the fruits of Smith and Porcher's expedition to Cyrene, 1860–61; the purchase in 1864 of the collection formed by the 6th Viscount Strangford, including the late archaic *kouros* known as the Strangford Apollo; the purchase in the same year of sundry statues at the sale of the residue of the Farnese collection; the substantial body of material from the Archaic and later temples of Artemis and other sites at Ephesus excavated by J. T. Wood between 1863 and 1874; and the sculpture excavated by R. P. Pullan at the site of the Temple of Athena Polias during the expedition to Priene of 1868–9 and presented to the Museum through the Society of Dilettanti.

These were considerable additions to an already unwieldy collection, but the principal preoccupation of Newton's Keepership was consolidation, rather than acquisition. While, therefore, he ensured that the collections of his Department expanded enormously through the increase of smaller antiquities, with regard to sculpture he felt that more should be done to achieve that 'scientific' arrangement first conceived by his predecessor. In keeping with this internal restraint on acquisition, it may be argued that the great age of British archaeological dilettantism was, in any case, over.[7] Certainly, the second part of the nineteenth century did not offer the same opportunities as those formerly exploited by that most telling combination of the diplomat-archaeologist acting in conjunction with the Royal Navy. By this means, the sheer volume of material assembled in the national repository had far outstripped expectations and confounded any attempt to prepare exhibition galleries in advance. Now 'want of space', became the perennial lament of the Keeper of Greek and Roman Antiquities. The great crisis of the 1850s had resolved that Athena should hold sway over Attica and the sculptures, including the all-important

Elgin Marbles, should be housed at Bloomsbury. There remained, however, the question of how best to accommodate them there.

The systematic reorganisation of the sculpture collections depended upon the provision of new galleries. During the 1850s the great debate had focused upon the prospect of transferring the collections to another site altogether. In the end it was resolved that the Natural History collections should go and the sculptures remain. The removal of the former, although it afforded additional space for the smaller antiquities crowded into the upper galleries, did nothing to relieve the situation of the sculptures on the ground floor. When, therefore, a committee appointed by the Trustees of the Museum to consider the Treasury's resolution to remove the Natural History collections from Bloomsbury met early in 1862, their report included detailed recommendations for adapting and enlarging the ground floor galleries.[8] These, in brief, were as follows:

1. Demolishing the principal staircase in order to enlarge the room (1 on Fig. 1) to the south running westward from the Front Hall.
2. Extending the length of the Egyptian Sculpture Gallery southwards by removing the partition walls of what were then the Trustees' Offices and Board Room.
3. Building over the ground to the west of the Board Room, backing onto the south wall of the Third Graeco-Roman Room.
4. Extending the Second Elgin Room northwards to meet the appendage to the north wing of the Museum, then occupied by the Insect Room on the lower and the Print Room on the upper floor (10 on Fig. 1); at the same time, adapting the floor levels of the latter so as to correspond with the proposed new gallery (9 on Fig. 1) to the south.
5. Filling in the plot of land (11 on Fig. 1) between the northern Assyrian slip room and the proposed extension to the Elgin Room.

These were the recommendations of the Trustees' Committee as submitted on 21 January 1862, and the successful arrangement of the classical sculptures was seen to depend upon how far they were carried out. Time and again the Keeper of Greek and Roman Antiquities and his sympathisers would invoke the text of the 1862 Report in future pleas for expansion of the galleries, and on 8 February 1868 a committee was appointed 'for carrying on communications with the Lords Commissioners of Her Majesty's Treasury relative to the execution of the plan adverted to in the Treasury Minute of 13 November 1861 and contained in the Report of the Committee of the Trustees, 21 January 1862.'[9]

Such were the aspirations, but how far were they realised? To take each in turn: although revived more than once, the removal of the grand staircase was too radical and expensive a proposal for acceptance by the Treasury. Nor was the extension southward of the Egyptian Sculpture Gallery ever carried out, while the plan for building permanent exhibition space on the open ground to the west of the Board Room also remained unfulfilled until the construction of the present New Wing

special exhibition gallery. In this place, however, a temporary shed-like building was erected in 1909 to accommodate a display of casts. Such a collection of casts of important sculptures in other European collections, in which to trace the progress of classical sculpture, had long been desired. Its eventual creation was belated and short-lived. In 1905 the Museum received an approach from the Principals of the University of London urging the need 'for educational purposes' of a good gallery of casts from antique sculptures,[10] and a year later the Board of Education proposed that the classical casts then housed at the Victoria and Albert Museum should be transferred to Bloomsbury.[11] Estimates were accordingly drawn up for the erection of a skylighted building of iron and asbestos cement.[12] The casts were received in the summer of 1907,[13] but the gallery was not completed until August 1909.[14] On 74
completion, the casts were arranged so that the visitor could trace the development of classical sculpture chronologically from the lions of the gateway at Mycenae to the reliefs of the Roman arch at Beneventum. Not all the available casts could, however, be accommodated, and those that were had been uncomfortably crammed in.

The Museum that had insufficient space for important original sculptures had always been reluctant to accommodate casts and, only twenty years after the Cast Gallery was opened to the public, the Keeper of Greek and Roman Antiquities, H. B. Walters, recommended dismantling it to make way for the series of early sculptures from Cyprus.[15] The Cast Gallery does not seem to have attracted art students particularly, and for teaching purposes Walters felt that they would be better placed at University College. In the long term a Royal Commission on Museums had recommended the setting up of a National Cast Museum, but this must have seemed a long way off. Accordingly, the evacuation of the Cast Gallery was completed and the contents dispatched, in part, to University College, the remainder to an uncertain future in the Museum basement, all except the cast of the Laocoon which went to the Ashmolean Museum in Oxford.[16]

Apart from this somewhat dubious success there were more positive additions arising out of the recommendations of the 1862 Committee. Thus the fourth proposal, to extend the Elgin Room northwards, was realised in 1873–4 (9 on Fig. 1), as we have already seen in Chapter 5. Then in 1889 the gallery to the north of this extension was adapted to bring it into sequence with the rest (10 on Fig. 1).[17] This last had been tacked onto the north-west corner of Robert Smirke's original quadrangle in 1842. It was constructed on three floors with a shallow basement, a ground floor given over to the Zoological Department, and an upper floor which served as the Print Room. The completion in 1884 of the White Wing[18] on the east side of the Museum had provided new accommodation for the Print Room and, with the earlier transfer of the Natural History collections, the odd appendage at the north-west angle of the Museum became vacant for other purposes. In 1887 the

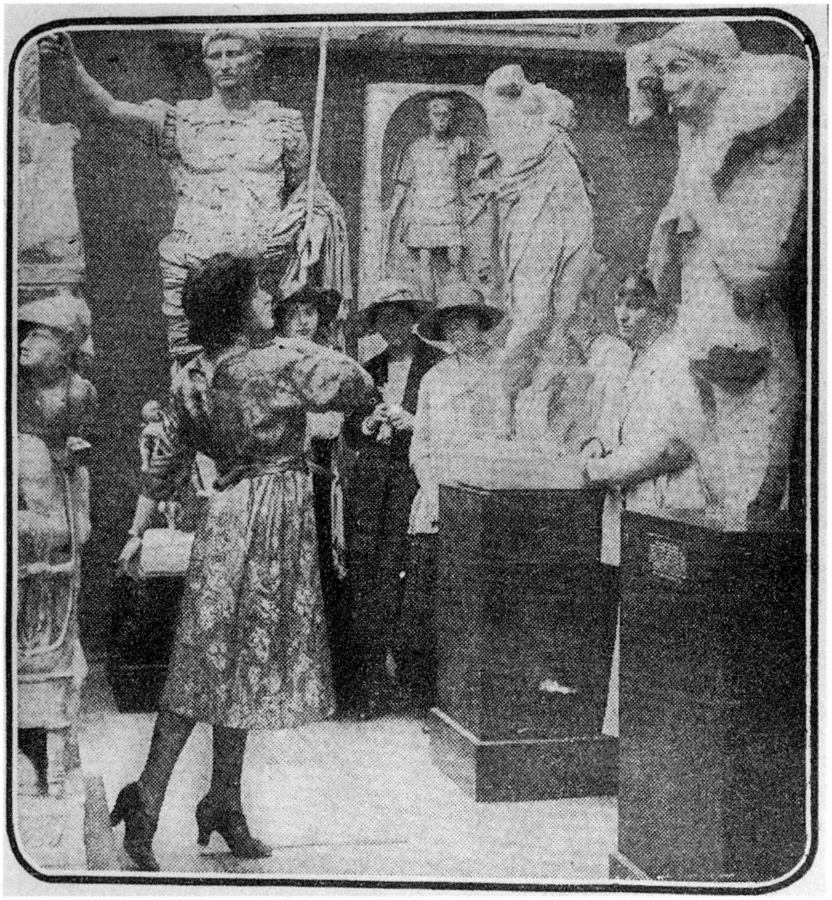

74 'Miss Helen May, the well-known dancing mistress', gives a lesson in the cast gallery. The Museum's cast gallery was short-lived: completed in 1909, the display was dismantled and the collection dispersed in 1935. Newspaper cutting dated 15 May 1920. British Museum, from a scrapbook in the Department of Greek and Roman Antiquities.

Treasury sanctioned the expenditure of £1,250 to alter the building for exhibiting sculpture.[19] The ground floor was accordingly raised to bring it to the level of the Elgin Room to the south, while the upper floor of the old Print Room was taken out. The Keeper of the day, Alexander Murray, determined that the Phigaleian
75 frieze should occupy this new space along with the Greek funerary stelae.[20] The latter had, in fact, been temporarily stored here since the removal of the Natural History collections. In the enlarged basement of the refurbished gallery were arranged a number of Roman sepulchral reliefs.

The rearrangement of the Phigaleian frieze left vacant space in the place formerly
76–7 occupied by those sculptures, and here the Nereid Monument was to find a home. Already in 1877–8 the Lycian sculptures had been removed from their cramped quarters in the old Lycian Room, so detested by one and all, and re-exhibited in a
78 new northern extension of the Front Hall.[21] This space had hitherto been open ground traversed by a corridor linking the Hall with the Reading Room. Now as a

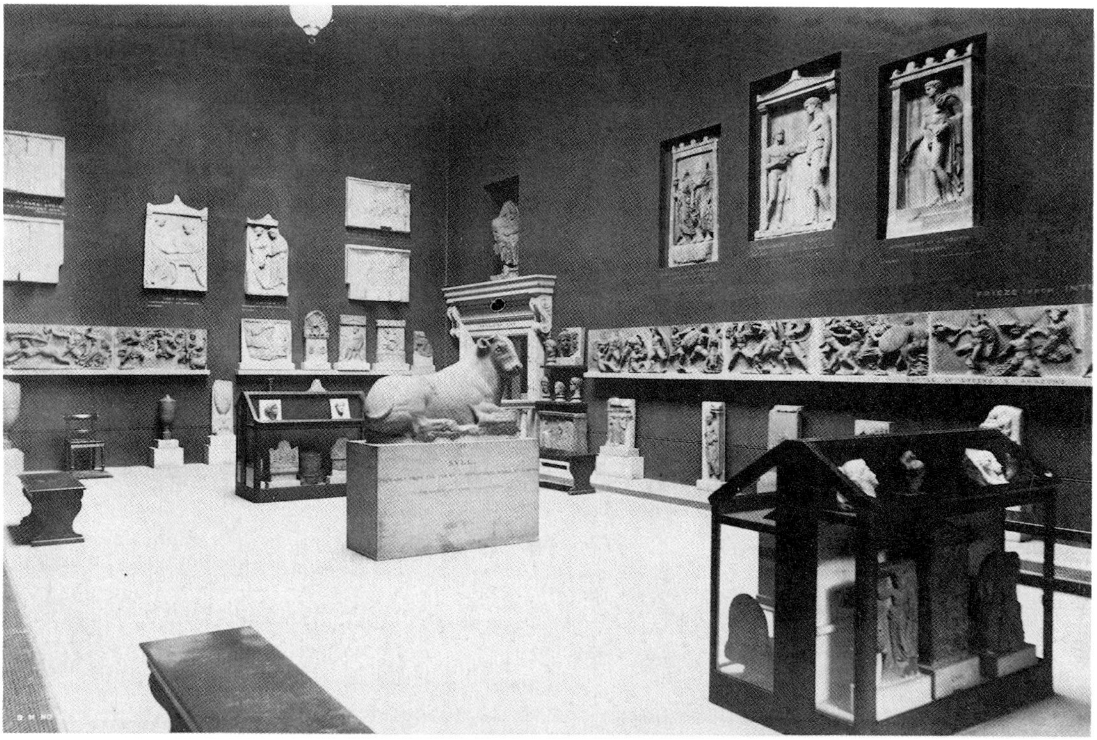

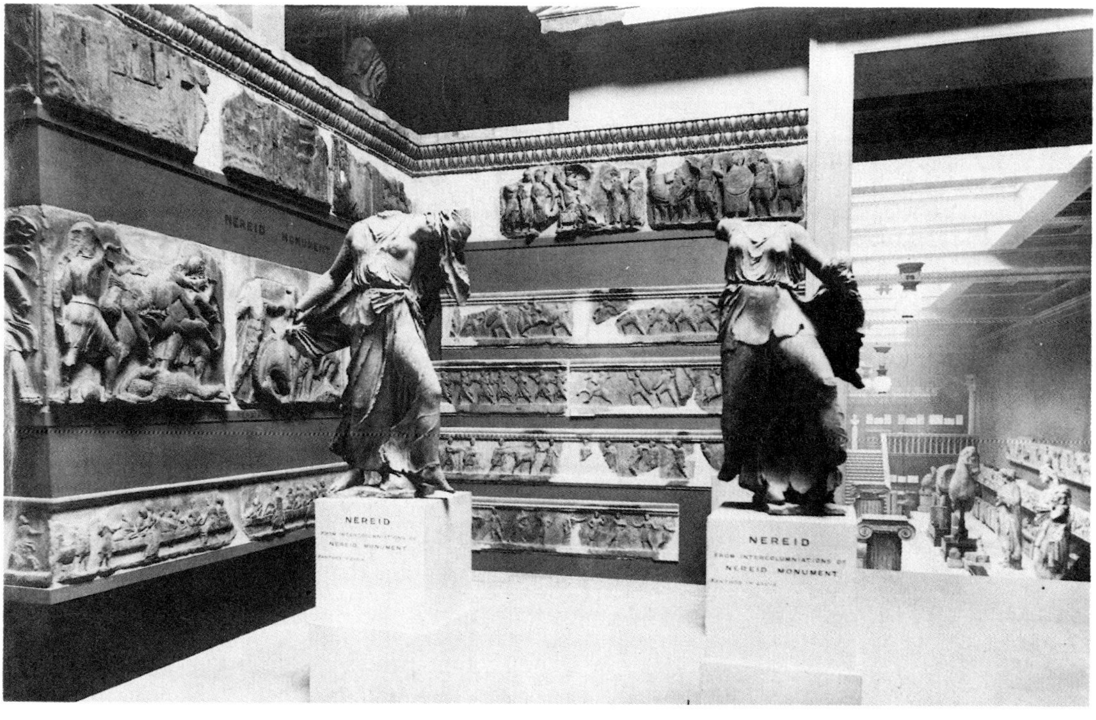
NEREID MONUMENT
NEREID
FROM INTERCOLUMNIATIONS OF
NEREID MONUMENT
NEREID
FROM INTERCOLUMNIATIONS OF
NEREID MONUMENT

75 (*Opposite, top*) The Phigaleian Marbles in the newly converted old Print Room (10 on Fig. 1), looking north-east, *c.*1890. This is now Room 10, where the Payava Tomb from Lycia stands. Photo The London Stereoscopic and Photographic Company. British Museum, Department of Greek and Roman Antiquities.

76 (*Opposite, bottom*) The Nereid sculptures in the vacated Phigaleian Room (12 on Fig. 1), looking north into the Mausoleum Room, *c.*1890. This is now Room 15. Photo The London Stereoscopic and Photographic Company. British Museum, Department of Greek and Roman Antiquities.

77 (*Right*) The Nereid sculptures in the vacated Phigaleian Room, looking west into the Elgin Room, *c.*1920. Photo British Museum, Department of Greek and Roman Antiquities.

78 (*Below*) The Lycian sculptures displayed in the space adjoining the Front Hall now occupied by the Bookshop, *c.*1888. T. Greenwood, *Museums and Art Galleries* (London 1888), p. 220.

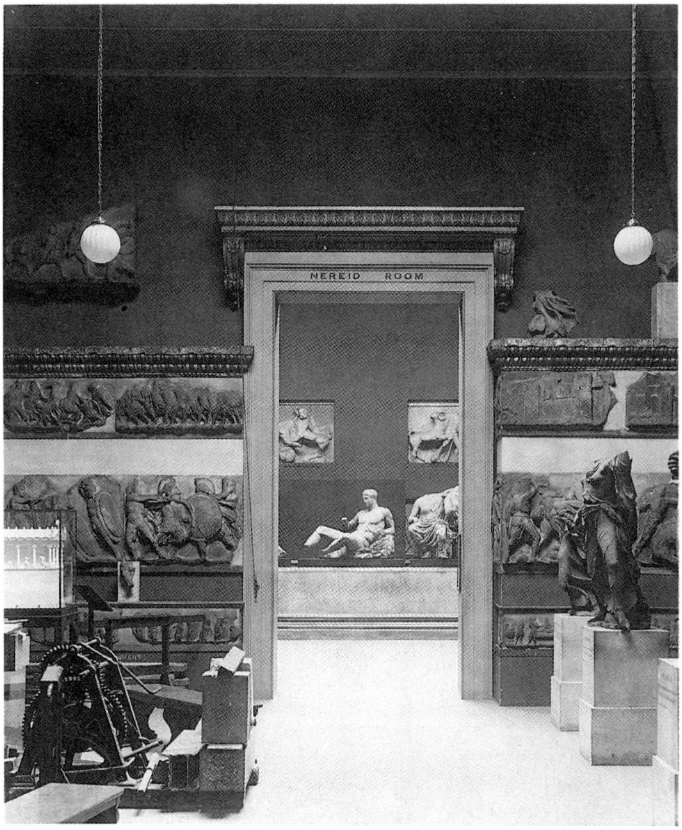

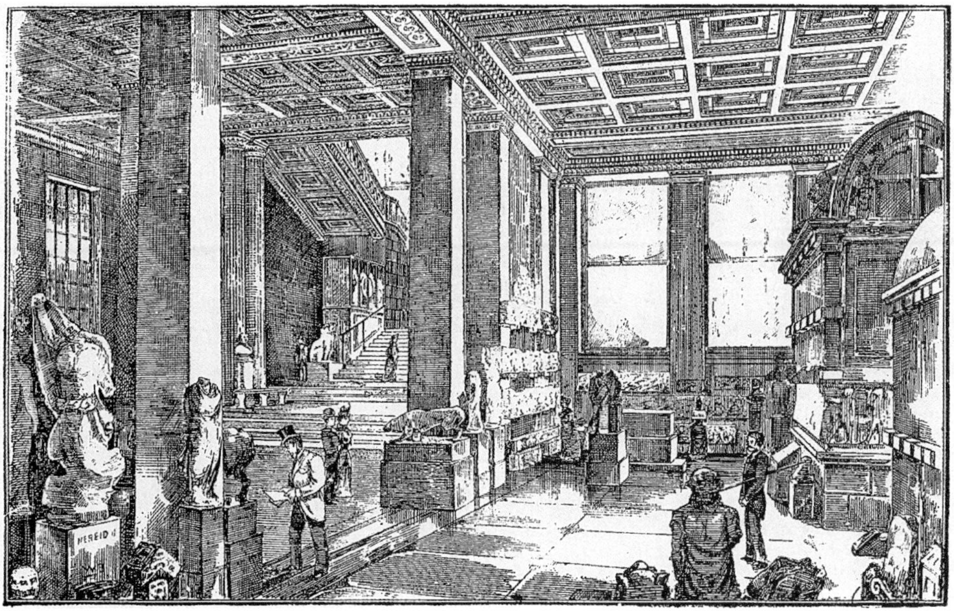

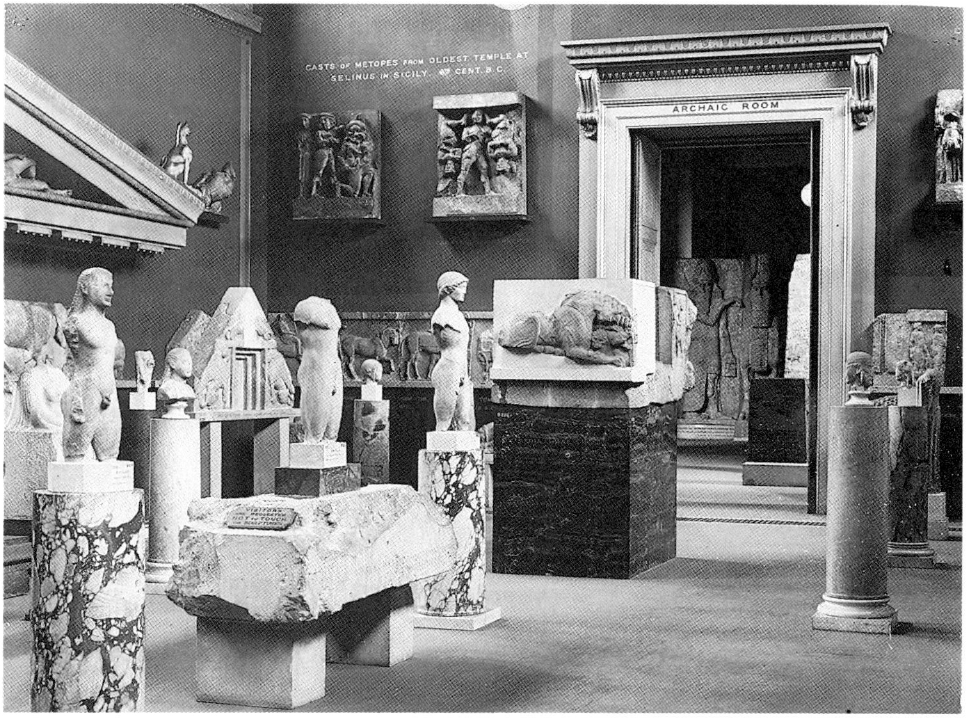

79 The Archaic Room (5 on Fig. 1), looking east into the Assyrian Transept, *c.*1930. This is now Room 3. Photo British Museum, Department of Greek and Roman Antiquities.

new extension to the Entrance Hall it would provide much-needed additional exhibition space. It did not, however, permit the separation of the Nereid Monument (or Ionic Trophy Monument, as it was then called) from the other Lycian monuments, and only when the Phigaleian sculptures migrated north (to 10 on Fig. 1) was the opportunity seized of presenting the Greek monument in isolation. The rearrangement was completed in 1891.[22]

The departure in 1878 of the Lycian sculptures from the room they had occupied since 1847 left this space vacant. Here Newton seized the opportunity of creating a room devoted to the Archaic period of Greek sculpture, vital to the chronological 79
sequence. Some twenty Archaic statues were moved from the old Phigaleian, Elgin and Graeco-Roman Rooms. In addition, the casts of metopes from Selinus and the

80 (*Opposite, top*) The Mausoleum Room (11 on Fig. 1) looking south, *c.*1890. This space is now divided by a mezzanine floor, with the Lecture Theatre in the basement and the Mausoleum sculptures displayed at ground-floor level. Photo The London Stereoscopic and Photographic Company. British Museum, Department of Greek and Roman Antiquities.

81 (*Opposite, bottom*) The Mausoleum Room looking north, *c.*1920. Photo by D. Macbeth. British Museum, Central Archive.

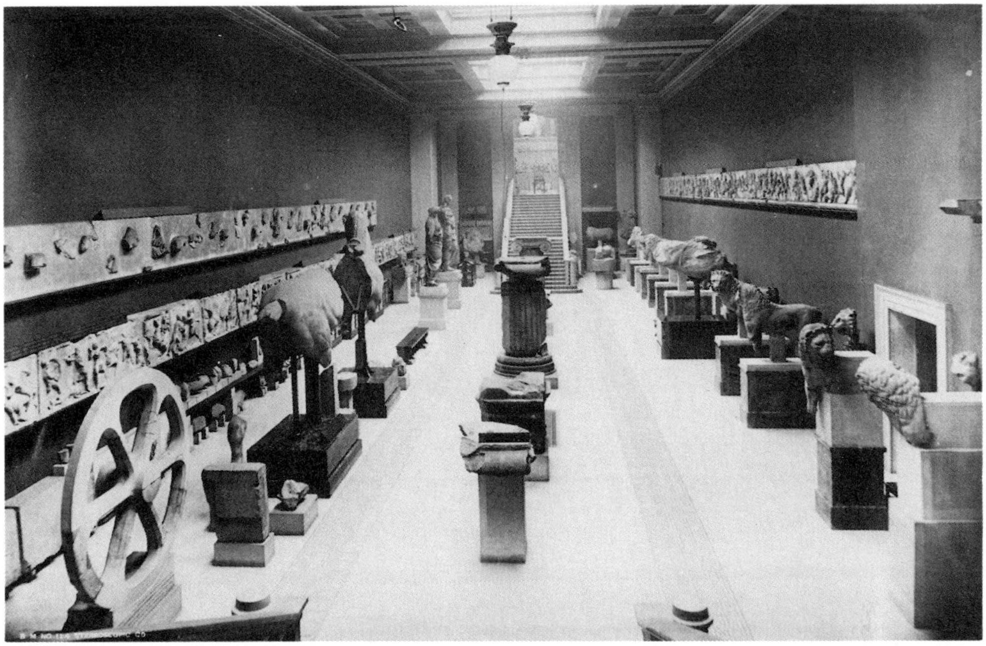

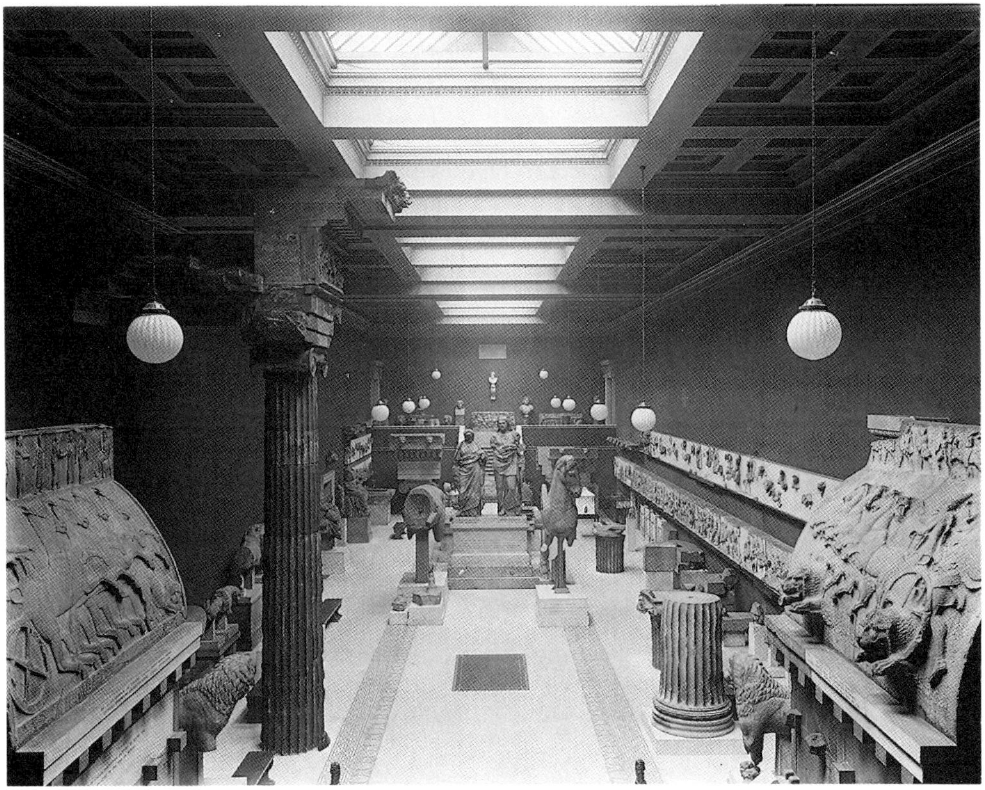

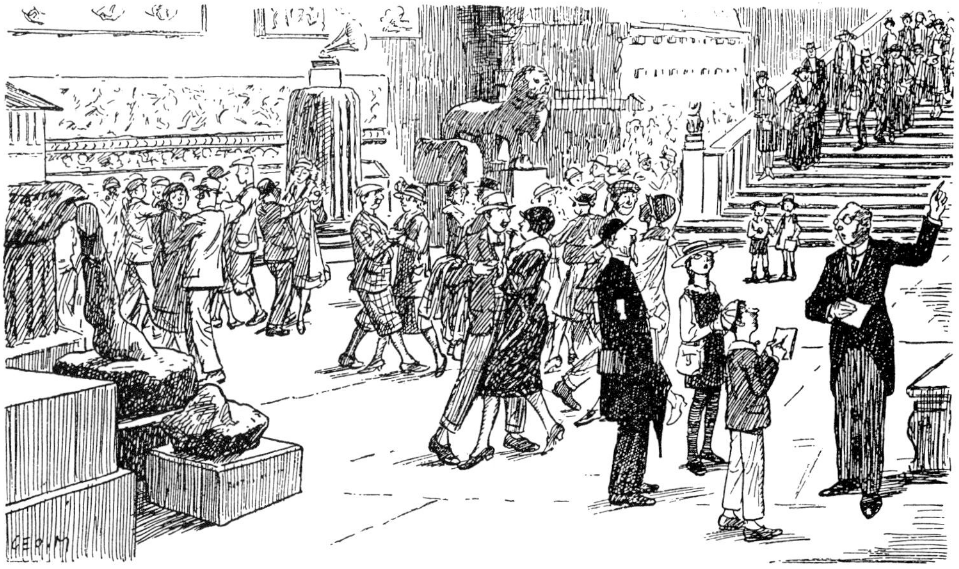

82 'London Improvements, A Lecture Dansante in a Museum'. This imaginary event is taking place in the Mausoleum Room, where, from the steps leading down to it, lectures were actually once delivered. *Mr Punch in London Town*, no. 150.

casts of the Aegina pediments were brought in to complete the scheme.[23] These casts would remain here until 1932, when they were removed to the Sepulchral Basement.[24]

The fifth and final proposal of the 1862 Committee was also to be fulfilled in the utilisation of the space to the west of the northern Assyrian slip-room (11 on Fig. 1), where in 1884, with only two years left to serve as Keeper of Greek and Roman Antiquities and only ten more years to live, Charles Newton realised his ambition in seeing the Mausoleum sculptures properly displayed together for the first time.[25] Already in 1869 what had previously been the First Elgin Room had been renamed the Mausoleum Room, and a number of the more important sculptures brought in Col. Pl. VII
from the sheds within the colonnade were displayed here.[26] By 1879 the condition of those sheds was such that substantial and expensive repairs were needed.[27] After much delay Newton persuaded the Trustees to erect a new shed, of brick with an iron roof 'in an inner court of the Museum'.[28] The Mausoleum sculptures remained 80–82
here a short time, however, before their transfer to the new room. This was a colossal space, built at basement level with grand staircases leading down into it at its Col. Pl. XIII
southern and northern ends (11 on Fig. 1). At the head of the northern staircase, a mezzanine was created. This gave access at its eastern end into the landing at the foot of the north-west staircase.[29] At the western end steps led up to a doorway that gave access into what was to become the new Phigaleian Room.[30] In 1889 a bust of

Newton himself, commissioned from the sculptor Edgar Boehm and presented to Newton by a number of his friends and pupils, was placed against the north wall of the mezzanine.[31] From this vantage point, long after his death in 1894, Newton's handsome features immortalised in stone would gaze down upon the work of a lifetime. Only in 1933 did the Keeper John Forsdyke apply to the Trustees for the removal of Newton's portrait. A new age had dawned and this 'modern' work so evocative of the Victorian past was considered an inappropriate ornament to the Museum as then conceived.

Further experiments in the Elgin Room

In the 1930s, as always, the arrangement of the Elgin Room would serve as the measure of taste. But before embarking upon a description of what was then proposed, for the sake of completing the story something must be said of the changes already made in that gallery since Newton's day. In 1886 Newton retired as Keeper of Greek and Roman Antiquities, and his successor Alexander Murray lost no time in initiating new changes in the Elgin Room. Ever since 1832, the pedimental sculptures had been exhibited on stone pedestals cased with wood, which had now become somewhat worn and, in any case, according to Murray, were 'never worthy of sculptures which attract universal admiration'.[32] New bases clad in stone were
83 ordered accordingly, and in his report dated 9 May 1888, Murray noted, 'the sculptures of the pediments of the Parthenon have been moved and placed on new pedestals'. This, it seems, applied strictly to the sculptures of the east pediment, for the west pediment sculptures were only placed on their new bases two years later.[33]

The peculiar status of the Elgin Marbles had provided particular problems of exhibition. Should they be displayed as art, or as archaeological parts of an architectural whole? The question had already been addressed more than once, and hitherto, although there had been a concerted effort to render the collection as complete as possible, the guiding principle had been aesthetic rather than archaeological. Now the tide began to turn, and within the limits imposed by the room itself the exhibition became increasingly architectural. Thus in 1902 Murray proposed to transfer the four metopes from the central division of the west wall of the Elgin Room to the east. There he hoped to combine them with the three casts of the Parthenon metopes already in the Elgin Room and to add to their number a further five casts 'of the best preserved metopes still on the Parthenon'. It had been a mistake, argued Murray, to arrange all the metopes in the British Museum in one line when they did not represent a continuous series but had, on the building, been separated by a number of additional sculptures, now lost.[34] (This proposal was never, in fact, carried out.)

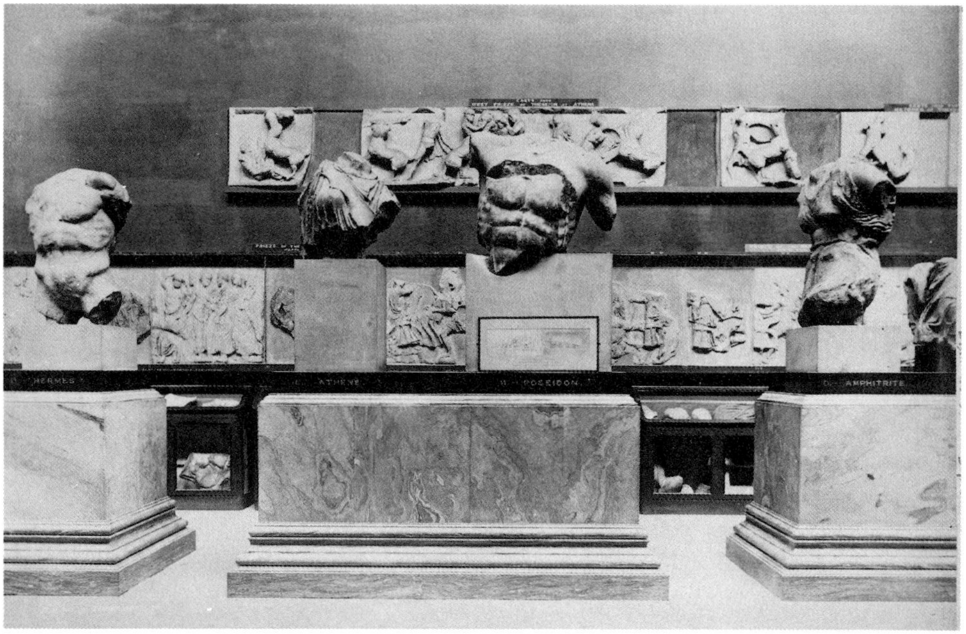

83 The Elgin Room, west pediment sculptures, *c.*1890. Photo The London Stereoscopic and Photographic Company. British Museum, Department of Greek and Roman Antiquities.

The casts from Athens never materialised, nor was the west pediment ever to be reconstructed in cast form in the gallery as Murray also suggested.[35] One consequence, however, of the desire to rationalise the Elgin Room was the gradual removal of the material that had either been there by virtue of comprising some part of the Elgin Marbles, or was deposited in the Elgin Room for want of a better place elsewhere. For a number of years such ancillary material had not been permitted in the principal Elgin Room and when, as in the case of the Caryatid, a special exception was made, the northern extension to the main room was seen as the proper place. So in 1905 Cecil Harcourt Smith, who succeeded Murray as Keeper – still maintaining the hope that the casts of additional metopes from Athens would be acquired – notified the Trustees of his intention to remove Elgin's casts of the Hephaesteum friezes to the northern annexe in order that the main room should contain practically nothing but Parthenon marbles and casts.[36] (This was not, in fact, done.)

The ultimate achievement of so many years of experimental endeavour in the

84 (*Opposite, top*) The Elgin Room, west pediment sculptures, *c.*1920. Photo British Museum, Department of Greek and Roman Antiquities.

85 (*Opposite, bottom*) 'Pheidias belongs to Peace': wartime measures against bombing in the Elgin Room, *c.*1915. Photo by D. Macbeth. British Museum, Central Archive.

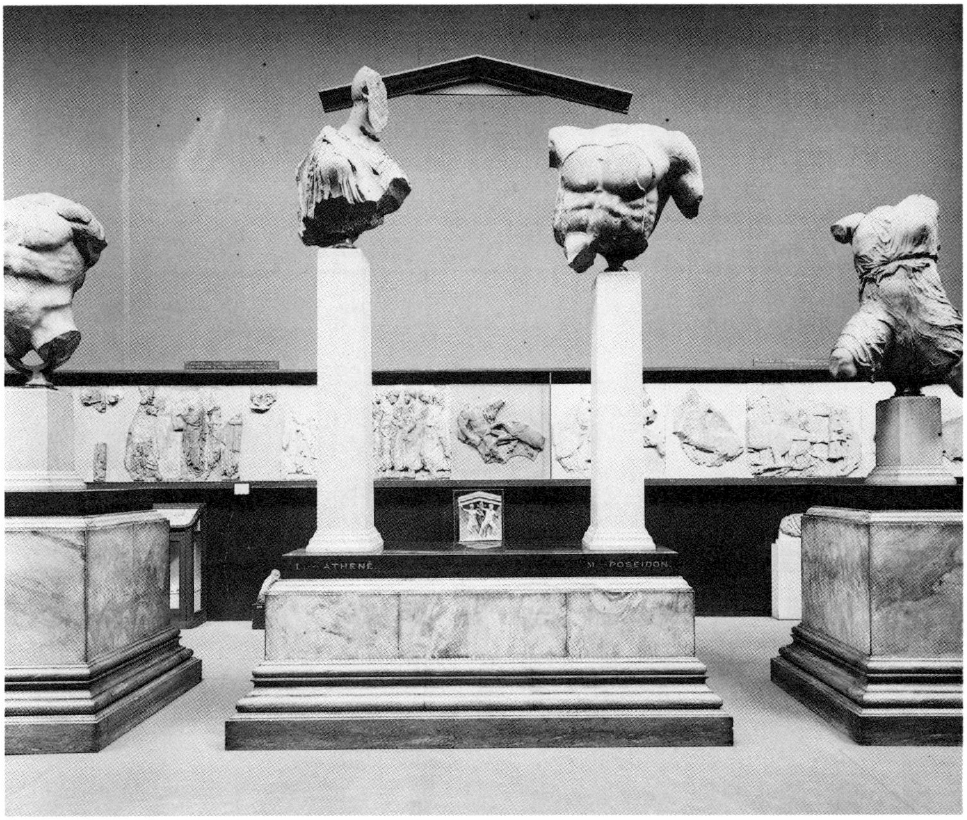
ATHENE.
POSEIDON.

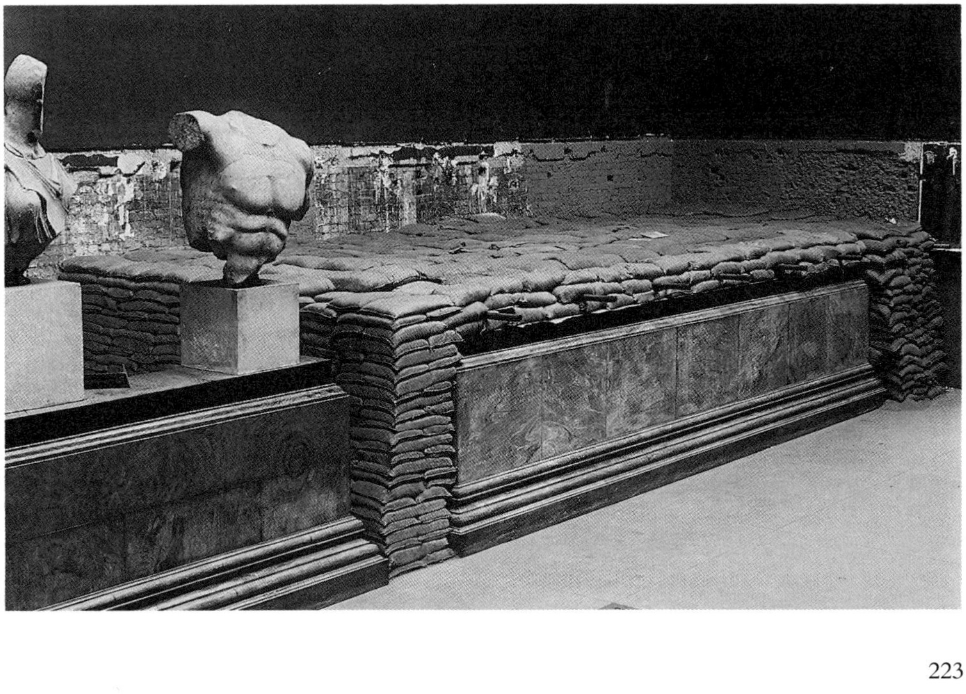

Elgin Room was the publication in 1910 of Arthur Hamilton Smith's monumental study of the Parthenon sculptures, including photographs of both the original marbles and casts in the gallery, supplemented by photographs of those sculptures still on the building. The aim was to present in one work the most complete record of the archaeological whole. The casts of select metopes still on the building never materialised, and in order to complete his publication Smith commissioned a new series of photographs of all the metopes extant in Athens using the new technique of telephotography.[37]

Meanwhile, Smith, now Keeper, also set about tackling the deficiencies, as he saw them, of the arrangement of sculptures in the gallery. Previously, it had been the wooden facings of the pedestals that were at fault: now Smith complained of the 'rough blocks of Portland stone' that supported the pediment sculptures. By these it 83
seems he meant the blocks placed under a number of the sculptures, as shown in photographs of the period. Furthermore, the placement of these sculptures was thought manifestly wrong. Not least, Smith had confirmed a suspicion mooted by Quatremère de Quincy as long ago as 1818 that the figure then identified as Iris and given to the east pediment, in fact belonged to the west.[38] In 1909 he reported to the Trustees: 'A study of the Elgin papers which Lord Elgin has been good enough to place in Mr Arthur Smith's hands has made it certain that the figure long attributed to the east pediment, belongs to the west.'[39]

Experiments were conducted with casts of the sculptures of the west pediment and a full-scale model was constructed in the Elgin Room. The aim was 'to place the torsos as far as possible in their true relative position, as shown by Carrey's drawing, and to correct the poses of each fragment.' In particular Smith wished to lift the pedimental sculptures 'to their correct heights in relation to the upper surface of the pedestal, which must be taken to represent the floor of the pediment.' The sculptures were to be raised on metal tubes allowing them to revolve, and these iron shafts 84
were to be masked with marble casing.[40] The Trustees gave their approval and in due course the scheme was completed.[41]

'Pheidias belongs to peace' as the ancient apocryphy has it,[42] and nearly a century after the Elgin Marbles were first brought to the British Museum the arrangement was dismantled when the outbreak of the First World War threatened their safety.[43] 85
After the war the sculptures were brought back to the Elgin Room and replaced on their former shelves and pedestals.[44] The pre-war programme of works amplifying the architectural context of the Parthenon sculptures continued, and in 1922 Smith drew the attention of the Trustees to the moulds and casts of the north-west angle of the entablature of the Parthenon, acquired around the middle of the previous century through the agency of the French Commission of Philippe Le Bas.[45] Smith proposed to strike new casts from those moulds and to carry out a reconstruction of 86
the entablature in the northern annexe to the Elgin Room. This he did, com-

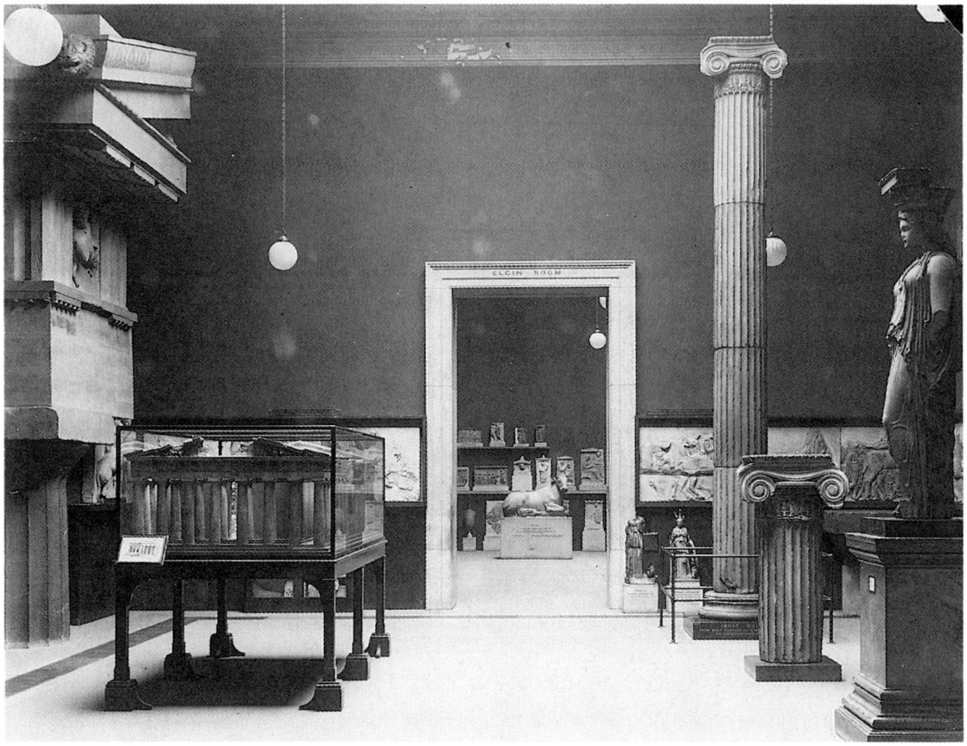

86 The north division of the Elgin Room, 1934. R. Lucas's model of the Parthenon is seen on the left, beneath the plaster-cast reconstruction of the architectural order of the Parthenon. Photo British Museum, Department of Greek and Roman Antiquities.

missioning further casts from Athens of the *regulae*, *guttae* and architrave below the Doric frieze.[46]

The nineteenth-century tradition of constant experiment in the Elgin Room, therefore, continued into the following century and the slow progress towards archaeological rationalisation went on as before. When at the end of the war, however, the Parthenon sculptures had emerged from the subterranean gloom of their makeshift shelters, they found themselves exposed to the scrutiny of a new generation.

The Garden of Eden

The Parthenon Marbles, being the greatest body of original Greek sculpture in existence, and unique monuments of its first maturity, are primarily works of art. Their former decorative function as architectural ornaments, and their present educational use as illustrations of mythical and historical events in ancient Greece, are by comparison accidental and trivial interests, which can indeed be better served by casts.

Such was the opening statement of three classical archaeologists, John Beazley, Donald Robertson and Bernard Ashmole, invited to report upon the proposed re-exhibition of the Parthenon sculptures by the Royal Commission on National Museums and Art Galleries of 1928.[47] Their meaning could not be plainer and the break with the past more clear. In a reply drawn up a year later, A. H. Smith, now in retirement, would observe that such an approach would 'imply a reversal of the policy that has been pursued for about a hundred years'.[48] Smith, as we have seen, was of the school that subscribed to the Parthenon sculptures as representing parts of an architectural whole: 'The Parthenon by universal consent was a consummate whole and the decoration of all its parts was designed with reference to the whole.' At the time of his writing the frieze consisted of sixty per cent original sculpture and forty per cent plaster. How long he had striven in the wake of his predecessors to render the frieze, in particular, as complete as possible!

The signatories of the report to the Royal Commission were, however, of another persuasion: 'The juxtaposition of marble and plaster is bound to be inharmonious.' They were for separating cast and original so as to present the sculptures in isolation, and in this they were successful.

In 1928 Sir Joseph Duveen had responded to the Royal Commission by offering, in addition to providing extensions to the Tate and National Portrait Galleries, to furnish a new exhibition gallery for the Elgin Marbles.[49] A Sub-Committee of Trustees was set up, and at first proceeded to deliberate upon various schemes drawn up by Sir Richard Allison.[50]

Duveen, however, submitted a scheme proposed by an American architect of his own choosing, J. Russell Pope.[51] Since Duveen was putting up the money, the
Trustees were obliged to dance to his tune, but in due course criticisms began to be 87
voiced over the apparent faults in Pope's design. In short, Pope seems to have begun by using the sculpture as an ornament to his own architectural design and not, as was required, subordinating the gallery to the needs of the sculpture. In particular he had placed the sculptures at inaccessible heights away from the immediate gaze of the spectator. Further, he proposed to treat the sculptures from the east pediment as though they comprised the entire composition without allowance for the great quantity of material lost from the centre.[52] Nevertheless, Beazley, Robertson and
Ashmole considered the scheme generally pleasing and a compromise was reached 88
over the aforementioned objections.[53]

By June 1934, all major differences being settled, Lord Duveen was ready to endorse the agreement legally binding him to his promises, but now an unforseen obstacle presented itself. The new gallery was to be built upon land purchased from the Bedford Estate in 1894. The houses occupying this land were leased to tenants and it was their gardens that would be sacrificed to make way for the new building. One individual by the name of Eden, tenant of 2 Bedford Square, proved particu-

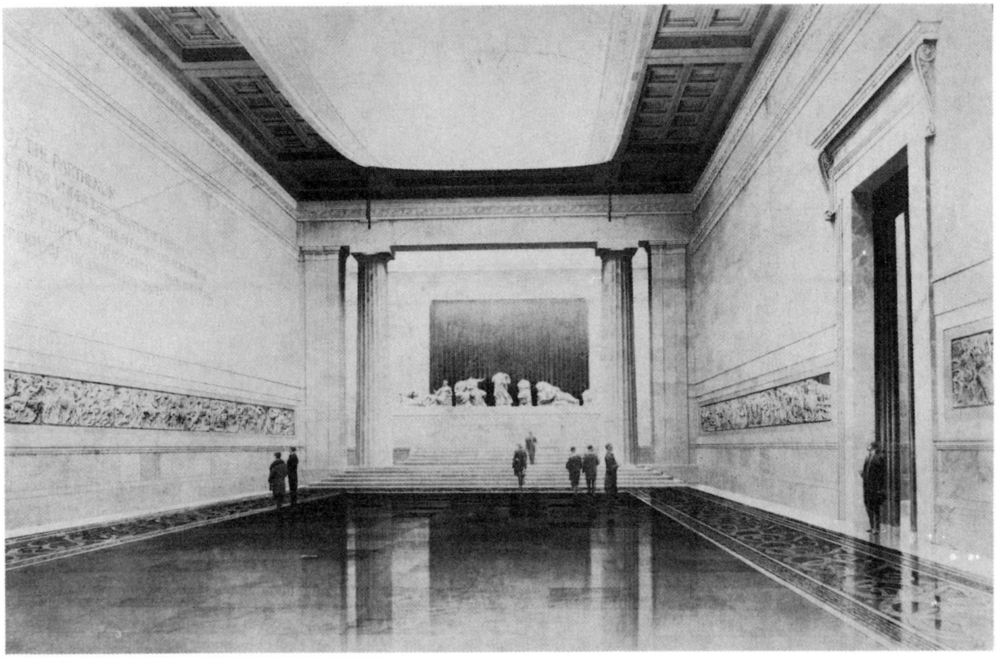

87 J. Russell Pope's unadopted 'Valhalla' for the Duveen Gallery, *c.*1933. British Museum, Central Archive.

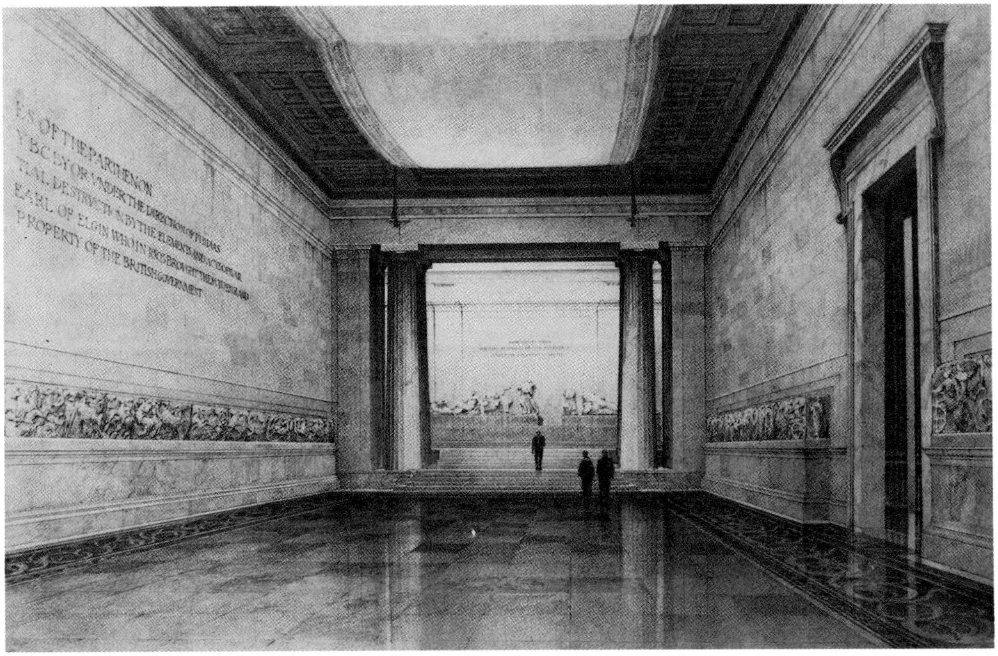

88 J. Russell Pope's revised scheme for the Duveen Gallery, *c.*1933–4. British Museum, Central Archive.

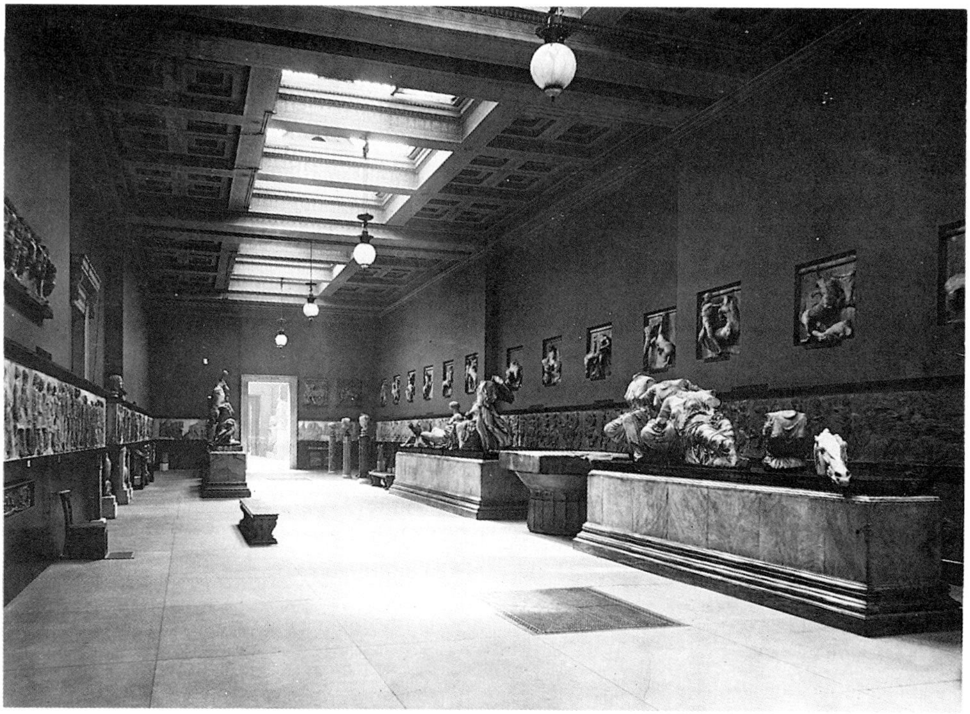

89 The Elgin Room looking south, *c.*1905. Photo by D. Macbeth. British Museum, Central Archive.

larly intransigent.[54] Against all persuasion and bribery the Garden of Eden would remain out of bounds for a further two years and the progress of the Duveen Gallery was delayed.[55] The new suite of rooms was at last completed by the beginning of 1939. Lord Duveen did not live to see it, and hardly had work begun on installing the sculptures than the Second World War necessitated a hasty general evacuation of the Museum. Not until 1962 was the scheme, first envisaged some thirty years earlier, eventually realised.[56]

The arrangement has now remained intact for a further thirty years, the name of Duveen emblazoned upon the west wall of the gallery having put an apparent end to experiment and achieved a permanence denied even to the greater name of Elgin. So ends the history of the exhibition of the Parthenon sculptures at the British Museum over some two centuries. Their story is inextricably bound up with that of the institution to which they belong. Although our perception of them in relation to the art of other cultures is no longer what it was in the nineteenth century, and the Egyptians and Assyrians are rightly now given their due, nevertheless our regard for them has never lessened. The 'Elgin Room' of the British Museum is still the inner sanctum of Bloomsbury's Temple of the Muses. It remains now, as it was sixty years ago, in the words of those who first conceived the present arrangment, 'one of the central places of earth'.[57]

The 1920s and 1930s had seen great changes in the sculpture galleries of the Greek and Roman Department. The dismantlement of the old Elgin Room was accompanied by a general attempt to exorcise what had come to be seen as Victorian gloom in favour of brighter, more airy galleries. Walls were repainted with light pastel shades; the collections were thinned so as to be more 'selective', and casts were largely banished. This was the age of Art Deco and the cult of modernism, when even that most conservative institution, the British Museum, felt the cutting edge of fashionable minimalism (compare Figs 90 and 47). And yet, what was done was not so radical as to challenge the essential premise on which the sculpture collections had been arranged in the nineteenth century. The Parthenon sculptures still reigned supreme and the ground floor of the western galleries was still devoted to tracing the progressive chronological sequence by which the great classical moment of the Parthenon had waxed and waned. That chronology was as imperfect as it had always been, but for all their inadequacies, the great western galleries on the ground floor of the Museum had continued to belong to the sculptures. Only later,

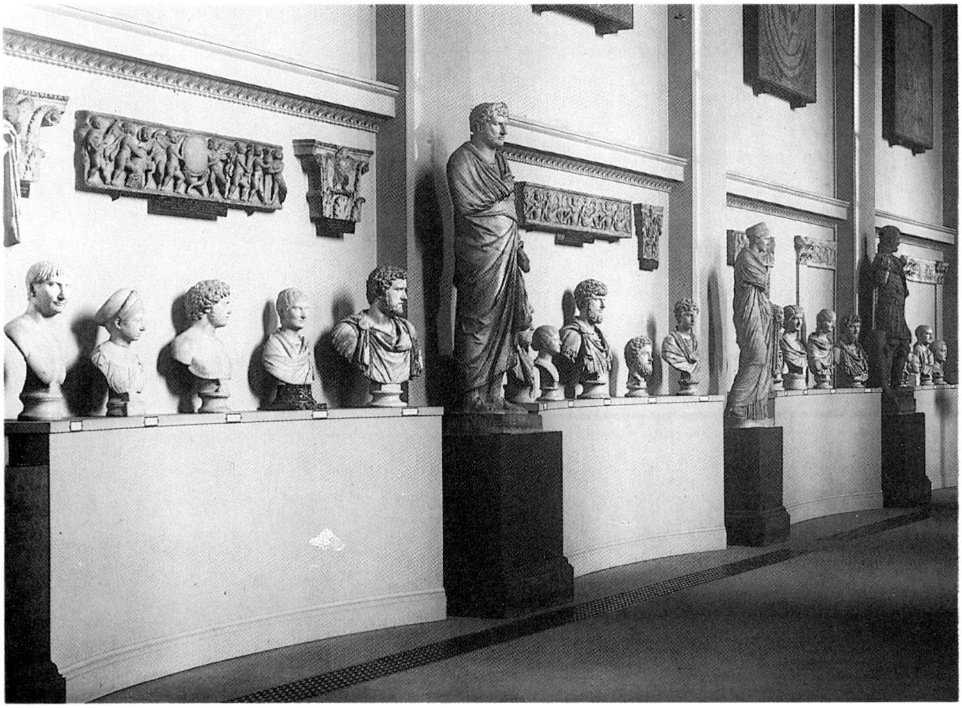

90 The Roman Gallery (1 on Fig. 1) looking east, after the marble pedestals had been removed 'to reduce the monotony', *c.*1931. Photo British Museum, Department of Greek and Roman Antiquities.

following the evacuation of the collection during the Second World War, did a real change come about.

Today, albeit in modified form, the Egyptian and Assyrian sculptures occupy much the same space as before, but the great series of classical sculptures is broken up. Where the Townley Marbles once graced the Graeco-Roman Rooms, now the space is filled with small objects illustrating the development of Greek prehistory. Where the Lycian marbles once jostled for elbow room and where were later to be found the Archaic sculptures and Aegina casts, now stand showcases filled with *Kleinkunst* illustrating the chronological and regional developments of archaic Greek culture. These changes reflect new advances and, correspondingly, new priorities in our understanding of Greek civilisation. The old Platonically inspired teleology is replaced with an open-ended system based upon a freer principle of cultural relativism. No longer is the art of one people judged the inferior of another, but each is taken on its own terms. The age when the history of art was regarded as one continuous chain tracing the progress of civilisation is over, and, although we may feel a sense of melancholy at its passing, it is better so.

Notes

Introduction

1. Herder and Winckelmann, see Podro, pp. 1–2, with bibliography at his note 3.

2. Mitter, p. 104.

3. Podro, *passim*. For Winckelmann's German followers see Turner, p. 42 and Michaelis (1908), chapter 11.

4. Turner, p. 213.

Chapter 1

1. For this ancient apocryphal reference to Pheidias, see Winckelmann, Preface to the Notes, 22. Contrary to the lexicon of Suidas, Winckelmann took it to mean that the arts flourish alone in a state of peace.

2. Gould, p. 65: 'The idea, latent for so long, is specifically stated in a letter from Thouin to Bonaparte that the French spoliation of Italy was the reward of military virtue over decadence and that it was strictly comparable with what the Greeks are supposed to have done to the Egyptians and the Romans in their turn to the Greeks . . . .'

3. For the circumstances surrounding the failure of England's attempt to secure the Aegina Marbles, see Stoneman, pp. 191–3, with bibliography.

4. Jenkins (Montpellier 1988 forthcoming).

5. F. Beaufort, *Karamania, or, a brief Description of the South Coast of Asia Minor and of the Remains of Antiquity* (London 1817).

6. D.V. Denon, *Voyage dans la Basse et la Haute Égypte pendant les Campagnes du général Bonaparte*, 2 vols (Paris 1802).

7. St Clair, p. 88: 'On 17 June General Hutchinson received the surrender of Cairo and the success of the Egyptian expedition was finally assured. On 6 July, Elgin obtained the firman he had asked for. Those two events were intimately connected.'

8. See Chapter 8 with note 10.

9. Gould, pp. 119–20, quotes a letter by Denon: 'What is most certain is that Mon. Hamilton has behaved in this matter like a maniac, that he has set on the entire destruction of the Museum and that he has got the support of Lord (sic.) Wellington in the execution of his project.' For Hamilton in Paris, see Smith (1916), pp. 331–2; Haskell and Penny, p. 115.

10. *The Gentleman's Magazine* vol. 86 (January–June 1816), p. 39.

11. Crook (1973), p. 405; Miller, pp. 124ff.

12. For the early history of the Museum see Edwards, *passim*; Miller, pp. 19–115; Caygill (1981), pp. 3ff.

13. *Diary*, 16 April 1691, vol. 5, p. 48.

14. Miller, pp. 60–61.

15. Ibid., pp. 99–100.

16. Haskell and Penny, p. 112.

17. Larrabee, p. 257; Gould, p. 80.

18. P.P. (1816), pp. 26–7; *The Museum of Classical Antiquities* 1 (1851), p. 403.

19. *The Gentleman's Magazine* vol. 87 (January 1817), p. 80.

20. For Plato on art, see Keuls and Murdoch. For later authors, see Cicero, *Orator*, II, 7–9; for Quintilian, see *Inst. Orator*, Book XII, 10, 7–9. For Reynolds, see *Discourses on Art*, ed. Robert Wark (New Haven and London 1975); for Flaxman, see Knowles and Mason.

21. Cited by Turner, pp. 43–4; see also Rothenberg, pp. 32–3.

22. *Orator* II, 9.

23. Pollitt, pp. 53–4.

24. Burke, pp. lviii-lix.

25. Plato's theory of *mimesis* is most fully developed in Books III and X of the *Republic*. See Murdoch, *passim*; Keuls, especially pp. 25–6; Pollitt, pp. 37–50.

26. Winckelmann (1764), Book IV, ch. ii, 9.

27. Beardsley, pp. 78–87; Pollitt, pp. 55–8.

28. Plotinus, *Enneads* V, viii, 1.

29. Winckelmann (1764), trans. G. H. Lodge (Boston 1872–3), vol. 3, p. 234.

30. Gombrich (1971), pp. 16–24; Pollitt, pp. 82–3. Isaiah Berlin, author of *Vico and Herder: Two studies in the History of Ideas* (London 1976), is quoted by Rossi, p. x.

31. For Mengs see Potts, *J. Warb.* (1980).

32. Winckelmann (1764), trans. G. H. Lodge (1880), vol. 4, pp. 363–4.

33. For Visconti, see Haskell and Penny, pp. 106–7; Rothenberg, pp. 135–8, 352–6, 438; Potts, *J. Warb.* (1980), pp. 172–3. For the modern positive approach to Roman copies see especially P. Zanker, *Klassizistische Statuen* (Mainz 1974).

34. Clarke and Penny, p. 13.

35. Michaelis (1908), pp. 24–6.

36. Rothenberg, p. 355. Visconti's response to the Elgin Marbles was privately printed under the title *Lettre de E. Q. Visconti à un Anglais* (April 1815) and used by Elgin in the purchase negotiations, see Smith (1916), p. 318.

37. Rothenberg, pp. 434–45.

38. Liscombe, pp. 34–9; Cummings, pp. 367–80; Cummings (1964), pp. 323–8; Rothenberg, pp. 230–53.

39. Liscombe, pp. 38–9, with note 19; see also Rothenberg, pp. 347–8.

40. Rothenberg, p. 5. On p. 255 Rothenberg acutely observes: 'For some critics direct confrontation with the Parthenon sculptures served only to confirm rather than to destroy their unshakable beau-idealist criteria for judging the merits of all antique sculpture. Even at close range they were still seeing Phidian sculpture through Greco-Roman eyes.' My only quarrel with Rothenberg's excellent book is that I think he underestimates the extent to which this was a general response.

41. Canova: P.P. (1816), Appendix no. 8, p. xxiii, Letter from Canova to Elgin, 10 November 1851. Nollekens: P.P. (1816), p. 68. Westmacott: ibid., pp. 83–4. Lawrence: ibid., p. 90.

42. Haydon, *Autobiography*, cited by Cummings (1963), p. 374.

43. Cummings (1963), p. 374.

44. Winckelmann (1765), p. 30. For an explanation of the term 'beau-ideal', see Rothenberg, p. 41.

45. See Quatremère de Quincy, p. 17, 'Les sculptures du Parthénon me semblent propres à remplir une immense lacune dans l'histoire du goût.'

46. P.P. (1816), p. 9. On the full significance of this passage see Rothenberg, pp. 423–5.

47. Quatremère de Quincy, pp. 30–31.

48. Ibid., p. 84; for a full history of the placement of the Iris see A. H. Smith, *Guide to the Sculptures of the Parthenon* (1908), p. 26.

49. Quatremère de Quincy, pp. 10–12; cf. Rothenberg, pp. 408–9.

50. Quatremère de Quincy, pp. 48–9.

51. Ibid., p. 92.

52. Ibid., pp. 21–2.

53. Newton (1849), p. 22. This important essay was not included in the collection published in 1880.

54. See note 31 above. See also Rothenberg, pp. 445–9, and Hitchens, pp. 85–9.

55. Rothenberg, p. 449.

56. Cummings (1963), pp. 373–5.

57. Haskell and Penny, p. 104: 'Clearly if Greek sculpture could not be imitated it could not be restored.' Elgin had hoped to restore his Marbles and offered the job to Canova in 1803, but he refused with the words 'it would be sacrilege in him or any man to presume to touch them with a chisel', *Memorandum* (1815 ed.), p. 39. See Rothenberg, p. 185, and St Clair, pp. 152–3. Elgin seems to have entertained notions of restoring the marbles until quite late in the proceedings leading up to their purchase for the nation, see Rothenberg, p. 351, note 301.

58. E. Oldfield, P.P. (N.G. 1857), 1768–9.

59. Haskell and Penny, p. 107.

Chapter 2

1. C. 2426, 11 November 1809, G.M. 1068, 10 February 1810.

2. G.M. 1044, 21 May 1808. C. 2387, 11 June 1808. Cf. Royal Academy Council Minutes IV, fols 42–3, 18 February 1808; fols 50–51, 56–8, 16 March 1808; fols 67–9, 5 July 1808. The Academicians were not subject to these rules. The facilities appear already to have been extended by 1823, when the hours were published in the *New Times*, 21 November 1823: 'On Tuesday and

Thursday in every week save the three holiday weeks of Easter, Whitsun, and Christmas, the Gallery of Antiquities is open to students of the Royal Academy and other artists.'

3. Prince Hoare is quoted by Cummings (1963), p. 369, the source being *Epochs of the Fine Arts* (1813), pp. 183–5. For the Academy casts, see Morgan, pp. 54–64, whence the quotation from *Annals of the Fine Arts*.

4. Three dozen ordered, see C. 2654, 8 March 1817.

5. C. 3436, 14 January 1832; O.R. 15, January 1832.

6. O.R. 57, 10 September 1856.

7. C. 9071, 9 August 1856; O.R. 57, 10 September 1856; O.R. 57, 30 October 1856; C. 9095, 1 November 1856; C. 9109, 22 November 1856.

8. Cf. O.R. 13, 13 February 1830.

9. Vol. 5 (1847), p. 145.

10. G. Scharf, *The Greek Court erected in the Crystal Palace* (London 1854). Thus E. Oldfield at the 1857 Parliamentary enquiry (1774–6, 26 March 1857) concluded that the Crystal Palace collection of casts was the finest in England and, with that at Paris, the best in the world.

11. Physick, pp. 15–17.

12. Macdonald, p. 177.

13. P.P. (1836), 1189.

14. P.P. (N.G. 1853), 8929–36.

15. P.P. (N.G. 1853), 9290–9325.

16. P.P. (N.G. 1853), 9326–9358.

17. This seems to have been a natural law, rather than one enshrined in the regulations themselves, which stated that: 'Each student, who offers himself for Admission into the Royal Schools shall present a Drawing or Model from some plaister cast to the Keeper, and if he thinks him properly qualified, he shall be permitted to make a Drawing or Model from some Cast in the Royal Academy, which if approved of by the Keeper and Visitor for the time being, shall be laid before the Council for their confirmation, which obtained he shall receive his letter of Admission as a student in the Royal Academy where he shall continue to draw after the plaister, till the Keeper and Visitor for the time being, judge him qualified to draw after the living models, when they shall have power to admit him', Hutchison, pp. 29–30, Morgan, pp. 39–42.

18. P.P. (N.G. 1857), 1671. The statue is probably BM Cat. Sculpture 1697, a reclining satyr. At the beginning of this century A. H. Smith had the restored extremities of the satyr removed. They were subsequently reinstated by B. F. Cook.

19. P.P. (N.G. 1857), 1749.

20. O.P. XXIII, 7 August 1840.

21. Pulsky and Newton in Chapter 4 below.

22. P.P. (N.G. 1853), 6538–41.

23. Thus Westmacott, P.P. (N.G. 1853), 9041–2; Loft, P.P. (N.G. 1853), 9334.

24. Jenkins (1990), *passim*.

25. For this painting see Chapter 5 below.

26. Jenkins (1984).

27. O.R. 9 October 1873; ibid., 26 January 1876; ibid. 23 January 1878.

28. O.R. 8 Nov. 1877; ibid., 8 May 1878; ibid., 6 July 1878.

29. O.R. 8 March 1886.

30. These seem to have been displayed for a period in the Elgin Room – see the undated catalogue of photographs supplied by The London Stereoscopic Company, preserved in the Library of the Greek and Roman Department of the British Museum. After 1909 they were probably transferred to the newly created gallery of casts, for which see Chapter 10.

31. O.R. 20 March 1889; C. 18192, 13 April 1889.

32. Macdonald, p. 265.

Chapter 3

1. Potts (Munich 1980), p. 270–71.

2. Ibid., pp. 269–75; cf. Seling, p. 109.

3. Quoted by Seling, p. 112.

4. Discussed in Chapter 6 below.

5. Ibid.

6. P.P. (N.G. 1853), Appendix VIII no. 39.

7. Fergusson, p. 20.

8. Chapter 5 below.

9. Ibid.

10. O.R. 51, 4 November 1853.

11. O.R. 61, 7 July 1858.

12. P.P. (N.G. 1853), 8359.

13. Newton to Panizzi from Genoa, Add. Ms 36, 720, f. 278.

14. Caygill (1987).

15. Potts (Munich 1980), p. 276.

16. Cook (1977), p. 60.

17. O.P. LXI, 30 December 1858, and see below.

18. Chapter 5 below.

19. Potts (Munich 1980), p. 276.

20. P.P. (N.G. 1857), 2494.

21. For polychromy see note 39 below.

22. *The Builder* 9 (15 February 1851), p. 99.

23. O.P. XXXVI, 19 December 1846.

24. Cf. C. 7113, 19 December 1846.

25. For the drawing, see Laing, p. 1382, fig. 1.

26. *The Builder* 7 (28 April 1849), p. 198.

27. O.P. XLVI, 8 June 1850; C. 8008, 12 June 1850.

28. C. 8045, 10 August 1850.

29. O.P. XLIV, November 1850.

30. O.R. 46, 21 February 1851.

31. C. 8163, 22 February 1851.

32. O.P. LXII, 5 March 1859.

33. *The Builder* 9 (26 April 1851), p. 259.

34. C. 8149, 8 February 1851; C. 8172–3, 8 March 1851.

35. O.R. 46, 11 June 1851; O.P. XLVI, 11 November 1851.

36. O.R. 48, 7 January 1852.

37. O.P. LI, 10 November 1854; C. 8755, 11 November 1854; C. 8763, 9 December 1854; O.P. LII, 12 January 1855 – Basement of the 'Roman Gallery'. Sub-Committee on Finance, p. 883, 19 January 1855 – Gallery of Romano-British Antiquities. O.R. 57, 9 July 1856 – The Roman Gallery.

38. O.P. LIV, 14 March 1857; O.P. LVII, 4 December 1857; O.R. 60, 6 January 1858; C. 9312, 9 January 1858; O.R. 62, 6 January 1859.

39. For the rediscovery of ancient polychromy, see the catalogue to the exhibition entitled *Paris, Rome, Athènes, Le Voyage en Grèce des Architectes Français aux XIXe et XXe Siècles*, École Nationale Supérieure des Beaux-Arts, 12 May – 18 July 1982, and other locations. See also, von Buttlar. For a useful overview of the early development of the subject by one of its chief exponents see Semper. In the same volume see the interesting review by E. Falkener of Owen Jones's proposals for colouring the interior of the Crystal Palace in Hyde Park (pp. 98–102). See also P. Dimitriou, *The Polychromy of Greek Sculpture: To the Beginning of the Hellenistic Period* (PhD thesis, New York 1951).

40. For an appraisal of this nineteenth-century investigation and an account of a modern reinvestigation, see Jenkins and Middleton (1988).

41. The effect of the preference for Gothic on British interest in polychromy is discussed by Semper, p. 231.

42. T. L. Donaldson, *et al.*, p. 2.

43. Klenze, P.P. (N.G. 1853), Appendix VIII no. 39. For Klenze's archaeological interest, see von Buttlar.

44. Smirke, 1oc. cit. in note 42 above, pp. 2–3.

45. C. 8741, 14 October 1854.

46. O.P. LIV, 8 May 1856.

47. Sub-Commmittee on Antiquities, 26 January 1858. For these changes see Chapter 5 below.

48. Cf. O.P. LIX, 26 January 1858; C. 9330–31, 13 February 1858.

49. C. 9383, 17 April 1858.

50. C. 9519, 12 February 1859; but see also Sub-Committee on Antiquities, 31 March 1858 and 5 March 1859.

51. O.P. LXI, 30 December 1858.

52. See Chapter 5 below.

53. See R. Westmacott jun. (1864), pp. 149–74.

54. For a modern assertion that these so-called patinas are, indeed, vestigial paint, see Jenkins and Middleton (1988); for the Victorian conviction that the ancient Greeks shared a preference for white sculpture, see Jenkyns, pp. 146–54.

55. See Chapter 5 below.

56. O.P. LXII, 5 March 1859.

57. Sub-Committee on Antiquities, 5 March 1859. Now Room 1, the alcoves filled with showcases.

58. O.P. LXIII, 9 April 1859.

59. O.R. 62, 5 May 1859.

60. O.P. LXIII, 30 May 1859.

61. C. 9606, 25 June 1859; cf. O.P. LXIV, 6 August 1859.

62. 'The Munich Glyptothek and the Redecoration of the British Museum', *Country Life* vol. 65 (19 January 1929), pp. 69–72.

63. Ibid.

64. F. Watson, 'The Tired Horse of Selene', *Guardian*, 28 September 1961. This was not quite accurate, since already by 1936 the walls of the Elgin Room below the frieze had been painted in a 'quiet stone colour', O.R. 5 February 1936.

65. See 'Elgin Marbles on View Again – Rearranged Display', *The Times*, 5 September 1949: 'In the large room the walls are now blue below the line of the sculptures, and white above. The walls of the smaller room are entirely blue.' The old marble bases for the pedimental sculptures were reused and we are given a description, not found elsewhere, of their colour: '... grey, blue and green Cipollino marble, upon which the white or cream (of various shades) of the Pentelic marble of the figures looks extremely well.'

66. C. 4486, 13 October 1928; C. 4608, 14 December 1929; O.R. 13 January 1930; O.R. 24 February 1930; Sub-Committee on Antiquities, 7 March 1930; O.R. 14 January 1931; O.R. 10 February 1931; Sub-Committee on Antiquities, 13 March 1931; C. 4753, 14 March 1931; O.R. 10 February 1932; O.R. 13 February 1934; O.R. 1 February 1939.

67. 'Blue-Mauve for a Goddess and Apple Green for Roman Busts. Colour Experiments. Brightening the British Museum', *Evening News*, 9 December 1931.

Chapter 4

1. Miller, pp. 192–3, 206–7; see Chapter 7 below.

2. Potts (Munich 1980), pp. 262–9.

3. Michaelis (1908), p. 45.

4. See Chapter 9 below.

5. Pulsky, p. 12.

6. Newton visited Museums in Germany and Italy in the autumn of 1848 and submitted to the Trustees of the Museum a report in manuscript which still survives in the library of the Greek and Roman Department. Subsequently a shorter version was published in *The Museum of Classical Antiquities* 1.3 (July 1851), pp. 205–27.

7. Potts (Munich 1980), p. 263; see also Seling, pp. 112–13, for the debate over the arrangement of the Glyptothek and Schinkel's Altes Museum.

8. Rothenberg, p. 259; Liscombe, p. 37, on the debate over the relative idealisation of the 'Theseus' from the Parthenon east pediment *qua* hero, and that of the Apollo Belvedere *qua* god. An ancient source for this distinction is Quintilian, *Inst. Orator*, Book XII, 10, 8, where he discusses the relative merits of Polycleitus as portrayer of ideal grace in human subjects, and Pheidias as the sculptor best suited to showing the dignity of the gods.

9. See Chapter 6 below.

10. Newton (1851), p. 214.

11. Winckelmann (1764), Preface, 1 and 2.

12. Ibid., Preface to the Notes, 7; for the problem in numismatics of establishing a chronology of pre-Imperial coinage, see Crawford, p. 125.

13. Ibid., Preface, 3–7 and 12.

14. For Scaliger, see Pfeiffer, pp. 113–20; for Winckelmann and Scaliger, ibid., pp. 119, 168 and 170. See also Bosanquet, pp. 188–9.

15. Rossi, p. 120.

16. Plotinus, *Enneads*, V. ii, 1–2.

17. Winckelmann (1764), Book I, ch. i, 2.

18. Ibid., Book I, ch. i, 6–8, 16.

19. J. B. Bury, *The Idea of Progress* (first published New York 1932).

20. An explanation was elicited from Westmacott by H. Ellis and later expanded by him: British Library Add. MS 38626, f. 202; cf. Crook (1972), p. 127.

21. Jenkins (1985), pp. 174–81, for this and the other Museum drawings by Stephanoff.

22. J. L. Stephens, *Incidents of Travel in Central America, Chiapas, and Yucatan* (London 1841).

23. The date of the Nereid Monument was at this time thought to be 100–150 years earlier than is now believed. Fellows had identified it as a trophy monument erected to celebrate the conquest of Xanthus by the Persian General Harpagus in 547 BC (Herodotus, I, 176). On this basis Fellows guessed the monument to have been set up by 'the followers of Harpagus, commemorating his victory and serving as a tomb for his heroes'. He went on to put its date in the lifetime of 'some of the conquerors' as not later than 500 BC – Fellows (1852), p. 469. The folly of this early date seems to have been general, see E. Hawkins, 'The Xanthian Marbles', *The Builder* 3 (1845), pp. 301–2. Even C. R. Cockerell was deceived, ibid.,

p. 63, transcript of a lecture: '... it was erected in the year 546 before our era, a century earlier than the Parthenon'. There is, therefore, good reason for Stephanoff to have treated the Nereid Monument sculptures as earlier than the Parthenon, but, like the Phigaleian Marbles, he no doubt also thought of them as aesthetically prior.

24. For Mexican antiquities in the Egyptian Gallery, see Sub-Committee on Antiquities, p. 13, 14 June 1828; cf. the complaints of Pulsky, p. 12.

25. Bury, pp. 254–5. In following Bury, I have grossly simplified Hegel's aesthetic philosophy, but as Bosanquet observes, 'It is undoubtedly difficult to get a net result out of Hegel'. For a useful summary see ibid., pp. 334–55, with Appendix I.

26. Jenkins (1985), p. 180, fig. 12.

27. S. Smirke, 'Remarks on the Assyrian Sculptures discovered by Dr. Layard etc', *The Builder* 8 (1850), pp. 160–61.

28. The casts of the Selinus metopes, five in all, were presented to the Museum by S. Angell in 1827: O.P. VI, 29 May 1827; ibid., 4 June 1827. Upon arrival they were deposited in the temporary Phigaleian Room: Sub-Committee on Antiquities, p. 13, 14 June 1828; *Synopsis* (1832), p. 179.

29. The casts of the Aegina sculptures were acquired from the studio of the sculptor Carl Wagner in Rome. Rev. Burgess, Chaplain to British Residents at Rome, acted as agent and processed an order on the British Museum's behalf, having first consulted with Thorvaldsen as to the quality of the moulds: C. 4191, 13 February 1836; C. 4253, 16 April 1836. The arrival of the casts was announced in September: C. 4358, 20 September 1836.

30. O.P. XXIII, 7 August 1840.

31. *Illustrations of the British Museum*, vol. I. f. 120, letter dated 5 April 1826.

32. Newton (1851), p. 206.

33. Pulsky, p. 12. He could not, however, bring himself to include the curiosities and instruments of the barbarous races of Africa and Oceania within his scheme.

34. Ibid., p. 15.

35. Ibid.

36. Haskell (1976), pp. 54–5; Hendy, pp. 34–5; cf. Gould, p. 109.

37. See below, Chapters 7 and 9. See also Reade (1987), p. 48; Haskell (1976), pp. 54–5; cf. Bohrer, *passim*.

38. Newton (1880), p. 66.

39. Ibid., pp. 48–9.

40. The entire passage is quoted below in Chapter 9.

41. C. Darwin, *On The Origin of Species etc.* (London 1859).

42. The MS is in the library of the Department of Greek and Roman Antiquities. A summary version was published subsequently in the first volume of the journal *The Museum of Classical Antiquities* (1851), pp. 205–27.

43. Newton (1851), p. 227.

44. Newton (1849), pp. 29–30.

45. For nineteenth-century German cast collections see Michaelis (1908), pp. 298–9, F.G. Welcker's at Bonn being the first. For the collection see *Akademisches Kunstmuseum der Universität Bonn, Verzeichnis der Abguss-Sammlung* (Berlin 1981). For nineteenth-century cast collecting in general see Conner.

46. For the Crystal Palace see Scharf (1854).

47. Note 45. A letter from Michaelis to C. T. Newton, in the library of the Greek and Roman Department of the British Museum, is dated Tübingen, 6 June 1872, and informs Newton that, having just been appointed Professor of Archaeology in the University of Strasbourg, Michaelis is anxious to build up a cast collection. He goes on to name what he regards as the main cornerstones of Greek art-history, viz. the Parthenon marbles, the Phigaleian frieze, the Mausoleum sculptures and the Aegina pediments.

48. Pulsky, p. 11, and see Chapter 9 below.

49. P.P. (1857–8), p. 501.

50. Dodds, p. 5.

51. Miller, pp. 239–44; Stearn, pp. 27–38.

52. Desmond, p. 426.

53. P.P. (1859), plan and report pp. 72–5.

54. Chapter 9 below.

55. Daniel, p. 28–67.

56. Michaelis (1908), p.viii, quoted in Turner, pp. 69–70.

57. Turner, especially pp. 36–76.

58. C. L. Woolley, *Excavation at Ur* (London 1954), cited by Ceram, p. 333.

Chapter 5

1. Most important is Smith (1916), which makes copious use of P.P. (1816); see also Rothenberg; St Clair; Vrettos; Cook (1984), ch. 4; Hitchens.

2. G.M. 1153.

3. C. 2654, 8 March 1817.

4. C. J. C. Reuvens, cited in H. D. Schreider, *Dutch Museums* 6 (Leiden 1981), p. 17.

5. C. 12577, 14 December 1872.

6. Smith (1916), pp. 352–5.

7. Liscombe *passim*; Cummings (1963 and 1964); Jenkins (1984), p. 176; Rothenberg, ch. 6.

8. Cf. Jenkins (1985), pp. 176–7.

9. B.M. Cat. Sculpture 1672, Elgin collection and said to come from the Acropolis.

10. Figures L and M.

11. Jenkins (1985), p. 175 and fig. 3.

12. For Aegina and Bassae, see Stoneman, pp. 179–201, with bibliography on pp. 313–14; see also Rothenberg, pp. 331–3, with notes.

13. Cockerell (1860). The book was to be published jointly with Haller, but the plan failed owing to the untimely death of the latter in Greece in 1817.

14. Cf. Michaelis (1908), p. 33.

15. For the temple see now Cooper.

16. BM Cat. Sculpture 510–19.

17. BM Cat. Sculpture 520–42. For the frieze see Hofkes-Brukker; see also Felten, pp. 80–106.

18. Stoneman, pp. 190–94.

19. O.P. III, 1 May 1814.

20. C. 2614, 11 November 1815.

21. O.R. 4, 9 March 1816; GR 1816.3–9.1. BM Cat. Sculpture 534.

22. GR 1825.11–12.2–3.

23. O.R. 4, 11 May 1816; C. 2634, 15 June 1816.

24. On Elgin's casts see Smith (1916), p. 236; Rothenberg, p. 147; Visconti (1816), p.xiv; Jenkins (1990).

25. The scarab is EA 74: Cook (1984) fig. 66; the Elgin Eros is BM Cat. Sculpture 1672, said to come from the Acropolis.

26. *Synopsis* (1832), pp. 179–80.

27. For T. Lawrence's casts see Chapter 6, note 93.

28. GR 1827.5–12.1–5. The casts were presented by S. Angell; see O.P. VI, 4 June 1827: '... we consider them to be about 600 years BC, and certainly among the very earliest specimens of Greek sculpture.' A year later they were deposited in the Phigaleian Room: Sub-Committee on Antiquities, p. 13, 14 June 1828.

29. C. 2657, 12 April 1817; letter from Elgin, O.P. IV, 10 May 1817; G.M. 1160, 10 May 1817.

30. C. 2662, 10 May 1817; North Frieze XXII 66; North Frieze XXXV 109.

31. O.R. 5, 14 March 1818.

32. *Synopsis* (1824), p. 142, no. 16.

33. O.R. 5, 13 June 1818.

34. C. 3129, 8 November 1828.

35. North Frieze XL 123 and 124.

36. O.R. 6, 9 December 1820; C. 2769, 13 January 1821. On the history of East Frieze VII see Marcadé and Pinatel in Berger pp. 338–42.

37. GR 1830.3–13.1. O.R. 13, March 1830; Cockerell's letter offering the fragment to the Trustees, and explaining the circumstances by which he acquired it, is preserved in *Letters on Antiquities*, 1757–1834, no. 98; see also S. P. Cockerell, pp. 262–3.

38. GR 1828.7–28.1–2. *Letters on Antiquities* 1757–1834, no. 90.

39. O.R. 14A, April 1831; C. 3348, 10 April 1831.

40. G.M. 1253, 25 February 1826.

41. O.P. VI, 25 March 1828.

42. Cf. C. 3105, 14 June 1828.

43. O.R. 11 December 1828.

44. Sub-Committee on Buildings, p. 34, 13 February 1830.

45. Sub-Committee on Buildings, p. 36, 4 March 1830.

46. Sub-Committee on Buildings, p. 37, 9 March 1830.

47. Sub-Committee on Buildings, 13 March 1830.

48. O.P. VII, 3 April 1830; cf. Sub-Committee on Buildings, p. 39, 12 May 1830.

49. O.R. 13, April 1831; C. 3348, 10 April 1831.

50. G.M. 1392, 9 July 1831.

51. O.P. IX, 8 July 1831.

52. O.R. 14A, November 1831.

53. C. 3447, 11 February 1832.

54. O.P. IX, 8 July, 1831; G.M. 1392, 9 July 1831.

55. C. 3481, 9 June 1832.

56. G.M. 1421, 14 July 1832.

57. This figure had been discussed as possibly coming from the east pediment of the Parthenon: Ellis, vol. 2, p. 70.

58. BM Cat. Sculpture 432.

59. The figure nearest the Sigeum inscription is BM Cat. Sculpture 2065.

60. The stone vase is BM Cat. Sculpture 2415; the bronze is GR 1816.6–10.12.

61. GR 1816.6–10.107. BM Cat. Inscriptions 1002.

62. BM Cat. Sculpture 433 and 434.

63. BM Cat. Sculpture 696 (left) and 683 (right). In front of the Caryatid is 690.

64. C. 3462, 10 March 1832.

65. O.P. X, 10 August 1833.

66. O.P. XIX, 5 August 1838; C. 4839–40, 10 May 1838.

67. O.P. XXI, 11 November 1839.

68. C. 5233, 16 November 1839.

69. O.R. 23, 20 November 1839; C. 5245, 7 December 1839.

70. C. 5337, 14 March 1840.

71. O.P. XXII, 21 March 1840.

72. C. 5346, 21 March 1840.

73. O.P. XXIX, November 1843.

74. C. 6335, 11 November 1843; cf. C. 3957, 31 March 1835.

75. O.P. XXIX, 7 December 1843; C. 6344, 9 December 1843.

76. C. 6472, 22 June 1844; cf. C. 6362, 10 December 1843; C. 6458, 8 June 1844.

77. O.R. 36, 24 January 1846.

78. C. 6875, 14 March 1846; O.R. 36, March 1846.

79. O.R. 36, April 1846 ff.

80. Fergusson, pp. 21–3.

81. C. 5480, 10 October 1840: BM Cat. Sculpture 326.27, part of West Frieze XIV, 27 – a fragment of the upper part of a figure from the frieze; BM Cat. Sculpture 342.15 – a leg of a centaur now incorporated in South Metope II; BM Cat. Sculpture 342.6 – the arm of a woman from one of the metopes.

82. O.P. XXVII, January 1842; C. 6110, 14 January 1843.

83. Ambrose Poynter was, in fact, the architect of St Catherine's Lodge.

84. GR 1843.5–29. 1–2.; BM Cat. Sculpture 3 and 4.

85. Letter from G. Scharf jun. to W. R. Hamilton, O.P. XLIV, 21 November 1850.

86. O.R. 45, 27 November 1850; C. 8112, 30 November 1850.

87. O.P. XLIII, 23 November 1849.

88. O.R. 43, 6 December 1849.

89. See Chapter 7 below.

90. Sub-Committee on Buildings, p. 471, 12 January 1850.

91. O.P. XLV, February 1851.

92. C. 8172–3, 8 March 1851.

93. O.P. XLV, 24 May 1851.

94. O.P. XLVII, 26 February 1852.

95. O.P. XLVIII, 18 June 1852.

96. O.R. 48, 25 June 1852.

97. O.P. XLVIII, 18 June 1852.

98. C. 8477, 13 November 1852; O.R. 50, January 1853.

99. O.R. 56, 10 January 1856.

100. Chapter 8 below.

101. Sub-Committee on Antiquities, 27 February 1856; C. 9027, 14 June 1856.

102. O.R. 56, 9 July 1856.

103. O.P. LIV, 9 August 1856.

104. C. 9072, 9 August 1856.

105. O.R. 58, 11 March 1857.

106. Sub-Committee on Antiquities, 22 May 1857; cf. O.R. 58, 10 June 1857; Sub-Committee on Antiquities, 19 June 1857.

107. O.R. 60, 6 January and 9 March 1858.

108. Sub-Committee on Antiquities, 20 June 1860; cf. O.P. LXVIII, 5 July 1860.

109. O.P. LXVIII, 6 July 1860.

110. Collected together in a volume in the library of the Department of Greek and Roman Antiquities, entitled *Elgin Room Arrangement, 1860–1930.* The contents are as follows:
1. Letter from R. Westmacott to A. Panizzi, 19 July 1860.
2. Memorandum by W. W. Lloyd, 13 July 1860.
3. Report by C. T. Newton, 1 March 1861.
4. Memorandum by W. W. Lloyd, 22 February 1861.
5. 'Suggestions for the new exhibition of the Sculptures of the Parthenon', J. D. Beazley *et al.*, September 1929.
6. 'Memorandum on the proposed new Elgin Room', A. H. Smith, 24 October 1930.

111. Sub-Committee on Antiquities, 29 April 1861.

112. Ibid., 24 May 1861.

113. C. 9966, 25 May 1861.

114. O.R. 24 August 1864.

115. C. 11538, 10 October 1868; C. 11555, 14 November 1868.

116. O.R. 9 February 1869; C. 11595, 13 February 1869.

117. O.R. 14 December 1868; O.P. LXIX, 20 May 1861.

118. Sub-Committee on Buildings and Antiquities, 15 December 1868; C. 11576, 9 January 1869; C. 11621, 10 April 1869.

119. P.P. *Returns* (1873), p. 14.

120. O.R. 10 October 1867.

121. O.R. 8 October 1873.

122. O.R. 8 November 1873.

123. Jenkins (1990), *passim.*

124. *Guide* (1875), p. 89.

Chapter 6

1. O.P. II, September 1801; *Ellis Scrapbook*, f. 70.

2. C. 2226, 6 August 1802; enclosed subsequently, C. 2245, 20 April 1804.

3. James, pp. 6–8.

4. C. 2228, 18 December 1802.

5. C. 962–3, 14 May 1803.

6. C. 964, 14 May 1803.

7. In addition to the design discussed below, it seems Saunders drew up a grandiose neo-Greek scheme which must have been rejected at an early stage. See the drawings acquired by the Department of Prints and Drawings from G. B. Shaw: 1984–1–21–2 (1–3).

8. Cook (1985), *passim.*

9. Cook (1977), pp. 57–66.

10. O.P. II, 6 May 1806.

11. EA 430; 510.

12. EA 498 (135★); 27; 136; 136A.

13. The hawk is EA 1420 (59★).

14. Cook (1977) p. 34; Cook (1985) p. 7.

15. Cook (1985), *passim.*

16. In their response to the Select Committee on the Elgin Marbles (P.P. 1816), both R. Westmacott and R. Payne Knight made a distinction between the Townley and Elgin Marbles by emphasising the commercial value of the former as 'furniture'. Westmacott, however (p. 84), considered the Elgin Marbles superior by virtue of their being a collection 'for Government and to form a school of study'. Payne Knight (pp. 102–4) was more equivocal.

17. Webster, p. 72, no 94; Cook (1977), pp. 38–9.

18. Michaelis (1882) p. 3.

19. Sloane: GR 1756.1–1.1.ff. Hollis: GR 1757.8–16.1★–26★. For Hollis, see Michaelis (1882), p. 69.

20. Hamilton: GR 1775.6–16.1.ff.

21. O.P. II, 3 April 1806.

22. O.P. II, 11 August 1806; ibid., 11 September 1806; C. 2295, 16 September 1806.

23. *Ellis Scrapbook*, f. 72; C. 2376, 9 April 1808; O.P. II, 14 April 1808.

24. Feinberg, pp. 37–8; Feinberg Millenson, p. 21; Jenkins (Buck's Vases, 1988) p. 450.

25. Cook (1985), fig. 1.

26. Westmacott (1808), p. 48.

27. *The Gentleman's Magazine* vol. 80 (July–December 1810), p. 209.

28. Feinberg, p. 200; Feinberg Millenson, pp. 119–20.

29. Feinberg, p. 211.

30. As the review in *The Gentleman's Magazine* noted, this created a deficiency of light in the Hamilton Room (XII), and was contrary to Sir William's own wishes that his vases should be seen in a 'strong light': C. 964, 14 May 1803.

31. Watkin, especially pp. 102–4; Waywell (1986), pp. 42–8.

32. O.P. IV, 10 March 1818; C. 2691, 14 March 1818.

33. For a full description of the proceedings, see Add. MS 41,580 ff. 165–85b; see also *The Times*, 30 August 1826.

34. EA 19.

35. Dawson and Uphill, pp. 23–4.

36. O.R. 5, 9 January 1819.

37. O.R. 5, 13 February 1819.

38. C. 2844, 14 June 1823.

39. G.M. 1180, 10 February 1821.

40. G.M. 1204, 15 March 1823.

41. The northern section of the Egyptian Sculpture Gallery, together with the Central Saloon, would be open to the public at the beginning of 1835.

42. O.P. V, 1 April, 4 and 8 May 1824: letters from Soane regarding the removal of the sarcophagus from the Museum. See also O.P. V, 10 November 1825, for a letter from Belzoni's widow.

43. O.P. IX, 27 December 1832.

44. O.R. 15, 11 July 1833.

45. Sub-Committee on Finance, p. 46, 5 March 1834.

46. O.P. XI, 11 April 1834.

47. C. 3820, 14 June 1834; O.P. XI, 20 June 1834.

48. *Synopsis* (1837) pp. 176–7; cf. O.P. XI, 30 July 1834.

49. O.P. X, 8 March 1833 ff.

50. O.P. XI, 30 April 1834.

51. O.P. XI, 8 July 1834.

52. O.R. 16, December 1834.

53. O.R. 17, January 1835.

54. For a description of the new room as completed, see *The Times*, 5 February 1838.

55. EA III. Budge, *Guide*, p. 227, from information supplied by S. Birch.

56. O.P. III, 13 July 1811; C. 2500, 13 July 1811.

57. C. 3176, 9 May; C. 3180, 16 May; C. 3183, 20 June.

58. O.P. XXX, 9 October 1844.

59. O.P. XV, 25 November 1836.

60. EA 90.

61. O.P. XVIII, 16 January 1838.

62. C. 5922, 21 May 1842.

63. C. 4910, 1 December 1838.

64. O.P. XIII, 20 October 1835.

65. This account is corroborated in a letter from J. G. Wilkinson, O.P. XIII, 20 October 1835, but is contradicted by Bonomi's version, for which see below.

66. O.P. XV, 9 September 1836.

67. O.P. XVI, 7 February 1837.

68. O.P. XVIII, 21 May 1838; C. 4771, 26 May 1838.

69. C. 4837, 28 July 1838.

70. O.P. XXV, 19 September 1846.

71. Cf. C. 7026, 10 October 1846; O.R. 37, 11 November 1846.

72. C. 7065, 14 November 1846.

73. C. 8427, 12 June 1852.

74. E.g. a year later by the Crystal Palace Company: O.P. XLIV, 2 April 1853.

75. See British Library Add. MS 30,129 f. 4, for a full description of the proceedings.

76. O.P. XXI, 13 December 1839; C. 5278, 11 January 1840.

77. O.P. XLII, 11 April 1849.

78. O.P. XLVIII, 28 September 1852; C. 8466, 9 October 1852.

79. C. 11225, 4 May 1867.

80. Budge (1926), p. 70; H. J. Shepstone in H. Golding (ed.), *The Wonder Book of Wonders* (London 1922), pp. 219–23, gives a lively account with contemporary photographs.

81. P.P. (N.G. 1857), 1592.

82. G.M. 1392, 9 July 1831; C. 3392, 14 September 1831.

83. O.P. XI, 14 June 1834; C. 2835, 14 June 1834; O.P. XI, 30 July 1834.

84. O.P. XI, 30 July 1834; C. 3856–7, 1 August 1834.

85. Cook (1977), p. 67.

86. *The Athenaeum*, 7 January 1837, pp. 6–7; H. Ellis, *The Library of Entertaining Knowledge, The British Museum: The Townley Gallery*, 2 vols (London 1836).

87. O.P. XI, 9 August 1834.

88. C. 3875, 11 October 1834; C. 3944, 14 March 1835; O.R. 17, May 1835.

89. O.P. XXV, 2 February 1842; O.R. 28, 12 February 1842.

90. *Ellis Scrapbook*, f. 320.

91. C. 6098, 14 January 1843; *Ellis Scrapbook*, f. 351, records the sale poster of scrap materials dated 20 April 1843.

92. O.R. 30, April and May 1843; *Synopsis* (1844), p. 76.

93. T. Lawrence's cast collection was presented to the Museum by the Royal Academy in 1831: O.P. IX, 23 July 1831; C. 3391, 14 September 1831. Although put up for sale at Christie's, 18 July 1822, it was purchased *en bloc* by an anonymous benefactor before the auction actually took place, and was subsequently deposited in the Royal Academy; see *The Times*, 19 July 1822, cf. Sub-Committee on Antiquities p. 168, 22 May 1839. Lawrence's casts were later returned to the Academy: C. 6354, 9 December 1843; O.P. XXX, 6 May 1844; C. 6438, 11 May 1844.

94. Sub-Committee Minutes, pp. 315–16, 318–19, 23 July 1846; O.R. July 1846.

95. C. 6953, 1 August 1846.

96. C. 6954, 10 October 1846.

97. O.R. 37, 11 November 1846; 9 December 1846.

98. O.P. XXXVI, 15 December 1846 for the sale-catalogue of scrap materials.

99. *Synopsis* (1848), pp. 96–105.

100. *Synopsis* (1844), pp. 81–3, 105–6.

101. *Synopsis* (1848), p. 113.

102. O.R. 49, 12 August 1852.

103. *Synopsis* (1852), pp. 82 and 91.

104. Fergusson, pp. 22–5.

105. Waagen, p. 39.

106. O.P. XL, 12 May 1848.

107. O.R. 47, 29 October 1851.

108. O.R. 49, 26 November 1852; O.P. XLVIII, 26 November 1852; C. 8484, 27 November 1852.

109. Sub-Committee on Antiquities, p. 546, 2 December 1852.

110. O.R. 49, 8 December 1852; ibid., 50, Annual Report, January 1853; also O.R. 52, January 1854 and 9 February 1854.

111. O.R. 49, 8 December 1852.

112. See especially the Synopsis for 1853.

113. S. Tillett, *Egypt Itself* (1984).

114. Ibid., p. 73.

115. Ibid., pp. 29 and 73.

116. O.P. XVIII, 5 January 1838.

117. C. 5277, 11 January 1840 – a figure Hay made up out of contempt for the manner in which he was being treated by the Museum. See also O.P. XXI, 12 December 1839; O.R. 24, January 1840.

118. Tillett, p. 80; O.P. XXIII, 26 July 1840.

119. C. 5311, 15 February 1840; C. 5346, 21 March 1840.

120. C. 5437, 25 July 1840; cf. O.R. 25, July 1840. See also Bonomi's list reproduced by Tillett, p. 88, note 10.

121. O.P. XXII, 20 January 1840.

122. C. 5552, 9 January 1841.

123. C. 5576, 13 February 1841; O.R. 26 May 1841.

124. O.R. 26, May 1841.

125. O.P. XXV, 14 October 1841; C. 5731–2, 13 November 1841; C. 5763, 11 December 1841.

126. O.P. XXVI, 30 June 1842.

127. C. 5982, 9 July 1842.

128. C. 6657, 26 April 1845; see the *Synopsis* for a detailed list.

129. O.P. XXXIV, 28 March 1846.

130. O.P. LVIII, 30 November 1857; O.R. 59, 30 November 1857.

131. O.P. XLVIII, 9 October 1852; cf. P.P. (1852), p. 318, 9 October 1852.

132. O.R. 52, January 1854; O.P. L, 11 March 1854.

133. Sub-Committee on Antiquities, p. 876, 1 July 1854.

134. O.R. 54, 10 January 1855.

135. O.R. 56, January 1856.

136. *Synopsis* (1855), p. 90.

137. *Synopsis* (1854), p. 92.

138. Sub-Committee on Antiquities, 15 May 1857; ibid., 22 May 1857.

139. O.P. LVIII, 10 July 1857.

140. C. 9426, 26 June 1858; O.R. 61, 7 December 1858.

141. For a concise survey see Kenworthy-Browne, pp. 334–53.

142. O.R. 58, 27 March 1857; C. 9174, 28 March 1857; Sub-Committee on Antiquities, 31 March 1857; C. 9266, 10 October 1857; C. 9288, 14 November 1857; O.R. 59, 9 December 1857; C. 9312, 9 January 1858; O.R. 62, 8 March 1859.

143. C. 7078, 28 November 1846.

144. O.P. XXXVI, 19 December 1846; C. 7112, 19 December 1846.

145. *Synopsis* (1844), p. 76.

146. O.R. 49, 12 August 1852.

147. O.R. 49, 29 July 1852; C. 8453, 14 August 1852.

148. O.R. 55, 6 July 1855.

149. O.R. 66, January 1861.

150. GR 1838.6–8.25–48. Facsimiles of wall-paintings from tombs 'on the road leading from Toscanella to Corneto, and at Bomarzo and Vulci'.

151. O.P. LIII, 2 November 1855; O.R. 58, January 1857.

152. A number of Etruscan cinerary urns were purchased from Campanari in 1838, and others were acquired from J. Russell in 1849.

153. Cf. Hubert Robert's 'Grande Galérie' of the Louvre in ruins (1796).

154. Newton to Panizzi, Add. MS 36,718, ff. 282–5, Bodrum, 6 March 1858.

Chapter 7

1. Fellows (1838), p. 1; Michaelis (1908), p. 93.

2. Fellows (1839); Fellows (1843), pp. 1–2; P.P. (1850), 1570.

3. C. 5017, 9 March 1839.

4. Cf. O.P. XX, March 1839.

5. O.P. XX, 11 March 1839.

6. O.P. XXI, 10 August 1839.

7. O.R. 23, September 1839; C. 5175, 21 September 1839.

8. O.P. XXI, 26 October 1839.

9. Fellows (1843), p. 2.

10. Fellows (1841).

11. O.P. XXIV, 31 May 1841.

12. O.P. XXIV, 8 June 1841.

13. O.P. XXIV, 10 June 1841.

14. O.P. XXV, September 1841; cf. ibid., 22 September 1841.

15. Collected together in O.P. XXV.

16. O.P. XXV, 29 December 1841.

17. O.P. XXIV, 8 June 1841.

18. Fellows (1843), pp. 7–9.

19. Fellows (1843), p. 43; C. 6054, 12 November 1842; C. 6092, 24 December 1842; cf. *The Athenaeum*, 24 December 1842.

20. C. 5098, 14 May 1842. This notebook – 'Copy of Memorandum Book kept at Xanthus, 1842' – is preserved in the library of the Greek and Roman Department.

21. C. 5908, 14 May 1842.

22. O.P. XXVII, 12 October 1842.

23. C. 5981, 9 July 1842.

24. O.R. 30, 1 January 1843.

25. C. 6092, 24 December 1842.

26. C. 6081, 10 December 1842.

27. C. 6109, 14 February 1843.

28. O.R. 30, February 1843; C. 6133, 11 February 1843.

29. O.P. XXVIII, 26 May 1843.

30. C. 6238, 10 June 1843.

31. C. 6251–3, 24 June 1843.

32. O.P. XXVIII, 20 May 1843.

33. P.P. (1850), 1816.

34. O.P. XXIX, 3 December 1843.

35. C. 6438, 11 May 1844; O.P. XXX, 30 March 1844.

36. O.P. XXX, 29 June 1844; C. 6475, 29 June 1844.

37. O.P. XXXI, 6 November 1844; C. 6519, 9 November 1844.

38. O.R. 30, May 1843; cf. O.R. 34, January 1845.

39. *Synopsis* (1844), p. 103.

40. *Synopsis* (1844), p. 94.

41. Jenkins (1985), pp. 178–9.

42. *Illustrations of the British Museum*, vol. I, f. 23.

43. O.P. XXX, 8 March 1844; C. 6403, 9 March 1844.

44. O.P. XXX, 9 May 1844; C. 6429, 11 May 1844; cf. O.P. XXX, 17 May 1844.

45. O.R. 32, April 1844; GR 1844.5–11.1 ff.

46. Cf. *Synopsis* (1844), p. 76.

47. O.P. XXXII, 2 June 1845.

48. C. 6697, 14 June 1845.

49. P.P. (1850), 1590 ff.

50. O.P. XXI, 8 November 1844; ibid. 9 November 1844; C. 6519, 9 November 1844. The document is preserved in the library of the Department of Greek and Roman Antiquities and is inscribed: 'An account of the position of the various objects about to be placed in the Lycian Gallery before their removal to this country, being a paper addressed to the Trustees of the British Museum by Mr Charles Fellows and illustrated by the drawings of Mr George Scharf and plans by Mr R. Hawkins.'

51. O.P. XXXIII, 28 June 1845; P.P. (1850), 1623 ff.

52. O.R. 35, June 1845; C. 6728–9, 28 June 1845.

53. P.P. (1850), 1749.

54. P.P. (1850), 1595; 1742.

55. C. 6728–9, 28 June 1845; P.P. (1850), 1624.

56. C. 6747, 12 July 1847.

57. P.P. (1850), 1626; C. 6756, 26 July 1845.

58. O.P. XXXIII, 28 June 1845.

59. O.P. LIV, 5 June 1856; cf. P.P. (1850), 1597.

60. For a list of these drawings see O.P. XXXI, 9 November 1844.

61. P.P. (1850), 1625.

62. P.P. (1850), 1727 ff.

63. P.P. (1850), 1836.

64. P.P. (1850), 1960.

65. P.P. (1850), 10877.

66. P.P. (1850), 1773; cf. ibid., 1960.

67. O.P. XXXI; C. 6519, 9 November 1844.

68. O.P. XXXI, 14 December 1844; cf. C. 6540–1, 14 December 1844.

69. O.P. XXXII, 20 May 1845; C. 6689, 24 May 1845; C. 6672, 10 May 1845.

70. C. 6711, 14 June 1845; O.P. XXXIII, 8 July 1845.

71. O.P. XXXIII, 1 August 1845; cf. C. 6767, 9 August 1845.

72. O.P. XXXV, 22 August 1846; C. 6989, 5 September 1846; O.P. XXXV, 10 September 1846; C. 7005, 19 September 1846; and further letters dated 16, 22 and 25 September. See also C. 7082, 28 November 1846.

73. O.P. XXXV, 29 September 1846; C. 7028, 10 October 1846.

74. O.P. XXXV, 24 October 1846.

75. O.P. XXXVI, 27 November 1846; C. 7082–3, 28 November 1846.

76. P.P. (1850), 1960.

77. O.P. XXXVI, 14 November 1846.

78. O.P. XXXVI, 11 December 1846; C. 7091, 12 December 1846.

79. C. 7151, 30 January 1847; C. 7165, 13 February 1847.

80. O.P. XXXVII, 5 June 1847; C. 7263, 5 June 1847.

81. O.P. XXXVII, 10 June 1847; P.P. (1850), 2058.

82. C. 7368, 4 December 1847.

83. C. 7165, 13 February 1847.

84. Gadd, p. 14. The seated figure is WA 118886.

85. Probably WA 1825.5–3.61 and 62.

86. Rich (1836).

87. Rich (1815).

88. Cf. Pallis, pp. 46–7.

89. Botta (1849).

90. O.P. XXXII, 23 March 1844.

91. O.P. XXXII, 11 March 1845.

92. Reade (1983), p. 6; cf. Layard, (1903), vol. I, p. 102.

93. Ibid. vol. I, pp. 306–7.

94. Gadd, p. 15.

95. Layard (1903), vol. II, ch. 2; Waterfield, ch. 6, 'Constantinople and Sir Stratford Canning'.

96. See Chapter 8 below.

97. O.P. XXXIV, 8 Jan. 1846; cf. Peel Papers, vol. CCCXCIV, BM Add. MS 40,574, ff. 21–6. The heads were sent to the British Museum pending Canning's return.

98. Another valuable source of information is Layard's copious letters written from Mosul or Nimrud to his patron at Constantinople, now British Library Add. MS 40,637.

99. O.P. XXXIV, 12 March 1846.

100. O.R. 39, 9 June 1846.

101. O.P. XXXV, 21 August 1846.

102. O.P. XXXV, 11 July 1846.

103. O.P. XXXVI, 19 August 1846.

104. O.P. XXXV, 21 April 1846. On comparisons between Greek and Assyrian art, see further Reade (1987), pp. 47–53.

105. O.P. XXXVIII, 4 August 1847.

106. O.R. 41, 8 November 1848; C. 7628, 11 November 1848.

107. C. 7629, 11 November 1849; O.R. 42, 19 January 1849.

108. Gadd, p. 56.

109. O.R. 42, 26 January 1849. A very faint sketch by G. Scharf in the Department of Prints and Drawings of the British Museum shows Assyrian bas-reliefs double banked down the centre of the Lycian Room basement.

110. WA 118886.

111. O.P. LXII, 10 August 1849; C. 7844, 18 August 1849.

112. Gadd, p. 57.

113. Layard, *Nineveh*, ch. XIII.

114. Gadd, p. 38.

115. Chapter 6.

116. O.R. 46, 8 January 1851.

117. O.P. XLI, 5 February 1849; cf. O.P. XLII, 20 March 1849.

118. Gadd, p. 54.

119. He was one of a number of artists to accompany the expedition including the unfortunate T. S. Bell, who was chosen to succeed Cooper and drowned while bathing: Gadd, pp. 69–71.

120. Gadd, p. 88.

121. O.R. 48, January 1852.

122. C. 7813, 30 June 1849.

123. O.R. 47, 11 October 1851.

124. Sub-Committee on Antiquities, p. 317–18, 23 July 1846.

125. O.P. XXXV, 15 August 1846.

126. C. 7078, 28 November 1846; O.P. XXXVI, 19 December 1846; C. 7112, 19 December 1846; cf. C. 7148, 30 January 1847. The columbarium was never occupied since it was later dismantled to provide the maximum possible space for the Assyrian sculptures from Nimrud – see Chapter 6.

127. O.P. XLI, 22 December 1848; C. 7670, 22 December 1848.

128. C. 7676, 13 January 1849; O.P. XLI, 2 February 1849.

129. The room under the Lycian Gallery was designated the 'Nimrud Room' in the *Synopsis* (1851), pp. 107–12; see also p. 91 for the Assyrian reliefs displayed in the room leading westwards from the Front Hall: O.R. 42, 23 February 1849; cf. O.R. 42, 7 March 1849.

130. Chapter 5.

131. O.R. 43, 6 December 1849; Sub-Committee on Buildings, p. 471, 12 January 1850.

132. O.R. 44, January 1850.

133. O.R. 43, 6 March 1850.

134. O.P. XLIV, 4 July 1850.

135. C. 8064, 8 October 1850.

136. C. 8078, 14 October 1850.

137. O.R. 46, 8 January 1851.

138. C. 8135, 11 January 1851.

139. O.R. 46, 7 April 1851.

140. C. 7594, 14 October 1848; O.R. 46, 9 April 1851; O.R. 47, 5 November 1851.

141. C. 8326, 22 November 1851.

142. O.R. of that date. An extract was printed in P.P. (1852), pp. 217–28.

143. O.R. 47, 5 December 1851; P.P. (1852), p. 219.

144. Sub-Committee appointed to consider and report as to the arrangement of Assyrian Sculptures, p. 517 ff, 6 December 1851; cf. p. 520, 17 December 1851.

145. O.R. 47, 10 December 1851; P.P. (1852), pp. 221–2. The plan for this proposal is printed with the extract of his report.

146. O.R. 48, 7 January 1852.

147. O.P. XLVIII, 25 June 1852; C. 8438, 26 June 1852.

148. O.R. 50, January 1853.

149. O.R. 52, 9 February 1854.

150. *Synopsis* (1856), pp. 136–57.

151. *Synopsis* (1856), p. 136.

152. WA 118807.

153. Gadd, p. 81.

154. WA 118898.

155. Probably WA 115040.

156. WA 118885.

157. WA 1846.7–2. ff.

158. Gadd, p. 107.

159. O.R. 54, 10 April 1855; O.R. 55, 6 July 1855; O.R. 56, January 1856 gives a summary list.

160. Gadd, pp. 107 and 116.

161. Gadd, pp. 116–19.

162. C. 9027, 14 June 1856.

163. O.R. 56, 8 July 1856; O.R. 57, 9 July 1856; C. 9053, 12 July 1856.

164. C. 8907, 8 December 1855; O.R. 56, 9 January 1856; Sub-Committee on Antiquities, p. 904, 16 February 1856; Sub-Committee on Antiquities, 22 February 1856; C. 8983, 26 April 1856; C. 9015, 7 June 1856.

165. O.R. 64, January 1860.

Chapter 8

1. O.P. XXIX, 29 January 1844; cf. O.P. XXX, 23 March 1844. Waterfield, p. 115.

2. Luttrell, p. 166.

3. Luttrell, p. 167.

4. Luttrell, p. 167. A 'new' fragment of the frieze recently discovered in the castle on Cos by N. Stambolides has been shown to join with the slab from Genoa: 'A new fragment from the Mausoleum of Halicarnassus', in *Festschrift for M. Andronikos* (Thessalonike 1986, in Greek).

5. Luttrell, p. 208, pl. 16.

6. Stanford and Finopoulos, pp. 89–98.

7. For the complexity of the process by which Dalton's engravings were published, see Stanford and Finopoulos, Appendix, pp. 232–3.

8. Luttrell, pp. 206–7; but see, Jenkins (1988), p. 195, note 35.

9. *Ellis Scrapbook*, f. 325.

10. For Canning see L. G. Byrne, *The Great Ambassador* (Ohio 1964); Stoneman, pp. 217–21; Layard (1903), vol. II, p. 101, describes in brief Canning's policy of supporting a liberal and pro-European faction in the Turkish Government under the leadership of Rashid Pasha.

11. C. 6874, 14 March 1846. For Canning's earlier attempts see Devereux, p. xiv; see also O.P. XXIX, 29 January 1844. Captain H. Edgell was the officer responsible for the eventual removal of the sculptures from the castle.

12. C. 6931, 11 July 1846. Canning is said to have discouraged use of the term 'Canning Marbles' for fear of attracting the oppobrium Elgin had brought to his own name.

13. O.P. XXV, 1 August 1846; O.P. XXXV, 23 August 1846; C. 6983, 5 September 1846.

14. O.P. XXXV, 9 September 1846.

15. C. 7028, 10 October 1846; C. 7045, 24 October 1846.

16. C. 7655, 2 December 1848.

17. C. 7762, 21 April 1849.

18. O.R. 46, 9 May 1851; C. 8208, 10 May 1851.

19. O.P. XLII, 19 July 1849.

20. For its early history see Newton (1862), p. 234; Luttrell, p. 205.

21. C. 7830, 21 July 1849; C. 7856, 3 October 1849.

22. Sub-Committee Minutes, 12 July 1859.

23. C. 9284, 14 November 1859.

24. C. 10798, 20 May 1865.

25. C. 10860, 29 July 1865.

26. For a brief biography, see *JHS* 14 (1894), pp. xlix–liv.

27. Ruskin, *Praeterita*, vol. I. ch. xi, 225; cf. vol. II: ch. viii. 155–7.

28. O.R. 24, January 1840.

29. Add. MS 34,582, f. 5.

30. O.R. 31, December 1843.

31. O.R. 46, 4 March 1851.

32. Add. MS 36,317, ff. 612–21, 9 November 1856.

33. O.P. XL, 29 July 1848.

34. O.R. 41, 11 October 1848.

35. Add. MS 34,582, f. 329, 9 January 1852.

36. O.P. XLVII, 31 January 1852.

37. Add. MS 30,998, 'Rhodes and Cos', 1853.

38. Add. MS 36,717, f. 54, 4 October 1854.

39. GR 1854.5–19.1–180. O.R. 54, 10 January 1855; cf. O.P. LI, 17 October 1854.

40. GR 1855.10–27.1–35. C. 8856, 23 June 1855; O.P. LII, 31 May 1855.

41. Newton (1865), vol. I, pp. 280 ff.; see also the lengthy report by Newton addressed to Lord Stratford de Redcliffe, as Canning was known after his elevation to the peerage, O.P. LIII, 31 January 1856; see further, *Archaeological Journal* 13 (1856), pp. 14–37; a copy of this last is bound into a volume in the library of the Department of Greek and Roman Antiquities labelled, 'Newton, *Ancient Art Calymnos*'.

42. GR 1856.8–26.1–729. O.R. 57, 9 July 1856; O.P. LIII, 3 March 1856.

43. Newton (1865), vol. I, pp. 333–6.

44. Newton (1865), vol. II, pp. 39 ff.

45. Newton (1862), p. 325.

46. Newton (1865), vol. II, p. 66.

47. Add. MS 36,717, ff. 468, 474–87, 497, 505, 511, 517, 519, 525. The manuscript catalogue is still preserved in the library of the Department of Greek and Roman Antiquities.

48. O.P. LIV, 8 August 1856; Newton (1862), p. 85.

49. *Antiquities of Ionia Published by the Society of Dilettanti*, Part 3 (London 1840), ch. I, being the belated publication of the expedition of 1812.

50. Newton to Panizzi, Add. MS 36,718, f. 274, 18 February 1858.

51. *Transactions of the Royal Society of Literature*, Second Series 5, part I, pp. 1–23; Newton (1862), p. 82; cf. O.P. XXXIX, 19 February 1848.

52. No. 1606, *Classical Museum* 5 (1848), pp. 170–201.

53. Newton (1862), p. 84.

54. Newton, *Papers*, no 1, p. 1, Bodrum, 14 December 1856.

55. Cf. C. 9070, 9 August 1856; C. 9081, 11 October 1856.

56. Newton (1862), p. 85.

57. Cf. O.P. LIV, 8 August 1856.

58. Murdoch Smith, p. 108.

59. See G. Feyler, 'Contribution à l'Histoire des Origines de la Photographie Archéologique', *Mélanges de L'École Française de Rome Antiquité* 99.2 (1987), pp. 1019–47.

60. Jenkins (1984), p. 178.

61. C. 7627, 11 November 1848.

62. O.P. XLII, 12 September 1849. The report itself is dated 18 January 1849.

63. O.P. LIV, 4 August 1856.

64. Cf. Davis, pp. 48–9.

65. O.P. LV, 6 November 1856; Newton to Panizzi, Add. MS 36,717, ff. 627–8, HMS *Gorgon*, 16 November 1856; Murdoch Smith, p. 24.

66. Newton, *Papers*, no 1, pp. 2–3; Newton (1862), pp. 325–32; Murdoch Smith, pp. 27–8.

67. Newton to Panizzi, Add. MS 36,717, ff. 627–8, HMS *Gorgon*, 16 November 1856.

68. Newton (1865), pp. 211–12.

69. Jenkins (1984), *passim*.

70. Newton, *Papers*, no 1, p. 3; Newton (1862), pp. 319–25; Murdoch Smith, p. 29; Newton to Panizzi, Add. MS 36, 17, ff. 651–8, 20 December 1856.

71. BM Cat. Sculpture 1112.

72. BM Cat. Sculpture 1111.

73. Newton, *Papers*, no 1, p. 5; Newton (1862), pp. 280–310; Murdoch Smith, pp. 30–32.

74. Newton (1865), vol. II, p. 83; Towsey's Diary, 7 and 8 January 1857.

75. Murdoch Smith, ch. 5; Murdoch Smith and Porcher, *passim*.

76. Murdoch Smith, ch. 6.

77. Murdoch Smith, p. 33.

78. Newton, *Papers*, no 2, p. 7.

79. Newton (1865), vol. II, p. 87.

80. Newton to Panizzi, Add. MS 36,717, ff. 627–8, 16 November 1856.

81. Newton to Panizzi, Add. MS 36,718, ff. 23–8, 15 February 1857.

82. Spratt (1856) reproduces the Admiralty Chart published 9 April 1851, showing the placement of what Newton later called Spratt's Platform. Newton subsequently adapted this chart for his own purpose.

83. Newton (1865), vol. II, p. 109.

84. Murdoch Smith, p. 49.

85. Cf. Newton (1865), vol. II, pp. 90–1.

86. Newton (1865), vol. II, p. 91.

87. Newton (1865), vol. II, pp. 91–2.

88. Newton (1862), p. 99.

89. On the find-places of the Mausoleum sculptures, see Jeppesen (1958), p. 21; Waywell (1978), pp. 3–13.

90. Waywell (1978), Cat. 34.

91. Ibid., Cat. 42.

92. Newton (1862), p. 90; (1865), vol. II, pp. 94–5; *Papers*, no 2, p. 8, 12 January 1857; Murdoch Smith, p. 41.

93. Newton (1862), pp. 99–100; (1865), vol. II, p. 95; *Papers*, no 5, p. 13, 3 April 1857; Murdoch Smith, p. 57; Waywell (1978), Cat. 33.

94. Newton (1862), p. 100; (1865), vol. II, pp. 95–6; *Papers*, no 5, p. 13, 3 April 1857, and no 9, p. 21, 12 June 1857. See also *Papers*, no 13, p. 33, 12 August 1857. See Cook (1989), pp. 35–7, on the unreliability of Newton's testimony.

95. Newton (1862), pp. 102–10; (1865), vol. II, pp. 108–12; *Papers*, no 7, pp. 14–15, 11 May 1857; ibid., no 9, pp. 21–2, 12 June 1857; Murdoch Smith, pp. 58–60.

96. Newton (1862), p. 102; (1865), vol. II, p. 109.

97. Cf. Jenkins *et al.* (1989), pp. 317–19.

98. Pliny, N.H., XXXVI, 30–31: 'In summo est quadriga marmorea, quam fecit Pythis'; cf. Luttrell and Jeppesen (1985), pp. 53ff.

99. Other wheel-parts were later to be discovered on the south side of the excavation: Newton (1862), p. 129; *Papers*, no 15, p. 46, 30 September 1857.

100. Waywell (1978), Cat. 401.

101. Waywell (1978), Cat. 26–7.

102. Murdoch Smith, p. 41 and cf. p. 49.

103. *Papers*, no 12, pp. 27–9.

104. See also Newton (1862), pp. 311–18; (1865), vol. II, pp. 138–42.

105. Newton (1862), p. 82.

106. Murdoch Smith, p. 55.

107. Newton (1865), vol. II, pp. 100–105; *Papers*, no 4, p. 10, 19 March 1857; cf. O.P. LVI, 28 February 1857; C. 9176, 28 March 1857.

108. O.P. LVI, 11 April 1857. This pledge was never carried out.

109. Newton (1865), vol. II, p. 113.

110. Newton to Panizzi, Add. MS 36,718, 3 June 1857.

111. O.P. LVII, 24 June 1857; the list was printed in *Papers*, no 11, pp. 24–7, 24 June 1857.

112. Newton to Panizzi, Add. MS 36,718, 22 June 1857.

113. Add. MS 36,718, ff.474–9, 24 November 1859.

114. O.R. 59, 5 August 1857.

115. C. 9312, 9 January 1858; O.R. 60, 18 January 1858.

116. O.P. LVII, 25 August 1857; O.P. LVII, 31 August 1857.

117. O.R. 61, 7 December 1858; O.P. LIX, 7 January 1858; C. 9328, 23 January 1858; O.R. 60, 7 February 1858.

118. O.R. 60, 21 April 1858; *Further Papers Respecting the Excavations at Bodrum*, 26 March 1858.

119. Newton to Panizzi, Add. MS 36,718, f. 173, 11 July 1857.

120. Jenkins and Middleton (1988), pp. 185–7.

121. Newton to Panizzi, Add. MS 36,718, ff. 220–1, 27 November 1857; cf. for paint on the coffers when first discovered, Add. MS 36,718, f. 261, 9 February 1858.

122. Cf. Towsey's Diary for red and blue on the frieze, 13 March 1857.

123. *Papers*, no 13, p. 32.

124. Newton to Panizzi, Add. MS 36,718, 27 November 1857.

125. Newton (1865), vol. II, pp. 160ff; *Further Papers*, no 3, p. 10.

126. Murdoch Smith, p. 106.

127. Newton to Panizzi, Add. MS 36,718, 3 September 1857 and 10 August 1857.

128. Newton to Panizzi, Add. MS 36,718, f. 431, HMS *Supply* at sea, 15 September 1858.

129. Newton to Panizzi, Add. MS 36,718, f. 263, 9 February 1858.

130. *Further Papers*, no 3, p. 10; Newton to Panizzi, Add. MS 36,718, f. 263, 9 February 1858.

131. *Further Papers*, no 3, p. 12; Newton to Panizzi, Add. MS 36,718, ff. 164–5, 9 February 1858.

132. *Further Papers*, no 3, p. 13; (1865), vol. II, p. 174.

133. Newton (1865), vol. II, p. 195.

134. Newton to Panizzi, Add. MS 36,718, ff. 282–5, 6 March 1858; Newton (1865), vol. II, pp. 177ff; *Further Papers*, no 4, p. 21.

135. *Further Papers*, no 3, p. 13, and no 4, p. 20; Newton to Panizzi, Add. MS 36,718, ff. 282–5, 6 March 1858 and f. 308, 6 April 1858.

136. GR 1859.12–26.447–460.

137. BM Cat. Sculpture 1301.

138. BM Cat. Sculpture 1314.

139. BM Cat. Sculpture 1303–1310.

140. BM Cat. Sculpture 1328–49.

141. BM Cat. Sculpture 1354–57.

142. BM Cat. Sculpture 1351.

143. BM Cat. Sculpture 1350; Newton (1865), vol. II, pp. 214ff.; Newton (1862), pp. 480ff.; Murdoch Smith, pp. 118ff.; *Further Papers*, no 6, pp. 24–7.

144. Newton to Panizzi, Add. MS 36,718, f. 359, 18 May 1858.

145. Murdoch Smith, pp. 119–33.

146. Newton (1862), pp. 485–511; (1865), vol. II, pp. 221–7; *Further Papers*, no 10, pp. 38–42.

147. On the down-dating of the Lion Tomb, see F. Krischen, *RM* 59 (1944), pp. 173–81.

148. *Further Papers*, no 9, p. 34; Newton (1862), pp. 537 ff.; (1865), vol. II, pp. 231 ff.; Newton to Panizzi, Add. MS 36,718, ff. 430–31, 15 September 1858.

149. *Further Papers*, no 1, p. 1; Newton (1862), pp. 527 ff; (1865), vol. II, pp. 147 ff.

150. Newton to Panizzi, Add. MS 36,718, ff. 273–4, 18 February 1858.

151. O.R. 60, 18 January 1859.

152. O.P. XLI, 23 November 1858 and 1 December 1858.

153. C. 9490, 11 December 1858.

154. O.R. 61, 7 December 1858.

155. C. 9490, 11 December 1858.

156. O.R. 62, 6 January 1859.

157. C. 9505, 22 January 1859.

158. C. 9513, 11 January 1859.

159. Newton to Panizzi, Add. MS 36,718, ff. 495–504, 14 December 1858.

160. Newton to Panizzi, Add. MS 36,718, ff. 571–7, 20 February 1859.

161. Murdoch Smith, p. 140.

162. *Further Papers*, no 17, pp. 94–5.

163. C. 9640, 6 August 1859.

164. C. 10816, 10 June 1865; C. 10848, 18 July 1865; Biliotti Papers in the library of the Greek and Roman Department, no 6, Mausoleum 1865, no 7, Budrum, Cos and Nisyros.

165. C. 10859, 29 July 1865.

166. C. 10770, 14 October 1865; cf. C. 10906, 9 December 1865.

167. C. 12283, 11 November 1871.

168. C. 12306, 9 December 1871.

169. Newton (1865), vol. I, pl. 1; O.R. 6 February 1879; ibid., 15 May 1879 BM Cat. Sculpture 1017.

170. O.R. 3 February 1869.

171. C. 9620, 9 July 1859.

172. C. 9620, 9 July 1859.

173. Newton to Panizzi, Add. MS 36,720, ff. 123–4.

174. O.P. LXV, September and October 1859, for several letters, and see also Greek and Roman Department Letter Books, 135–6, 19 September; 137, 20 September; 138, 20 September; 143–5, 26 September.

175. C. 9675, 12 November 1859.

176. O.P. LXVI, January 1860.

177. O.P. LXVII, 28 March 1860.

178. O.P. LXVII, 2 April 1860.

179. C. 9749, 14 April 1860.

180. O.R. 64, January 1860.

181. C. 9995, 13 July 1861.

182. O.P. LXV, 30 November 1859.

183. BL Manuscripts, Egerton Papers, 3815, f. 128.

184. Newton to Panizzi, Add. MS 36,717, ff. 612–21.

185. Newton to Panizzi, Add. MS 36,718, f. 501, 14 December 1858.

186. Miller, pp. 299–300; cf. C. 9842, 10 November 1860; C. 9851–2, 8 December 1860.

187. Newton to Panizzi, Add. MS 36,720, ff. 485–8. His successor to the Consulship in Rome was Joseph Severn. Newton was then betrothed to Severn's second daughter Mary: W. Sharp, *The Life and Letters of Joseph Severn* (London 1892), p. 214. Mary Newton died in 1866.

188. C. 9834, 27 October 1860.

189. C. 9889, 26 January 1861; C. 9896, 2 February 1861.

190. C. 9897–8, 2 February 1861.

191. C. 9904, 9 February 1861; C. 9914, 13 February 1861; Miller, p. 300.

192. Ruskin, *Praeterita* vol. II, ch. viii, 151–4.

Chapter 9

1. See anonymous report in *The Traveller*, 19 February 1824: 'Particulars and Estimate of the Designs for the New Buildings of the British Museum'.

2. O.R. 30, March 1843.

3. *The Builder* 1 (16 December 1843), pp. 542–3.

4. O.R. 37, 4 September 1846; cf. Sub-Committee Minutes, p. 315, 23 July 1846; C. 6988, 5 September 1846.

5. Maunde Thompson, f. 151.

6. P.P. (1852), pp. 213–19, report dated 3 July 1851; cf. O.R. 47, where the manuscript version is undated.

7. P.P. (1850), 10576.

8. Ibid., 10585.

9. Fergusson, p. 11.

10. G.M. 1211, 26 June 1823.

11. Add. MS 43, 231, ff. 135–8; *Ellis Scrapbook*, f. 115: cutting from *The Times*, dated 29 March 1825, an article on the possible formation of a National Museum of Sculpture and Paintings; see also Miller, p. 195.

12. *Ellis Scrapbook*, f. 120, letter dated 5 April 1826.

13. P.P. (N.G. 1853).

14. Quoted by Hendy, p. 34.

15. Hendy, p. 27.

16. P.P. (N.G. 1853), 9051.

17. P.P. (N.G. 1857), 2207.

18. P.P. (N.G. 1857), 2253–91.

19. Hendy, p. 37.

20. P.P. (N.G. 1857), 2474.

21. Subsequently included in Newton (1880), pp. 39–72.

22. P.P. (N.G. 1853), 8284.

23. P.P. (N.G. 1857), 1526.

24. P.P. (N.G. 1857), 1608.

25. P.P. (N.G. 1857), 1670.

26. P.P. (N.G. 1853), 8946.

27. P.P. (N.G. 1857), 1660–61.

28. P.P. (N.G. 1853), 8359.

29. Crook (1972), pp. 105–6.

30. Potts (Munich 1980); P.P. (N.G. 1853), 9359–9417, and Appendix VIII.

31. *Mechanics Magazine, Museum Register, Journal and Gazette*: 'The New Buildings at the British Museum' (Thomas Watts), vol. 36, 1836–7, pp. 454–9.

32. Miller, p. 185; Sir Frederic Madden, Keeper of Manuscripts, 1837–66.

33. O.P. XLIII, 30 November 1849; *The Builder* 8 (22 June 1850), pp. 295–6; see also Crook (1973), p. 418, for this and other schemes; also Miller, p. 185.

34. C. 7898, 8 December 1849.

35. Miller, pp. 185–8.

36. Vol. 17, p. 157; a copy is preserved among the Panizzi Papers, 1853, f. 270.

37. C. 8592, 13 August 1853; Madden, O.R. 51, 1 November 1853; S. Smirke, O.P. L, 2 November 1853; Hawkins, O.R. 51, 4 November 1853; Panizzi, O.R. 51, 5 November 1853; Ellis, O.R. 51, 10 November 1853.

38. C. 9239, 11 July; Sub-Committee on Buildings, 13 July 1857.

39. Sub-Committee on Buildings, 11 November 1857.

40. O.R. 56, 10 January 1856.

41. Add. MS 36,718, ff. 104–25, 13 May 1857.

42. *Ellis Scrapbook*, f. 119: journal cutting dated 21 March 1826 and labelled 'Representation'.

43. P.P. (N.G. 1853), 7854.

44. Add. MS 36,718, f. 499, 14 December 1858; and see Miller, especially pp. 239–44, where the story of the eventual transfer of the Natural History collections to South Kensington is chronicled.

45. P.P. (1857–8), pp. 499–503.

46. O.P. LXI, December 1858; printed in P.P. (1859), pp. 68–70.

47. See especially the article published in *The Builder* 17 (1 January 1859), p. 6: 'British Museum – The Christmas Holidays'.

48. P.P. (1859), p. 51.

49. For the full reference to this, see Chapter 10.

50. Miller, pp. 243–4; Maunde Thompson, ff. 153–61.

Chapter 10

1. For Stephens see Chapter 4, note 22.

2. The casts were formerly at South Kensington, where they were displayed in the Architectural Court. In 1893–4 they were transferred together with the original sculptures to the British Museum, but it seems some casts were returned to storage at South Kensington in 1895: C. 19651, 9 March 1895. By 1922 some or all of these casts seem to have returned to Bloomsbury when, towards the end of that year, a temporary exhibition of casts and original sculptures brought by Maudslay from Copan and Yaxchilan was opened on the upper floor of the Museum: Sub-Committee on Antiquities, 11 March 1922; C. 3914, 8 April 1922; C. 3972, 9 December 1922; C. 3986, 13 January 1923. For Maudslay and the Maya, see I. Graham in *Collectors and Collections, British Museum Yearbook* 2 (London 1977), pp. 137–55.

3. Hawkins, O.P. XV, 14 July 1836.

4. C. 14920, 13 December 1879; C. 15056, 10 April 1880; C. 12502, 13 July 1872.

5. For Stephanoff see Chapter 4.

6. P. Mitter, *Much Maligned Monsters: The History of European Reaction to Indian Art* (Oxford 1977).

7. The progress and development of archaeological science is the major theme of Michaelis (1908) – see especially ch. 11; see also Stoneman, *passim*.

8. See the privately printed paper 'British Museum: At a Meeting of the Committee appointed at the Special General Meeting of the Trustees on the 3rd December, to consider the Treasury Minute of 13 November, 1861'.

9. Sub-Committee Minutes, 4 April 1868, for a full summary; cf. ibid., 4 November 1874; O.R. 4 October 1874; 9 November 1878; 15 July 1879; 17 June 1882; 13 May 1885; 20 February 1886.

10. O.R. 7 July 1905; C. 2107, 8 July 1905.

11. C. 2244, 28 July 1906. These were largely the collection built up by Walter Copland Perry – see his *Descriptive Catalogue of the Collection of Casts from the Antique in the South Kensington Museum* (London 1887).

12. Cf. C. 2303, 9 February 1907; C. 2309, 23 February 1907; C. 2450, 11 April 1908; C. 2475, 13 June 1908.

13. O.R. 4 July 1907; 3 August 1907; 1 November 1907 – deducting casts from originals already in the British Museum and casts duplicated in the Museum's cast collection, A. H. Smith enumerated the Victoria and Albert casts as consisting of 85 statues and groups; 72 reliefs, or series of reliefs; 59 busts and heads; 1 sarcophagus, and 38 statuettes, comprising in all 255 items.

14. The casts were temporarily stored at one end of the Mausoleum Room and elsewhere – O.R. 3 February 1908; O.R. September 1908; O.R. 18 February 1909; O.R. 5 October 1909; C. 2629, 9 October 1909. The gallery had been opened to the public on 23 August. A guide to the collection was drawn up by F. N. Pryce: *A Guide to the Collection of Casts in the Department of Greek and Roman Antiquities in the British Museum* (London 1913).

15. O.R. 24 February 1930; Sub-Committee on Antiquities, 7 March 1930; cf. C. 4754, 14 March 1931.

16. O.R. 2 January 1934; C. 9035, 13 January 1934; C. 5044, 10 February 1934: the casts were transferred as a loan so as not to prejudice the possibility of incorporating them at some future date in a National Museum of Casts. C. 5102, 13 October 1934; C. 5178, 11 May 1935; O.R. 1 June 1935.

17. Constructed between 1839 and 1842: O.R. XX, January 1839; O.P. XXVI, 13 May 1842. Cf. Griffiths and Williams, pp. 20–3.

18. Caygill (1982).

19. C. 17799, 14 January 1888; C. 17839, 11 February 1888.

20. O.R. 2 November 1888; completed a year later: O.R. 5 November 1889.

21. O.R. 12 July 1877; O.R. 12 June 1878; C. 14336, 15 June 1878; completed by September 1878: O.R. 17 September 1878.

22. O.R. 7 April 1891.

23. O.R. September 1878; C. 14473, 26 October 1878; O.R. 5 March 1879. The arrangement was completed in 1879 but further additions and alterations would be carried out: O.R. 10 January 1889; O.R. 11 December 1889; O.R. 4 February 1909; 5 March 1909; C. 4608, 14 December 1929; C. 4753, 14 March 1931.

24. O.R. 1 January 1930; O.R. 5 December 1932.

25. C. 16900, 13 December 1884: the Mausoleum Room was opened to the public on 17 November.

26. C. 11595, 13 February 1869.

27. Sub-Committee on Buildings, 9 November 1878; ibid., 15 July 1879; C. 14530–31, 24 December 1878.

28. C. 14768, 12 July 1879; O.R. 8 March 1880. The sheds on the colonnade were removed in the course of the year: C. 15347, 11 December 1880.

29. Griffiths and Williams, loc. cit., note 17.

30. The Phigaleian Room was reached from the Mezzanine by a flight of steps. Presumably these were necessitated by the raising of the floor level when the old Insect Room was converted in 1889.

31. O.R. 5 November 1889. Now displayed in the lobby of the Department of Greek and Roman Antiquities.

32. O.R. 27 September 1886.

33. O.R. 11 December 1889 and 4 February 1890.

34. O.R. 20 February 1902; O.R. 21 January 1903; O.R. 21 February 1904.

35. O.R. 17 February 1904; O.R. 3 March 1904.

36. O.R. 24 February 1905.

37. O.R. 18 February 1909; O.R. 25 February 1909; O.R. 5 May 1909.

38. For this see Chapter 1, note 48.

39. O.R. 18 February 1909.

40. O.R. 7 June 1909; 29 September 1909; C. 2635, 9 October 1909; O.R. 4 November 1909; O.R. 3 May 1910.

41. C. 2718, 11 June 1910; O.R. 18 February 1911.

42. Chapter 1, note 1.

43. O.R. 2 March 1915; O.R. 3 March 1915; Sub-Committee on Antiquities, 13 March 1915; O.R. 3 April 1915; C. 3358, 10 April 1915; O.R. 6 July 1918.

44. O.R. 3 December 1919; O.R. 10 February 1920; see also O.R., pp. 128 ff., 1920: full reports on the Museum during the war.

45. O.R. 4 December 1922; Jenkins (1990).

46. C. 3973, 9 December 1922; O.R. 1 May 1923; O.R. 1 May 1923; C. 4016, 12 May 1923; O.R. 29 October 1923.

47. Printed as 'Suggestions for the new exhibition of the sculptures of the Parthenon' and dated September 1929.

48. *Memorandum on the Proposed New Elgin Room*, privately printed and dated 24 October 1930.

49. C. 4486, 13 October 1928.

50. Sub-Committee on proposed new Elgin Room, 27 November 1928; ibid., 30 January 1929; 4 May 1929.

51. C. 4618, 11 January 1930; C. 4670, 14 June 1930.

52. Sub-Committee on Elgin Room, 17 June 1930; 1 April 1931; C. 4678; 28 June 1930; C. 4680, 12 July 1930.

53. Sub-Committee on Elgin Room, 8 May 1931; ibid., 16 November 1931; ibid., 9 March 1932; C. 4895, 9 July 1932; C. 4973; 10 June 1933.

54. C. 4996, 14 October 1933; C. 5079, 9 June 1934.

55. C. 5118, 10 November 1934; C. 3135, 12 January 1935; C. 5291, 11 July 1936; C. 5302, 10 October 1936.

56. After the war, while bomb damage in the Duveen Gallery was repaired, the Parthenon sculptures were reinstalled from 1949 in the old Elgin Room and what are now Rooms 9 and 10 – see the plan on the back cover of B. Ashmole, *A Short Guide to the Sculptures of the Parthenon in the British Museum, Elgin Collection* (London 1949).

57. Beazley, Robertson, Ashmole, loc. cit., note 47.

Chronology of Principal Events

Summer 1802 Egyptian sculptures captured at Alexandria arrive in Museum.

September 1806 Arrival of the Townley Marbles purchased 1805.

June 1808 Opening of the Townley Gallery.

October 1815 Arrival of the Phigaleian Marbles purchased 1814.

February 1817 Opening of the temporary exhibition of the Elgin and Phigaleian Marbles.

January 1819 Head of Ramesses II displayed in the Townley Gallery.

1823 R. Smirke draws up plans for the new Museum.

1825–8 Schinkel's Altes Museum (designed 1823) built at Berlin.

1830 Completion of Klenze's Glyptothek, Munich.

1831 Temporary Elgin Room demolished.

July 1832 Permanent Elgin Room opened.

Summer 1834 Egyptian sculpture installed in the north division of the new west wing.

1836 First contract drawn up for the commercial supply of casts from the Museum.

1839 The Elgin Room is coloured red.

September 1841 Excavations commence for the new South Front.

December 1842 First consignment of Lycian sculptures arrives.

Winter 1842 Townley Gallery partly demolished.

November 1844 Second delivery of Lycian sculpture.

September 1846 Arrival of the 'Canning Marbles' (Mausoleum frieze).

December 1846 The remainder of the Townley Gallery is demolished.

1846–50 The Graeco-Roman sculptures are exhibited in the gallery leading westwards from the Front Hall (later Roman Gallery) and in the Grand Central Saloon.

June 1847 Arrival of the first Assyrian sculptures from Layard's excavations.

December 1847 Lycian Gallery opened to the public.

1849 The Front Hall is decorated in archaeological polychromy.

1850–51 The Graeco-Roman sculptures are rearranged extending into the First Graeco-Roman Room.

1852 Installation completed of the Assyrian sculptures in the southern side-gallery.
South Front of the Museum completed.

1852–3 Select Committee on National Gallery investigates future of the collections.

February 1854 Arrangement of the Assyrian sculptures completed in the south and north side-galleries and the Assyrian Transept.
Egyptian sculptures rearranged to occupy both divisions of the west wing.

1855 Graeco-Roman sculpture galleries completed.

Summer 1856 Sculptures of the west pediment of the Parthenon transferred to the First Elgin Room.

1857 Further sculptures transferred to the First Elgin Room, including the east pediment.

Further investigation into proposals for a new National Museum of Art.

Round Reading Room completed.

July 1857 The *Gorgon* arrives at Woolwich with her cargo of sculpture from Halicarnassus.

August 1857 The first sheds are erected under the colonnade.

The *Curacao* arrives with her cargo of sculpture and mosaics from Davis's excavations at Carthage.

1858 Alcoves introduced into the Second Graeco-Roman Room.

November 1858 The *Supply* arrives with further antiquities from the excavations of Newton in Asia Minor and Davis in Tunisia.

1859 Arrangement of the Sepulchral Basement completed.

Assyrian sculptures arranged in the Assyrian Basement Gallery.

October 1860 Edward Hawkins retires.

January 1861 Department of Antiquities divides three ways with Newton as Keeper of Greek and Roman Antiquities.

Summer 1861 Sculptures arrive from Smith and Porcher's excavations at Cyrene.

January 1862 Committee appointed to consider the future of the Museum in light of the Treasury decision to evict the Natural History collections.

1863–74 J.T.Wood conducts excavations on the site of the Temple of Artemis at Ephesus.

1864

6th Viscount Strangford's collection purchased, including the 'Strangford Kouros'.

Sculptures purchased from the sale of the Farnese Collection.

1868–9 R.P.Pullan excavates Temple of Athena Polias at Priene.

January 1869 First Elgin Room renamed the Mausoleum Room.

1873 The Elgin Room is extended northwards, and the Parthenon frieze is rearranged and glazed.

1877–8 Lycian sculptures transferred to the Front Hall.

1879–80 Mausoleum sculptures transferred from the colonnade sheds to the shed newly erected on the west side of the Reading Room.

1883 Transfer of the Natural History collections to South Kensington completed.

1884 Mausoleum Room completed.

1889 Phigaleian Marbles rearranged in the new gallery adapted from the old Print Room.

1890 Museum fully lit by electricity.

1891 Nereid Monument rearranged in the old Phigaleian Room.

August 1909 Gallery of casts opened.

1915–16 Galleries dismantled as precaution against wartime bombing.

April 1918 Parthenon Frieze removed to the Post-Office Tube.

Summer 1918 Temporary wartime exhibition arranged in the galleries, including a mock-up of the Elgin Room using the storecasts.

Autumn 1919 The Elgin Room and the other sculpture galleries reinstated.

1928 Sir J. Duveen responds to the Report of the Royal Commission on National Museums and Art Galleries by offering funds for the re-exhibition of the Parthenon sculptures.

February 1939 Transfer of the Parthenon sculptures into the new gallery commences, but is discontinued at the outbreak of war.

Bibliography

PRIMARY WORKS

Trustees' Papers

The principal sources are the papers of the Trustees of the Museum housed in the Museum's Central Archive. For these the following abbreviations are used:

C. = Minutes of the Standing Committee of Trustees.

G.M. = Minutes of the General Meeting of Trustees.

O.P. = Original Papers, being the various letters and original reports.

O.R. = Officers' Reports, being the reports of the various officers of the Museum to the Trustees. After July 1805 these are bound separately from the Papers. From 1861 onwards volume numbers are not cited for the Officers' Reports, since the copies referred to are the unnumbered series kept in the library of the Department of Greek and Roman Antiquities.

Parliamentary Papers and House of Commons Papers, Reports etc.

The other major source of primary documents is the various Parliamentary Reports, for which the abbreviation is usually P.P. and the date in brackets, as follows:

P.P. (1816) = *Report from the Select Committee of the House of Commons on the Earl of Elgin's Collection of Sculptured Marbles etc.* (printed as a separate volume for John Murray, 1816).

P.P. *Returns*, being the annual report of the Trustees to the House of Commons printed and bound in sequence.

P.P. (1835) = *Report of the Select Committee on the Condition, Management and Affairs of the British Museum; together with Minutes of Evidence, Appendix and Index.* 6 August 1835, VII.1. See also 1836, X.1.

P.P. (1836) = *Report from the Select Committee on Arts and their Connexion with Manufactures, with the Minutes of Evidence, Appendix and Index.* 1836, IX.1.

P.P. (1850) = *Report of the Commissioners appointed to enquire into the Constitution and Government of the British Museum; with Minutes of Evidence.* 1850, XXIV.

P.P. (1852) = *Communications made by the Architect and Officers of the British Museum to the Trustees respecting the Enlargement of the Building of that Institution; and Communications between the Trustees and the Treasury upon the same subject, subsequent to the period when the Commissioners upon the Constitution and Management of the British Museum presented their Report to Her Majesty.* 1852, XXVIII.201.

P.P. (N.G.1853) = *Report of the Select Committee on the Management of the National Gallery; also to consider how Collective Monuments of Antiquity etc. possessed by the Nation may be preserved, judiciously augmented and advantageously exhibited to the Public; with Proceedings, Evidence, Appendix and Index.* 1852–3, XXXV.

P.P. (N.G.1857) = *Report of the Commissioners on the Site for the National Gallery; with Evidence, Appendix and Index.* 1857, Session 2, XXIV.

P.P. (1857–8) = *Communications made by the Architect and Officers of the British Museum to the Trustees, and between the Trustees and the Treasury.* 1857–8, XXXIII.373.

P.P. (1859) = *A Copy of all Communications made by the Officers and Architect of the British Museum and the Trustees respecting the Want of Space for exhibiting the Collections in that Institution, as well as respecting the Enlargement of the Buildings, – And of all Minutes of the Trustees and all Communications between the Trustees and the Treasury upon the same subject (the whole subsequent to and in continuation of Parliamentary Paper no 379 of Session 1857–8).* XIV. 51.

Other Primary Printed and Manuscript Material

Ellis Scrapbook, a volume of miscellanea compiled by Henry Ellis, Principal Librarian, 1827–56.

Fellows, C. *Copy of a Memorandum Book kept at Xanthus 1842* (MS in library of Department of Greek and Roman Antiquities.

Fellows, C. *An Account of the Position of the Various Objects about to be placed in the Lycian Gallery before their Removal to this Country being a Paper addressed to the Trustees of the British Museum by Mr. Charles Fellows and illustrated by the Drawings of Mr. George Scharf and Plans by Mr. R. Hawkins, London 1844* (MS in library of Department of Greek and Roman Antiquities).

Guides: The *Synopsis of the Contents of the British Museum*, discontinued in 1856, was superseded by the series of *Guides*. These fell into the category of general surveys of the exhibitions or, alternatively, they dealt with specific galleries. The general *Guide* seems to have been first published in 1859 and went into various editions. Among the specific *Guides* was that to the Elgin Room, first published in two parts by C. T. Newton in 1881.

Illustrations of the British Museum – a miscellany of pictorial reference material, two volumes in the Central Archive and another in the library of the Department of Greek and Roman Antiquities.

Letters: (1) Letters 1757–1834, a bound volume in the library of the Department of Greek and Roman Antiquities, entitled *Letters on Antiquities 1757–1834*; (2) *Original Letters 1861–1966*, in a series of bound volumes in the library of the Department of Greek and Roman Antiquities. (3) *Correspondence 1826–1860*, a series of bound volumes in the library of the Department of Western Asiatic Antiquities.

Maunde Thompson, Edward, BL Add. MS 30,080.

Memorandum on the Subject of the Earl of Elgin's Pursuits in Greece (1810, 1811 and 1815).

Memoranda on the arrangement of the Elgin Marbles, privately printed and gathered together in a bound volume entitled *Elgin Room Arrangement, 1860–1930*, in the library of the Department of Greek and Roman Antiquities: these are listed in Chapter 5, note 110.

Newton, C. T. Manuscript account of Newton's sojourn in Rome, January 1849.

Newton, C. T. *Letters to Rev. P. Bliss 1839–52*. British Library Additional Manuscripts.

Newton, C. T. *Letters to A. Panizzi 1854–72*. British Museum Additional Manuscripts.

Newton, C. T. *Drawings and Plans of Discoveries at Halicarnassus etc.* 1856–1859. British Library MS 31,980.

Newton, C. T. *Papers Respecting the Excavations at Budrum*, printed copies of Newton's dispatches to the Foreign Secretary, December 1856 – December 1857.

Newton, C. T. *Further Papers respecting the Excavations at Budrum and Cnidus*, in continuation of the last, December 1857 to July 1859. This bound with the last into a volume, with plans, in the library of the Department of Greek and Roman Antiquities.

Synopsis = *Synopsis of the Contents of the British Museum* (63 editions, 1808–56).

SECONDARY WORKS

The following abbreviations are used in the citation of periodicals:

JHS = *Journal of Hellenic Studies*

J. Warb = *Journal of the Warburg and Courtauld Institutes*

RM = *Römische Mitteilungen*

Note that articles in *The Builder* referred to in the notes are not listed in the general bibliography, the majority being anonymous.

Ancient Marbles, Description of the Collection of Ancient Marbles in the British Museum, 11 vols (1812–61).

Ashmole, see Beazley.

Beardsley, M. C. *Aesthetics from Classical Greece to the Present: a short history* (Tuscaloosa and London 1966).

Beaufort, F. *Karamania, or, a brief Description of the South Coast of Asia Minor and of the Remains of Antiquity* (London 1817).

Beazley, J., Robertson, D. and Ashmole, B. 'Suggestions for the new exhibition of the Sculptures of the Parthenon' (privately printed, September 1929).

Berger, E. (ed.) *Parthenon-Kongress Basel*, Papers of the congress, 4–8 April 1982, 2 vols (Mainz 1984).

Bohrer, F. N. 'Assyria as Art: A Perspective on the Early Reception of Ancient Near Eastern Artifacts', *Culture and History* 4 (Copenhagen 1989).

Bonomi, J. *Nineveh and its Palaces* (London 1975).

Bosanquet, B. *A History of Aesthetic* (2nd edition, London 1904).

Botta, P. E. *Monuments de Ninive*, 5 vols (Paris 1849).

Britton, J. *Illustrations of the Public Buildings of London* (London 1825).

Budge, E. A. *A Guide to the Egyptian Sculpture Galleries* (London 1909).

Budge, E. A. *Cleopatra's Needles and other Egyptian Obelisks* (London 1926).

Burke, J. *William Hogarth, The Analysis of Beauty* (Oxford 1955).

Bury, J. *The Idea of Progress* (New York 1932).

Buttlar, A. von. 'Klenzes Beitrag zur Polychromie-Frage', in *Ein Griechische Traum: Leo von Klenze der Archäologe*, exh. catalogue, Munich, 6 December – 9 February 1986.

Caygill, M. *The Story of the British Museum* (2nd edn, London 1992).

Caygill, M. 'William Who's Building?', *British Museum Society Bulletin* 40 (Summer 1982).

Caygill, M. 'How the British Museum saw the Light', *British Museum Society Bulletin* 55 (Summer 1987).

Ceram, C. W. *Gods, Graves and Scholars* (reprinted London 1984).

Clarke, M. and Penny, N. *The Arrogant Connoisseur: Richard Payne Knight 1751–1824* (Manchester 1982).

Cockerell, C. *The Temples of Jupiter Panhellenius at Aegina and of Apollo Epicurius at Bassae near Phigaleia in Arcadia* (London 1860).

Cockerell, S. P. *Travels in southern Europe and the Levant 1810–1817. The Journal of C.R. Cockerell R.A.* (London 1903).

Connor, P. 'Cast-collecting in the nineteenth century: scholarship, aesthetics, connoisseurship' in *Rediscovering Hellenism*, ed. G.W. Clarke (Cambridge 1989), pp. 187–235.

Cook, B. F. 'The Townley Marbles in Westminster and Bloomsbury', in *Collectors and Collections, British Museum Yearbook* 2 (London 1977), pp. 34–78.

Cook, B. F. *The Elgin Marbles* (London 1984).

Cook, B. F. *The Townley Marbles* (London 1985).

Cook, B. F. 'The Sculptors of the Mausoleum Friezes', in *Architecture and Society in Hekatominid Caria. Proceedings of the Uppsala Symposium*, 1987, ed. T. Linders and P. Hellstrom, *Boreas* 17 (Uppsala 1989), pp. 31–42.

Cooper, F. *The Temple of Apollo at Bassai* (New York and London 1978).

Crook, J. M. *The British Museum* (London 1972).

Crook, J. M. 'The British Museum' in *History of the King's Works*, ed. H.M. Colvin (London 1973), pp. 403–21.

Crawford, M. H. 'From Borghesi to Momsen: The Creation of an Exact Science', *Warburg Institute Surveys and Texts* 21, *Medals and Coins from Bude to Momsen* (London 1990).

Cummings, F. 'B. R. Haydon and his School', *J. Warb* 26 (1963), pp. 367–80

Cummings, F. 'Phidias in Bloomsbury etc.', *The Burlington Magazine* 104 (July 1964), pp. 323–8.

Daniel, G. *One Hundred and Fifty Years of Archaeology* (2nd edition 1975).

Davis, N. *Carthage and her Remains* (London 1861).

Dawson, W. R. and Uphill, E. P. *Who was Who in Egyptology* (London 1972).

Desmond, A. *The Politics of Evolution* (Chicago and London 1989).

Devereux, W. B. *Views on the Shores of the Meditteranean* (London 1847).

Dodds, E. R. *The Ancient Concept of Progress and Other Essays on Greek Literature* (Oxford 1973).

Donaldson, T. L. 'Report of the Committee appointed to examine the Elgin Marbles', *Transactions of the Royal Institute of British Architects*, 1st series 5.2 (1837–42), pp. 100–108.

Donaldson, T. L. *et al.* 'On Polychromatic Embellishments in Greek Architecture', *Proceedings of the Royal Institute of British Architects*, 1st Series (1851–2), being the proceedings of three separate meetings; 12 and 26 January and 9 February.

Edwards, E. *Lives of the Founders of the British Museum 1570–1870* (London 1870).

Ellis, H. *The Library of Entertaining Knowledge, The British Museum: The Townley Gallery*, 2 vols (London 1836).

Feinberg, S. G. *Sir John Soane's Museum: an Analysis of the Architect's House-Museum in Lincoln's Inn Fields, London* (PhD Thesis, University of Michigan, Ann Arbor, 1979).

Feinberg Millenson, S. G. *Sir John Soane's Museum* (Michigan 1987).

Fellows, C. *A Journal written during an Excursion in Asia Minor* (written 1838, published London 1839).

Fellows, C. *An Account of Discoveries in Lycia, being a Journal kept during a Second Expedition in Asia Minor* (written 1840, published London 1841).

Fellows, C. *The Xanthian Marbles, their Acquisition and Transmission to England* (London 1843).

Fellows, C. *Introductory Remarks to Lycia, Caria, Lydia, illustrated by Mr. George Scharf with descriptive letter-press by Sir Charles Fellows* (London 1847).

Fellows, C. *Travels and Researches in Asia Minor, more particularly in the Province of Lycia* (London 1852).

Felten, F. *Griechische tektonische Friese archäischer und klassischer Zeit* (Vienna 1984).

Fergusson, J. *Observations on the British Museum, National Gallery and National Record Office* (London 1849).

Feyler, G. 'Contribution à l'Histoire des Origines de la Photographie Archéologique', *Mélanges de L'Ecole Française de Rome Antiquité*, vol. 99.2 (1987), pp. 1019–47.

Flaxman, J. *Lectures on Sculpture* (2nd edition London 1838).

Gadd, C. J. *The Stones of Assyria, The Surviving Remains of Assyrian Sculpture, their Recovery and their Original Positions* (London 1936).

Gombrich, E. *The Ideas of Progress and their Impact on Art* (New York 1971).

Gould, C. H. M. *Trophy of Conquest. The Musée Napoléon and the Creation of the Louvre* (London 1965).

Gratziu, see Jenkins (1989).

Griffiths, A. and Williams, R. *Department of Prints and Drawings in the British Museum, a User's Guide* (London 1986).

Haskell, F. *Rediscoveries in Art. Some Aspects of Taste, Fashion and Collecting in England and France* (London 1976).

Haskell, F. and Penny, N. *Taste and the Antique* (Yale 1981).

Hendy, P. *The National Gallery* (London 1960).

Hitchens, C. *The Elgin Marbles: should they be returned to Greece?* (London 1987).

Hofkes-Brukker, C. *Der Bassai-Fries* (Munich 1975).

Hutchison, S. *The History of the Royal Academy* (2nd edition, London 1986).

James, H. *The British Museum and Ancient Egypt* (London 1981).

Jenkins, I. 'Frederic Lord Leighton and Greek Vases', *The Burlington Magazine* 125 (October 1983), pp. 597–605.

Jenkins, I. 'G. F. Watts' Teachers: George Frederic Watts and the Elgin Marbles', *Apollo* 120 (September 1984), pp. 176–81.

Jenkins, I. 'James Stephanoff and the British Museum', *Apollo* 121 (March 1985), pp. 174–81.

Jenkins, I. 'Adam Buck and the Vogue for Greek Vases', *The Burlington Magazine* 130 (June 1988), pp. 448–57.

Jenkins, I. 'British Reception of the Durand Vases sold in Paris in 1836' (forthcoming in *Proceedings of Colloque International: Anticomanie*, Montpellier, 9–12 June 1988).

Jenkins, I. 'Acquisition and Supply of the Casts of the Parthenon Sculptures by the British Museum 1835–1939', *The Annual of the British School of Archaeology at Athens* 85 (1990), pp. 89–114.

Jenkins, I. and Middleton, A. 'Paint on the Parthenon Sculptures', *The Annual of the British School of Archaeology at Athens* 83 (1988), pp. 183–207.

Jenkins, I., Gratziu, C. and Middleton, A. 'Dati Preliminari sulle Relazioni fra Patine e Policromia nei Fregi del Mausoleo di Alicarnasso', *Atti del Convegno: Le Pellicole ad Ossalato – Origine e Significato nella Conservazione delle Opere d'Arte*, Milan, 25–6 October 1989.

Jenkyns, R. *The Victorians and Ancient Greece* (Oxford 1980).

Jeppessen, K. *Paradeigmata – Three Mid-Fourth Century Main Works of Hellenic Architecture Reconsidered* (Jutland Archeological Society Publications 1958).

Jeppessen, K. see also Luttrell.

Jones, O. *An Apology for the Colouring of the Greek Court at the Crystal Palace.* (London 1854).

Kenworthy-Brown, J. 'Private Skulpturen-Galerien in England 1730–1830', in K. Vierneisel and G. Leinz (eds), *Glyptothek München 1830–1980* (Munich 1980)

Keuls, E. *Plato and Greek Painting* (London 1978).

Knowles, J. *Life and Writings of Henry Fuseli*, 3 vols (London 1831).

Laing, A. 'Penny Plain or Tuppence Coloured', *Country Life* 175 (17 May 1984), pp. 1382–3

Larrabee, S. A. *English Bards and Grecian Marbles* (New York 1943).

Layard, A. H. *Nineveh and its Remains*, 2 vols (London 1849).

Layard, A. H. *Discoveries in the Remains of Nineveh and Babylon* (London 1853).

Layard, A. H. *Autobiography and Letters*, ed. W.N. Bruce (London 1903).

Liscombe, R. W. 'The Commencement of Real Art', *Apollo* 103 (January 1976), pp. 34–9.

Lovejoy, A. O. *The Great Chain of Being: A Study of the History of an Idea* (Cambridge, Mass. 1936).

Lucas, R. C. *Remarks on the Parthenon being the result of studies and enquiries connected with the production of Two Models of that Noble Building* (Salisbury 1845). Reviewed by C. T. Newton, *The Classical Museum* 3 (1846), pp. 443–6.

Luttrell, A. and Jeppessen, K. *The Maussolleion at Halikarnassos*, vol. II, *The Written Sources* (Moesgaard 1985).

Macdonald, S. *The History and Philosophy of Art Education* (London 1970).

Mason, E. C. *The Mind of Henry Fuseli* (London 1951).

Michaelis, A. *Ancient Marbles in Great Britain* (Cambridge 1882).

Michaelis, A. *A Century of Archaeological Discoveries* (London 1908).

Middleton, see Jenkins (1988 and 1989).

Miller, E. *That Noble Cabinet* (London 1973).

Mitter, P. *Much Maligned Monsters: The History of European Reaction to Indian Art* (Oxford 1977).

Morgan, H. *A History of the Growth of the Royal Academy Schools from the beginning of the Academy to 1836, with special reference to Academic Teaching and Condition* (PhD Thesis, University of Leeds, 1984).

Murdoch, I. *The Fire and the Sword* (Oxford 1977).

Murdoch Smith, R. *The Life of Major-General Sir Robert Murdoch Smith*, by his son-in-law W. K. Dickson (Edinburgh and London 1901).

Murdoch Smith, R. and Porcher, E. A. *History of the Recent Discoveries at Cyrene made during an Expedition to the Cyrenaica in 1860–61* (London 1864).

Newton, C. T. 'On the Sculptures of the Mausoleum at Halicarnassus', *The Classical Museum* 5 (1848), pp. 170–201.

Newton, C. T. *On the Method of the Study of ancient Art*, read at the meeting of the Oxford Art Society, 14 November 1849 (Oxford 1850).

Newton, C. T. 'Remarks on the Collections of ancient Art in the Museums of Italy, the Glyptothek at Munich and the British Museum', *The Museum of Classical Antiquities* 1 (1851), pp. 205–27.

Newton, C. T. 'Excavations and Discoveries at Calymnos', *Archaeological Journal* 13 (1856), pp. 14–37.

Newton, C. T. *A History of Discoveries at Halicarnassus, Cnidus and Branchidae*, 2 vols, the second in two parts (London 1862).

Newton, C. T. *Travels and Discoveries in the Levant* (London 1865).

Newton, C. T. *Essays on Art and Archaeology* (London 1880).

Osborn, H. *From the Greeks to Darwin: An Outline of the Development of the Evolution of an Idea* (London 1894).

Pallis, S. A. *The Antiquity of Iraq. A Handbook of Assyriology* (Copenhagen 1956).

Paris, Rome, Athènes: Le Voyage en Grèce des Architectes Français Aux XIXe et XXe Siècles, exh. cat., École Nationale Supérieure des Beaux-Arts, 12 May – 18 July 1982, and other locations.

Penny (1981), see Haskell.

Penny (1982), see Clarke.

Perry, W. C. *Descriptive Catalogue of the Collection of Casts from the Antique in the South Kensington Museum* (London 1887).

Pfeiffer, R. *History of Classical Scholarship from 1300 to 1850* (Oxford 1976).

Physick, J. *The Victoria and Albert Museum: The History of its Building* (London 1982).

Podro, M. *The Critical Historians of Art* (Yale and London 1982).

Pollitt, J. J. *The Ancient View of Greek Art: criticism, history and terminology* (Yale 1974).

Porcher, see Murdoch Smith.

Potts, A. 'Greek Sculpture and Roman Copies: Anton Raphael Mengs and the Eighteenth Century', *J. Warb* 43 (1980), pp. 150–73.

Potts, A. 'Die Skulpturenaufstellung in der Glyptothek', in Vierneisel, K. and Leinz, G. (eds), *Glyptothek München 1830–1980* (Munich 1980), pp. 258–83.

Pryce, F. *A Guide to the Collection of Casts in the Department of Greek and Roman Antiquities in the British Museum* (London 1913).

Pulsky, F. 'On the Progress and Decay of Art; and on the Arrangement of a National Museum', *The Museum of Classical Antiquities* 2 (1852), pp. 1–15.

Quatremère de Quincy, A.-C. *Lettres adressées à M. Canova sur les Marbres d'Elgin, ou les Sculptures du temple de Minerve à Athènes* (Rome 1818).

Reade, J. *Assyrian Sculpture* (London 1983).

Reade, J. 'Reflections on Layard's Archaeological Career', Proceedings of the symposium: *Austen Henry Layard tra l'Oriente e Venezia*, ed. F. M. Fales and B. J. Hickey (Rome 1987), pp. 47–53.

Reynolds, J. *Discourses on Art*, ed. R. Wark (New Haven and London 1975).

Rich, C. J. *Memoir on the Ruins of Babylon* (London 1815).

Rich, C. J. *Narrative of a Residence in Koordistan, and on the site of Ancient Nineveh, with a Journal of a Voyage down the Tigris to Bagdad etc.*, edited by his widow (London 1836).

Robertson, see Beazley.

Rossi, P. *The Dark Abyss of Time: The History of the Earth and the History of Nations from Hooke to Vico* (first published Milan 1979; English translation Chicago and London 1984).

Rothenberg, J. *'Descensus ad Terram': The Acquisition and Reception of the Elgin Marbles* (New York and London 1977).

Ruskin, J. *Praeterita: Outlines of scenes and thoughts perhaps worthy of memory in my past life* (London 1949, first published in 3 vols, 1885–1900).

St Clair, W. *Lord Elgin and the Marbles* (2nd edition, Oxford 1983).

Scharf, G. *Observations on the Peculiarities of Sculptures seen on the Monuments of Ancient Lycia* (London 1847).

Scharf, G. *The Greek Court erected in the Crystal Palace* (London 1854).

Seling, H. 'The Genesis of the Museum', *The Architectural Review* 14 (1967), pp. 103–14.

Semper, G. 'On the Study of Polychromy and its Revival', *The Museum of Classical Antiquities* 1 (1851), pp. 228–46.

Sharp, W. *The Life and Letters of Joseph Severn* (London 1892).

Shepstone, H. J. 'London's Most Ancient Monument', in H. Golding (ed.), *The Wonder Book of Wonders* (London 1922).

Smith, A. H. 'Lord Elgin and his Collection', *JHS* 36 (1916), pp. 163–372.

Smith, A. H. 'Memorandum on the Proposed new Elgin Room' (privately printed 24 October 1930).

Spratt, T. 'On Halicarnassus', *Transactions of the Royal Society of Literature*, second series 5, part I (1856), pp. 1–23.

Stambolides, N. 'A new fragment from the Mausoleum of Halicarnassus', in *Festschrift for M. Andronikos* (Thessalonike 1986, in Greek).

Stanford, W. B. and Finopoulos, E. J. *The Travels of Lord Charlemont in Greece and Turkey 1749* (London 1984).

Stearn, W. T. *The Natural History Museum at South Kensington* (London 1981).

Stoneman, R. *Land of Lost Gods* (London 1987).

Tillett, S. *Egypt Itself* (London 1984).

Turner, F. *The Greek Heritage in Victorian Britain* (Yale 1981).

Visconti, E. Q. *Lettre à un Anglais* (London 1815).

Visconti, E. Q. 'Catalogue of the Elgin Marbles, Vases, Casts and Drawings prepared from the Manuscript of M. Visconti.', appended to P.P. (1816).

Visconti, E. Q. 'Memoir on the Sculptures of the Parthenon', appended with the last to P.P. (1816).

Vrettos, T. *A Shadow of Magnitude: The Acquisition of the Elgin Marbles* (New York and Toronto 1974).

Waagen, G. *Treasures of Art in Great Britain*, 3 vols (1854).

Waterfield, G. *Layard of Nineveh* (London 1963).

Watkin, D. *Thomas Hope, 1769–1831, and the Neo-Classical Idea* (London 1968).

Waywell, G. B. *The Free-Standing Sculptures of the Mausoleum at Halicarnassus in the British Museum* (London 1978).

Waywell, G. B. *The Lever and Hope Sculptures* (Berlin 1986).

Webster, M. *Johann Zoffany 1733–1810*, exh. cat., National Portrait Gallery (London 1976).

Westmacott, R. *Account of the Arrangement of the Collection of Antique Sculpture lately placed in the British Museum* (London 1808).

Westmacott, R. jun. 'On Colouring Statues: a Paper read at Cambridge at the Meeting of the Archaeological Institute of Great Britain and Ireland in 1854', *The Archaeological Journal* 12 (1855), pp. 22–46.

Westmacott, R. jun. *The Schools of Sculpture, Ancient and Modern* (Edinburgh 1864).

Williams, see Griffiths.

Winckelmann, J. J. *Reflections on the Painting and Sculpture of the Greeks* (trans. H. Fuseli, London 1765).

Winckelmann, J. J. *A History of Ancient Art among the Greeks* (1764) partially translated by G. H. Lodge (London 1850) with various editions of a later complete translation published in Boston and Cambridge, Mass.

Index